"*The Dark Side of Leadership: A Cross-Cultural Compendium* offers a profound exploration of the complexities and challenges of leadership across different cultures. It provides invaluable insights into leadership's often-overlooked negative aspects, making it a must-read for anyone looking to understand the full spectrum of leadership dynamics. The authors' thorough research and engaging writing style make complex concepts accessible and thought-provoking. This book is a truly enlightening read for both aspiring and seasoned leaders."

Assad Tavakoli, *W.T. Brown Endowed Chair and Distinguished Professor of Economics, Broadwell College of Business and Economics, Fayetteville State University, North Carolina, United States*

"Power often carries a destructive streak that eats away at organizational effectiveness. This book contributes a timely reminder, especially as far-right leaders appear to be on the ascendancy in many parts of the world, casting long shadows of narcissism, hubris, corruption, nepotism, lack of empathy, and Machiavellianism, issues which this book deals with in great detail. This book is an excellent compendium and reminder of the devastating effect of the dark side of leadership. It is a compelling read for leaders and all those interested in organizational progress."

Felix Maringe, *Professor of Higher Education, University of Kigali, Rwanda*

The Dark Side of Leadership: A Cross-Cultural Compendium

The corporate landscape is rife with instances of leaders who have left a trail of sinister outcomes.

In the last three decades, the research in leadership and organisational sciences has expanded in theoretical and typological breadth to include the dark side. These works have aimed at uncovering the complex interplay of personalities, power dynamics, and organisational cultures that can lead to destructive and unethical behaviours in the workplace. While there are volumes of literature on leadership, there is a dearth of research that integrates dark leadership and cross-cultural norms, perspectives, variances, and interventions. *The Dark Side of Leadership: A Cross-Cultural Compendium* is a collaborative and transdisciplinary venture that draws on the knowledge and experiences of practitioners and scholars across the globe to explore the contentious and evolving subject of dark leadership. The primary consideration of this book is to explore dark side leadership conceptualisations and manifestations across contexts and provide insights into traits, processes, and outcomes, as well as interventionist paradigms. Hofstede's research demonstrates the fundamental role of national and organisational culture in shaping leadership behaviour. This book comprehensively documents cross-cultural cases, perspectives, and research on the dark side of leadership.

The Dark Side of Leadership: A Cross-Cultural Compendium

With Lessons for Leaders

Edited by
Adebukola Oyewunmi, Gill Owens, and Ogechi Adeola

Routledge
Taylor & Francis Group
A PRODUCTIVITY PRESS BOOK

Designed cover image: Shutterstock

First published 2025
by Routledge
605 Third Avenue, New York, NY 10158

and by Routledge
4 Park Square, Milton Park, Abingdon, Oxon, OX14 4RN

CRC Press is an imprint of Taylor & Francis Group, LLC

Library of Congress Cataloging-in-Publication Data
Names: Oyewunmi, Adebukola, editor. | Owens, Gill (Psychologist), editor. | Adeola, Ogechi, editor.
Title: The dark side of leadership : a cross-cultural compendium : with lessons for leaders / edited by Adebukola Oyewunmi, Gill Owens, and Ogechi Adeola.
Description: New York, NY : Routledge, 2025. | Includes bibliographical references and index. | Summary: "The corporate landscape is rife with instances of leaders who have left a trail of sinister outcomes. In the last three decades, the research in leadership and organizational sciences has expanded in theoretical and typological breadth to include the dark side. These works have aimed at uncovering the complex interplay of personalities, power dynamics, and organizational cultures that can lead to destructive and unethical behaviors in the workplace. While there are volumes of literature on leadership, there is a dearth of research that integrates dark leadership and cross-cultural norms, perspectives, variances and interventions. The Dark Sides of Leadership: A Cross-Cultural Compendium is a collaborative and transdisciplinary venture that draws on the knowledge and experiences of organizational science practitioners and scholars across the globe to explore the contentious and evolving subject of dark leadership in the workplace. The primary consideration of this book is to explore dark-side leadership conceptualizations and manifestations across national contexts and provide insights into cultural peculiarities in traits, processes, and outcomes, as well as interventionist paradigms. Social psychologists agree that the dimensions of individual worldviews shrink or broaden based on socialization and Hofstede's research demonstrates the fundamental role of national and organizational culture in shaping leadership behavior. There is currently no book that comprehensively documents cross-cultural cases, perspectives, and research on dark leadership. The authors intend to bridge this gap with this transdisciplinary book"— Provided by publisher.
Identifiers: LCCN 2024057833 (print) | LCCN 2024057834 (ebook) | ISBN 9781032757018 (hardback) | ISBN 9781032757001 (paperback) | ISBN 9781003475262 (ebook)
Subjects: LCSH: Leadership—Moral and ethical aspects. | Leadership—Psychological aspects. | Leadership—Cross-cultural studies.
Classification: LCC HD57.7 .D3937 2025 (print) | LCC HD57.7 (ebook) | DDC 658.4/092—dcundefined
LC record available at https://lccn.loc.gov/2024057833
LC ebook record available at https://lccn.loc.gov/2024057834

ISBN: 9781032757018 (hbk)
ISBN: 9781032757001 (pbk)
ISBN: 9781003475262 (ebk)

DOI: 10.4324/9781003475262

Typeset in Garamond
by codeMantra

To the Father of lights, without variableness or shadow of turning
and all the unrelenting advocates of the bright side of leadership

Contents

Foreword ... x

Preface ... xiii

Acknowledgements ... xv

Notes on the Editors ... xvi

Notes on Contributors ... xviii

THEME I DARK SIDE LEADERS: WHO THEY ARE AND WHAT THEY DO

1 **The Hunt for Prey: A Playbook of Psychopathic Leadership** ... 3
ADEBUKOLA OYEWUNMI

2 **Unveiling the Dark Leadership in *Star Wars*** ... 18
GILL OWENS

3 **Categorical Error and the Dark Side of Leadership** ... 25
WALE OLAJIDE AND OLUFEMI OLUWATAYO

4 **Apparently Great Start – Evidentially Disastrous Finish: The Longitudinal Nature of Failure in Psychopathic Leadership** ... 33
CLIVE R. BODDY

5 **Exploring the Shadows of Dark Side Leaders** ... 47
SHAMAILA GULL AND ROOHI IMTIAZ

THEME II THE PROCESS OF DARK LEADERSHIP

6 **The Process of Dark Leadership: Reflections from a Norwegian Military Community of Practice** ... 59
JOHAN BERGH

7 **Discursive Practices of Dark Side Leaders: Reflections from Pakistan and Colombia** 70
LUIS J. SERRANO-TAMAYO AND JABRAN KHAN

8 **The Toxic Triangle of Leadership** 82
GODBLESS AKAIGHE AND ISAIAH ADISA

9 **Ethical Behaviour Beyond Convergent Calculative Thinking: From Modern to Meaningful Leadership** 94
MEHRDAD SARHADI

10 **Leadership: Disruption and Influence** 106
LISA C. BAREFIELD

THEME III THE CONTEXT OF DARK LEADERSHIP

11 **Dark Triad and Leadership: A Perspective on the Causes and Consequences in Family Business Environments** 117
JOSÉ RICARDO ANDRADE

12 **Bending the Rules of the Game: Dark Entrepreneurship in a Capitalist System** 133
GBEMISOLA OGBOLU AND SUZANNE HAGUE

13 **Voluntary Veils and Community Camouflage: Finding Darkness in the United Kingdom's Voluntary, Community and Social Enterprise Sector** 144
JENNIFER HAGAN AND LUCY PHILIPSON

14 **The Dark Side: A Philosophical Analysis of Leadership in Nigeria's Arts and Entertainment** 161
OLAMILEKAN "LAYCON" AGBELESHE

15 **Does Culture Influence Dark Leadership Manifestation? A Hofstede Exploration of Nigeria** 173
OGECHI ADEOLA, OBINNA MUOGBOH, ISAIAH ADISA, AND BERNADINE BUKOMEKO

16 **Culture and the Politics of Leadership: Insights from Iraqi-Kurdistan** 185
BALEN MOHAMMED

17 **Unveiling the Unfelt Snakes: Understanding the Dark Side of Leadership in Asian Culture** 192
SAMYIA SAFDAR, NAMRA MUBARAK, AND SHAZIA FAIZ

18 Toxic Leadership across Cultures: A Bitter Pill to Swallow 202
OLUWATOBI OMOTOYE, EMMANUEL MOGAJI, AND ZACCHEAUS OLONADE

THEME IV CONTEMPORARY AND EMERGING ISSUES

19 The Invisible Manager: The Dark Side of Digital Leadership in the Nordic Context 215
KATERYNA MALTSEVA REIBY AND INGVILD SAGBERG

20 My Boss Is Horrible: A Cursory Social Media Content Analysis of Perceptions and Perspectives of the Dark Side of Leadership in the Workplace 230
EBES AZIEGBE-ESHO

21 Combating Digital Manipulation: A Cross-Cultural Analysis of Enterprise Leadership in China and the United Kingdom 243
YUAN ZHAI

THEME V INTERVENTIONIST PARADIGMS

22 Navigating the Dark Side of Leadership: Insights from Nigeria's Public Sector 257
SHERIFF F. FOLARIN, UGOCHUKWU D. ABASILIM, AND MOSTAFA M. JALAL

23 Leadership and the Bankruptcy of Integrity 271
MATTHEW N. O. SADIKU AND JANET O. SADIKU

24 Self-Awareness: A Path to the Bright Side of Leadership 280
MAHADIH KYAMBADE, BRIDGET NAMUBIRU, AFULAH NAMATOVU, MONICA TUSHABE, AND REHEMA KAGERE

25 Strategic Interventions for Addressing Dark Side Leadership 288
DEASI-ANN WILLIAMSON

26 Afterword 301

Index 303

Foreword

Like many academic fields, leadership studies have a tendency to develop ostensibly new models and concepts that turn out to be "old wine in new bottles". Research into dark leadership may not wholly avoid this trap but the present collection manages to at least dodge it because the contributors treat dark leadership as something that (a) has always been with us and (b) is not conveniently marked off from other forms of leadership. An illustration of both points can be found in the stress on Machiavellianism as a feature of dark leadership. While dark leaders may have few compunctions about manipulating and exploiting workers, it is unhelpful to imagine that manipulation and exploitation by leaders are new or unique to dark leadership. The Marxist claim that profit is unpaid labour draws attention to inherent exploitation, even in situations where both parties are happy with the exchange. Even the best of employers treat workers as a means to an end and the workers expect to be paid as little as possible and fired if they no longer serve the organisation's purposes. This is as true for organisations with charitable aims as it is for cut-throat businesses, and leaders at all levels experience pressure to achieve outcomes that might seem to be most readily achieved by resorting to dark leadership behaviours.

All leadership involves setting a direction and influencing others to follow it, which inevitably begs the question of whether the direction is well chosen and whether people would be wise to follow it. This is largely neglected not only within the mainstream leadership literature but also in everyday organisational life. Discussions of dark leadership often illustrate the issues with infamous organisational cases like *Theranos*, but this obscures how common some aspects of dark leadership can be. The late Jerry B. Harvey used the ordinary example of downsizing in a university department to illustrate the ease with which a leader might "go to the dark side" without really recognising the step being taken. Many UK departments are currently downsizing to cope with financial difficulties; most are related to sector-wide problems, but some are unique to individual institutions and arise from poor decisions taken by VCs with eyes on their careers and/or legacies and ears closed to concerns raised by staff and unions (and sometimes even their senior management colleagues) about the wisdom of their decisions. And when a reluctance to listen is paired with a willingness to bully and silence critics, we can observe dark leadership in this humdrum setting, perhaps attesting to Sayre's 3rd law ("The politics of the university are so intense because the stakes are so low").

When considering whether the ends justify the means, an area of particular danger for thinking on dark leadership is motivated reasoning, leading us to see strong leadership when we approve of the ends but dark leadership when we do not. An especially vivid example is the importance placed by some on the left on making a clear distinction between Stalin and Hitler. Both men intentionally caused the deaths of millions, but the deaths caused by Stalin are sometimes framed as the regrettable side effect of a necessarily forceful drive to modernise the Soviet Union. Their desire to argue over which mass murder was worst is, for some, a reluctance to acknowledge the reality of the Soviet era, but for others, it is about sustaining an argument against the criticism that communism is in practice as brutal as fascism. While this is an extreme example, social media provides constant illustrations of the same leadership behaviours being judged completely differently depending on whether the leader is perceived as being on the side favoured by the person posting.

The chapters here draw upon a range of theoretical perspectives to examine leadership in a range of settings, most obviously in different cultures and regions, but also in different types of organisations, in politics, in popular culture, in education, and in the media. The cross-cultural nature of the compendium is an important contribution in itself. The idea that different styles of leadership might be more or less effective in different cultural settings has been extensively explored within cross-cultural management. It would be bold to suggest that dark leadership may be the most appropriate approach in some settings, and yet, Western governments for much of the 20th century pursued a line on diplomacy and international relations which tacitly accepts this – while ironically in the 21st century, their critics (at home and in the Global South) sometimes make a similar case. The story of the rise and fall of Saddam Hussein illustrates this well. Saddam was at different times viewed as a dangerous revolutionary, a Soviet lackey, someone the West could do business with, a valuable counterweight to Iranian power, a major source of regional instability, and (after his fall) the only person who could have held Iraq together. Yet throughout he was also understood to be a ruthless individual willing to use extreme violence to achieve his aims. Many of the same foreign policy hawks who justified supporting this dark leader eventually came to the view that he had to go. We might add that many of those who were appalled by American support for a monster like Saddam eventually came to the view that leaving him in charge of Iraq was a necessary evil if the country was to avoid descending into chaos. Both sides are guilty of treating dark leadership as something that might be appropriate in certain settings (settings where they don't live, of course). These discussions draw our attention to the use of power within leadership and raise the question of whether there are any circumstances in which elements of dark leadership might be viewed as an appropriate way to lead.

Having argued that dark leadership can be found in a range of settings, I want to conclude by considering the extent to which dark leadership might be more common in our own practice than we recognise. In the movie *The Big Easy*, Remy McSwain, a likeable but corrupt cop, tangles with Anne Osborne, a highly principled district attorney. Osborne is infuriated by McSwain's behaviour and his attitude – McSwain is still proud of being a cop and does not really seem to think he's doing much wrong. After one particularly egregious incident of corruption, Osborne loses her temper: "*You still think it's funny, don't you? Why don't you just face it, Remy? You're not one of the good guys anymore.*" Anyone who follows whistleblowing cases as I do will come across countless examples of leaders who still think they're a "good guy" despite appalling wrongdoing taking place on their watch (and in many cases under their direction). And they continue to think of themselves as good guys even as they engage in vindictive reprisals against the whistleblower. This pattern seems to be worst among leaders of organisations who make claims of a moral purpose, e.g., charities, religious groups, health and social care, and activist organisations. Those who abhor dark leadership in principle will also be least likely to accept they are at times guilty of practising it. If we go back to the *Star Wars* example, the idea of turning to the dark side is a major and largely irrevocable change. Perhaps in reality, we all channel a dark side occasionally and maybe a little more often than we care to admit. The question, "Am I still one of the good guys?" may be a useful prompt for self-reflection for anyone in a leadership position.

Professor John Blekinsopp
Oslo New University College, Norway
Northumbria University, United Kingdom

Preface

This little light of mine, I am going to let it shine.
–*Harry Dixon Loes*

At every point in history, personalities and institutions have embodied the dark side of leadership. Think of dictators and totalitarians, wars and genocides, social injustice and human rights abuse, white-collar crimes, and corporate scandals. Today, the social landscape remains rife with leaders who continue to leave a trail of sinister outcomes. The examples of leaders from the dark side are seemingly more than those from the bright side. In the last three decades, the research in leadership and organisational sciences has expanded in theoretical and typological breadth to encompass the negative dimensions of leadership.

Defining the dark side of leadership is contentious. While some definitions are founded on the negative implications of the construct, others focus on the process rather than the effects; the last category captures both the effects and the process. Some studies have explored the complex interplay of personality, culture, process, and damaging outcomes of the dark side of leadership. Others offer an alternative perspective, arguing that there are benefits to the dark side. The multitude of theories, methodological perspectives, and findings in the field underscores the shift from the utopian and optimistic accounts of leader–follower interactions. Despite the broad exploration, a noticeable gap remains, a comprehensive resource for practitioners and practice-based researchers, encapsulating cross-cultural cases, perspectives, and actionable interventions. *The Dark Side of Leadership: A Cross-Cultural Compendium* is a transdisciplinary venture that draws on the experience and scholarly apparatus of practitioners and researchers. We are excited about our contributors whose backgrounds cut across Africa, the Americas, Asia, and Europe with interesting and extensive professional experience in the military, psychiatry and healthcare, media and entertainment, higher education, engineering, non-profit, political science and public policy, human resource management, consulting, law, marketing, and project management.

In line with the aim of the book, five main themes emerged. The first theme centres on the multi-level conceptualisations of dark leadership, antecedents, motivation, manifestations, and liabilities for individuals, teams, and organisations. The second theme explores some dynamics of leader–subordinate interactions in the workplace; values, follower responses, and perceptions; and the impact of interactions. The third theme discusses contextual factors, national culture, and themes of convergence and divergence in cross-cultural analysis and how they impact leader–follower interactions and the manifestations of the dark side. The fourth theme assesses emerging issues of social media and information technology, the dark side of digital leadership, and the role of the United Nation's Sustainable Development Goals (SDGs). The fifth and final theme provides interventionist paradigms for mitigating the dark side of leadership. Each chapter concludes with a kaleidoscope of actionable lessons and principles for leaders and aspiring leaders.

Weaving a rich tapestry of insights and interventions, this book is a roadmap for timely reflection on leadership, to check ourselves before we wreck ourselves and to check our leaders before they wreck us. This book offers organic perspectives on our individual and collective responsibility to advocate and epitomise the bright side of leadership in our personal and corporate spaces.

Acknowledgements

We acknowledge the contributors who have shared thoughtful perspectives and proffered interventions to *The Dark Side of Leadership*. We are grateful to everyone, who at one point or the other, has sown the seed of the bright side in our personal development and leadership journey. Last but surely not least, our families and friends deserve special mention for their love and support.

Notes on the Editors

Adebukola Oyewunmi is the founder of and lead trainer at Characom Leadership Consulting. An advocate of the bright side of leadership, she has facilitated notable local and international workshops on leadership effectiveness in the private and public sectors. She has years of experience working as a banking consultant in one of the United Kingdom's major financial institutions. She holds master's and doctorate degrees in strategic human resource management and industrial relations. Her research interests include leadership development, organisational psychology, and ethical behaviour. Her collaborations span Africa, Europe, and North and South America. She is a facilitator of Global Futures Literacy Network and has served as an assessor for the Mandela Washington Fellowship for Young African Leaders, a programme funded by the United States Government. She is an associate editor and a member of the editorial board of two reputable international journals. She is an academic fellow of the Chartered Institute of Personnel Development and currently lectures at the Teesside University International Business School, United Kingdom.

Gill Owens is a highly experienced chartered psychologist with an impressive professional trajectory spanning over 40 years. Her extensive expertise encompasses both the private and public sectors, as well as higher education. Throughout her career, she has embarked on the successful launch, operation, and sale of businesses, underscoring her entrepreneurial flair while honing her robust business acumen. Her fascination with dark leadership stemmed from her encounters with senior organisational leaders who showcased a markedly distinct leadership style from her supportive approach. Her transition into academia provided the perfect platform for her to delve deeper into this area of interest, evolving it into a central theme in her research. Furthermore, she conducted engaging seminars with MBA students, integrating her practical insights to deliver interactive sessions. At the core of all her professional pursuits, she has consistently upheld the value of demonstrating kindness. This ethical and compassionate approach has not only underpinned her decision-making but also greatly informed her teaching and research endeavours.

Ogechi Adeola is a professor of marketing and deputy vice-chancellor at the University of Kigali, Rwanda. She holds an adjunct professorship at Torrens University Australia. Her research has been published in top journals such as the *Journal of International Business Studies*, *Annals of Tourism Research*, *Tourism Management*, *Journal of Business Research*, *Industrial Marketing Management*, *Psychology and Marketing*, and *International Marketing Review*. Her co-authored papers won Best Paper Awards at international conferences from 2016 to 2019 consecutively, and she received the prestigious Emerald Literati Award for Outstanding Paper in 2022. She was honoured with the Most Influential Women 2024 Sustainability Award by the World Association for Sustainable Development (WASD) for her contributions to women's empowerment and sustainable development. In 2025, the International Hospitality Institute (IHI) recognised her among the 50 Most Influential Educators in Global Hospitality and Travel.

Notes on Contributors

Ugochukwu D. Abasilim, PhD, is a senior lecturer of public administration and serves as the postgraduate coordinator in the Department of Political Science and International Relations at Covenant University, Nigeria. With over a decade of academic and research experience, his expertise spans public administration, public personnel management, organisational leadership, public service ethics, and e-governance. He is committed to advancing knowledge and fostering public sector leadership through teaching and impactful research.

Isaiah Adisa is a management researcher and consultant. He has co-edited books and written several book chapters and journal articles published in recognised outlets. His research interests cut across human resource management, organisational behaviour, marketing, and gender studies. He is currently a doctoral student at the Business School, King's College, London.

Olamilekan "Laycon" Agbeleshe, is a Nigerian rapper, singer, songwriter, and the 2020 winner of Big Brother Nigeria Lockdown show. He is a member of the Recording Academy and co-owner of *Jive*, a music discovery platform. As one of the most followed public figures on social media in Nigeria, Laycon's fanbase and audience cuts across all demographics. He holds a bachelor's in philosophy from the University of Lagos, Nigeria, and a master's in international relations from the University of Portsmouth, United Kingdom. He also does significant philanthropic work through the Laycon Cares Foundation, a foundation focused on good governance, quality education, and climate action.

Godbless Akaighe is a lecturer in leadership at the School of Business, University of Leicester, UK. He earned his PhD in management (emphasis in work psychology) from The University of Sheffield, UK. He is an associate editor for the *Journal of Organisational Effectiveness: People and Performance*. His research interests are in organisational leadership and followership. Specifically, his research focuses on the dark side of leadership, workplace relationships, employee well-being, team dynamics, and gender in leadership. His research has been published in reputable peer-reviewed journals.

José Ricardo Andrade is a professor of organisational behaviour and human resource management at the Miguel Torga Higher Institute in Coimbra, Portugal, and a researcher at the Centre for Advanced Studies in Management and Economics. He is also a human resources manager and director of the human resources department of a Portuguese industrial group.

Lisa C. Barefield is pursuing her doctorate focusing on leadership at Teesside University International Business School. She recently completed a pilot study titled "Transformational Leadership and Brand Reputation: Employee Perceptions in the UK Finance and Accountancy Sector" and is now expanding her research to further develop the findings. She also works for Teesside University Online Ltd, delivering online study support guidance for MSc in aviation management and MA in leadership.

Johan Bergh is an associate professor in organisation and leadership at Oslo New University College. He is a Commander Senior Grade (Ret.) in the Royal Norwegian Navy and was formerly Head of Department, Military Leadership at the Norwegian Command and Staff College. He has been a project manager for the Norwegian Armed Forces' Basic Pedagogical View and has co-edited the Norwegian Chief of Defences' View on Military Leadership.

Clive R. Boddy has been a researcher in corporate psychopathy and psychopathic leadership since 2005. He has two doctorates, two books, eight book chapters, and fifty-six refereed academic papers on the subject. He is currently deputy head of the School of Management at Anglia Ruskin University and has previously been professor of management at the University of Tasmania in Australia and professor of leadership at Middlesex University in the United Kingdom.

Bernadine Bukomeko is an experienced academic at the University of Kigali, Rwanda, with a strong background in development economics, statistics, and monitoring and evaluation. He holds a Master of Science in Development Economics and a Postgraduate Certificate in Monitoring and Evaluation from Uganda Martyrs University. He is committed to leveraging data-driven insights to advance sustainable development and deliver innovative solutions across diverse communities.

Ebes Aziegbe-Esho is a senior lecturer at the Nigerian University of Technology and Management and a **senior research** associate at the University of Johannesburg, South Africa. Her research interests include investigating issues around human capital, the core factors that enable businesses to succeed through variance decomposition studies in business strategy, and international business. She earned her doctorate in management, specialising in business strategy, from Lagos Business School, Pan-Atlantic University, Nigeria. Before venturing into research and academia, she worked in different banks in Nigeria.

Shazia Faiz is an accomplished **associate** professor in the Department of Management Sciences at Capital University of Science and Technology (CUST), Pakistan. Her research interests are focused on leadership, organisational politics, and workplace dynamics. Her work delves into how leadership influences employee attitudes and behaviours, and how political dynamics shape organisational culture.

Sheriff F. Folarin has put in over 24 years in the African and global university space. He worked as a full professor of international relations and politics at Covenant University, Nigeria, for over 18 years. He served as a visiting scholar at Texas State University in 2022 and returned as a visiting professor to the Department of Political Science, where he currently teaches. He also serves as the associate editor-in-chief of the *American Society for Public Administration Journal* and *Good Governance Worldwide*. His experience across Africa and the United States has earned him peer recognition and academic awards, including invitations to speak at high-level international and national strategic conferences, the National War College in Rwanda, where he is a regular guest of the government. Among his awards are the Carnegie African Development Fellowship Program in 2015 and the United States Institutes on US Foreign Policy in 2007.

Shamaila Gull has extensive experience working as an academic/researcher in the higher education sector. Her academic career spans Pakistan, Switzerland and the UK. She completed her doctorate with a focus on sustainable business practices. Her teaching and research portfolio encompasses a wide range of themes in the domains of management, leadership and sustainability. She endeavours to promote academic knowledge exchange through her scholarly writings. She is currently affiliated with Teesside University International Business School as a senior lecturer in business.

Jennifer Hagan has many years of experience in the UK voluntary sector in fundraising, partnerships, project management, and communications, mainly in health and the natural environment. Her academic expertise and research interests lie in organisational behaviour and research methods, specifically ethics, diversity, volunteering and voluntary sector management, well-being, and heritage. Her publications and PhD thesis focused on the sustainability of volunteering in the Tees Valley region of the United Kingdom.

Suzanne Hague is a principal lecturer, facilitator, and researcher, with over 10 years of experience in philanthropy and entrepreneurship research. Her PhD investigated the motivational base of entrepreneurs. It considered how certain individuals recognise opportunities, whereas others do not. She subsequently tracked the entrepreneur's life course to identify what stimulated the individual to become a philanthropist. Dark entrepreneurship and the importance of legitimacy emerged as some of the key findings. Beyond her research, she teaches organisational sustainability and entrepreneurial leadership; she also leads executive education within the Business School.

Roohi Imtiaz is a lecturer and researcher with over 12 years of experience. Her professional trajectory encompasses comprehensive engagement in teaching, research, and administrative capacities in esteemed higher education institutions in Pakistan, the UAE, and the UK. She has led and collaborated on several projects with multicultural frameworks. Her interest centres on leadership, and she has published widely in reputable peer-reviewed journals.

Mostafa M. Jalal is a Graduate Research Assistant and Master of Public Administration (MPA) student in the Department of Political Science, at Texas State University.

Rehema Kagere is a lecturer at Makerere University Business School, Uganda. She holds a master's in business administration. Her research interests are technological innovation, business administration, leadership, governance, and business ethics.

Jabran Khan is a lecturer in project management at Cardiff Metropolitan University, United Kingdom. Before this, he held teaching positions at Bahria University and the University of Lahore in Islamabad, Pakistan. With a PhD in project management from Universiti Sains Malaysia, his academic journey has been marked by notable achievements, including receiving the prestigious SANGGAR SANJUNG Award for outstanding journal publications in 2020. His scholarly work can be found in esteemed international journals such as the *International Journal of Project Management*, *International Journal of Managing Projects in Business*, *Project Management Journal*, *IEEE Transactions on Engineering Management Journal*, *Journal of Business Research*, and the *Leadership and Organisation Development Journal*. Additionally, he serves as an expert reviewer for various international journals, further showcasing his dedication to advancing knowledge in the field of project management.

Mahadih Kyambade is an academician and lecturer in the Department of Leadership and Governance at the Makerere University Business School, Uganda. He is currently pursuing a PhD in responsible leadership and governance and holds a bachelor's in leadership and governance, a bachelor's in law, and a master's of science in leadership from Makerere University. His research focuses on themes related to leadership, governance, psychological safety, gender diversity, higher education, and policy.

Emmanuel Mogaji is an academic researcher focusing on the ABCDE of Marketing – Advertising, Branding, Communication, Digital, and Ethics, particularly within the transportation, education, and financial services sectors. He has published peer-reviewed journal articles, edited special issues and books, and presented his research at many national and international conferences. His work has appeared in esteemed journals such as *Industrial Marketing Management*, *Technological Forecasting & Social Change*, *European Journal of Marketing*, *Journal of Consumer Behaviour*, *Journal of Services Marketing*, *International Journal of Bank Marketing*, and *Telematics and Informatics*.

Namra Mubarak is a dedicated lecturer in the Department of Strategy and Marketing at Cardiff School of Management with over six years of academic experience. She holds a PhD in project management from Universiti Sains Malaysia, ranked #147 in the QS World Ranking. In addition to her teaching duties, she leads modules and actively participates in various academic committees. Her research, focused on project success factors, leadership styles, and personality traits, has been published in top-tier journals such as the *International Journal of Project Management* and the *Project Management Journal*. Recognised with multiple awards, including a research excellence award, she also serves as a reviewer for prestigious journals and has presented her work at numerous international conferences.

Balen Mohammed has over a decade of experience in leadership, media, education, and event management. He is a dynamic professional with a strong background in business administration and extensive involvement in youth development, public affairs, and digital marketing. Fluent in Kurdish and English, with proficiency in Persian and Arabic languages, he brings a global perspective to his work and excels in cross-cultural communication. He is currently pursuing a postgraduate degree in international management at Teesside University with research interest in global business practices and cross-cultural management.

Obinna Muogboh holds a BSc in electronic engineering from the University of Nigeria and an MSc and a PhD in industrial engineering from the University of Pittsburgh, USA. He is a faculty member at the Lagos Business School, Pan-Atlantic University, Nigeria, and the pioneer director of the doctorate programme. He has consulted and researched for various organisations in Nigeria and abroad, including multilateral agencies such as UNIDO. He is a member of the Institute for Operations Research and the Management Sciences (INFORMS). He also worked at INSEAD, France, as the 2009 INSEAD African Faculty fellow.

Afulah Namatovu is a lecturer in information management at the Makerere University Business School, Uganda. Her research focuses on information technology, leadership, and gender issues in organisations.

Bridget Namubiru holds a master's in leadership and governance from Makerere University, Uganda, and is currently pursuing her PhD. She is currently a senior lecturer at the Makerere University Business School in Uganda. Her research interests are in leadership, governance, management, business, and work ethics.

Gbemisola Ogbolu is a senior lecturer and a beacon of expertise in her field. With a profound passion for academia, enterprise, and research, she has dedicated her career to advancing knowledge, working with SMEs, and nurturing future professionals. Specialising in sustainable innovation, entrepreneurship, and strategy, her contributions have significantly impacted both the academic community and wider society. Beyond her scholarly endeavours, she is known for her mentorship, adeptly leading students with profound insight and knowledge. Her commitment to excellence and innovation serves as an inspiration to all who have the privilege of working with and learning from her.

Wale Olajide (FPAN, PHF) is a professor of philosophy and former deputy vice-chancellor of Ekiti State University, Nigeria. He lives in Northampton, United Kingdom.

Zaccheaus Olonade is a lecturer and academic researcher in the Department of Employment Relations and Human Resource Management at Osun State University, Nigeria. His research focuses on organisational behaviour, human resource management, and employment relations.
He has published peer-reviewed journal articles and books, presenting his work at many national and international conferences.

Olufemi Oluwatayo is a consultant psychiatrist at Oxford Health NHS Trust and a former medical director of Lakeside Hospital, Wyboston, Bedfordshire, United Kingdom. He was previously a Welcome Research fellow and lecturer at the University of Manchester.

Oluwatobi Omotoye is an academic researcher with an interest in dysfunctional leadership, leadership development, human resource management, and organisational behaviour. He has published peer-reviewed journal articles and has presented his work at numerous national and international conferences. He is currently a doctoral candidate at IESEG School of Management, University of Lille.

Lucy Philipson brings 20 years of experience from the international charity sector with a specialisation in responsible leadership and sustainable development initiatives. Bridging the gap between community-led decision-making and corporate philanthropy, her interest is driven by global inequity, ethics, and authenticity. She has broad experience in NGO management, and her key interests include ESG, CSR, education, climate-smart agriculture, and gender equity.

Kateryna Maltseva Reiby has a PhD in business and economics (with specialisation in Marketing) from BI Norwegian Business School. In her research, she studies how humans interact with technologies like wearables, gamified platforms, performance management systems, and AI. She has published in journals such as the *Journal of Management Inquiry*, *Computers in Human Behaviour*, and *The Information Society*. Kateryna is an associate professor at Oslo New University College, teaching courses on digital transformation and digital technologies.

Janet O. Sadiku earned a bachelor's in nursing science in 1980 from the University of Ife, now known as Obafemi Awolowo University, Nigeria. She holds a master's from Juliana King University, Houston, Texas, USA. She has worked as a nurse, educator, and church minister in Nigeria, the United Kingdom, Canada, and the United States. She has co-authored several books and articles.

Matthew N. O. Sadiku is a professor emeritus in the Department of Electrical and Computer Engineering at Prairie View A&M University, Prairie View, Texas, USA. He is the author of several books and papers. His areas of research interest include computational electromagnetics, computer networks, and marriage counselling. He was the recipient of the 2000 McGraw-Hill/Jacob Millman Award for outstanding contributions in the field of electrical engineering. He is a life fellow of the Institute of Electrical and Electronics Engineers.

Samyia Safdar is a lecturer in strategy at Teesside University, UK. She earned her PhD in business management with a specialisation in HR and management from the University of International Business and Economics, China. She has previously served as an assistant professor at leading institutions in

Pakistan, showcasing her extensive academic and professional experience. Her research interests are diverse, encompassing leadership, psychological factors, project management, employee performance, organisational behaviour, and cross-cultural management. She has an impressive portfolio of publications in esteemed journals recognised by ABS, ABDC, and Web of Science.

Ingvild Sagberg has a PhD in organisational psychology from the University of Oslo, Norway. Her research interests include organisational socialisation and onboarding, work role transitions, HRM, leadership, and work environment. She has published in journals such as *Nordic Psychology* and *Scandinavian Journal of Work and Organisational Psychology*. Ingvild is an associate professor at Oslo New University College, teaching in the fields of leadership, human resource management, and organisational psychology.

Mehrdad Sarhadi is a lecturer of project management at Teesside University, Middlesbrough, United Kingdom. He holds a PhD, an MSc in project management, and a BSc in architectural engineering. His research explores how philosophy and social sciences can provide new insights into different areas of management studies, such as management paradigmatic changes, management education, ethical behaviour, and sustainable management. His publications appear in the *Project Management Journal*, the *International Journal of Managing Projects in Business*, and the *Journal of Legal Affairs and Dispute Resolution in Engineering and Construction*.

Luis J. Serrano-Tamayo served for 30 years in the Colombian Navy until the rank of Navy Captain. He is currently a lecturer in project management at Cardiff Metropolitan University, United Kingdom. He has taught project management at the University of Manchester in the UK and other high-profile Colombian universities. He obtained his Project Management Professional (PMP) certification 10 years ago, demonstrating his 20+ years of experience in project management positions, leading projects in a portfolio of £500+ million in the defence, R&D, education, shipbuilding, and infrastructure sectors. During this time, he created a series of Project Management Offices (PMO) and mathematical decision-making models for the optimal selection of procurements in defence projects, negotiating multiple technology transfer agreements with organisations worldwide, and undertaking highly complex projects.

Monica Tushabe holds a master's in leadership and governance from Makerere University and is currently pursuing her PhD. She is a senior lecturer at Makerere University Business School, Uganda. Her research interests are leadership, governance, gender diversity, women's representation, and business ethics.

Deasi-Ann Williamson brings over 17 years of invaluable experience from her tenure at the National Health Service (NHS), in England. She has held various impactful roles, culminating in her appointment as a commercial operations executive. There, she spearheaded effective functions and governance, optimising service delivery. Her commitment to excellence and organisational development led her from frontline clinical practice (Modern Matron) to the board rooms (Private Commercial and County Council). Her dedication to innovation was recognised by the Department of Health England and City Fringe, acknowledging her team for Innovation in Practice and Community Engagement and Development. At the senior level, she played a pivotal role in preparing a prominent Central London NHS Trust for GDPR Compliance and Readiness in 2018.

Yuan Zhai holds a PhD in business management from the University of Sunderland, an MSc in engineering business management from Warwick University, and a BEng in electrical and electronic engineering from Imperial College London. He is passionate about bringing unique perspectives to teaching and research. As guest editor-in-chief for special issues in the *International Journal of Organisational Analysis* and the *Journal of Management Development*, he has demonstrated his expertise in digital transformation, environmental sustainability, and management development. His consulting engagements that include organising food production safety training and facilitating cooperation between UK and Chinese institutions demonstrate his commitment to fostering international collaboration and knowledge exchange.

I

DARK SIDE LEADERS: WHO THEY ARE AND WHAT THEY DO

Chapter 1

The Hunt for Prey: A Playbook of Psychopathic Leadership

Adebukola Oyewunmi

Introduction

Viewed with a superficial lens, the corporate environment presents a vista of structure, strategy, and goal achievement. This becomes even more vivid with the introduction of charismatic orators in leadership, and the common usage of metaphoric language such as corporate family, corporate soul, core values, compelling vision, and similar semantics. Beneath this sublime representation, is a corporate jungle where the existence of some individuals is dependent on their predatory prowess. The natural order of the animal kingdom is unamenable to the principles of ethics and the morality of good and evil but in corporate spaces where these principles are lauded, the manifestations of predation remain prevalent. In his treatise, *Leviathan*, Hobbes (1996) describes self-interest as the most potent driver of human behaviour. The proponents of Adam Smith's capitalism also advocate the centrality of rational self-interest to economic viability. At its extreme, the capitalist ethos of modern organisations is underpinned by irrational self-interest and associated with leader psychopathy (McHoskey, 1999; Boddy, 2017).

Predation is an art that comes naturally to the psychopath. Criminal psychopaths are often profiled as monstrous, deranged, cold-blooded personalities lurking in the shadows or behind the keyboard, waiting to execute sinister intentions. The psychopathic leader (also known as the successful psychopath) lurks in the open, a master of impression management, charming and charismatic yet predatory. Other components of this behavioural

DOI: 10.4324/9781003475262-2

toolkit include manipulation, grandiosity, emotional detachment, sabotage, victimisation of others, parasitic attitude, criminal versatility, and every other trait that comes to mind when you imagine a snake in a suit (Babiak & Hare, 2006; Côté et al., 2011).

The consequences of this repertoire of traits are dire on multiple levels (e.g., Oyewunmi et al., 2018). Some writers, such as Dutton (2012), counter the view that psychopathic leaders are wholly evil, stating that there is a bright side to their personalities that is potentially beneficial to organisations. The argument suggests that the traits of charm, confidence, communication skills, ruthlessness, and ambitions without the constraints of emotional attachment are fundamental to the achievement of personal and corporate goals. Hence, there is wisdom in leader psychopathy that non-psychopaths can learn from. This position is why organisations are attracted to dynamic, ambitious individuals with psychopathic tendencies. Dutton's (2012) perspective raises important questions. What is charisma and ambition without character? If psychopathic traits reinforce the achievement of organisational goals but continuously undermine the personhood and well-being of others, does this not translate to the normalisation of predation in the corporate space? Important points are made on the social imperative to harness the *functional* traits of psychopaths (Dutton, 2012; Maccoby, 2007), but not much insight is provided on navigating the dysfunctional traits and how victims can protect themselves.

There are diverse instances of dark side traits covering toxic, abusive, despotic, Machiavellian, sadistic, destructive, and psychopathic leadership in nations and organisations. With the widespread shift in values, increasing social anomie and the capitalist extremes of competitive struggle and materialism, interest in the dark side of leadership will continue to grow. This chapter presents a portrait of the psychopathic leader and reflects on their predatory process. Most importantly, it discusses the necessity for victims to protect themselves from the damaging effects of psychopathic leadership. In a subsequent chapter, Clive Boddy explains the rise of psychopathic leaders, their initial supposed success, and their eventual disastrous finish. Unfortunately, a typical pattern in their disastrous finish is dragging others with them on their way down. An adage from Achebe's (1958) *Things Fall Apart*, says that since hunters have learned to shoot without missing, birds must learn to fly without perching. They can protect themselves from being prey by the swiftness of flight, hiding from view, or fighting back. These are the tenets of self-preservation, and failure to act is ceding existence to the predator. Therefore, it is the moral responsibility of the individual and collective to push back against the predation of psychopathic leaders so that we are *no longer prey for the beasts of the land but dwell in safety and without fear* (Ezekiel 34:28 New King James Version).

The Predator Playbook

There is significant literature that details the traits of psychopathic leaders. A portrait of such a leader will outline charismatic features with veiled intentions etched in the frozen cockles where a heart theoretically exists. Hare (2003) describes four trait quadrants comprising interpersonal (glib, superficial, grandiose sense of self-worth, pathological lying, and manipulative), affective (lack of remorse, emotional shallowness, lack of empathy, and failure to accept responsibility), lifestyle (stimulation seeking, impulsive, irresponsible and parasitic attitude) and anti-social (behavioural problems, juvenile delinquency, and criminal versatility). The difference between psychopathic and non-psychopathic leaders is the extent to which the former will go to achieve goals, their tendency for unethical behaviour, and the predatory abuse of others.

Predation is a process whereby members of an animal group consume members of a less powerful group of animals. The predator evolves, camouflages, and attacks the prey for its sustenance. The prey also evolves and camouflages to avoid being nourishment to the predator. The most skilled predators live, reproduce, dominate, and threaten the existence of less powerful species in the ecosystem. From the standpoint of ecological biology, predator-prey interaction is a food web subject to the laws of the wild (Burak et al., 2018). This interaction can also be observed in human groups. Aside from the physiological, humans have diverse needs related to security, relationships, self-esteem, social status, financial success, material acquisition, and other extrinsic goals. Broadly, there are two ways of meeting these needs and achieving extrinsic goals: ethically – aligning with good conscience and the natural laws that guide human conduct or unethically – abusing, manipulating, taking undue advantage of others, objectifying relationships while pursuing personal goals. The latter is what human predators do; it is the trademark of psychopathic leaders.

The psychopathic leader's camouflage of charisma provides the social currency and authority to influence others. The intensity of charm, social ease, and dominance they demonstrate is perceived as presence, attractiveness, success, reliability, and role-model worth. Charisma is from the Greek χάρισμα (khárisma) and is loosely translated as "favour freely given" or "gift of grace" that describes personal magnetism that has a profound effect on others. This *gift* can either be used to lead others for good or astray. A critical component of what is referred to as charisma is communication skills, non-verbal and verbal. Psychopathic leaders are masters of non-verbal communication (Ten Brinke et al., 2017). Depending on the setting, they mimic and evoke emotions in dynamic social performances where they are often the main characters. This skill may involve subliminal non-verbal communication through eye contact, gestures, facial expressions, tone, tempo, and cadence. Such performative behaviour helps them *light up a room* and *charge* their audience. They typically build an influence network by identifying pawns and patrons through one-on-one interactions, a phenomenon known as the psychopathic bond which is predicated on deceit and manipulation.

Verbal communication style is also definitive and predictive of psychopathy (Sneiderman, 2006). While the relationship between communication and personality is complex and may be moderated or mediated by several variables, research suggests a familiar linguistic profile of psychopathic leaders (Endres, 2004). Their verbal communication is characterised by linguistic intelligence, talkativeness, elaborate vocabulary, ability to narrate self-aggrandising stories that assert their dominance and massage their ego, and the use of metaphors and figurative expressions because they are useful for deceptive behaviour (Klaver et al., 2007). They also employ rhetorical questions, contrasts, lists, repetition, and alliteration (Woodworth et al., 2012). The language of psychopathic leaders is described as *hollow;* employed fluidly, creatively, and convincingly (Cleckley, 1976). They may act like they are invested when using emotional words but are disconnected from the emotional valence (Brites, 2016). There is a positive relationship between charisma and psychopathy (e.g., Paulhus & Williams, 2002). While this does not imply that all charismatic individuals are psychopathic or vice versa, it indicates that psychopathic leaders are less likely to be detected or punished for their unethical behaviours. With the changing dynamics in the business environment, the leader is redefined as a charismatic hero with a messianic zeal to navigate organisational change and achieve significant outcomes. However, charisma does not always denote character. In his biography of Hitler, Kershaw (2008) states that "the mass appeal of the charismatic leader has only an indifferent relation to the leader's actual personality and character attributes. Perceptions are more important than reality".

Nonetheless, armed with charisma and charm, they typically launch a compelling vision and communicate it convincingly to their followers. The vision presents an idealised venture, organised goals and objectives, integrated structures, and activities founded on norms that reinforce. Symbols, construction, and delivery are critical to follower commitment. While such visions seem well-defined, there are important what, why, and how questions that should be interrogated. Several leaders have risen and fallen because a compelling vision is not always authentic, realistic, or constructive. The psychopathic leader exaggerates, deflects questions and criticisms using anecdotes, and controls the narrative by magnifying positive information and relegating the negative (Conger, 1990).

Followers continue to pursue the vision, make sacrifices, and adjust their behaviour and values. The insularity to opposing views and one-way top-down communication clouds their judgement. For some, access to the leader is everything. It empowers and helps them compensate for their insecurities by identifying with the dynamic persona of the leader. Such hypercompliant *corporate yes-men* fan the flames of the status quo and profess unending loyalty to the convictions and actions of the psychopathic leader. Others eventually realise that their opinions do not matter. In this arrangement, *Rule Number 1 is that the leader is always right. Rule Number 2 is, when the leader is wrong, refer to Rule Number 1.* The commitment to the vision is measured by compliance with the directives of the leader. Of course, commitment and compliance are not always synonymous. Motivated by a devotion to the leader, being part of a greater purpose, or drive for self-actualisation, followers pursue the vision at the expense of a gradual decline in personal autonomy and introspection.

Psychopathic leaders require their followers to express solidarity with the vision continuously. Team meetings, inductions, retreats, and other corporate events include sessions dedicated to reinforcing the vision. Organisational culture is designed and deployed as the collective programming of the mind (Hofstede et al., 2010) by top management to shape cognitive processes and modify behaviour. As culture architects, these leaders promote monoculturalism and groupthink yet project an illusion of choice and noble ideals (Lalich, 2004). The line between corporate culture and corporate cultism soon fades because of dysfunctional norms, the relegation of followers' voices, overdependence on the superior wisdom of the leader, and the use of culture as control. The leaders continue legitimising the system by constructing a narrative that complements their perception of reality. The authority, loyalty, and respect they enjoy provide a conducive environment to perpetrate diverse forms of misconduct. Boddy (2011) argues that the unethical practices of corporate psychopaths are significantly responsible for white-collar crimes and the 2008–2009 global financial crisis. These leaders use selective moral disengagement by reframing unethical behaviour as acceptable or justifiable without self-condemnation (Bandura & National Inst of Mental Health, 1986). The constellation of psychopathic traits (e.g., lack of empathy, criminal versatility, pathological lying) and the use of figurative language to sanitise behaviour make it easy to foster a culture where followers condone and perpetrate unethical practices.

Zimbardo (2007) identified three schemas of dark-side behaviours – *bad apples*, *bad barrels*, and *bad barrel makers*. Bad apples, such as psychopathic leaders are individuals lacking moral character, with dark traits and intentions. These traits are not exclusive to dark-side leaders; followers who possess them are comfortable with the unethical culture and leverage it for their self-interest. Bad apples can corrupt the system, making it a bad barrel. Individuals without dark traits or intentions eventually become complicit because of the prevailing culture. When good apples over-commit to a psychopathic leader, it impairs their ethical judgement as they begin to accept ethical lapses they originally would not tolerate. Social learning theory indicates that individuals learn behaviours by modelling environmental influences (Bandura, 1977). When others are rewarded for demonstrating unethical behaviours, it further reinforces the observer's modelling. Bad apples foster a bad barrel context; bad barrel makers are the dark side leaders who create toxic contexts, normalise unethical practices, and benefit from them, disregarding consequences. The psychopathic leader can disregard or misrepresent consequences by not taking responsibility and minimising their role in circumstances that have led to negative outcomes. They spin misleading narratives that blame victims for the consequences of their psychopathic behaviours. These tactics are defensive mechanisms that help them to perpetuate their ambitions while projecting a positive self-image. It is important to highlight that individual actors are embedded in broader socio-cultural contexts that influence worldviews and decisions. This promotes the institutionalisation of norms, eventually redefining and legitimising them as the new benchmarks for other actors. No behaviour is context-free, and when organisations operate in environments where ethical and regulatory frameworks are lacking, weak or contradictory, it provides the latitude for the dark side to thrive.

In wildlife, predator-prey interaction is significantly impacted by ecological conditions, the population of predator species, the hunting behaviour of predators, and prey vulnerability. These factors are mirrored in the corporate ecosystem and greatly determine the cascading of costly outcomes on multiple levels. Some of the far-reaching consequences are noted in the correlation between dark-side leadership styles and depersonalisation, heightened emotional exhaustion, and decreased personal accomplishment (Oyewunmi et al., 2018); psychological distress (Restubog et al., 2011); alcoholism (Bamberger & Bacharach, 2006); paranoia (Lopes et al., 2019); work deviance and unethical behaviour (Mitchell & Ambrose, 2007), employee withdrawal, decreased commitment and turnover (Boddy et al., 2021); suicide ideation (Liu et al., 2023) and several other destructive outcomes. These should awaken individual and collective consciousness to the reality that predators prey on the vulnerable. To not be a prey, we must develop different adaptations for self-preservation.

No Longer Prey: Redefining the Culture of Followership

Culture is one of the most significant factors in the leader-follower process. At the macro level, sociocultural values and expectations play an important role in developing worldviews and formulating frames of reference. Over time, group members share common beliefs about adaptation or response to the environment. Inevitably, this social conditioning is expressed in conduct and becomes the cultural capital that impacts every facet of the organisation. The conceptualisation of the leader-follower process and the characteristics of both roles is rooted in the patterned way of thinking. Hofstede's (1991) extensive research demonstrates the impact of cultural dimensions on organisations. Dimensions such as individualism-collectivism and power distance have an indelible effect on leader-follower exchange. Psychopathic leader tendencies and the actions or inaction of followers are impacted by these cultural factors. For instance, Boddy et al. (2015) explain that dark-side leaders thrive in individualistic cultures/countries where excessive self-interest to the point of greed may be undetected. Individualism is a cultural value that describes a sense of autonomy, achievement motivation, the pursuit of personal ambition, competition, innovative behaviour, and social status (e.g., Gorodnichenko & Gerard, 2011). Social psychologists have also established that individualism correlates with the overestimation of one's ability and opportunistic conduct (e.g., Oyserman et al., 2002).

The *Theranos* case exemplifies extreme individualism and its effects on leader-follower exchange (Tourish & Willmott, 2023). Driven by greed and an inflated sense of self, Elizabeth Holmes, the CEO, convinced herself and others that her biotech company, *Theranos*, had developed a revolutionary technology that would change the future of blood testing. It was claimed that *the Edison machine* (described as a medical laboratory on a chip) could test a patient's blood for various ailments, and patients would be able to analyse their results without medical oversight (Williams, 2022). However, the technology never worked, and the company relied on the industry-standard technology purchased from other biotech companies – the same technology that *Theranos* claimed would lose relevance due to the revolutionary *Edison*. Yet, the corporate board was composed of formidable personalities in business and politics expected to provide some oversight in organisational processes. This was unlikely to happen since many of the board members had no expertise in the biotech industry (Tourish & Willmott, 2023). In 2015, *Theranos* was exposed as a massive fraud following a series of investigations and eventually filed for bankruptcy in 2018 (Jennings, 2022). Before then, Holmes had been named the youngest female billionaire in the history of Wall Street with *Theranos* having a value of US$10 billion (Tourish, 2023).

The leadership of *Theranos* was defined by behaviour and thought control, non-communication across teams, a pervasive culture of silence fostered by Non-Disclosure Agreements, and punishment for dissent. The hyper-individualistic style disregarded the adverse impact of decisions on clients, employees, shareholders, and the biotech industry by focusing solely on personal ambitions. Employees would have struggled to reconcile the imperfections of Edison and Holme's charismatic rhetoric of the blood testing technology being *"the most important thing humanity has ever built… everyone needs to work as hard as humanly possible to deliver it"* (Carreyrou, 2018, p. 103). Such a vision offers an identity of relevance for followers, a privilege to be a part of something groundbreaking that motivates personal sacrifices sometimes beyond rationality. This process often starts at the point of recruitment when individual resistance is likely at its highest (Tourish & Vatcha, 2005). In the classic predatory style, the psychopathic leader inculcates a compelling but flawed vision and sets the stage for control mechanisms under the guise of collaboration for a greater cause (Oyewunmi et al., 2024). While the cognitive strain, ego depletion, and crisis of conscience may cause some followers to confront leadership, others may remain silent. In the case of Theranos, two employees eventually blew the whistle, exposing the fraudulent and life-threatening practices of the company.

In collectivist and high-power distance cultures, psychopathic tendencies in leadership are amplified. The cultural values emphasise existential inequalities, social hierarchy, conformity, group identity, and loyalty. Dissent, questioning, or offering perspective is often perceived as an attempt to embarrass those in authority. In many African contexts, the legacies of monarchical and paternalistic regimes continue to impact the conception of leadership. Leaders are considered superior, and followers are expected to defer to their authority. In contexts where these cultural orientations are combined with socio-economic gaps, silence in the face of leader excesses is a survival strategy. The Asian philosophies of Confucianism and paternalism also highlight a hierarchical social structure embedding values such as loyalty (zhong), harmony (he), and personal connections (guanxi) (Warner, 2010). Leader-follower exchange in organisations is characterised by an authoritarian style, controlled flow of information, the ambiguity of leader intentions, an expectation of employee loyalty, maintaining power imbalance, and the perception of the leader as an exemplary figure. The interplay of these values in both contexts presents a fertile field for psychopathic leadership as followers "are less attuned to unfairness committed by authority figures because they perceive these actions as part of their role-defined privilege" (Li & Cropanzano, 2009, p. 793). Faced with the dilemma of the *morality of loyalty* to the group versus the *morality of principle* (acting according to ethical principles), followers in these cultural contexts may tend towards the former alternative. An overbearing sense of group identity and prioritisation of group interest encourages conflict avoidance.

The corporate prey playbook is defined by silence, a lack of mental boundaries, rationalising toxic leader behaviour, programmed obedience, making apologies when not needed, and a lack of situational awareness. Predatory leaders exploit these follower attitudes, enabling them to leverage and abuse their positions of authority. A prey posturing makes followers vulnerable to the antics of psychopathic leaders, creating a siege or conflicted consciousness that tramples self-esteem and personal freedom. What, then, do we do when the predator is constantly on the prowl? Shall we continue to serve the dark lords? (Landay et al., 2019). There is a lot we can learn from the wild about prey defence. Animals have well-defined senses to detect predators and escape in time. Clear vision, hearing, and smell help to sense the slightest movement or action from a distance. They use warning signs and signals to alert other group members. Some have venom and adapted body parts that serve as defence mechanisms to create boundaries and ward off threats. Swiftness of flight, hiding from view or watchfulness, they do what they can to ensure self-preservation.

Followership is central to individual and organisational life but the romanticisation of leadership minimises our consideration of the integral role of followers. The traditional assumption is that followers are passive members whose role is to do the bidding of an influential leader. This view minimises the role of the follower as a significant co-determinant of leader effectiveness. It also informs the construction of follower identity – the psychological framework for cognitive and behavioural processes and the interpretation of social roles. Therefore, if followers portray a prey identity of subservience, predatory leaders will continue to exploit them for inordinate ambitions. A reassessment of identity and recognition of the significant role of followership is critical, especially with the evolution of organisations. Followers are leaders whether in alternative social arrangements or self-leadership. Leaders can also be followers reporting to others in a chain of command. Understanding the fluidity of these roles should inform a reconstruction of the prey-follower identity to an assertive follower identity that identifies and questions the psychopathic tendencies of leadership.

A questioning culture requires that followers reflect on the compelling visions of their leaders before over-aligning and investing themselves regardless of whatever charismatic spectacle presented to win their allegiance. Assertive followership will create a reciprocal effect on leader-follower behaviour and flatten the curve. Identity is fundamental and even in contexts with declined psychological safety where voice behaviour may be silenced, followers must not become psychologically comfortable with the prey identity. Creating support networks of like-minded followers would provide a channel for expressing concerns, information sharing, strategic coping mechanisms, and ultimately gaining a measure of control. Such networks are beneficial in unlearning the acceptance of psychopathic leadership, increasing self-esteem, and reducing vulnerability. The first rule of working with a psychopathic leader is to distance emotions and set psychological boundaries. The second is to identify social support and coping mechanisms. The third rule is to exit the department, organisation or system once the right opportunity presents itself.

Lessons for Leaders

In many parts of the world, event halls are filled with people attending conferences, seminars, and training sessions to *learn and relearn the art of leadership*. Yet, the responsibility of rising to a personal example of the bright side remains challenging. Everyone is a leader whether or not they hold a title or position. Fundamentally, we are responsible for leading ourselves. Therefore, we must adapt our worldviews, cognitive processes and develop our social intelligence to accommodate the service dimension of leadership. T. S. Eliot (1927, p. 8), noted that "humility is the most difficult of all virtues to achieve". We must all learn to see ourselves accurately, and non-defensively without misrepresenting our strengths or weaknesses. This does not connote low self-esteem or self-disparagement. There should be a departure from the traditional, prosaic, and materialistic objectives that dominate business thinking. Organisations should be viewed as a network of interdependent relationships collaborating towards the shared aim of sustainability for all stakeholders.

To protect followers from psychopathic leadership and other shades of the dark side, it is imperative to initiate and follow through on ethical codes of conduct, zero-tolerance policies, and disciplinary structure (Manesh et al., 2024). Leader-follower trust can only be established on a progressive culture of respect for all, transparency, credibility, and inclusion (Oyewunmi & Oyewunmi, 2022; Oyewunmi et al., 2021). There is value in instituting procedural justice systems and implementing systems for checks and balances. This will promote distributive justice and moderate self-serving behaviours. By creating flatter structures and participative systems, accountability implicitly becomes a part of leadership and other relational processes. Specialised training interventions on constructive voice and leadership development and opportunities for followers to provide honest feedback to leaders without fear are components of this culture. Leadership development interventions are generally effective when they focus on the creation of new self-schemas. Such interventions should, therefore, be concerned with advancing group-serving values as the standard leadership self-schemas.

Conclusion

Samuel T. Coleridge (1992) wrote, "water, water, everywhere and not a drop to drink". There are leaders everywhere, but not many have the substance to foster the trust, psychological safety, and wellbeing of followers. A Native American story of two wolves represents a metaphor for the dark and bright sides of leadership. A man narrates to his son that there are two wolves inside each of us. One wolf is on the dark side – greedy, abusive, egotistical, manipulative, guilty, and lying. The other wolf represents the bright side, an embodiment of virtues and positive emotions. The dominant one is the one we feed. For the bright side of leadership to become the norm rather than a pipe dream, we need to completely rethink current models and recognise the fluidity, interdependence, and authority of both leadership and followership. The dark side requires apathy to thrive; it flourishes when silence is salient, and followers are isolated. Its severity is the initiation of others and the reproduction of dominance. We empower it when we condone the psychopathic status quo. It gets stronger when we do not provide genuine feedback, hold leaders accountable for their actions, and allow the few courageous persons who speak up to be intimidated or shamed. Shall we remain prey to the psychopathic predator? The answer should be a unanimous and resounding negative.

References

Achebe, C. (1958). *Things Fall Apart.* London: Heinemann.

Babiak, P., & Hare, R. D. (2006). *Snakes in Suits: When Psychopaths Go to Work.* New York: Regan Books/Harper Collins Publishers.

Bamberger, P. A., & Bacharach, S. B. (2006). Abusive supervision and subordinate problem drinking: Taking resistance, stress and subordinate personality into account. Human Relations, 59(6), 723–752. https://doi.org/10.1177/0018726706066852

Bandura, A. (1977). *Social Learning Theory.* Englewood Cliffs, NJ: Prentice-Hall.

Bandura, A., & National Inst of Mental Health. (1986). *Social Foundations of Thought and Action: A Social Cognitive Theory.* Upper Saddle River, NJ: Prentice-Hall, Inc.

Boddy, C. R. (2011). The corporate psychopaths theory of the global financial crisis. Journal of Business Ethics, 102, 255–259. https://doi.org/10.1007/s10551-011-0810-4

Boddy, C. R. (2017). Psychopathic leadership: A case study of a corporate psychopath CEO. Journal of Business Ethics, 145, 141–156. https://doi.org/10.1007/s10551-015-2908-6

Boddy, C. R., Malovany, E., Kunter, A., & Gull, G. (2021). Employee well-being under corporate psychopath leaders. In S. Dhiman (Ed.), The Palgrave Handbook of Workplace Well-being (pp. 843–869). Palgrave Macmillan/Springer Nature. https://doi.org/10.1007/978-3-030-30025-8_74

Boddy, C., Miles, D., Sanyal, C., & Hartog, M. (2015). Extreme managers, extreme workplaces: Capitalism, organisations and corporate psychopaths. Organisation, 22(4), 530–551. https://doi.org/10.1177/1350508415572508

Brites, J. (2016). The language of psychopaths: A systematic review. Aggression and Violent Behaviour, 27, 50–54. https://doi.org/10.1016/j.avb.2016.02.009

Burak, M. K., Monk, J. D., & Schmitz, O. J. (2018). Eco-evolutionary dynamics: The predator-prey adaptive play and the ecological theatre. The Yale Journal of Biology and Medicine, 91(4), 481–489.

Carreyrou, J. (2018). *Bad Blood: Secrets and Lies in a Silicon Valley Startup*. New York: Alfred A. Knopf, Inc.

Cleckley, H. (1976). *The Mask of Sanity*. St. Louis, MO: Mosby.

Coleridge, S. T. (1992). *The Rime of the Ancient Mariner*. New York, NY: Dover Publications.

Conger, J. A. (1990). The dark side of leadership. Organisational Dynamics, 19(2), 44–55. https://doi.org/10.1016/0090-2616(90)90070-6

Côté, S., DeCelles, K. A., McCarthy, J. M., Van Kleef, G. A., & Hideg, I. (2011). The Jekyll and Hyde of emotional intelligence: Emotion-regulation knowledge facilitates both prosocial and interpersonally deviant behaviour. Psychological Science, 22(8), 1073–1080. https://doi.org/10.1177/0956797611416251

Dutton, K. (2012). *The Wisdom of Psychopaths: What Saints, Spies, and Serial Killers Can Teach Us About Success*. Toronto, ON: Anchor Canada.

Endres, J. (2004). The language of the psychopath: Characteristics of prisoners' performance in a sentence completion test. Criminal Behaviour and Mental Health, 14(3), 214–226. https://doi.org/10.1002/cbm.588

Gorodnichenko, Y., & Gerard, R. (2011). Which dimensions of culture matter for long-run growth? American Economic Review, 101(3), 492–498.

Hare, R. D. (2003). *The Hare Psychopathy Checklist-Revised* (2nd ed.). Toronto, ON: Multi-Health Systems.

Hobbes, T. (1996). In J. C. A. Gaskin (Ed.), *Leviathan*. New York: Oxford University Press.

Hofstede, G. (1991). *Cultures and Organisations: Software of the Mind*. London: McGraw-Hill.

Hofstede, G., Hofstede, G. J., & Minkov, M. (2010). *Cultures and Organisations, Software of the Mind: Intercultural Cooperation and Its Importance for Survival* (3rd ed.). New York: McGraw-Hill.

Jennings, A. (2022). Theranos: Case Study and Examination of the Fraud Triangle. Finance Undergraduate Honors Theses. Retrieved from https://scholarworks.uark.edu/finnuht/72

Kershaw, I. (2008). *Hitler: A Biography*. New York: W.W. Norton & Co.

Klaver, J. R., Lee, Z., & Hart, S. D. (2007). Psychopathy and nonverbal indicators of deception in offenders. Law and Human Behaviour, 31(4), 337–351. https://doi.org/10.1007/s10979-006-9063-7

Lalich, J. (2004). *Bounded Choice: True Believers and Charismatic Cults*. Berkeley, CA: University of California Press.

Landay, K., Harms, P. D., & Credé, M. (2019). Shall we serve the dark lords? A meta-analytic review of psychopathy and leadership. The Journal of Applied Psychology, 104(1), 183–196. https://doi.org/10.1037/apl0000357

Li, A., & Cropanzano, R. (2009). Do East Asians respond more/less strongly to organizational justice than North Americans? A meta-analysis. Journal of Management Studies, 46(5), 787–805. https://doi.org/10.1111/j.1467-6486.2009.00825.x

Liu, J., Ran, G., Zhang, Q., Li, Y., & Zhang, Q. (2023). The association between callous-unemotional traits and suicide ideation among youth: A conditional process analysis. Journal of Affective Disorders, 328, 245–254. https://doi.org/10.1016/j.jad.2023.02.063

Lopes, B. C., Kamau, C., & Jaspal, R. (2019). Coping with perceived abusive supervision: The role of paranoia. Journal of Leadership & Organizational Studies, 26(2), 237–255. https://doi.org/10.1177/1548051818795821

Maccoby, M, (2007). *Narcissistic Leaders: Who Succeeds and Who Fails*. Boston, MA: Harvard Business School Press.

Manesh, M., Tavakoli, A., Oyewunmi, A. E., & Pillay, S. (2024). Ethical decision-making in East Africa: Predictors of whistleblowing intention. Society and Business Review, 19(3), 424–454. https://doi.org/10.1108/SBR-03-2022-0067

McHoskey, J. W. (1999). Machiavellianism, intrinsic versus extrinsic goals, and social interest: A self-determination theory analysis. Motivation and Emotion, 23(4), 267–283. https://doi.org/10.1023/A:1021338809469

Mitchell, M. S., & Ambrose, M. L. (2007). Abusive supervision and workplace deviance and the moderating effects of negative reciprocity beliefs. Journal of Applied Psychology, 92(4), 1159–1168. https://doi.org/10.1037/0021-9010.92.4.1159

Oyewunmi, A. E., Adedeji, O., & Adegbuyi, A. (2024). Spiritual intelligence in the workplace: is there a dark side? Journal of Organizational Change Management, 37(4), 704–716. https://doi.org/10.1108/JOCM-06-2023-0255

Oyewunmi, A. E., Akinnusi, D. M., & Oyewunmi, O. A. (2018). Of predators and preys: Corporate psychopathy and employee burnout as parallels. Periodica Polytechnica Social and Management Sciences, 26(2), 149–156. https://doi.org/10.3311/PPso.11810

Oyewunmi, A. E., Esho, E., & Oyewunmi, O. A. (2021). Spiritual intelligence and employee outcomes in an African sample. Journal of Management, Spirituality & Religion, 18(2), 151–171.

Oyewunmi, A. E., & Oyewunmi, O. A. (2022). Speaking silence: Abusive supervision, subordinates' citizenship behaviour, and whistleblowing intention. *Sage Open*, *12*(1), 1–13. https://doi.org/10.1177/21582440221079912

Oyserman, D., Coon, H. M., & Kemmelmeier, M. (2002). Rethinking individualism and collectivism: Evaluation of theoretical assumptions and meta-analyses. Psychological Bulletin, 128(1), 3–72. https://doi.org/10.1037/0033-2909.128.1.3

Paulhus, D. L., & Williams, K. M. (2002). The dark triad of personality: Narcissism, Machiavellianism and psychopathy. Journal of Research in Personality, 36(6), 556–563. https://doi.org/10.1016/S0092-6566(02)00505-6

Restubog, S. L. D., Scott, K. L., & Zagenczyk, T. J. (2011). When distress hits home: The role of contextual factors and psychological distress in predicting employees' responses to abusive supervision. Journal of Applied Psychology, 96(4), 713–729. https://doi.org/10.1037/a0021593

Sneiderman, A. J. (2006). *Word Usage Patterns in Psychopathic Jail Inmates* (Doctoral dissertation, George Mason University). (UMI No. 3195564).

Ten Brinke, L., Porter, S., Korva, N., Fowler, K., Lilienfeld, S. O., & Patrick, C. J. (2017). An examination of the communication styles associated with psychopathy and their influence on observer impressions. Journal of Nonverbal Behaviour, 41(3), 269–287.

Tourish, D. (2023). The Leadership of Elizabeth Holmes: Lessons from the Dark Side of Silicon Valley. https://ilaglobalnetwork.org/the-leadership-of-elizabeth-holmes-lessons-from-the-dark-side-of-silicon-valley/

Tourish, D., & Vatcha, N. (2005). Charismatic leadership and corporate cultism at Enron: The elimination of dissent, the promotion of conformity and organizational collapse. Leadership, 1(4), 455–480. https://doi.org/10.1177/1742715005057671

Tourish, D., & Willmott, H. (2023). Despotic leadership and ideological manipulation at Theranos: Towards a theory of hegemonic totalism in the workplace. Organization Studies, 44(11), 1801–1824.

Warner, M. (2010). In search of Confucian HRM: Theory and practice in Greater China and beyond. International Journal of Human Resource Management, 21, 2053–2078.

Williams, M. (2022). Elizabeth Holmes and Theranos: A play on more than just ethical failures. Business Information Review, 39(1), 23–31. https://doi.org/10.1177/02663821221088899

Woodworth, M., Hancock, J. T., Porter, S., Hare, R., Logan, M., O'Toole, M. E., & Smith, S. (2012). The language of psychopaths: New findings and implications for law enforcement. FBI Law Enforcement Bulletin, 81 (July Issue), 28.

Zimbardo, P. (2007). *The Lucifer Effect: Understanding How Good People Turn Evil.* New York: Random House.

Chapter 2

Unveiling the Dark Leadership in *Star Wars*

Gill Owens

Introduction

George Lucas created the *Star Wars* universe, which is a vast and enduring science fiction franchise that has left an indelible mark on popular culture. Over four decades after the release of the first film, *Star Wars IV: A New Hope*, in 1977, the success of the *Star Wars* story still lies in its ability to transcend global cultures by capturing the hearts and minds of its fan base. The films have been one of the most popular film franchises in cinematic history and one of the most profitable, with an estimated $20 billion being brought in by the end of the ninth edition (Britannica, 2023). The *Star Wars* series of films explores the universal themes of heroism, redemption, and the battle between good (light) and evil (dark). It has inspired generations to stand up for what's right and to believe in the power of hope. The mythical energy field of the Force that permeates the *Star Wars* galaxy is central to the narrative of the story. The force has two aspects: The Light side, associated with peace and selflessness, and the Dark side, associated with aggression and selfishness.

Darth Vader is an iconic and formidable figure in the "Star Wars" saga, towering over his adversaries with an imposing presence. Conceived by the visionary George Lucas, Vader's character embodies a rich depth that provides profound insights into the complexities of authority and influence. This chapter will consider how Darth Vader serves as a compelling representation of dark leadership, examining the broader impact of such leadership within

 DOI: 10.4324/9781003475262-3

organisational contexts. Also, scholarly theories offer a strong structure for comprehending the various aspects of Vader's leadership approach and its consequences.

The Leadership Style of Darth Vader

The character of Darth Vader, originally known as Anakin Skywalker, presents a powerful and intricate narrative arc that vividly portrays the transition from a compassionate and principled leader to a malevolent figure of darkness. His journey, heavily guided and manipulated by Emperor Palpatine, serves as a poignant example of how a Jedi Knight, committed to upholding peace and justice, succumbs to the temptations of the dark side and ultimately becomes a Sith Lord driven by a thirst for authority and supremacy. This transformation stands as a sombre reminder of the corrupting influence of power and the grave repercussions of forsaking moral ideals (Giurge et al., 2021). It showcases how even the noblest aspirations can be tainted by the allure of power, ultimately leading to a leadership approach characterised by deceit, manipulation, and the imposition of fear.

In examining Darth Vader's leadership style, we find that it is characterised by traits often associated with the Dark Triad, a term used in psychology to describe narcissism, Machiavellianism, and psychopathy (Paulhus & Williams, 2002). His narcissistic tendencies are evidenced by his grandiose sense of self-importance and unwavering belief in his exceptional destiny, which causes him to perceive others as mere tools for achieving his own ends or as barriers to be ruthlessly removed. According to Campbell and Baumeister (2006), leadership rooted in narcissism often leads to a lack of empathy and an excessive focus on self-promotion, ultimately overshadowing the well-being of the group or organisation. This prioritisation of self-interest over the common good erodes team solidarity and fosters a toxic work environment.

Vader's Machiavellianism is on full display through his deceitful and strategic mindset, showcasing his willingness to manipulate and betray to achieve his goals (Genau et al., 2022). This is best illustrated by his ultimate act of betrayal against Emperor Palpatine. Machiavellian leaders are known to prioritise personal gain and power over ethical considerations, often resorting to deceit and manipulation to maintain their authority (Sendjaya et al., 2014). Vader's interactions with his subordinates and peers reflect a calculated pursuit of power, with little consideration for loyalty or honesty. Vader displays prominent psychopathic characteristics, demonstrating a pronounced absence of empathy, impulsivity, and a propensity for antisocial conduct. Leadership psychopathy is distinguished by callous behaviour, a lack of guilt, and an inability to establish authentic emotional bonds (Boddy, 2017). Vader's callous actions, such as dealing with subordinates' shortcomings through execution, serve as evidence of his lack of empathy and disregard for others' well-being (Holt & Marques, 2012). This conduct fosters an environment of fear and compliance, further cementing his authoritarian rule.

According to researchers Einarsen, Aasland, and Skogstad (2007), dark leadership can be defined as a persistent pattern of behaviour characterised by actions that deliberately undermine the organisation's objectives and have a detrimental impact on the morale and performance of its members. This style of leadership is typified by traits such as authoritarianism, narcissism, and a lack of empathy, which collectively contribute to creating a toxic work environment. As a result, the long-term consequences of dark leadership can be profoundly negative for both individuals and the organisation.

The concept of dark leadership extends beyond academic inquiry and is a prevalent theme in cultural narratives, as exemplified by characters like Darth Vader. In popular culture, such characters provide a vivid representation of the consequences of unethical leadership, offering a lens through which the complexities of power and leadership can be explored. Darth Vader's transformation from a heroic figure to a symbol of tyranny and fear illustrates the potential for leadership to go awry when ethical principles are abandoned in favour of personal power and control. This narrative serves as a cautionary tale about the dangers of dark leadership and the importance of maintaining ethical standards in positions of authority.

It is evident that Darth Vader's leadership had profound impacts on the Galactic Empire, serving as a compelling case study of the destructive potential of dark leadership. The atmosphere within the Empire under Vader's rule was dominated by fear and suppression, creating an environment where subordinates were primarily concerned with avoiding punishment rather than contributing meaningfully to organisational objectives. This oppressive climate stifled creativity, discouraged initiative, and fostered a culture of compliance over innovation (Stanojevic et al., 2020). Such an environment not only limited the potential for growth and progress within the Empire but also had detrimental effects on the well-being of its members. Tepper (2000) identified abusive supervision as a key component of dark leadership, highlighting the detrimental impact of such behaviours. Research indicates that such leadership behaviours lead to decreased job satisfaction, increased stress, and higher turnover rates among employees. In the context of the Galactic Empire, it is clear that Vader's use of intimidation and punishment as tools of control exacerbated these issues, leading to a disengaged and demoralised workforce.

The consequences of Vader's leadership style were not only limited to the operational efficiency of the Galactic Empire but also had far-reaching implications, creating an unstable organisational environment where loyalty and morale were low. The impact of dark leadership can have wide-ranging and long-lasting effects, impacting both the success of an organisation and the well-being of its members. The atmosphere of fear created by Vader's leadership style has a profound impact on the dynamics within the organisation. This fear-based compliance has a chilling effect on open communication and constructive feedback. As a result, employees are hesitant to voice dissenting opinions or propose alternative solutions. This reticence deprives the organisation of diverse perspectives and hampers the free flow of ideas that are essential for innovation and adaptability (Cullen et al., 2013). Consequently, the organisation finds itself unable to tap into the collective intelligence of its members, leading to strategic blind spots and ineffective responses to external challenges.

Such a leadership environment prioritises internal control and stability over adaptability and responsiveness. This focus on maintaining strict hierarchical control limits the organisation's ability to pivot in the face of new challenges or opportunities. The Empire's preoccupation with suppressing dissent rather than fostering a culture of open dialogue and collaboration undermines its strategic positioning and competitive edge. As a result, the organisation becomes increasingly insular, missing out on the benefits of diverse perspectives and the creative potential of its members. In essence, the emphasis on rigid control within the leadership structure can stifle innovation and hinder the organisation's capacity to swiftly respond to changes in the external environment. Instead of nurturing an environment where ideas can flourish and individuals are empowered to voice their opinions, the organisation faces the risk of stagnation and potential missed opportunities. This can ultimately impact the organisation's ability to remain agile and competitive within its industry.

Northouse (2018) underlines the importance of a balanced approach to effective leadership, which involves a delicate interplay between control and flexibility. According to Northouse, leaders should establish a sufficient level of structure to maintain organisational coherence and provide direction while also fostering an environment of flexibility that encourages innovation and adaptability. This equilibrium is vital for successfully navigating the intricate and uncertain nature of dynamic work environments. In contrast, the leadership style attributed to Vader heavily favours control and suppression, failing to harness the potential of subordinates. This approach leads to an organisational structure that lacks resilience and struggles to adapt and prosper in the face of change.

In popular culture, Vader is one of the most recognisable figures symbolising the dark side of power and authority. His transformation from Anakin Skywalker, a promising and heroic figure, to Darth Vader, a tyrannical enforcer, underscores the corrupting influence of power and the moral compromises that often accompany it. His character has become a pervasive symbol, encapsulating the dangers of unchecked power and the complexities of leadership ethics (Giurge et al., 2021). This narrative resonates with audiences, offering a cautionary tale about the perils of losing one's ethical bearings in the pursuit of power. The iconic imagery associated with Vader—his black armour, deep voice, and menacing presence—further cement his role as an archetype of dark leadership.

Vader's story reminds us that ethical dilemmas are often present in leadership roles. His journey serves as a cautionary tale of how ethical intentions can give way to unethical actions, especially when leaders prioritise personal power over the well-being of those they lead. This is in line with ethical theories in leadership studies, which emphasise the importance of integrity, transparency, and accountability (Bauman, 2013). Vader's narrative calls for a deeper consideration of the role of ethical decision-making in leadership and prompts us to reflect on how leaders' values and actions can profoundly impact their followers and organisations. Vader's journey also serves as a powerful example of the potential for redemption, carrying significant implications for the study of leadership ethics. His eventual transition back to the light side of the Force underscores the profound prospect of ethical rehabilitation, even for individuals deeply entrenched in dark leadership practices. This aspect strongly underscores the significance of self-reflection, accountability, and the capacity for transformation in leadership approaches (Branson, 2007).

Lessons for Leaders

Dark leadership can present itself in many ways within an organisational culture and is experienced by numerous employees; however, the language used to describe these experiences varies, and many are not aware of the terminology linked to dark leadership. Darth Vader's character serves as a powerful case study of dark leadership, providing a narrative that highlights the complexities and dangers of this leadership style. His portrayal has significantly influenced both popular and academic understandings of leadership, illustrating how cultural symbols can inform theoretical discussions. Vader's character encapsulates key aspects of dark leadership, including authoritarianism, narcissism, and the detrimental effects on organisational health and employee well-being. His story also offers valuable lessons on the ethical responsibilities of leaders and the potential consequences of prioritising power over principles. The impact of Darth Vader on the concept of dark leadership underscores the importance of examining both the positive and negative aspects of leadership. By bringing these issues into the public consciousness, his character encourages a more nuanced and comprehensive understanding of leadership, ethics, and the responsibilities inherent in positions of power. As such, Darth Vader remains a compelling and enduring figure in discussions about the nature of leadership and the ethical challenges it presents.

References

Bauman, D. C. (2013). Leadership and the three faces of integrity. *The Leadership Quarterly*, 24(3), 414–426. https://doi.org/10.1016/j.leaqua.2013.01.005

Boddy, C. R. (2017). Psychopathic leadership: A case study of a corporate psychopath CEO. *Journal of Business Ethics*, 145, 141–156. https://doi.org/10.1007/s10551-015-2908-6

Branson, C. M. (2007). Improving leadership by nurturing moral consciousness through structured self-reflection. *Journal of Educational Administration*, 45(4), 471–495. https://doi.org/10.1108/09578230710762463

Britannica. (2023). The Editors of Encyclopaedia. "2023: The Year in Review". Encyclopaedia Britannica. https://www.britannica.com/topic/2023-The-Year-in-Review.

Campbell, W. K., & Baumeister, R. F. (2006). Narcissistic personality disorder. In J. E. Fisher & W. T. O'Donohue (Eds.), *Practitioner's guide to evidence-based psychotherapy* (pp. 423–431). Springer Science + Business Media. https://doi.org/10.1007/978-0-387-28370-8_42

Cullen, K. L., Edwards, B. D., Casper, W. C., & Gue, K. R. (2013). Employees' adaptability and perceptions of change-related uncertainty: Implications for perceived organisational support, job satisfaction, and performance. *Journal of Business Psychology*, 29, 269–280.

Einarsen, S., Aasland, M. S., & Skogstad, A. (2007). Destructive leadership behaviour: A definition and conceptual model. *The Leadership Quarterly*, 18, 207–216. https://doi.org/10.1016/j.leaqua.2007.03.002

Genau, H. A., Blickle, G., Schütte, N., & Meurs, J. A. (2022). Machiavellian leader effectiveness: The moderating role of political skill. *Journal of Personnel Psychology*, 21(1), 1–10. https://doi.org/10.1027/1866-5888/a000284

Giurge, L. M., van Dijke, M., Zheng, M. X., & De Cremer, D. (2021). Does power corrupt the mind? The influence of power on moral reasoning and self-interested behaviour. *The Leadership Quarterly*, *32*(4), 101288. https://doi.org/10.1016/j.leaqua.2019.03.003

Holt, S., & Marques, J. (2012). Empathy in leadership: Appropriate or misplaced? An empirical study on a topic that is asking for attention. *Journal of Business Ethics*, 105, 95–102.

Northouse, P. G. (2018). *Leadership: Theory and Practice* (8th ed.). Thousand Oaks, CA: Sage Publications.

Paulhus, D. L., & Williams, K. M. (2002). The dark triad of personality: Narcissism, Machiavellianism and psychopathy. *Journal of Research in Personality*, 36(6), 556–563. https://doi.org/10.1016/S0092-6566(02)00505-6

Sendjaya, S., Pekerti, A., Hartel, C., Hirst, G., & Butarbutar, I. (2014). Are authentic leaders always moral? The role of machiavellianism in the relationship between authentic leadership and morality. *Journal of Business Ethics,* 133, 125–139.

Stanojevic, A., Akkerman, A., & Manevska, K. (2020). The oppressive boss and workers' authoritarianism: Effect of voice suppression by supervisors on employees' authoritarian political attitudes. *Contemporary Politics*, 26(5), 573–595.https://doi.org/10.1080/13569775.2020.1801168.

Tepper, B. J. (2000). Consequences of abusive supervision. *Academy of Management Journal*, 43(2), 178–190. https://doi.org/10.2307/1556375.

Chapter 3

Categorical Error and the Dark Side of Leadership

Wale Olajide and Olufemi Oluwatayo

Introduction

Beyond the error of perception by researchers, the drama of leadership is essentially inscrutable specifically because of its drivers: motive and interest. While the latter is ceremonially made public when contestants throw in their hats, the former is only ever known to the subject. The dark side of leadership becomes obvious, accompanied by people's discontent as a result of deliverables deficit with attending horrible consequences between the leader's promises and the expectations of *the led*, a reality which unknown to *the led* is nonetheless on course and in one accord with the motive of the leader. A good case is that of Heinrich Himmler and the SS as he secretly, without making his motive known to the Reich, systematically plots and executes the Holocaust. The same stories are found in George Orwell's Animal Farm and among a host of European and third-world nations where suddenly tyranny, oppression, treasury looting, high-jacking of the judiciary and the rule of law, systematic ethnic cleansing, corruption, personality cult movements, and assassinations hold sway and the rhetoric on democracy and servicing the public interest rage on.

All of the world's population where demonstrative leadership is absent would correctly pass for a colony, a herd, or a loose tribe lacking centralised direction where positive thinking, reasoned judgment, and opinion do not exist. Leadership is about instituting direction, mounting opinions and policies, crafting vision and purpose, and setting templates and frameworks

DOI: 10.4324/9781003475262-4

of service and action for meeting the needs of those being led. The world population, however, is not a herd or a colony of mindless robots. There are groups made of conscious human beings, institutions, organisations, governments, and sects that are led and supervised by those that are called leaders, people of the same kind, taken from among those that are being led and only given the privileged role because their vocation is different; the vocation of leadership. This chapter submits that far from being solely an external exhibitionist craft, leadership is a subjective private mental art whose origin is domiciled in the human brain. It is its root, its source, specifically located in the DNA, the molecule that carries the genetic information for the development and functioning of the organism, which is described as our genetic autobiography (Venter, 2008).

If leadership is all about mentally sourced actions and the cause and effect that derive from their relations, it is appropriate to assert that everything, the totality of what we think, do, or refrain from doing, is determined by the brain, inclusive of those primary psycho-social dispositions which we shall soon discuss, namely, interest and motives (Swaab, 2015). The brain determines our potential and limitations; it is the sum of our individual character to the extent that we can correctly say that we are our brains. It is what makes everyone of us who we are and what makes us different from each other in millions of ways. In other words, our personality is determined by our genetic makeup and the life experience stored in different parts of our subconscious mind, it is where our interests and motives are formed and stored.

Leadership is a process that is driven and exemplified by groups of individuals who are referred to as leaders by virtue of position, character, and attitude. Where and when leadership is perceived as an objective, homogeneous, end-to-end process that is out there to be analysed, studied, or critiqued, it must be assumed that an error has been committed because it is not the case. Again, whenever leadership is perceived, interpreted, and understood as an external phenomenon for interrogative study, a duplicate error must be assumed to have been committed because leadership is neither of the former description nor about the latter. This error of perception, interpretation, and judgment commits a categorical mistake, the ontological or semantic error of ascribing a thing to a category to which it does not belong, thereby suggesting that it does, thus inadvertently precipitating a misinterpretation and misunderstanding that essentially distorts meaning, defaces praxis and frustrates the pursuit of knowledge and truth (Ryle, 1949).

Interest and motive drive leadership. The former is generally made public while the latter is always private and unannounced because the public to which leadership interest is announced is operationally satisfied at the level of the content of interest that has been made public. It is sufficient that the candidate who is interested in seeking, for example, a political position announces his or her interest. That is all that is required to gain attention and acceptance and guarantee followership. It is all that is required by the people to believe that he or she is not a joker who has come to take them for a ride. Interest is what informs followership and is made explicit in the letter of manifesto and agenda for action. It is what drives political campaigns and, in the end, wins or loses elections. Whatever the type, form, scope, or level of leadership, be it family, institutional organisations, religious communities, or fraternities, the template is the same; interests are *ab initio* announced and made public but never motive. It is never announced, never made public, but rather, it evolves gradually, revealing its character through policy pronouncements, decrees, and actions that are adjudged good if they promote the people's well-being or evil if otherwise.

Interest is essentially subjective, and it is always made public with the full consciousness and awareness of the subject that announces the specific interest. The process is made formal, for example, in politics by purchasing a registration form, seeking nomination of party headship, sourcing for referees, and taking part in party primaries where party delegates elect their preferred candidate to represent their party and their interest. It is this process that makes authentic the hitherto confessed interest of the subject and the desire to become a leader endowed with the authority and power to lead. The two concepts of authority and power go together, the latter mapping out the boundaries of legitimate pronouncements and actions to be obeyed. The reference here is not inclusive of personal authority, which is generic, the type of authority that every human species ontologically has by right to be what he or she or is created to be, a disposition that is only made possible through self-discovery.

In the sphere of leadership and rulership, authority is accompanied by an implicit power mandate that is vested in the leader to act, lead, and be obeyed. Authority without power is essentially defective and deficient; it is reigning without ruling. Yet, when both run amok and become victims of dark motives such as greed, iron-fist dictatorship, authoritarianism, and totalitarianism show up as veritable hallmarks. The abuse of power and the misuse of authority turn the leader and man of authority into a monster to be feared and detested. Such naked use of power and authority corrupts absolutely. At the family, organisational or institutional levels, the story shamefully is the same.

Motives are sourced from the brain, albeit with help from the environment. As Venter (2008) rightly observes, without understanding the environment in which species exist, life as we know it cannot be understood. An organism's environment is ultimately as unique as its genetic code, unknown and undetected, hidden in the subconscious, remaining strictly personal, waiting to be ignited. This is the reason why in most cases, the followership is always caught by surprise by the betrayal of trust, pitiable victims of a rude awakening, as *the lamb* suddenly becomes a devouring deranged roaring lion. The life and times of Adolf Hitler, Joseph Stalin, Mao Zedong, Benito Mussolini, Robert Mugabe, Idi Amin, Mobutu Sese Seko, Sani Abacha, Ferdinand Marcos, and Augusto Pinochet are veritable examples of leadership gone seriously wrong. Modern management policies in all sectors underscore the need for psychiatric tests for new entrants, just as marriage counsellors canvass similar tests for intending couples to prevent horrible instances of domestic violence. However, the character is a major precursor to whatever findings such mental evaluations might reveal and what motives the subject might be nurturing to spring on followership. Munroe (2015) submits that "the most valuable component of (visible) leadership is not power, position, influence, notoriety, fame, talent, gifting, dynamic oratory, persuasiveness, intellectual superiority, academic achievement or management skills. It is a character, the cradle of credibility". Leadership without character is a sham, a great disaster waiting to happen, so equally hidden motives. For illustrative purposes, compare the life and times of Heinrich Himmler and the SS, who secretly, without making his motives known to Adolf Hitler and the Reich, systematically plotted and executed six Jews with that of the South African President Late Nelson Mandela, whose interest and motive for leadership was service, a vow that remained unbroken till his death.

The Interplay of Interests and Motives: A Reflection

Some years ago, following a restructuring in a private hospital that caters to long-stay patients with mental health needs, a new role of Director of Operations was created. This post was primarily to head the nursing team and assist the hospital Director in the day-to-day running of the hospital. At the time, there were concerns about the standard of nursing care and the unprofessional laissez-faire culture amongst nurses and support workers, who were the largest workforce in the hospital and the front-line care providers. There was a culture of cosy friendships with the nurse managers allocating bank shifts to their "pals" and booking in their friends and associates via a sole locum agency that the hospital uses to cover shortages. The idea was to break up this culture and improve the overall standard of nursing care in the hospital.

After an extensive recruitment process, a lady with an MBA from a prestigious Business School and what seemed like a track record of achievements in leadership positions with experience in the private health sector was appointed. She appeared to be a no-nonsense character whose strength was in following due process and staying the course whilst implementing change even when unpopular. Within a couple of months of her resumption, she was noticed to have a peculiar style of leadership. She liked to see people as either good or bad and would pick her favourites among them. She had a couple of female nurses that she quickly became close to and would repeatedly ask them about the performance of the other managers, who were all males, and the other staff. She would obtain information from them, use that information to manipulate other staff, and threaten them with disciplinary measures to get them to do what she wanted. She was issuing queries and adopting due processes with certain nurses whilst leaving her favourites untouched. Very soon, it became an open conversation in the hospital that she had her "untouchable" nurses who could do no wrong. Her style was basically to play the staff against each other in what can be colloquially described as "divide and rule". She also tended to see men as bad and a threat to her.

She tried to lead a change in the rota pattern, i.e., to stop nurses and support workers from being on permanent night shifts and to change the shifts to thrice daily instead of the previous twice daily long shifts. She also moved staff around to break the cosy relationships and friendships. Based on this leadership style, she was unable to achieve the targeted goals, but rather, she made the environment toxic, culminating in a breakdown of trust among the nursing team and the hospital management. There was a perceptible reduction in morale, and within 6 months of her appointment and a couple of months of implementing the changes, several nurses and support workers resigned, whilst some went on long-term sick as a result of "work-related stress". The hospital ended up requiring significantly more agency staff as it was impossible to replace those leaving immediately due to a national shortage of medical workforce personnel at the time.

With the reforms unravelling rapidly and the situation getting worse, her attitude soon became untenable. She resigned from the job 12 months after she was appointed. She was so unpopular that she negotiated to leave immediately and did not serve the mandatory 3-month notice period on her contract. The fallout significantly contributed to the hospital's inability to provide effective and safe services to its patients and meet its obligations to the commissioners. The cost of running the hospital also skyrocketed because of increased agency staff usage. Eventually, the owners of the company decided that the risk of running a hospital like that was too high, and it was no longer financially profitable. The hospital shut down a year after the reforms began and 6 months after she resigned.

In view of this reflection, a cursory look at what went wrong and why her leadership was so toxic is instructive. The first issue was her background. She was a pharmacist before she went into management. She was employed primarily to lead nurses. Immediately, there was the question of authenticity in whatever decision she made as far as the nurses were concerned as the narrative was – 'you are not a nurse, you are not one of us, how can you understand what we are going through and help us to work better'. The second was her people skills and being able to pick up on subtle social cues and know what is appropriate to say or not to say in certain situations. There was a clue of this during her job interview when she was given the opportunity to ask questions. She inquired from a panel member how long he had been working there if he had considered moving on, and why he had not moved! There was a telling look on the face of the other panelists as the question felt intrusive coming from someone who was attending a job interview!

Third, her style of categorising people into good or bad and having favourites was divisive and set up the nursing staff against each other. In the weeks before her departure, it was discovered that she was having significant challenges in her personal life as she was going through a separation from her partner, whom she had been with for about a year. One day she collapsed at work and had to be rushed to a nearby hospital for treatment. When her partner was informed, he refused to go and see her expressing the view that there was nothing wrong with her and that she had collapsed deliberately to get his attention as she had been manipulating him to remain in the relationship. He reportedly ended the relationship and moved out of the home they shared soon afterward.

In this example, the personality traits of this leader influenced the way she operated and made decisions. Her motives were driven by these traits but were entirely unconscious as she appeared impervious to them even when she was encouraged to self-reflect. Her experience with her partner also probably led to her making sweeping misogynistic allegations against male managers in the hospital.

Would the relationship challenges that this leader had in her personal life have given a clue of what to expect from her? Could a closer look at her personality have given a better insight into her leadership style? Would a personality test have provided some objective evidence and identified some red flags of dark leadership? These questions logically lead us to the issue of how far we can go along this path of probing people's personal lives and backgrounds before entrusting them with leadership positions. There is the question of moral acceptability too. Interestingly, it is already the case that in some sensitive leadership positions, especially in military or security positions, detailed background checks and personality tests are routinely done. We know that politicians talk a lot about their personal lives and their upbringing to convince us that we can trust them with leadership positions, but what about their unconscious motives that they do not even know influence their decisions? As already inferred, most motives are hidden even from the dark leader.

Perhaps, it is, therefore, probable and plausible to argue from theory and practice that there is no art to finding elements of dark motives in the face of any leader, and neither is it ever the case that in all forms of leadership, the morning will predict the day. Human beings drive the relationship processes of governance, leadership, and followership and it is always about interests, desires, and motives. What is instructive, however, is to be mindful. While our mindfulness might not entirely cancel out horrible, devastating manifestations of the dark sides of leadership, at least, it ought to limit the surprises and devastating horrible impacts that often generally follow. The usefulness of personality tests to help identify these leaders remains a cogent interest that requires further research.

Lessons for Leaders

Leadership is essential for a community to exist to provide direction and framework for the peaceful co-existence of its inhabitants and for the community to fulfil its mission, function, grow, and thrive. Without leadership, the community will be in utter chaos. Consequently, every leader must understand that their position as leader is based on trust in their truthfulness and sincerity when they register their interests to serve. They must not betray the trust or else they undermine the privilege to lead. Leadership comes with authority and power. The leader expresses his or her interests during the quest for the position, but their motives are largely unknown. The motives only start manifesting once the leadership position is attained. Slowly and steadily, motives drive authority and power, which evolve into dictatorship, authoritarianism, and eventually totalitarianism, the hallmark of dark leadership. Conscious efforts must be made by every leader to walk away from the temptation to abuse authority and power in all forms. Leadership is a mental art whose origin is located within the mind, with the deeper subconscious playing a crucial role. Thus, a closer look at the mind and how it controls behaviour may give us insight into the dark side of leadership. A route that can be explored is the closer scrutiny of the background of leaders and the use of personality tests. Every leader must exhibit openness, humility, and readiness for self-discovery and self-understanding, accompanied by their willingness to accept whatever is found and manage it.

References

Munroe, M. (2015). *Power of character in leadership: How values, morals ethics and principles affect leadership*. New Kensington, PA: Whitaker House.

Ryle, G. (1949). The concept of mind. *British Journal for the Philosophy of Science*, *1*(4), 328–332.

Swaab, D. (2015). *We are our brains: From the womb to Alzheimer's*. London: Penguin Books Limited.

Venter, C. (2008). *A life decoded: My genome, my life*. London: Penguin Press Service.

Chapter 4

Apparently Great Start – Evidentially Disastrous Finish: The Longitudinal Nature of Failure in Psychopathic Leadership

Clive R. Boddy

Introduction

In an authoritative literature review of what was then deemed to be known and unknown about psychopaths in the workplace, Smith and Lilienfeld (2013) suggested that there may be adaptive and positive features of the syndrome of psychopathy as far as leadership is concerned. Their paper posited the existence of positive as well as negative psychopathic leadership outcomes stemming from such traits as the fearless dominance and boldness of psychopaths and possibly resulting in increased persuasiveness and the ability to set an agenda for the future (Smith & Lilienfeld, 2013). This view is echoed in a minority of press reports about psychopaths with, for example, suggestions that financial market traders who are psychopathic may be more effective because they are unswayed by emotional considerations or that some professionals need to be coldly rational to do their jobs well (Crawford, 2013).

DOI: 10.4324/9781003475262-5

In line with this viewpoint, recent papers suggest that psychopaths, with their lack of emotional responsiveness, maybe the only true rational economic human or homo economicus, as described in classical economic theory (Boddy, 2023a; Yamagishi et al., 2014). Such people may end up rich and powerful but their lack of human connectivity and absence of meaningful relational bonds with others may mean that this is not a version of success that many of us would aspire to. Therefore, a viewpoint equating psychopathy with success begs the question of at what point in time such positive outcomes are to be measured and for whom the results of psychopathic leadership are judged to be positive. Using case studies examining organisations that were run by people with highly psychopathic traits, this chapter explains how psychopathic leaders may initially be deemed to be successful but that this success does not continue longitudinally.

The reason for these questions is that corporate psychopaths are hypothesised to be good at creating a positive impression when first met and at presenting a credible and attractive vision of the future (Babiak & O'Toole, 2012; Babiak, 1995; Boddy et al., 2021a). Indeed, recent research suggests that to those employees with psychopathic leaders, the initial impression created by those leaders was one of poise, calm, sociability, rationality, and friendliness (Boddy, 2023c). This was to the extent that they were more highly evaluated on these characteristics than truly transformational leaders were by their subordinates. In other words, at the first meeting, most people cannot tell the difference between psychopathic leaders who are going to prove destructive, and transformational leaders who are going to be effective.

Those who have worked with colleagues with heightened levels of psychopathic traits, estimate that such people can manipulate their image to appear attractive on first meeting but that this impression is not necessarily maintained over time (Boddy et al., 2010; Boddy, 2006). Thus, at one point in time, a psychopathic leader may be judged to be successful on many measures and by many supporters but may eventually reveal outcomes that are negative for everyone, except for the psychopath. The central argument of this chapter is therefore that regardless of how charming and successful corporate psychopaths appear to be when first met, no matter how appealing they look and how many awards they win, no matter how often they appear to be leadership stars; the final result is often one of employee abuse, organisational destruction, and societal impoverishment (Boddy et al., 2015).

Known outcomes for employees who have superiors who are psychopathic include reduced employee well-being (Boddy, 2014; Boddy et al., 2021b), reduced employee job satisfaction (Boddy & Taplin, 2015, 2016), and increased levels of employee burnout (Oyewunmi et al., 2018). Employees are bullied and abused by their psychopathic superiors (Valentine et al., 2017; Boddy, 2011) which creates stress and employee withdrawal. The cold, emotionless psychopath, creates an environment marked by negative emotions and stress (Boulter & Boddy, 2021). This may mean the employer could be legally liable for the distress caused to employees by the psychopathic leader (Sheehy et al., 2021). Psychopathic organisational leadership is further associated with self-serving behaviour, reduced corporate social responsibility, and the illegal disposal of toxic waste (Boddy et al., 2010, 2022; Ray & Jones, 2011). This behaviour is theorised to have negative impacts on global sustainability and reduced future prospects for the successful survival of humanity (Boddy, 2023b).

An example of the phenomenon of psychopathic leadership is described below with regard to three political psychopaths. Two other examples come from the corporate sphere. These examples illustrate how psychopathic leaders may be seen as initially successful but how this appearance disintegrates over time.

Political Psychopaths and the Largest Loss of Life in Human History

Time magazine's Man of the Year in 1936 was a country leader, Adolf Hitler, who had been diagnosed as a psychopath in 1933 (Lavik, 1989; Crawford, 2013) as were his two deputies, Rudolf Hess in 1941 and Hermann Goering, later in 1946 (Boddy, 2021; Gilbert, 1948). They had nevertheless initially started to transform their country's fortune, eliminating widespread unemployment, creating a motorway system that was the envy of the world, and re-establishing a sense of national pride and identity to the people of the country concerned (Brendon, 2000). Such strong tyrannical leadership is appealing to those people who see the world as a dangerous place and who expect their leader to be able to protect them from this danger (Mirowska et al., 2022). This helps to explain the popularity among a large minority of followers and voters, of psychopathic and tyrannical leaders.

A couple of years later, this trio was at the height of their popularity in their home country, but 6 years after that, the estimations of their success were revised significantly downwards. The results of their leadership included the destruction of much of Europe, the deaths of up to 80 million people, and the institutionalisation of mass murder with crimes so obscene that even the more reflective members of this brutal leadership team wept during their trials in Nuremberg when they were confronted with the horrific evidence of what they had done (Brendon, 2000). Nonetheless, the psychopathic members of the Nazi elite, such as Goering, joked and laughed through parts of the trial thus displaying the complete lack of remorse and indifference to the fate of other people that typify the psychopathic imagination (Boddy, 2021). Thus, initially, this trio of psychopathic political leaders appeared to be successful, but this later came at great cost to the rest of humanity.

Corporate Psychopaths and the Largest Fraud in USA History

As an example, from the corporate sphere, the top three people at Enron have all been described as having some psychopathic characteristics. Enron was an award-winning organisation, as were the top people within it. In 2001, Enron was one of the world's largest energy-trading, electricity, natural gas, and communications companies, with reported revenues of $101 billion in 2000 (Walker, 2005; Boddy, 2015, 2020). Enron had all the trappings of success, a modern office block in Houston, corporate jets, political connections, rave reviews in the media, and a rising share price.

While portraying itself as led by smart and effective people (Langbert, 2010), Enron embodied a ruthless and bullying approach to customers and employees, together with fraudulent accounting practices and reckless management and leadership. This entailed the adoption of far-fetched business plans which frequently failed, and well-honed political lobbying for commercial advantage (Boddy, 2020; Langbert, 2010). For example, Ken Lay, Chairperson of Enron, was a financial supporter and friend of President George Bush. Enron looked successful and fooled Wall Street investors and financial journalists alike, gaining numerous awards and honours as it did so. In terms of estimations of its success, Enron was ranked at number 22 for the best companies to work for in the Fortune.com 2001 ranking of the top 100 best companies in the USA. Similarly, Fortune magazine named Enron "America's Most Innovative Company" for 6 years in a row, 1996–2001. Enron was also placed at no. 18 overall on the list of the nation's 535 "Most Admired Companies" and ranked among the top five in "Quality of

Management," "Quality of Products/Services" and "Employee Talent" and the "100 Best Companies to Work for in America," 1999, 2000, and 2001.

In 2000, Enron received two prestigious awards from Financial Times Energy as the recipient of the group's most valued award, "Energy Company of the Year". Enron also received an award for the "Boldest Successful Investment Decision" for *EnronOnline*. The Financial Times acknowledged Enron's entrepreneurial skill in creating and launching a global, easy-to-transact, internet-based system for trading commodities. Enron ranked No. 25 on Fortune's year 2000, all-star list of most admired companies that "demonstrate a new-economy-style growth strategy while maintaining an old-economy approach to fiscal responsibility." Fortune also named Enron the most innovative company in the world and ranked it second in ability to attract, develop and retain talent. In this, Fortune evaluated companies in 27 industries globally, collecting feedback from executives, board members, and analysts. In addition to innovativeness and the ability to attract and keep people, companies were judged on the quality of products and services, quality of management, long-term investment value, financial soundness, community responsibility, use of corporate assets, and global business judgement. Global Finance declared Enron the world's best global company in the energy sector in its September 1999 issue. Companies were selected based on how well they are managed, their impact on competitors, return on invested capital, and global reach. Additionally, Enron was mentioned as one of 'Ten Stocks to Last the Decade' according to Fortune magazine and was described as having 'exceptional management.' Just over a year later, Enron was bankrupt with its exceptional management being under investigation for fraud and a variety of other crimes.

'Business Week' named Enron Chairman and CEO Ken Lay as one of the top 25 managers of 1999. Ken was recognised in 1999 for establishing Enron as the leading U.S. marketer of electricity and natural gas. 'Financial Intelligence' also listed Ken as one of the top CEOs in America. According to the journal, Ken's leadership, inventiveness, and business philosophy enabled Enron to grow from a small natural gas company in Houston into one of the world's largest integrated electricity and natural gas companies. In 1998, a Lifetime Achievement award was presented to Ken at the 26th Annual Energy Daily Congress dinner. He was cited by the nominating committee for his "unmatched vision, strategy and courage" in the energy industry. In his speech accepting the award, Lay mentioned "a lot of very creative, bright people who work around me." Ken Lay also won the Texas Energy

Pioneer Award in 1998 for his outstanding contributions and innovations in natural gas, and the Horatio Alger Award in 1998. This award recognises a lifetime of achievement and community service.

Jeffrey Skilling, Enron's CEO after Ken Lay moved to a Chair position and was named number 2, in the top 50 CEOs of 2001. In a report of this achievement, Jeffrey Skilling was described as a 'hypersmart, hyperconfident' CEO. Skilling mentioned a combination of open discourse and firm decision-making — "loose-tight," as chief financial officer Andy Fastow terms it, as an ingredient of its success. "I'm not sure he has a nonstrategic bone in his body," says Kenneth Lay, Skilling's predecessor. The company vision statement originally read "Become the world's leading energy company." Skilling grandiosely changed it to read "Become the world's leading company." Skilling was described as having a laissez-faire management style but one which quickly transformed into bullying if he was challenged. This is typical of the psychopath who allows employees to do what they want unless it opposes their desires or questions their self-serving direction of travel (Boddy et al., 2015). As one example of his management skills, Skilling organised a scavenger hunt for senior Enron managers in the Australian outback in 1996. Looking to win, he raced his Land Cruiser at nearly 100 miles an hour for 30 minutes before realising that no one was following him. He stopped. It took an hour for the guide to catch up and inform Skilling that he had indeed left the others behind but that he had gone the wrong way.

The Accurate Version of Enron's Success

At the turn of the last century, Enron was an excessively admired, award-winning, and frequently praised gas and energy supply and trading conglomerate based in Houston, USA. Enron was described as being a darling of Wall Street because of its apparent success and ever-growing share price. The scandal that subsequently unfolded at Enron was a scandal of toxic leadership and fraud involving the systematic and prolonged portrayal of a robust financial picture at the firm which was completely unrelated to the reality of its actual revenue and profitability status (Boddy, 2015). Financial records were fabricated, and Enron's success was largely falsified. In the first year of this century, Enron went bankrupt and was the largest bankruptcy and auditing failure in US history at the time, involving over $63 billion in corporate assets. Enron had reportedly bullied and pressured its auditors to coerce it to ignore financial reporting issues. The scandal entailed toxic leadership, fraud, grandiose lying, personal greed, and a lack of concern by the agents involved, over the consequences of their actions on the employees, shareholders, or any other stakeholders of the corporation (Boddy, 2020). Various investigators have presented explanations for why Enron went bankrupt. However, many of these explanations are mechanistic. They answer the question of how events unfolded rather than why and arguably do not address the behavioural roots of the events which underpin the technicalities of the failure.

Enron may have failed because it credited profits up to 20 years ahead of when those profits could reasonably be expected to be realised, because it was very much in debt and too short-term in orientation, or it was fraudulent or persuasive in presenting an illusion of financial accomplishment. However, attributes like personal greed, ruthlessness, and an unethical approach to business underpinned Enron's approach to management and these behaviour and outcomes. These traits of greed, a lack of ethics, and ruthlessness are among the key attributes of the corporate psychopath (Boddy, 2020). In December 2001, after losing money for years and then declaring losses of $1.2 billion in an off-balance sheet equity fund, Enron went bankrupt. The share price quickly went from $90.75 to $0.26. Enron is therefore linked to unethical behaviour, toxic leadership, and corporate psychopathy for many reasons, one of which is that Fastow, the CFO at Enron, was described as displaying several of the traits of the corporate psychopath. These included setting up fraudulent entities to make deals with Enron to keep various financial liabilities off the official company books, thus displaying untruthfulness and a cheating personality (Boddy, 2020). Corresponding with the theory that corporate psychopaths create chaos and confusion in their immediate environment to hide their true intentions from view, Enron fashioned a web of special-purpose financial entities whose transactions were not appropriately reflected in the balance sheet. This made for a lack of transparency in the accounts and represented a structure that was "an extraordinarily complex piece of financial engineering."

Further, many of Enron's transactions appeared to be designed to enable the manufacture of flattering financial statements rather than to describe authentic business transactions. For example, Enron created a complicated web of over 700 related companies and deals to hide the true extent of their debt. These dealings allowed Enron to obscure market losses and mislead analysts. It has been noted that this obfuscation via organisational complexity may be a common characteristic of corporate psychopaths (Boddy, 2020). Enron and its leaders demonstrated several traits of toxic leaders; for example, they were narcissistic in that they overtly sought praise and admiration and referred to themselves as the world's greatest corporation, even though this was largely a pretence. Enron was also Machiavellian as an organisation, as it manipulated events at the expense of others to further its interests. Corporate psychopathy was also evident as Enron and its leaders lied without conscience, remorse, or regret and at the expense of others to gain personal wealth and power. The culture within Enron was ruthless and intra-personally competitive and, for example, 15%–20% of the "worst performing" employees were dismissed every year, creating a vicious culture of brutal in-fighting (Van Niel & Rapoport, 2004). This led to a cruel, immoral, and venomous corporate culture where employees attacked one another rather than supporting each other. Theoretically, corporate psychopaths, like other toxic leaders, use divide-and-conquer tactics such as this to divert attention away from their self-serving activities, which may include fraud. An anxious, in-fighting workforce is easier to dominate and manipulate and less likely to speak out against malpractice.

Corporate psychopaths employ close control of their environment, and Enron was also marked by enforced conformity and the penalising of dissent (Tourish & Vatcha, 2005). Meanwhile, Enron's manipulation of the US energy markets led to large reported profits for that division of the business, while their clients paid unprecedented amounts for it. Further, customers such as schools, businesses, and households suffered power disruptions and complete blackouts (Clarke, 2005). Enron was further characterised by its selfish and rude culture, and the leadership can be described as toxic because the tone at the top of Enron was reportedly one of ruthlessness, arrogance, bullying, stage management, and lying. Further, it was one where unethical practices were encouraged and rewarded (Tonge et al., 2003). Enron was also reportedly well known for bullying analysts who disagreed with its optimistic estimation of prospects. Objectors and whistle-blowers were persecuted or forced out of their positions, and in the face of this mistreatment, very few internal or external accountants, auditors, or analysts raised any suspicions concerning Enron's falsely inflated revenues. Internal whistle-blowers were reportedly demoted or transferred to other posts (Boddy, 2020). Subordinates cannot often do very much to defend themselves against bad managers, and an examination of Enron appears to confirm this because whistle-blowers were easily reassigned and silenced (Tourish & Vatcha, 2005).

While Enron was manipulative and dishonest, creating illusory revenues and profits, Ken Lay, (the CEO) similarly encouraged employees to believe that the stock price was buoyant while simultaneously selling (2001) millions of dollars of his own shares in Enron. Lay had also previously cashed in $123.4 million in stock options in 2000. The scale of deception at Enron was so great and so stage-managed that it fooled investment analysts for years. Lay repeatedly hosted Wall Street analysts to the sixth floor of the HQ building where a fake trading floor of energy services dealers was set up. Computer screens were connected to receive bogus data, and dealers talked to each other in teleconference rooms and by telephone, making pretend deals whereas no real business was conducted (Boje et al., 2006). Analysts were both hoodwinked and impressed.

Of the top managers at Enron, Ken Lay, Jeff Skilling, and Andy Fastow, all three have been mentioned as candidates embodying elevated psychopathy. Enron's Skilling was described by Frank Perri in 2013 as possessing the traits of a corporate psychopath being manipulative, glib, lying, bullying, egocentric, and lacking in remorse (Perri, 2013). Fastow has also been described as displaying many of the traits of a corporate psychopath. Lay (CEO, Chair) died before he could be sentenced for securities fraud while Skilling (one-time COO and CEO) was initially sentenced to 24 years in prison for securities fraud and insider trading. Andrew Fastow (CFO) testified against other Enron executives and pleaded guilty to money laundering, fraud, and conspiracy and was sentenced to 5 years in prison.

Correspondingly, Enron's tone at the top was depicted by inside managers as being one where acceptable practice included lying and deception, as long as money was apparently being made, and top executives were reported to be aggressive and greedy. Further, when Lay was confronted with one executive who questioned the reality of Enron's financial statements, that executive was replaced. This applied to external critics as well and an external auditor who questioned whether Enron's business was supported by sound financial performance was removed from the audit team. Thus, Enron as a corporation arguably displayed all the signs of being a toxic and psychopathic entity while its CEO also displayed many of the same signs himself.

That Enron ran a regular employee dismissal scheme demonstrates a callous and cold indifference to the fate of others; again, this is a characteristic of corporate psychopaths. It also demonstrates ruthlessness, as does Lay's misleading of investors in claiming that Enron was fundamentally strong when Lay and the CFO were aware that financial disaster was approaching. The example of Enron illustrates how toxic, irresponsible leadership can bring down the largest corporations, as well as their multinational partners. This case also illustrates the devastating destructiveness of toxic leaders. Enron's bankruptcy made thousands of employees unemployed and emptied the company's pension fund, meaning that more than 20,000 employees lost their retirement savings. Thus, once again a trio of leaders with psychopathic traits, this time in the corporate sphere, appeared to be successful, but this later came at great cost to other stakeholders and the rest of society.

Another Record Fraud in USA History

Like Enron and its leaders before him, American financier Bernard Lawrence Madoff's much-admired investment company (Bernard L. Madoff Investment Securities LLC) proved to be fraudulent; it was a Ponzi scheme involving up to US$63 billion in real or apparent assets (Boddy, 2024; Greenspan, 2009). Madoff attracted investors from America and around the world, by reporting that his scheme generated large, regular returns through an investing strategy called *Splitstrike Conversion*. However, Madoff merely placed his client's funds into a bank account and used that to pay existing clients who wanted to withdraw funds from the scheme. Madoff gained clients via his reputation, seeming respectability, charm, and apparent exclusivity – you had to be invited to be a client. As a Wall Street insider and ex-chair of Nasdaq, Madoff had an authoritative reputation.

During the global financial crisis of 2007/2008, clients wanting to withdraw funds at scale meant payments could not be made because of a reduced inflow of investment cash, and Madoff confessed in November 2008 to his sons that the scheme was fraudulent. He was arrested the next day and eventually sentenced to 150 years in prison and was ordered to pay $170 billion to cover client losses. He died in prison in 2021. Madoff displayed the core traits of psychopathy including callousness, manipulativeness, cruelty, and arrogance (Crego & Widiger, 2022), overlaid and hidden by the charm, sociability, and allure of the corporate psychopath (Boddy et al., 2023a). Madoff was considered a sophisticated investor who made money on investments regardless of environmental conditions and this appealed to the avarice of his investors who sought above-average returns (Berkowitz, 2012; Creswell & Thomas, 2009).

Lessons for Leaders

All that glitters is not gold – psychopathic and toxic leaders may appear appealing and sociable extroverts delivering alluringly attractive and outstanding levels of success, but closer inspection often reveals the transitory, illusive, fraudulent, and unsustainable nature of this apparent success. The charm and showmanship of the psychopathic can fool investors, employees, and voters for significant periods of time but eventually, the truth of the situation is revealed. Profits are illusory; revenues over-claimed, successes insubstantial and organisational destruction, more or less, inevitable.

Previously hyperbolic descriptions of some of the 20th century's most lauded exemplars of modern capitalism can be read in better perspective now that the full facts are known. That Skilling raced his employees in a car across Australia at 100 mph for 30 minutes in the wrong direction looks less like the behaviour of a competitive, strategically attuned leader and more like the actions of a reckless and impulsive show-off. Similarly, the "loose-tight" decision-making utilised at Enron, as described by Enron's Chief Financial Officer, Andy Fastow, sounds like a contradiction in terms. A nonsense phrase coined by superficial and obfuscating leaders.

This chapter argues that Smith and Lilienfeld's view that psychopathic leaders may sometimes be successful as leaders on some measures may be correct, but this will only be the case in the short to medium term. To establish the veracity of this conjecture, leaders who are estimated to embody psychopathic traits will have to be researched over time to see if initial views of their success are maintained over the longer term. Similarly, popular political and corporate leaders who are estimated to be psychopathic can be tracked over time to see if their perceived success in leadership is maintained longitudinally.

References

Babiak, P. (1995). When psychopaths go to work: A case study of an industrial psychopath. *Applied Psychology: An International Review*, *44*, 171–188.

Babiak, P., & O'toole, M. E. (2012). The corporate psychopath. *FBI Law Enforcement Bulletin*, *81*, 7–11.

Berkowitz, M. (2012). The Madoff paradox: American Jewish sage, saviour, and thief. *Journal of American Studies*, *46*, 189–202.

Boddy, C. R. (2006). The dark side of management decisions: Organisational psychopaths. *Management Decision*, *44*, 1461–1475.
Boddy, C. R. (2011). Corporate psychopaths, bullying and unfair supervision in the workplace. *Journal of Business Ethics*, *100*, 367–379.
Boddy, C. R. (2014). Corporate psychopaths, conflict, employee affective well-being and counterproductive work behaviour. *Journal of Business Ethics*, 121, 107121.
Boddy, C. R. (2015). *Unethical 20th-Century Businesses and Their Leaders: Were Enron and Its CEO Corporate Psychopaths? The Value of Pluralism in Advancing Management Research, Education, and Practice: Management and Business History Track*. United Kingdom: Portsmouth University, British Academy of Management.
Boddy, C. R. (2020). Enron scandal. In: Poff, D. C. & Michalos, A. C. (Eds.), *Encyclopedia of Business and Professional Ethics* (pp. 648–651). Cham: Springer International Publishing.
Boddy, C. (2021). Populism and political personality: What can we learn from the dark triad personality of hermann goering? *The Journal of Psychohistory*, *49*, 12–31.
Boddy, C. R. (2023a). Is the only rational personality that of the psychopath? Homo Economicus as the most serious threat to business ethics globally. *Humanistic Management Journal*, *8*, 1–13.
Boddy, C. R. (2023b). Moving sustainability towards flourishing for all: The critical role of (toxic) leadership. *Business and Society Review*, *128*(4), 591–605. https://doi.org/10.1111/basr.12309
Boddy, C. R. (2023c). Transformational and psychopathic leadership: Graphical and statistical differences. *Cultivating Leadership for a Thriving Future*, International Leadership Association Conference, Vancouver, Canada.
Boddy, C. R. (2024). Insights into the Bernie Madoff financial market scandal which identify new opportunities for business market researchers. *International Journal of Market Research*, *66*, 149–167.
Boddy, C., Boulter, L., & Fishwick, S. (2021a). How so many toxic employees ascend to leadership. In Örtenblad, A. (Ed.), *Debating Bad Leadership: Reasons and Remedies* (pp. 69–85). Palgrave Macmillan.
Boddy, C. R., Ladyshewsky, R., & Galvin, P. G. (2010). The influence of corporate psychopaths on corporate social responsibility and organizational commitment to employees. *Journal of Business Ethics*, *97*, 1–19.
Boddy, C. R., Malovany, E., Kunter, A., & Gull, G. (2021b). Employee well-being under corporate psychopath leaders. In: Dhiman, S. (Ed.), *The Palgrave Handbook of Workplace Well-Being* (pp. 843–869). Cham: Palgrave Macmillan/Springer Nature. https://doi.org/10.1007/978-3-030-30025-8_74
Boddy, C., Miles, D., Sanyal, C., & Hartog, M. (2015). Extreme managers, extreme workplaces: Capitalism, organizations, and corporate psychopaths. *Organization*, *22*, 530–551.

Boddy, C. R., & Taplin, R. (2015). The influence of corporate psychopaths on job satisfaction and its determinants. In: Lange, T. (Ed.), *Sustainable HRM and Employee Well-Being. An International Research Symposium*, November 4th/5th, 2015. Sydney, Australia: Australian Catholic University.

Boddy, C. R., & Taplin, R. (2016). The influence of corporate psychopaths on job satisfaction and its determinants. *International Journal of Manpower, 37*, 965988.

Boddy, C. R., Taplin, R., Sheehy, B., & Murphy, B. (2022). Finding psychopaths in white-collar jobs: A review of the evidence and why it matters. *Society and Business Review, 17*, 217–235.

Boje, D. M., Gardner, C. L., & Smith, W. L. (2006). (Mis)Using numbers in the Enron story. *Organizational Research Methods, 9*(4), 456–474. https://doi.org/10.1177/1094428106290785

Boulter, L., & Boddy, C. (2021). Subclinical psychopathy, interpersonal workplace exchanges and moral emotions through the lens of affective events theory (AET). *Journal of Organizational Effectiveness: People and Performance, 8*, 44–58.

Brendon, P. (2000). *The Dark Valley: A Panorama of the 1930s*. London: Jonathan Cape, Random House.

Clarke, T. (2005). Accounting for Enron: Shareholder value and stakeholder interests. *Corporate Governance: An International Review, 13*(5), 598–612.

Crawford, A. (2013). The Pros to Being a Psychopath [Online]. Accessed on 14.03.2013 at https://www.smithsonianmag.com/science-nature/the-pros-to-being-a-psychopath-96723962/

Crego, C., & Widiger, T. A. (2022). Core traits of psychopathy. *Personality Disorders: Theory, Research, and Treatment, 13*, 674–684.

Creswell, J., & Thomas, L. (2009). The Talented Mr. Madoff [Online]. New York. Accessed on 12.10.2012 at https://www.nytimes.com/2009/01/25/business/25bernic.html?

Gilbert, G. M. (1948). Hermann Goering, amiable psychopath. *The Journal of Abnormal and Social Psychology, 43*, 211–229.

Greenspan, S. (2009). Fooled by Ponzi: How Bernard Madoff made off with my money, or why even an expert on gullibility can get gulled. *Skeptic (Altadena, CA), 14*, 20–26.

Langbert, M. B. (2010). Managing Psychopathic Employees. Cornell HR Review. Retrieved from Cornell University, ILR School site: https://ecommons.cornell.edu/items/37aff090-5f02-48bb-b36e-350cf8221fc8

Lavik, N. J. (1989). A psychiatrist who confronted Nazism. *Political Psychology, 10*, 757–765.

Mirowska, A., Chiu, R. B., & Hackett, R. D. (2022). The allure of tyrannical leaders: Moral foundations, belief in a dangerous world, and follower gender. *Journal of Business Ethics, 181*, 355–374.

Oyewunmi, A. E., Akinnusi, D. M., & Oyewunmi, O. A. (2018). Of predators and preys: Corporate psychopathy and employee burnout as parallels. *Periodica Polytechnica Social and Management Sciences, 26*, 149–156.

Perri, F. S. (2013). Visionaries or false prophets. *Journal of Contemporary Criminal Justice*, *29*, 331–350.

Ray, J. V., & Jones, S. (2011). Self-reported psychopathic traits and their relation to intentions to engage in environmental offending. *International Journal of Offender Therapy and Comparative Criminology*, *55*, 370–391.

Sheehy, B., Boddy, C., & Murphy, B. (2021). Corporate law and corporate psychopaths. *Psychiatry, Psychology and Law*, *28*, 479–507.

Smith, S. F., & Lilienfeld, S. O. (2013). Psychopathy in the workplace: The knowns and unknowns. *Aggression and Violent Behavior*, *18*, 204–218.

Tonge, A., Greer, L., & Lawton, A. (2003). The Enron story: You can fool some of the people some of the time. *Business Ethics: A European Review*, *12*(1), 4–22.

Tourish, D., & Vatcha, N. (2005). Charismatic leadership and corporate cultism at Enron: The elimination of dissent, the promotion of conformity and organizational collapse. *Leadership*, *1*, 455–480.

Valentine, S. R., Hanson, S. K., & Fleischman, G. M. (2017). The spiralling and spillover of misconduct: Perceived workplace bullying, subclinical psychopathy, and businesspersons' recognition of an ethical issue. *Employee Responsibilities and Rights Journal*, *29*, 221–244.

Van Niel, J. D., & Rapoport, N. B. (2004). Dr. Jekyll & Mr. Skilling: How Enron's public image Morphed from the most innovative company in the Fortune 500 to the most notorious company ever. In: Rapoport, N.B. & Dharan, B.G., eds. *Enron: Corporate Fiascos and Their Implications*. New York: Foundation Press, 77–93.

Walker, I. (2005). Psychopaths in Suits. ABC Radio National Background Briefings. Australian Broadcasting Corporation. Accessed on-line on 11.09.2005 at 7.18 pm at https://www.abc.net.au/rn/talks/bbing/stories/s1265568.htm

Yamagishi, T., Li, Y., Takagishi, H., Matsumoto, Y., & Kiyonari, T. (2014). In search of Homo economicus. *Psychological Science*, *25*, 1699–1711.

Chapter 5

Exploring the Shadows of Dark Side Leaders

Shamaila Gull and Roohi Imtiaz

Introduction

Leadership has an ever-increasing significance due to its pivotal role at all social levels (Ballı & Çakıcı, 2019). The influencing nature of leadership underscores the achievement of collective goals and hence, puts leaders on apedestal. Leaders are expected to provide support systems for employees to accomplish organisational goals. However, unethical or destructive leaders portray dysfunctional dispositions in the workplace exhibiting the 'dark side' of their personalities (McCleskey, 2013). Such leaders are called 'dark side leaders'. In many cases, dark side leaders are unworthy individuals who successfully occupy leadership positions and fail to justify their roles as leaders (Burke, 2006). The multifaceted study of these leaders and their derailed behaviour is known as 'dark leadership'. The unethical behaviours of leaders impact large societal segments, including politics, religion, and work life, necessitating the examination of dark traits of leadership (Liu, Liao, & Loi, 2012).

Dark side leaders are everywhere, and comprehensive studies are needed to understand how they adversely impact leadership (McCleskey, 2013). These leaders recurrently indulge in the denigration of their followers for no apparent reason and destabilise the regular working of an organisation (Fascia, 2018). Higgs (2009) categorised dark behaviours into four themes: abuse of power, inflicting damage on others, excessive control, and breaching rules for personal needs. Leaders who frequently display these

DOI: 10.4324/9781003475262-6

behaviours are perceived as deceitful and overly ambitious. Unfortunately, the dark behaviours exhibited by leaders may also result in a reciprocating effect on the followers of such leaders, thus making the organisational environment more damaging (Hogan & Hogan, 2001). It is pertinent to comprehensively explore the shadows of dark side leaders to avoid enduring negative organisational outcomes. This requires an in-depth understanding of the personality traits of these leaders, the impact of their dark behaviour on organisations, and important lessons for leaders to learn.

The Personality of Dark Side Leaders: A Reflection

Although leadership is often revered for its positive attributes, such as charisma, integrity, vision, and empathy, it is important to highlight the dark tendencies originating from the personality characteristics of leaders. Lurking beneath the surface lies a side of leadership characterised by personalities marked as 'dark' (Hogan & Hogan, 2001). Despite their diverse origin, negative personality traits termed as 'Dark Triad' portray several characteristics with varying behavioural tendencies. This dark triad involves Narcissism, Psychopathy, and Machiavellianism, socially aversive personalities that have drawn the most empirical attention (Kowalski, 2001). These dark side personalities can wield profound and detrimental effects on organisations, their employees, and society at large.

Narcissism

Dark side leaders exhibit traits of narcissism, such as self-importance, a sense of entitlement, and a lack of empathy for others (Khoo & Burch, 2008). They prioritise their own needs and desires over the well-being of their followers, often resorting to manipulative and exploitative behaviours (Grijalva & Harms, 2014). Consider the example of Elizabeth Holmes (Former CEO of 'Theranos') who exemplifies narcissistic leadership traits - a narcissistic leader who consistently sought admiration, took credit for the achievements of others, and promoted her brand image to gain investors. She avoided the scrutiny of her proprietary blood testing technology and misrepresented it to the investors. Her narcissistic personality led to unethical practices affecting her company's customers and the dismissal of employees who disagreed with her decisions. Consequently, the company folded up due to the dark personality traits of the leader.

Psychopathy

Psychopathic leaders, on the other hand, display characteristics such as deceitfulness, impulsivity, and lack of conscience (Mathieu, Babiak, & Hare, 2020). Once part of an organisation, they show no ethical boundary and go to any extent to gain power and prestige. Some of the common behaviours displayed by psychopaths include bullying, fraudulent actions, lack of empathy for others, increased absenteeism, lower morale, decreased productivity, and damaging the work environment (Cote, 2018). Imagine a manager who lies to the stakeholders for personal gain and shows no regret for unethical decisions; much like Bernie Madoff, the mastermind behind one of the largest Ponzi schemes in history. Madoff operated a fraudulent investment scheme for decades, promising high returns to investors while using new investors' funds to pay returns to earlier investors. His psychopathic personality resulted in self-destruction, business failure, and financial loss to thousands of investors (Henriques, 2011).

Machiavellianism

Machiavellian leaders are skilled strategists who prioritise their personal interests characterised by an unethical mindset and power hunger (Cote, 2018). In his book 'The Prince', Niccolò Machiavelli argues that leaders must put results over principles, and it is possible to achieve remarkable things while operating under unethical principles (Machiavelli, 1891). Machiavellian leaders manipulate others to cause interpersonal conflicts, shift loyalties, and use contingent rewards and punishments to get their desired results (Furnham, Richards, & Paulhus, 2013). These leaders engage in unscrupulous practices that put organisations at risk (Becker & Hair, 2007). Consider a leader like Scott Thompson (former CEO of Yahoo) forming alliances with certain employees to gain power and undermine rivals. Thompson, deemed to be a 'forthright, straightforward and likable guy' by the board members, falsely claimed to have a degree in computer science on his resume (Stewart, 2012). Hence, leaders may seem charismatic and enthusiastic, but their dark behaviours often result in a counterproductive work environment instead of creating a positive influence on followers (Hogan, Hogan, & Kaiser, 2010). Although there are no easy fixes for destructive behaviours borne by leaders, still organisations can avoid the worst outcomes by fostering self-awareness, offering positive behavioural choices, and encouraging ethical leadership practices (Burke & Fox, 2016).

Shadows of Dark Side Leaders on Organisation

The prominent leadership models of the 1980s argue that it is impossible to generalise the effectiveness of leaders because "leadership depends on the situation" (Strube & Strube, 1981). The mainstream leadership models portray positive psychological characteristics of leaders predicting elevated levels of performance (Alvesson & Einola, 2019), ignoring the reality of dark behaviours displayed by many leaders (Kaiser & Craig, 2014). A famous book written by Dixon (1976) on ten major British military disasters claims that each disaster could be attributed to the damaged personalities of the commanders in charge. Dixon's examples are distressing and prove a direct connection between personality and dark behaviours. Bentz's (1990) research explores various negative effects of leadership derailment on organisations. His findings showed that some executives considered job security, promotions, and rewards as their main objectives resulting in futile decision-making, relinquished responsibility, and lack of interaction with employees. The focus of such executives is to develop personal relationships for their upward mobility. Such leaders fail to build teams, implement organisational vision, and communicate a shared purpose to stakeholders.

Palmer (1998) argues that the unethical motivations of leaders generate unethical behaviours, which culminate in negative outcomes for the organisations. These unethical motivations are demonstrated in terms of (a) insecurity – when leaders are perceived as unassertive, socially withdrawn, and possessed by their own selfish needs, (b) functional disbelief – when leaders think that organisations cannot function without their involvement. Some of the common problems faced by dark side leaders are unhealthy interpersonal relationships, stress, burnout, and purposeless actions (Palmer, 1998). Undoubtedly, this kind of behaviour creates unfavourable consequences for both the leaders and their followers; (c) fear – when leaders have varied emotions such as anxiety, terror, nervousness, and concern (Goleman, 1998). The fear of chaos may prompt a leader to avoid regulations, interaction with followers, and the promotion of creativity (Palmer, 1998), and (d) denying failure – when leaders cease to accept failures and avoid making timely decisions (McCall & Lombardo, 1983).

Schyns and Schilling (2013) studied the effects of toxic leadership by conducting a meta-analysis of 57 studies. The analysis showed that toxic or destructive leadership induces negative attitudes towards the leader, deficient performance, increased levels of turnover, poor psychological health, and higher levels of resistance and tension among followers. Another study by Mehraein, Visintin, and Pittino (2023) indicated that dark side leadership negatively influences employee creativity and innovation. This negative influence is caused by the authoritative and narcissistic nature of leaders resulting in leader-follower detachment. Additionally, a study of 392 employees in the United States of America found that dark side leaders negatively influence the emotions of employees and enhance counterproductive behaviours (Yue, Qin, & Men, 2023). Considering the findings of these and other related studies, organisations need proactive approaches for identifying the unethical motivations within the dark side leaders to redeem the shadows of their dark behaviours (Cote, 2018).

Cross-Cultural Perspective of Dark Side Leaders

Scholars believe that culture plays a pivotal role in explaining the dark behaviours of leaders (e.g., Lee, Yun, & Srivastava, 2013). Several researchers have studied the 'Dark Triad' from the perspective of cultural differences. Studies conducted by Hofstede (1980, 1991) categorised cultures in terms of their individualistic or collectivist environment. People who belong to individualistic cultures tend to be more independent, self-oriented, and rational in their social interactions (Hofstede, 1991). A few examples of countries with individualistic cultures are the USA, Germany, Australia, and South Africa. In collectivist cultures, people are group-oriented and have social interactions based on relationships (Bhawuk, 2018; Hofstede, 1991). Some collectivist countries include China, Japan, India, Ghana, Pakistan, and Indonesia. These cultural differences not only impact but also help to explain the cognitions, motivations, and behaviours of people.

A cross-cultural study on the dark triad was conducted by Ma, Born, Petrou, and Bakker (2021) on a set of Chinese and American employees. The findings of this study revealed that psychopathic traits are negatively correlated to work outcomes among employees of both countries due to the highly unethical and deceitful personality of psychopaths. However, dark shadows of narcissism are stronger in the USA primarily due to individualistic culture which allows narcissists to focus on themselves and work toward their own goals. Machiavellian characteristics are more dominant among Chinese employees because the social interdependence in collectivist cultures offers more opportunities for Machiavellians to manipulate people and create interpersonal conflicts. Schmitt et al. (2020) conducted cross-cultural research on the 'dark triad' by collecting evidence from Germany and China. The findings of this study indicate that narcissistic and Machiavellian characteristics are more common among German respondents, especially German females, while German males are more prone to psychopathic behaviour. There were no significant findings about Chinese respondents exhibiting dark personality traits related to emotional manipulation.

A study conducted in Pakistan found that Machiavellianism and psychopathy are significantly correlated with counterproductive work behaviours (Rizvi & Siddiqui, 2023). The findings of the study proposed the integration of psychometric testing into the recruitment processes of organisations to identify candidates with dark personality traits. Furthermore, Chamorro-Premuzic and Sanger (2016) have studied leadership traits in different geographical regions revealing that leaders in China, Indonesia, UAE, Thailand, and much of Latin America (Mexico, Brazil, Columbia) exhibit narcissist characteristics to occupy upper ranks in organisations through the exploitation of other people and self-projection. Machiavellian leaders who encouraged conflicts for their personal goals were more commonly observed in countries like Malaysia and Indonesia. Although this study by Chamorro-Premuzic and Sanger (2016) was not based on Hofstede's cultural differences, it signifies the importance of micro-level analysis of culture to identify the factors that may promote dark behaviours.

Lessons for Leaders

Leaders can become effective and positive in their approach by seeking feedback about their performance, recognising and paying attention to their mistakes, learning from those mistakes, and displaying humility (McCall, Lombardo, & Morrison, 1988). By obtaining 360-degree feedback for what they do, leaders not only improve their relationships with their followers and other stakeholders but also mitigate the risks associated with the dark side of their personality. Similarly, self-awareness can be effective in making the dark side brighter. Understanding the tendency to manipulate others and acknowledging the need for deeper insight into their personalities can help leaders manage the impact of their behaviour. Different personality assessment tools such as HDS (Hogan Dark Side) and MLQ (Multifactor Leadership Questionnaire) can be considered in identifying dark side personality characteristics and applying appropriate support strategies (Cote, 2018). Organisations need to take a proactive stance on using personality assessment tools to screen leaders.

Leaders must be trustworthy, honest, and authentic in their leadership approach. Such leaders focus intentionally on displaying empathy for their followers, honouring mutual respect, and empowering others (Hale & Fields, 2007). Behaviour, being the essence of defining good or bad leadership, has ethics as its foundation. Positive leaders have ethics at the core of leadership, while dark side leaders tend to display unethical behaviours, generating destructive outcomes for organisations (Burns, 1978). Organisations endowing an ethical culture can avoid factors causing leadership derailment. Appropriate coaching and leadership development programs are imperative to undo the effects of unethical and detrimental behaviours.

Conclusion

Unscrupulous leaders occupying leadership positions tend to display derailed behaviours exposing the dark side of their personalities. Narcissism, psychopathy, and Machiavellianism describe the dark personality traits of leaders within the realm of the 'Dark Triad'. Each dark personality trait presents its unique set of challenges and risks, from the grandiosity and pomposity of narcissism to the callousness of psychopathy and manipulation of Machiavellianism. There is a dire need to comprehend the potential impacts of the shadowy behaviours demonstrated by the dark side leaders in organisations. Adopting a proactive approach to avoid the development and emergence of dark behaviours can facilitate organisations to prevent the counterproductive and destructive effects of dark leadership. To attain this, coaching and leadership development programs can be employed along with validated personality assessment tools.

A cross-cultural perspective on dark leadership was also presented for an elaborative understanding of dark side leaders and their dark behaviours across diverse cultures. Identifying the cultural factors which encourage dark behaviours among leaders can lower the incidence of dark side leaders within organisations. Organisations must put in place constructive behavioural alternatives to address counterproductive and destructive behaviours. Systematically understanding the reality of dark side leaders and active strategies can reduce the prevalence of their dark shadows.

References

Alvesson, M., & Einola, K. (2019). Warning for excessive positivity: Authentic leadership and other traps in leadership studies. *The Leadership Quarterly, 30*, 383–395.

Ballı, E., & Çakıcı, A. (2019). Karanlık Liderlik: Otel İşletmelerinde Bir Araştırma. *Turkish Studies, 14*, 155–173.

Becker, J. A., & Hair. (2007). Machiavellians' motives in organizational citizenship behaviour. *Journal of Applied Communication Research, 35*, 246–267.

Bentz, V. J. (1990). Contextual issues in predicting high-level leadership performance: Contextual richness as a criterion consideration in personality research with executives. In K. E. Clark, & M. B. Clark (Eds.), *Measures of Leadership* (pp. 131–143). West Orange, NJ: Leadership Library of America.

Bhawuk, D. (2018). Individualism and collectivism. In K. Y. Yun (Ed.), *The International Encyclopaedia of Intercultural Communication* (pp. 920–929). Hoboken: Wiley-Blackwell.

Burke, R. J. (2006). Why leaders fail: Exploring the dark side. *International Journal of Manpower, 27*, 91–100.

Burke, R. J., & Fox, S. (2016). *Human Frailties: Wrong Choices on the Drive to Success*. New York: Routledge.

Burns, J. M. (1978). *Leadership*. New York: Harper & Row.

Chamorro-Premuzic, T., & Sanger, M. (2016, May 06). *What Leadership Looks Like in Different Cultures*. Harvard Business Review. https://hbr.org/2016/05/what-leadership-looks-like-in-different-cultures

Cote, R. (2018). Dark side leaders: Are their intentions benign or toxic? *Journal of Leadership, Accountability and Ethics, 15*, 42–65.

Dixon, N. F. (1976). *On the Psychology of Military Incompetence*. Basic Books.

Fascia, S. (2018). The value of dark leadership. *Journal of Strategy, Operations & Economics, 3*, 1–6.

Furnham, A., Richards, S. C., & Paulhus, D. L. (2013). The dark triad of personality: A 10-year review. *Social and Personality Psychology Compass, 7*, 199–216.

Goleman, D. (1998). *Working with Emotional Intelligence*. New York: Bantam Books.

Grijalva, E., & Harms, P. D. (2014). Narcissism: An integrative synthesis and dominance complementarity model. *Academy of Management Perspectives, 28*, 108–127.

Hale, J. R., & Fields, D. L. (2007). Exploring servant leadership across cultures: A study of followers in Ghana and USA. *Leadership, 3*, 397–417.

Henriques, D. B. (2011). *The Wizard of Lies: Bernie Madoff and the Death of Trust*. New York: Times Books.

Higgs, M. (2009). The good, the bad and the ugly: Leadership and narcissism. *Journal of Change Management, 9*, 165–178.

Hofstede, G. (1980). *Culture's Consequences: International Differences in Work-Related Values*. Newbury Park, CA: Sage.

Hofstede, G. (1991). *Cultures and Organizations: Software of the Mind*. London: McGraw-Hill.
Hogan, R., & Hogan, J. (2001). Assessing leadership: A view from the dark side. *International Journal of Assessment and Selection*, *9*, 40–51.
Hogan, R., Hogan, J., & Kaiser, R. (2010). Management derailment: Personality assessment and mitigation. In S. Zedeck (Ed.), *American Psychological Association Handbook of Industrial and Organization Psychology* (pp. 555–575). Washington, DC: American Psychological Association.
Kaiser, R. B., & Craig, S. B. (2014). Destructive leadership in and of organizations. In D. V. Day (Ed.), *The Oxford Handbook of Leadership and Organizations* (pp. 262–286). Oxford: Oxford University Press.
Khoo, H. S., & Burch, G. S. (2008). The 'dark side' of leadership personality and transformational leadership: An exploratory study. *Personality and Individual Differences*, *44*, 86–97.
Kowalski, R. (2001). *Behaving Badly: Aversive Behaviours in Interpersonal Relationships*. Washington, DC: American Psychological Association.
Lee, S., Yun, S., & Srivastava, A. (2013). Evidence for a curvilinear relationship between abusive supervision and creativity in South Korea. *The Leadership Quarterly*, *24*, 724–731.
Liu, D., Liao, H., & Loi, R. (2012). The dark side of leadership: A three-level investigation of the cascading effect of abusive supervision on employee creativity. *Academy of Management Journal*, *55*, 1187–1212.
Ma, G. X., Born, M. P., Petrou, P., & Bakker, A. B. (2021). Bright sides of dark personality? A cross-cultural study on the dark triad and work outcomes. *International Journal of Selection and Assessment*, *29*, 510–518.
Machiavelli, N. (1891). *The Prince*. Oxford: Oxford University Press.
Mathieu, C., Babiak, P., & Hare, R. D. (2020). Psychopathy in the workplace. In A. R. Felthous & H. Saß (Eds.), *The Wiley International Handbook on Psychopathic Disorders and the Law* (2nd ed., pp. 607–644). John Wiley & Sons Ltd. https://doi.org/10.1002/9781119159322.ch27
McCall, W. M., & Lombardo, M. M. (1983). *Off the Track: Why and How Successful Executives Get Derailed* (Technical Report No. 21). Greensboro, NC: Centre for Creative Leadership. https://doi.org/10.35613/ccl.1983.1083
McCall, M. W., Lombardo, M. M., & Morrison, A. M. (1988). *The Lessons of Experience: How Successful Executives Develop on the Job*. Lexington, Mass: Lexington Books.
McCleskey, J. A. (2013). The dark side of leadership: Measurement, assessment, and intervention. *Business Renaissance Quarterly*, *8*, 35–53.
Mehraein, V., Visintin, F., & Pittino, D. (2023). The dark side of leadership: A systematic review of creativity and innovation. *International Journal of Management Reviews*, *25*, 740–767.
Palmer, P. J. (1998). Leading from within. In L. C. Spears (Ed.), *Insight on Leadership: Service, Stewardship, Spirit and Servant Leadership* (pp. 197–208). New York: Wiley & Sons Inc.

Rizvi, S. U., & Siddiqui, D. A. (2023). Dark triad and counterproductive work behaviour in Pakistan: The mediatory role of perceived organizational fairness complemented by organizational climate. *International Journal of Social Science & Entrepreneurship*, *3*, 545–568.

Schmitt, H. S., Sindermann, C., Li, M., Ma, Y., Kendrick, K. M., Becker, B., & Montag, C. (2020). The dark side of emotion recognition – Evidence from cross-cultural research in Germany and China. *Frontiers in Psychology, 11*, 1–15.

Schyns, B., & Schilling, J. (2013). How bad are the effects of bad leaders? A meta-analysis of destructive leadership and its outcomes. *Leadership Quarterly*, *24*, 138–158.

Stewart, J. B. (2012). In the undoing of a C.E.O: A puzzle. The New York Times.

Strube, J. J., & Strube, J. E. (1981). A meta-analytical investigation of Fiedler's model of leadership effectiveness. *Psychological Bulletin*, *90*, 307–321.

Yue, C. A., Qin, Y. S., & Men, L. R. (2023). The dark side of leadership communication: the impact of supervisor verbal aggressiveness on workplace culture, employee–organization relationships and counterproductive work behaviours. *Corporate Communications: An International Journal*, *29*, 405–429.

II

THE PROCESS OF DARK LEADERSHIP

Chapter 6

The Process of Dark Leadership: Reflections from a Norwegian Military Community of Practice

Johan Bergh

Introduction

In this reflective essay, I explore and reflect on one personal experience that affected me deeply as a senior commissioned officer in the Royal Norwegian Navy (RNA). I will relate this to Military Communities of Practice (MCoPs); the concept itself is referred to as 'Community of Practice' (CoP), which has been described as a type of informal learning organisation (Li et al., 2009). CoPs have been used in the education and business sectors for the past four decades (e.g., Wenger, McDermott & Snyder, 2002). Currently, it appears there is relatively little practice-related research when it comes to research about CoPs in a Norwegian military setting. Therefore, this contribution may put practical knowledge to the test of reflection. I will also introduce the concept of *samhandling* (e.g., Bergh & Boe, 2018), which is closely related to leadership (Torgersen & Steiro, 2009). The English equivalents of the term samhandling have embedded both key elements of group and team theory, and elements of general leadership theory (Horn & Walker, 2008; Jans et al., 2013).

DOI: 10.4324/9781003475262-8

Samhandling is, among other things, about gaining experience and learning from each other during the process (Torgersen & Steiro, 2009). This leads me to my introductory story.

A Short Story

I was one day summoned to a meeting with our top manager, an admiral whom I thought I knew pretty well. We had been colleagues for a long time. Before the meeting, I was ordered to present a recommendation for a case that the admiral underlined as very important for the institution's further business. Of course, I did as ordered. In this meeting, my line manager was present along with several other higher-ranking officers. We had prepared our recommendation thoroughly. At least, we thought so. After my presentation, the admiral, for some reason, went ballistic and was extremely unhappy with what I had presented. Yet, as far as I recall, I had presented what the admiral had requested in the first place. I wondered if maybe the admiral had lost it. Maybe it was a matter of losing control?

Shortly after my presentation, the admiral gave me a rough reprimand in front of all present officers and thereafter ordered me out of the meeting. I remember the admiral shouted: 'Get out!' So, I left the building and waited outside for my line manager. I was shaken and stirred, but my line manager comforted me just outside, at the top of the stairs. He also said that I did a good job. I am still grateful for that. I was disappointed and somewhat disillusioned. Why be scolded when I had followed orders? I was dazed and confused. My relationship with the admiral was never the same after that. And to this day, I wonder how this came to be. Therefore, it is important to me, in the light of learning and practice improvement, that I reflect on what was, for me, a very disturbing leadership encounter. Maybe my experience with this kind of toxic leadership behaviour can resonate with other leaders, be they military or civilian. This episode, therefore, calls for a few investigative reflections.

Original Reflection

Reflection is considered a process or activity that is central to developing practices (Dewey, 1933, 1938; Loughran, 1996). It also retains connotations of thinking processes and contemplative self-examination (Leitch & Day, 2000).

The introductory story connects with various aspects of toxic leadership. As a former department head for military leadership for several years, I was a practitioner, teacher, supervisor, and senior advisor to the admiral. All these functions were now at risk, at least from my perspective. In hindsight, the experience has brought me increasing insight into reflective practice research. Reflective practice is a way of elucidating life phenomena in everyday life, in practices, in work, in professions, in cooperation with others, in research, and in all kinds of activities (Lindseth, 2023, p. viii).

During my perennial career as a commissioned officer, I have encountered quite a few officers who had toxic traits and inclinations. But I was a bit surprised that a high-ranking admiral would treat a fellow officer and senior colleague in that way. In my experience, there seem to have been more military officers who focused on administration and procedures rather than on leading people. I find this paradoxical since all commissioned officers who graduated from any military academy in Norway are thoroughly trained not only to accomplish a mission but also, and equally importantly, to take care of their people in the process (e.g., Forsvaret, 2012). Why did the admiral, in this 'mission process', not also support a subordinate – me? This has puzzled me for years.

I have, as have many fellow officers, been and remain curious about how certain people are promoted to strategic management positions. For instance, in Norges Bank Investment Management[1] (NBIM), managers are now promoted due to their professional skills *and* people skills (Danielsen, 2023). I now teach project management, and I always tell my students this: If you are to succeed with any project, you must master the two **F**s – '***F****ag*[2] *og* ***F****olk*' (translated from Norwegian: subjects and people). This notion is consistent with up-to-date project management theory, which in turn is related to recognised organisational and leadership theories (e.g., Andersen, 2018). As I write this, it becomes evident to me that in this case, the admiral may somehow have missed the perspective on people. I wonder why that might be. Some additional reflections are, therefore, in order.

Critical and Theoretical Reflections

There appears to be a lack of a clear understanding of critical reflection, as it is a contested term reflecting the ideology of the user (Lucas, 2012). Fook (2006) suggests work needs to be done from a 'common basis of understanding' so that the practice of critical reflection can be refined and improved. Beyond question, this experience took place in an MCoP. I believe my experience with the admiral has several layers or aspects to it. For instance, how did the experience in the meeting affect me? And also later, outside at the top of the stairs? What did I expect, or did I really expect that? One thing stands out clearly: my line manager, who was also an admiral, comforted me unsolicited afterward. This made a big difference for me. Why? you might ask. It was because he showed empathy *in praxis*.

Empathy skills allow leaders to understand other people's perspectives and opinions, making the work environment more enjoyable and productive (Voss, Gruber & Reppel, 2010). To me, his comfort made a big difference in the sense that I had trust in him. Trust is a crucial element of effective leadership (Burke et al., 2007). As such, he exercised so-called resonant leadership, which appeals to me. In resonant leadership, leaders are mindful and optimistic and show empathy by focusing on the social and emotional needs of their followers (Faeq, Zyad & Hassan, 2022). In my case, this was a buffer against the apparent toxicity. What was at stake was my very liberty – my right to express myself in the face of a high-ranking officer without fear of consequences.

As a senior advisor to the admiral, and also a department head, I expected to be taken seriously. Obviously, that did not happen. As a department head, I was responsible for teaching 'good' military leadership. I also expected my superior officers to practice the same. The disappointment that I experienced that day at the meeting has made me reflect on what we were taught at the Norwegian Naval Academy. We were taught to lead by example – and (mostly) through dialogue. This experience proved to be the opposite. I have often wondered if it was my fault that it all went so terribly wrong. This, in turn, diminished my self-confidence at least to a certain degree. In leadership, self-confidence (or self-esteem, author's note) is widely regarded as an essential characteristic.

I will emphasise one reflection on leadership. I have had the opportunity to engage in writing and practising the Norwegian military organisation's leadership values and beliefs. Zheng et al. (2022) argue that ethical leaders, by facilitating followers' internalisation of organisational values, further engage followers' integrity identity. For me, integrity has been a bedrock in my leadership *praxis*. Ethics (e.g., honesty and integrity – which also implies trust) are intertwined with military leadership (e.g., Lagacé-Roy, 2008). As Peter Drucker (1986) puts it: 'Management is a discipline. But management is also people' (p. 6). Writing and practising our leadership values and beliefs also made me aware of other leaders' behaviour. I may, at this point, have strayed somewhat from the chapter's focus, namely dark or toxic leadership. I will, therefore, make a slight turn towards the dark side.

Toxic Leadership Behaviour

Dark, destructive, or toxic leadership has fascinated scholars and practitioners for decades (e.g., Mackey et al., 2021). Williams (2005) notes that toxic leadership appears in degrees, from the clueless who cause minor harm to the overtly evil who inflict serious damage. I wonder if the admiral's behaviour had to do with so-called 'derailed leadership'; that is, tyrannical or incompetent leadership (Arnulf, 2020). I am, to this day, not sure what went through the mind of my top manager that day. The admiral exercised what is commonly called 'workplace bullying' (e.g., Sischka, Schmidt & Steffgen, 2021). The regulation of extreme emotional expression is expected to facilitate team interaction and presumably allow for an easier exchange of ideas (Zaccaro, Rittman & Marks, 2001).

In my extensive military career, I have maybe been somewhat naïve in my expectations about leadership in MCoPs. It turns out that my experiences coincide with Mintzberg's (1985) view that organisations are areas of politics and conflicts. Ferris et al. (2007) also emphasise the need for social astuteness, or cleverness, in dealing with others. I find astuteness very intriguing. I shall explain why. To be astute in leadership is, for me, similar to Professor P. O. Brunstad's (2009) understanding of virtues and leadership. He has for several years researched and taught leadership at the Royal Norwegian Naval Academy. In his book, *Klokt Lederskap* (Wise Leadership), he states that the goal of wise leadership is to preserve one's integrity, the common good, and the dignity of our fellow humans. This stands in stark contrast to the admiral's behaviour. Toxic leadership behaviour in any circumstance will, at some point, poison both the individual's and the company's performance (e.g., Tate, 2009). With this in mind and my previous personal experience with the admiral, I came to realise that at this point in my military career, there was a certain discrepancy: a notion that something inner did not agree with the exterior (see, for example, Lindseth, 2020). That is, my inner evidence told me that the exterior, which was the meeting experience, did not agree with my own military leadership beliefs and praxis to date.

According to Lindseth (2020), inner evidence is an insight into a connection (author's translation), and we can only have inner evidence in the respective practical contexts and businesses. If we are to understand and develop our practical knowledge, we, therefore, need inner evidence. We must put our practical knowledge to the test of reflection. To conclude this part, I will emphasise the following: every leader, either military or civilian, should reflect on their leadership praxis, either alone or together with other competent persons. Reflection is considered essential to professional practice (Plack & Greenberg, 2005). Samhandling is necessary to achieve this.

Samhandling in a Military Community of Practice (MCoP)

Samhandling is both a mindset and a working method. The closest translation of samhandling is 'interaction' or 'joint action' (Torgersen & Steiro, 2018). Samhandling can be seen from a perspective of valuing interaction and trust as a means of developing organisations and efforts in the community. Therefore, it resonates with CoPs as mentioned earlier. Samhandling also implies that one must be aware that each participant contributes with their unique situational understanding. It is focused on interaction, complementary skills, and competencies and how to utilise them (p. 50). As such, samhandling an MCoP may well result in fruitful conversations between the competent and the inexperienced. This should, therefore, not be taken lightly.

Also, in activity theory or business theory, it is clearly stated that the various participants complement each other in the overall development process. Therefore, these theories also resonate with perspective-taking which is fundamental to social interaction (Decety & Sommerville, 2003). Perspective-taking can be organised into three distinct categories—perceptual, social-cognitive, and affective (Underwood & Moore, 1982). Perspective-taking in an MCoP, therefore, encompasses all categories. If one considers the above, then it becomes clear that officers in an MCoP should master, or at least have a certain degree of understanding of, both inner and outer environments. That is, they must have a certain situational awareness (e.g., Endsley, 1995).

Wenger et al. (2002) define CoPs by three structural elements: domain, community, and practice. Community describes the net of relationships, the shared identity, and the sense of belonging among members. The presence of these elements creates a social context in which individuals continuously make sense of their practices, negotiate meaning, and exchange perspectives. Another important element is, of course, *practice*, which refers to the actual activities in which members collectively engage. Within an MCoP, the situation seems to be somewhat similar. So far, there is only a relatively small amount of material about MCoPs, especially from a Norwegian perspective. Sookermany (2011) states among other things, that '…a military community of practice, consisting of individuals situated in a defined context with particular skills who as a community are able to solve the military tasks assigned to them…' (p. 480). Participation that is based on dialogue, sharing of narratives, and looking for relevant metaphors is the personal struggle that will develop one's (military) professional judgement (Sookermany, 2017).

For military officers, accomplishing missions or tasks is the main focus. But it also includes the human perspective. Yet, as our present Chief of Defence states in his view on leadership (2020): 'Accomplishing missions and taking care of our people. So basic and simple, but at the same time so challenging…' (p. 4, author's translation). He, therefore, emphasises both the task/mission and the human factor. Sometimes the latter part seems to be omitted. I have sometimes found the lack of a human perspective disturbing.

Conclusions, and Lessons for Leaders

This personal essay is based on experiences in Norwegian MCoPs and may, therefore, not be applicable worldwide. Yet in any encounter with toxic leaders, I have wondered: Is there anything we can do? This may seem like a rhetorical question, and I therefore rely on Professor Linda Lai (2022) at Oslo Business School. She claims that there are three options when you encounter toxic leaders. One, you can pick a fight and try to change the situation by raising your voice. Two, you can lie low and be silent and try to protect yourself as best you can. Three, you change jobs (recommended). As I see it, her research has a clear message to any toxic leader: if you practice toxic leadership, you may find yourself lacking employees at some point. It may not be very effective. Me, I laid low. Maybe it was not the wisest thing I have done. But the admiral's rank and posture intimidated me at the time. I often regret that I did not stand up for myself. As such, I was a victim of my insecurities. Maybe because of my military 'upbringing'? I wonder: If I, as one of many commissioned officers over the years have been intimidated by high-ranking officers, can the whole system become poisoned?

As a former participant in MCoPs, I have for several years claimed that one of the Norwegian military's greatest hindrances to effective communication is an officer's visible rank. My experiences, which include both inner and outer evidence, tell me that trying to engage in frank and real dialogue can be somewhat complicated. Many of my fellow officers, including me, have, at times, been very careful with how we express ourselves. Why? Mostly due to fear about our future careers. Fear has, at times, rendered me numb and powerless. To quote Frank Herbert (1965): 'Fear is the mind-killer. Fear is a little-death that brings total obliteration.'

As I have reflected upon earlier, being a military commissioned officer in an MCoP, integrity is at least important. Integrity can be described as credible communication, a strong sense of justice, and consistency of word and action (Mayer, Davis & Schoorman, 1995). Integrity increases trust, as it provides consistency of word and action, and makes people's behaviour more predictable (Adams & Webb, 2002). When toxic leaders say one thing and do the other, I and many others get confused. Can we then trust them?

I have, at times, somewhat naïvely expected from my superior officers that they will be trustworthy, frank, and supportive. I have also experienced false dialogue, or no dialogue at all, distrust, silencing, fear, and loathing in some MCoPs. I have had several interesting conversations with my former colleagues over the years. Like I, they also have encountered high-ranking officers who, out of ignorance or sheer ill will, either did not follow up with them at all or focused on trivialities.

As a leader and practitioner in various MCoPs, I have had the opportunity to form and educate many young NCO[3] and officers. I have not succeeded with all of them. In my opinion, for further professional development of MCoPs, or any CoP for that matter, all leaders, military or civilian, should engage in liberating, not limiting, praxis. Samhandling, for the sake of practice improvement, is therefore all leaders' responsibility at all levels in any organisation. There is enough evidence that toxic leaders poison both individuals and the organisations they operate within. My final conclusion is that any high-ranking leader, military or civilian, wherever they operate, should at least give their subordinates a break. I, and most of my fellow officers have only been concerned about doing a good job. I sincerely wish they would take that attitude more often into consideration.

Notes

1 The aim of NBIM is to ensure responsible and long-term management of revenue from Norway's oil and gas resources so that this wealth benefits both current and future generations of Norway. https://www.nbim.no/en/organisation/about-us/

2 Do NOT confuse this word with any slang.

3 Non-commissioned officers.

References

Adams, B. D., & Webb, R. D. (2002). Trust in small military teams. In *7th International command and control technology symposium,* Quebec City, Quebec, pp. 1–20.

Andersen, E. S. (2018). *Prosjektledelse: et organisasjonsperspektiv* (*Project management: An organisational perspective*). 2. utg. Bergen: Fagbokforlaget.

Arnulf, J. K. (2020). *Hva er ledelse* (*What is leadership*). 2nd ed. Bergen: Universitetsforlaget.

Bergh, J. & Boe, O. (2018). Samhandling and trust in military leadership structures. In G.-E. Torgersen (Ed.), *Interaction: 'samhandling' under risk. A step ahead of the unforeseen* (pp. 319–338). Oslo: Cappelen Damm Akademisk. https://doi.org/10.23865/noasp.36.ch17

Brunstad, P. O. (2009). *Klokt lederskap: Mellom dyder og dødssynder* (*Wise leadership: Between virtues and mortal sins*). Oslo: Gyldendal Norsk Forlag.

Burke, C. S., Sims, D. E., Lazzara, E. H., & Salas, E. (2007). Trust in leadership: A multi-level review and integration. *The Leadership Quarterly, 18*(6), 606–632.

Danielsen, T. (2023). *Anthropological gaze, stories, and reflections on NBIM culture.* Technical Report.

Decety, J., & Sommerville, J. A. (2003). Shared representations between self and other: A social cognitive neuroscience view. *Trends in Cognitive Sciences, 7*, 527–533.

Dewey, J. (1933). *How we think.* Boston, MA: D.C. Heath & Co Publishers.

Dewey, J. (1938). *Experience and education.* New York: Macmillan.

Drucker, P. F. (1986). *Management: Task, responsibilities, practices* (p. 6). New York: Truman Talley Books.

Endsley, M. R. (1995). Toward a theory of situation awareness in dynamic systems. *Human Factors, 37*(1), 32–64.

Faeq, D. K., Zyad, K., & Hassan, R. (2022). Impact of resonant leadership in reducing workplace bullying: A case from Sulaymaniyah Chamber of Commerce & Industry. *International Journal of Research in Business and Social Science* (2147–4478), *11*(6), 264–276.

Ferris, G. R., Treadway, D. C., Perrewe, P. L., Brouer, R. L, Douglas, C., & Lux, S. (2007). Political skill in organisations. *Journal of Management, 33*(3), 290–320.

Fook, J. (2006). Beyond reflective practice: Reworking the "critical". In *Critical reflection, Presented at the meeting of the professional lifelong learning: beyond reflective practice*, Leeds.

Forsvaret. (2012). *FSJ grunnsyn pa ledelse i Forsvaret* (The Norwegian Armed Forces Chief of Defence basic view of leadership in the ArmedForces). Oslo: Norwegian Armed Forces Defence Staff.

Herbert, F. (1965). *Dune.* Philadelphia: Chilton Company.

Horn, B., & Walker, R. W. (Eds.) (2008). *The military leadership handbook.* Toronto: Canadian Defence Academy Press.

Jans, N., Mugford, S., Cullens, J., & Frazer-Jans, J. (2013). *The chiefs – A study of strategic leadership.* Centre for Defence Leadership and Ethics, Australian Defence College.

Lagacé-Roy, D. (2008). Mentoring. In Horn, B. & Walker, R.W. (Eds.), *The military leadership handbook* (pp. 378–390). Toronto: Dundurn Press.

Lai, L. (2022). Hvordan kan man håndtere giftige ledere? (How can one handle toxic leaders?) BI Business Review. https://www.bi.no/forskning/business-review/articles/2022/06/hvordan-kan-man-handtere-giftige-ledere/

Leitch, R. & Day, C. (2000). Action research and reflective practice: Towards a holistic view. *Educational Action Research*, *8*(1), 179–193.

Li, L. C., Grimshaw, J. M., Nielsen, C., Judd, M., Coyte, P. C., & Graham, I. D. (2009). Evolution of Wenger's concept of community of practice. *Implementation Science: IS*, *4*, 11. https://doi.org/10.1186/1748-5908-4-1

Lindseth, A. (2020). Dosenten i et FoU-perspektiv. Refleksiv praksisforskning som en vei mot dosentkompetanse (The docent in a R&D perspective. Reflective practice research – about the importance of research towards docent competence). In C. C. Bachke & M. Hermansen (Eds.), Å satse på dosenter. *Et utviklingsarbeid* (*Commitment to docents. A developmental work*) (Chapter 4, pp. 75–101). Oslo: Cappelen Damm Akademisk. https://doi.org/10.23865/noasp.109.ch4

Lindseth, A. (2023). Preface - historical background of reflective practice research. In M. N. Weiss & G. H. Helskog (Eds.), *Reflective practice research in higher education pedagogies* (pp. vii–x). Wien: Lit Verlag.

Loughran, J. J. (1996). *Developing reflective practice: Learning about teaching and learning through modelling*. Great Britain, London: Falmer Press.

Lucas, P. (2012). Critical reflection. What do we really mean? In *Proceedings of the Australian Collaborative Education Network* (ACEN), *National Conference*. Deakin University, Geelong, Australia.

Mackey, J. D., Ellen III, B. P., McAllister, C. P. & Alexander, K. C. (2021). The dark side of leadership: A systematic literature review and meta-analysis of destructive leadership research. *Journal of Business Research*, *132*, 705–718.

Mayer, R., Davis, J., & Schoorman, F. (1995). An integrative model of organizational trust. *Academy of Management Review*, *20*(3), 709–734.

Mintzberg, H. (1985). The organization as political arena. *Journal of Management Studies*, *22*, 133–154.

Plack, M. M., & Greenberg, L. (2005). The reflective practitioner: Reaching for excellence in practice. *Paediatrics*, *116*(6), 1546–1552.

Sischka, P. E., Schmidt, A. F., & Steffgen, G. (2021). The effect of competition and passive avoidant leadership style on the occurrence of workplace bullying. *Personnel Review*, *50*(2), 535–559.

Sookermany, A. M. (2011). The embodied soldier: Towards a new epistemological foundation of soldiering skills in the (post) modernized Norwegian armed forces. *Armed Forces & Society*, *37*(3), 469–493.

Sookermany, A. M. (2017). Military education reconsidered: A postmodern update. *Journal of Philosophy of Education*, *51*(1), 310–330.

Tate, B. W. (2009). Bad to the bone: Empirically defining and measuring negative leadership. Available from ProQuest Dissertations & Theses Global. (304989652). Retrieved from https://nwulib.nwu.ac.za/login?url=https://search-proquest-com

Torgersen, G.-E., & Steiro, T. J. (2009). *Ledelse, samhandling og opplæring i fleksible organisasjoner* (*Leadership, interaction and training in flexible organizations*). Stjørdal: Læringsforlaget.

Torgersen, G.-E., & Steiro, T. J. (2018). Defining the term samhandling. In G.-E. Torgersen (Ed.), *Interaction: 'samhandling' under risk. A step ahead of the unforeseen* (pp. 39–54). Oslo: Cappelen Damm Akademisk. https://doi.org/10.23865/noasp.36.ch2

Underwood, B., & Moore, B. (1982). Perspective-taking and altruism. *Psychological Bulletin*, *91*(1), 143.

Voss, R., Gruber, T., & Reppel, A. (2010). Which classroom service encounters make students happy or unhappy? *International Journal of Educational*, *24*(7), 615–636.

Wenger, E., McDermott, R., & Snyder, W. M. (2002). Seven principles for cultivating communities of practice. *Cultivating Communities of Practice: A Guide to Managing Knowledge*, *4*, 1–19.

Williams, D. F. (2005). *Toxic leadership in the US Army* (pp. 1–27). Carlisle: US Army War College.

Zaccaro, S. J., Rittman, A. L., & Marks, M. A. (2001). Team leadership. *The Leadership Quarterly*, *12*(4), 451–483.

Zheng, Y., Epitropaki, O., Graham, L., & Caveney, N. (2022). Ethical leadership and ethical voice: The mediating mechanisms of value internalization and integrity identity. *Journal of Management*, *48*(4), 973–1002.

Chapter 7

Discursive Practices of Dark Side Leaders: Reflections from Pakistan and Colombia

Luis J. Serrano-Tamayo and Jabran Khan

Introduction

The term leadership has been studied for decades; plenty of theories have been established regarding this, but primarily emphasise positive leadership, and minimal research is focused on dark leadership (Bass & Avolio, 1990; Khan et al., 2022). In this chapter, we discussed how dark leadership seriously threatens organisations. The discussion is based on the literature and practical examples, mainly from Pakistan and Colombia. Dark side leaders have been described according to their characteristics. On the one hand, by using adjectives attached to their personality. In this first list, we may find adjectives such as arrogant (Borden et al., 2018), abusive (Oyewunmi & Oyewunmi, 2022), narcissistic (Ong et al., 2016), manipulative (Delani, 2019), toxic (Mergen & Ozbilgin, 2021). On the other hand, adjectives that include the prefix un or dis show what they lack. In this second list, we may find adjectives such as unethical (Hassan et al., 2023), unfair (Liu et al., 2017), disengaged (Bonner et al., 2016), and discouraging (Bush et al., 2021). However, these adjectives present specific characteristics that depict what a dark side leader is.

This chapter analyses the consequences of different dark side leaders based on a revision of literature and presents a case of dark side leaders'

DOI: 10.4324/9781003475262-9

discursive practices, especially the terms they usually use in organisational settings. The objective of the chapter is to develop a framework, including the main criteria that leaders must consider revising to determine whether the terms they use are on the dark or bright side. The following section is divided into three parts. The first part presents the impact of dark side behaviours; the second part explores how dark side leaders behave in the Southeast Asia region; and the third part is a case study about how discursive practices manifest in a military organisation, making cross-cultural connections around dark side leaders. The lesson for leaders is a framework, presented as a filter, to recommend to leaders a self-critical analysis of their use of words. The chapter concludes with a recap of the most relevant considerations of dark side leaders and some recommendations for the leaders to move from the dark to the bright side.

Dark Side Leaders in Practice: A Reflection from Pakistan

In the current era of a competitive and digital world, the organisation's success depends heavily on the role of leaders (Mubarak et al., 2024). As world dynamics change rapidly, organisations need to develop an approach to adjust to these changes; the role of leadership is crucial. Organisations need a proactive approach to respond to change in the competitive and disruptive technological era. To promote such a culture, everyone is involved in the process of promoting creativity and innovation and building a positive culture. However, with the presence of dark leadership, it is not possible, as such leaders undermine the culture of collaboration, information exchange, support, and feedback in the organisations (Neuman & Baron, 2005). Leaders with such traits influence the employees and the entire organisation negatively (Skogstad et al., 2007). Previous research has focused on the positive forms of leadership (e.g., inclusive, ethical, authentic, transformational, and empowered leadership). However, limited attention is paid to the dark side of leadership (Furtner et al., 2017; Khan et al., 2022). Dark side leadership promotes such behaviour in followers (e.g., passive behaviour, criminal acts, manipulation, and corruption). These qualities were found in different leadership styles (e.g., despotic, passive, autocratic, and destructive leaders) (Khan et al., 2022; Kurtulmuş & Kurtulmuş, 2019; Tepper, 2007). The presence of dark leaders is not only in the literature but there are examples from real-life practice. For instance, well-known company Enron leaders make false information in the accounting books for temporary benefits. As an outcome, we have seen the downfall of these companies. According to Tepper (2007), 13.6% of employees are affected by destructive leadership styles, with associated costs of approximately US$ 23.8bn.

One common trait of the dark side in Pakistan's high-power distance culture is despotic leadership. Despotic leaders are interested in dominating their employees and always think of and work toward their self-interest. They are arrogant, deceptive, and forceful and take credit for the contributions of others (Schmid et al., 2019; House & Howell, 1992). These characteristics are common among Pakistani leaders, as they always put themselves ahead of their followers and organisations' goals. Over time, this dark side behaviour is observed and modelled by followers. They never consider the public welfare and the organisation's goals; they always compromise on their duties and engage in corrupt practices. For instance, Pakistan International Airlines reported a $338 million loss in 2022 due to corruption and dark side leadership. In addition, there are several examples of political leaders who use manipulative tactics to attract followers for their personal interests leading to high corruption, weak governance, and limited attention to public welfare. Why do leaders adopt dark side leadership styles? To a certain extent, there is evidence in the literature. Many scholars point out that the personality of a leader is the source of dark leadership. O'Boyle et al. (2013) found that Machiavellianism and narcissism are dark leaders' traits. Interestingly, researchers have stated that the dark side is not a personality disorder, but it is the typical personality of the leader (Hogan & Kaiser, 2005; Hogan et al., 2011; Oyewunmi et al., 2024). The concept of organisational greed can also play an integral role in promoting dark leadership (Coser, 1974). Numerous examples of greedy institutions are available, such as the army, political parties, and family businesses. These organisations demand a great deal from their personnel, such as long working hours, competence, continual availability, profound dedication, and loyalty, but they provide little in return. Military organisations might be considered greedy, as they require their members to be willing to give up their lives for the organisation. Due to this, position holders may become dark leaders to their subordinates. The following case explores the discursive practices of dark side leaders in a military organisation.

Dark Leadership through Discursive Practices - A Case from the Colombian Militia

There are mostly two types of leaders. Some leaders are transformational and charismatic role models that everyone wants to emulate, and hopefully become. Other leaders are authoritarian and even rude. Sometimes, it is the same person, but in different moments. Although subordinates say they do not want to be authoritarian leaders but transformational leaders, they tend to replicate more authoritarian leadership than transformational leadership. This perception illustrates the urgent need to analyse the so-called "dark side leaders," who are also known as toxic, abusive, sycophant, and narcissistic, and the potential harm they can cause in organisations. In direct response to the need for a practice-oriented analysis of dark side leaders, this case explores their actions in a real-world setting. Various perspectives, such as discourse, materiality, and identity work, can be adopted when analysing leaders in practice. For this chapter, we examine the dimension of discourse, specifically exploring how dark side leaders use certain terms and their communication style. Our research draws from the rich culture of the military, where leadership is the very essence of the profession. Through the. ethnographic work of one of the authors, who was an insider in a military organisation in Colombia for 30 years, we have identified a series of terms that encapsulate some of the most notable behaviours of dark side leaders, including humiliation, contempt, and authoritarianism. However, we feel compelled to issue a warning to the reader as these terms may hit close to home. We hope this self-reflection will serve as a catalyst for change and growth.

Term One: "In my times..."

There are several "in my times" for toxic leaders when intergenerational differences exist. For example: *"In my times, we could do that easily"*, *"In my times, we were really hard workers"*, *"In my times, we could do the double this generation can do"*, *"In my times, we were truly men"*. The idea behind "*in my times...*" is to extol the characteristics of a previous generation against the younger generation. This creates a feeling of hopelessness. It leads to a vicious circle that creates a Pygmalion effect, in which the incapability of the younger generation becomes a self-fulfilling prophecy. Interestingly, this could happen from younger to older generations as well, for example, when referring to the use of technology. The biggest problem is that using the term generates a strong division that may ultimately affect the performance of others. How many times have we used the intergenerational gap to diminish others, consciously or unconsciously? What examples come to my mind when I hear about the intergenerational gap? Have I been a victim of the intergenerational gap? How have I felt?

Term Two: "The one that was before me did nothing"

Dark side leaders tend to minimise the success of those who were in the same position before them. This tactic helps them maximise every small victory, projecting a Messiah persona because, in their view, the former leader did nothing. The problem is that new leaders will work with pretty much the same people the former leader worked with before; so, when the dark side leader minimises and ridicules the work of the former leader, he is doing the same to the subordinates. This behaviour is normally accompanied by an abusive and narcissistic style, which tends to hoard all the victories and successes because of their leadership. However, in the event of failure, they are looking for a guilty person to condemn and sanction. How many times have we played the Messiah role, projecting that the only good started when we got in the leadership position? Am I aware that if I rant about the leader before me, I am also ranting about my work team? Am I recognising the achievements of my work team? Am I the leader who takes responsibility when something goes wrong, or do I look for someone to blame?

Term Three: "The one who commands is the one who commands, even if he commands badly"

The logic of this term is normally associated with the respect that needs to be given to the superior, even if we do not agree or if we think the leader is not right. In this case, there is neither unity of command nor harmony of action; the superior imposes the will on the subordinate, whose only duty is to obey. The biggest problem here is where the red line is. There can be certain tolerance to some "bad command" associated with routine tasks, some misguided words, or certain undesirable attitudes, but what happens if this bad command leads others to commit crimes? The extreme reference is that in WWII, Nazi soldiers hid behind the fact they were only undertaking orders from their superiors. However, how often have we followed orders from our superiors, knowing it was not the right path? Have we confronted our leader to defend what we firmly think is correct?

Term Four: "That is YOUR problem"

Dark side leaders abandon their subordinates and give them poor guidance. As they are usually ignorant, when the subordinates go to them and ask for advice, they dispatch the subordinate with the expression: "That is YOUR problem". This abandonment from the leader usually goes with: "*Give me solutions, no problems*"; "*Don't tell me about the pains of the birth, show me the creature*". These types of statements are intrinsically related to the famous Machiavelli statement: "*The goal justifies the means*". As the dark side leader does not give advice, instructions, clear orders, and ethical considerations, the subordinate will try to fulfil the entrusted mission by resorting to any available means, which usually borders on or even exceeds the limits of ethics and the law. How often have we shied away from our leadership responsibilities using similar terms?

Term Five: "In military life, you don't see your parents die or your children born"

The idea behind this narrative is that duty is above family, which is supposed to be one of the supreme altruisms that sometimes involve military life. If the military has sworn the flag, he/she needs to be available at any time, even at the expense of family needs or commitments. So, when the subordinate asks for permission to attend a personal event, in addition to a no answer, his/her loyalty and commitment to the institution, the mission, or the team are called into question. It may be true that sometimes, the mission, i.e. the needs of the work, might need this kind of commitment. However, if the scenario is not a matter of life and death, as usually are 99% of the scenarios in organisational life, there is no need to use these kinds of terms because they create hard feelings against the leader and the organisation, which become the inflection point in which the person realises there is a separation between their organisational and individual identity. If the person chooses their individual identity, sooner or later, he/she will abandon the organisation as they cannot tolerate the environment anymore. If the organisational identity is chosen, personal lives are affected adversely.

Have you ever denied permission to a subordinate who needed to do a personal errand? Was it really essential to deny that permission? Did you really know what the personal situation of that subordinate was? How would you have felt if you had been the one who had been denied that permission?

The above examples come from military life, but the reader will easily identify that they apply to different types of organisations in which similar terms are used daily. Although this section presents a series of reflection questions that work as lessons for leaders, in the following section, we propose a framework that will help leaders evaluate whether they are on the dark side or the bright side according to their discursive practices.

Lessons for Leaders

In the previous section, we have seen some of the consequences that dark side leaders may cause in organisations. We have seen undesirable conduct, such as the despotic leader, in the Southeast Asia region. In the case of Colombia, there are different discursive practices manifested as terms used daily in organisational life that produce a series of consequences to organisations, such as divisions, hopelessness, offences, and mistrust. The lessons for leaders are orientated to the needed awareness in their oral expression, especially in the terms they use. The terms that leaders use become part of their identity. Therefore, the framework in Figure 7.1 depicts a series of criteria, or filters, with a corresponding question to help leaders move from the dark to the bright side in their communication.

Hope/Hopelessness

Leaders are supposed to inspire their organisations and enthusiastically show the right path. Therefore, the first communication that leaders must make clear to their work team is the sense of hope. Rude expressions such as "that is YOUR problem" generate a feeling of disconnection and hopelessness in team members.

Intergenerational

The use of intergenerational terms such as "in my times…" generates immediate division, disconnection, and a sense of growing hopelessness. When leaders use this expression or similar to express the separation between

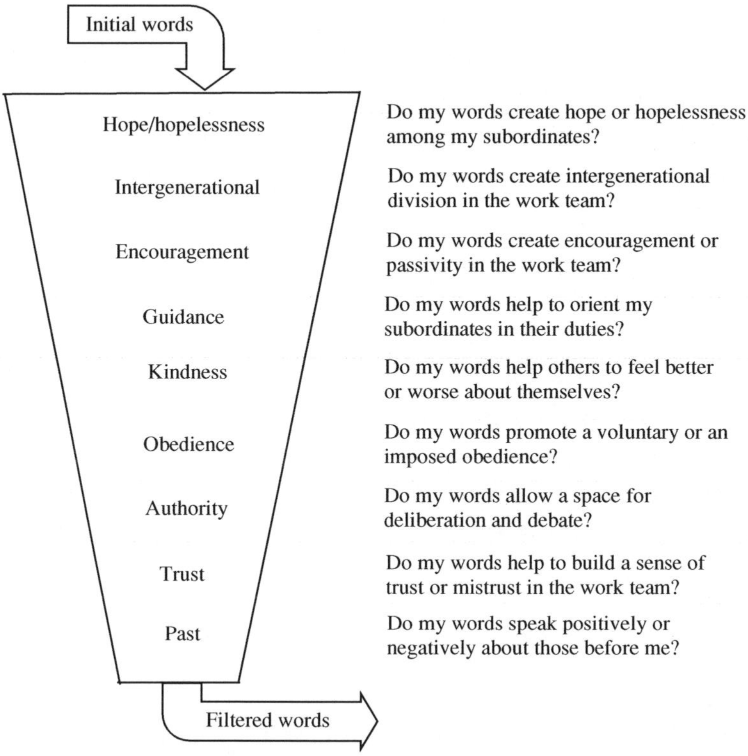

FIGURE 7.1 Filters to avoid becoming a dark-side leader through the use of words.

two worlds, they create non-reconcilable groups that are confronted by one another instead of working together toward the same goal.

Encouragement

Leaders must be aware of the Pygmalion syndrome, which works both ways. If team members are diminished, humiliated, and insulted with words such as stupid, incompetent, incapable, and so on, the person affected will end up representing that image sooner or later. However, if the leader is there to help their crew achieve the best version of themselves, the team members will achieve that vision.

Guidance

Leaders do not need to know everything, but they always must have words of guidance. When a team member reaches a leader asking for guidance, one of the most effective ways to push him/her away forever is to tell him/

her, "that is your problem" or "give me solutions, not problems". At this moment, the person who asked for guidance knows that they cannot count on the leader. Second, as the dark side leader is not giving advice, he /she is opening the door to achieve the goal by any means, which may lead to catastrophic consequences.

Kindness

Good leaders know their team members' struggles and family contexts. When a team member asks for permission to do a personal errand, try to help by always allowing that permission. If the situation is not critical and, as a leader, you should not allow the permission, instead of using the terms associated with the organisational commitment being above personal matters, analyse together what could be the best path to follow.

Obedience

Leaders must ask themselves how their orders are received. Are they received enthusiastically? Are they received with apathy? Are they received with resentment? The words leader use in their daily terms will construct their identity. As a leader, if you have to give an unpopular order, always use positive verbs instead of negative ones. If only negative words come to your mind, use a dictionary of antonyms, rearrange your words, write them down, rehearse your speech, and think how you would feel with the unpopular order. These small steps will go a long way in increasing your empathy.

Authority

Deliberation and discussions are needed in high-performance teams to reach decisions that represent the voice of members. Dark side leaders do not care about deliberation; they impose their authority over the rest, but doing so is missing many opportunities from their team that might help to reach the objectives sooner and easier. Team members who feel they are part of decision-making will work much better than those who work with imposed orders.

Trust

The construction of trust takes a long time, and its destruction takes seconds. Do not use terms that could destroy what took you a long time to build. Dark side leaders who speak badly about former leaders immediately create a sense of mistrust in their team members. Focus on what you can achieve in the future and build a strong and trustworthy relationship with your team.

Past

Dark side leaders tend to be anchored to the past and lack a vision of the future, one of the essential components of bright side leaders. Those leaders who speak badly about those who were in the same position before, are also speaking badly about themselves and their incapacity to improve a situation. In addition, they are speaking badly about the work team who previously worked with the former leader. When the dark side leader speaks badly about the past, the work team starts to think that the work they did in the past, in which they probably put plenty of effort, is worth nothing to the new leader. This feeling in the old members of the team generates division, resentment, and disillusion with the leader.

Conclusion

In this chapter, we mainly focused on how dark side of leadership manifests in practice, influencing organisational results and the performance of teams. The chapter is based on a discussion of examples from Southeast Asia and Latin America. From the literature and the case study, we found that the dark side of leadership negatively influences the organisation and has a long-term impact on subordinates. Moreover, we explored the discursive practices of dark leadership, and we found a series of criteria and self-reflection questions for helping leaders move from the dark to the bright side of leadership, especially through their discursive practices. Considering the above discussion, we provided a framework with criteria and questions associated with leadership values such as kindness, trust, guidance, and encouragement, which will contribute to transforming toxic and dark work environments into positive and healthy ones.

References

Bass, B. M., & Avolio, B. J. (1990). Developing transformational leadership: 1992 and beyond. *Journal of European Industrial Training*, *14*(5), 21. https://doi.org/10.1108/03090599010135122

Bonner, J. M., Greenbaum, R. L., & Mayer, D. M. (2016). My boss is morally disengaged: The role of ethical leadership in explaining the interactive effect of supervisor and employee moral disengagement on employee behaviors. *Journal of Business Ethics*, *137*, 731–742.

Borden, L., Levy, P. E., & Silverman, S. B. (2018). Leader arrogance and subordinate outcomes: The role of feedback processes. *Journal of Business and Psychology*, *33*, 345–364.

Bush, J. T., Welsh, D. T., Baer, M. D., & Waldman, D. (2021). Discouraging unethicality versus encouraging ethicality: Unraveling the differential effects of prevention-and promotion-focused ethical leadership. *Personnel Psychology*, *74*(1), 29–54.

Coser, L. A. (1974). *Greedy institutions: Patterns of undivided commitment*. The Free Press.

Delani, S. (2019). Manipulative leadership and the effect towards its subordinate as portrayed in Orson Scott Card's novel. *Journal of Linguistics, Literature, and Culture*, *1*(1), 27–34.

Furtner, M. R., Maran, T., & Rauthmann, J. F. (2017). Dark leadership: The role of leaders' dark triad personality traits. In *Leader Development Deconstructed* (pp. 75–99). Springer International Publishing/Springer Nature. https://doi.org/10.1007/978-3-319-64740-1_4

Hassan, S., Kaur, P., Muchiri, M., Ogbonnaya, C., & Dhir, A. (2023). Unethical leadership: Review, synthesis and directions for future research. *Journal of Business Ethics*, *183*(2), 511–550.

Hogan, J., Hogan, R., & Kaiser, R. B. (2011). Management derailment. In S. Zedeck (Ed.), *APA handbook of industrial and organizational psychology, 3. Maintaining, expanding, and contracting the organization* (pp. 555–575). American Psychological Association. https://doi.org/10.1037/12171-015

Hogan, R., & Kaiser, R. B. (2005). What we know about leadership. *Review of General Psychology*, *9*(2), 169–180.

House, R. J., & Howell, J. M. (1992). Personality and charismatic leadership. *The Leadership Quarterly*, *3*(2), 81–108.

Khan, J., Mubarak, N., Khattak, S. A., Safdar, S., & Jaafar, M. (2022). Despotic leadership and IT project efficiency: The role of resilience. *International Journal of Managing Projects in Business*, *15*(3), 449–468.

Kurtulmuş, B. E., & Kurtulmuş, B. E. (2019). *The dark side of leadership* (pp. 9–24). Springer International Publishing.

Liu, H., Chiang, J. T. J., Fehr, R., Xu, M., & Wang, S. (2017). How do leaders react when treated unfairly? Leader narcissism and self-interested behavior in response to unfair treatment. *Journal of Applied Psychology*, *102*(11), 1590.

Mergen, A., & Ozbilgin, M. F. (2021). Understanding the followers of toxic leaders: Toxic illusion and personal uncertainty. *International Journal of Management Reviews*, *23*(1), 45–63.

Mubarak, N., Khan, J., Bashir, S., & Safdar, S. (2024). Dark side of leadership and information technology project success: The role of mindfulness. *Journal of Managerial Psychology*, *39*(3), 304–322.

Neuman, J. H., & Baron, R. A. (2005). Aggression in the workplace: A social-psychological perspective. In S. Fox & P. E. Spector (Eds.), *Counterproductive work behavior: Investigations of actors and targets* (pp. 13–40). American Psychological Association. https://doi.org/10.1037/10893-001

O'Boyle, E. H., Forsyth, D., Banks, G. C., & Story, P. A. (2013). A meta-analytic review of the dark triad–intelligence connection. *Journal of Research in Personality*, *47*(6), 789–794.

Ong, C. W., Roberts, R., Arthur, C. A., Woodman, T., & Akehurst, S. (2016). The leader ship is sinking: A temporal investigation of narcissistic leadership. *Journal of Personality*, *84*(2), 237–247.

Oyewunmi, A. E., Adedeji, O., & Adegbuyi, A. (2024). Spiritual intelligence in the workplace: Is there a dark side? *Journal of Organizational Change Management*, *37*(4), 704–716. https://doi.org/10.1108/JOCM-06-2023-0255

Oyewunmi, A. E., & Oyewunmi, O. A. (2022). Speaking silence: Abusive supervision, subordinates' citizenship behavior, and whistleblowing intention. *Sage Open*, *12*(1), 215824402210799. https://doi.org/10.1177/21582440221079912

Schmid, E. A., Pircher Verdorfer, A., & Peus, C. (2019). Shedding light on leaders' self-interest: Theory and measurement of exploitative leadership. *Journal of Management*, *45*(4), 1401–1433.

Skogstad, A., Einarsen, S., Torsheim, T., Aasland, M. S., & Hetland, H. (2007). The destructiveness of laissez-faire leadership behavior. *Journal of Occupational Health Psychology*, *12*(1), 80.

Tepper, B. J. (2007). Abusive supervision in work organizations: Review, synthesis, and research agenda. *Journal of Management*, *33*(3), 261–289.

Chapter 8

The Toxic Triangle of Leadership

Godbless Akaighe and Isaiah Adisa

Introduction

Negative personality traits have become prominent in mainstream organisational research, but it is not a new phenomenon (Harms & Spain, 2015). The term dark personality describes a set of socially adverse traits, a lack of concern for the feelings of others, a socially aversive personality, and malevolent and self-serving behaviour patterns. The literature suggests that dark personality traits have both sub-clinical and clinical dimensions (e.g., Paulhus & Williams, 2002). The sub-clinical dimension presupposes that the personality traits are not at a level that requires clinical intervention or therapy. In this instance, individuals with such manifestations can function in everyday life in relationships with others, while the reverse is the case for clinical manifestations of dark personality traits (see Paulhus, 2014; Spain et al., 2014). However, the dark personality traits extend beyond the dark triad of Narcissism, Machiavellianism, and psychopathy. For example, perfectionism, which in many instances has been studied outside the dark triad characteristics, has received limited research in organisational settings (e.g., Ozbilir et al., 2015). Perfectionism is the mental need of individuals to mould themselves into an idealised image of flawlessness (Horney, 1950).

Dark leadership, also known as destructive leadership, is a phenomenon that has gained increasing attention in recent years due to its negative impact on both leaders' and followers' work outcomes (e.g., Elbers et al., 2023).

 DOI: 10.4324/9781003475262-10

The seeming neglect of this aspect of leadership in organisations has allowed unethical leaders to thrive (Hmieleski & Cole, 2023). Understanding the dark side of leaders' traits is important to mitigate the harmful effects of dark leadership in organisations. This chapter contributes to the existing literature on dark leadership by identifying the personality traits associated with it. This chapter answers the key question of what personality traits dark (or destructive) leaders possess and how they demonstrate these traits. The following section discusses the dark personality traits and factors associated with dark leadership in organisations. We further review a theoretical underpinning of dark leadership and show how dark leadership traits are demonstrated in organisations. Finally, we present a case study and some lessons for organisational leaders.

Dark Personality Traits

Dark personality traits, often referred to as the dark triad of personality, describe the complex nature of dysfunctional characteristics that have been theorised to have serious implications for individuals and organisations (Paulhus & Williams, 2002; Ternes et al., 2019). The dark triad personality traits include Narcissism, Machiavellianism, and Psychopathy, which have distinct theoretical roots but share some related characteristics. What is dark about dark personality traits is the intensity of desire to promote oneself above others, in disregard towards the feelings and well-being of others, which can cause harm to other individuals (Paulhus & Williams, 2002; Harms & Spain, 2015).

Narcissism: This is usually the first trait to be mentioned in conversations about the dark triad; a "personality trait entailing a grandiose sense of self, paired with self-affirmative strategies and disregard for others" (Braun, 2017, p. 5). It originates from the Greek mythology story of a young male hunter named Narcissus, who was so much in love with his beauty, that he constantly admired himself in the reflection of water and later died of heartbreak because he could not entice his image (see Freud, 1957/1914). Narcissism is rooted in insecurity, inflated self-view, ego reinforcement, and a sense of entitlement (Jones & Paulhus, 2014) that a person possesses, such that everything around the person and what others say should revolve around them through admiration and adoration (Schyns, 2015). Narcissism is further characterised by an inflated and unstable self-view, self-admiration, attention-seeking, self-aggrandisement, arrogance, and exploitative tendencies (Campbell & Foster, 2007). Narcissistic individuals desire to grab the headlines. They manifest a tendency to amplify their performance and potential beyond what is the norm in a bid to draw attention to themselves (Arpaci et al., 2018). Narcissism has been studied widely in the leadership field in relation to various outcomes. In the workplace context, leader narcissism has been positively linked to workplace bullying (Tokarev et al., 2017), employee job stress, leader volatile and risky decision-making (Chatterjee & Hambrick, 2007).

Machiavellianism: This describes a personality trait of manipulation, deceit, callousness, and emotional detachment from others, in the pursuit of serving oneself and personal gains (e.g., Christie & Gies, 1970). Machiavellianism is a conduct that involves exploiting other people's interests for personal gains. In the workplace, individuals high on Machiavellianism are interested in their personal gain, potentially at the detriment of others at the receiving end of their actions, which jeopardises the well-being of people who work with them. The origin of Machiavellianism is linked to the Italian diplomat Niccoló Machiavelli, who, in his book *The Prince in 1953,* discusses that for the acquisition and maintenance of power, the use of immoral means is often expected and justifiable, including assassinating political opponents. This is a total disregard for morality and ethics in the pursuit of power and control (Christie & Gies, 1970). Since then, Machiavellianism in principle and character has become associated with achieving self-serving goals with disregard for rules (Muris et al., 2017). Machiavellianism shares similar features with narcissism in some ways, such as the pursuit of selfish gains, self-aggrandisement, and exploitation of other people in the pursuit of personal interest (Paulhus & Williams, 2002). However, it is differentiated at its core by the fact that it is a fundamentally manipulative and callous personality (Christie & Gies, 1970).

Psychopathy: It has its roots in psychiatry (clinical and forensic psychology) and is described in the literature as a personality trait characterised by callousness, lack of empathy, selfishness, exploitation, specious charm, and arrogant and deceitful behaviour. Psychopathy as a concept is used to describe a group of patients under clinical observation who exhibited prolonged antisocial behaviour, coldness, low level of empathy, fear, remorse, and anxiety (e.g., Muris et al., 2017). From a non-pathological perspective, psychopathy as the last addition to the dark triad, fundamentally describes a cheating personality (Paulhus & Williams, 2002). Psychopaths are characterised by thrill-seeking, low anxiety, and behaviour associated with little forethought and reflection (Paulhus & Williams, 2002). Psychopathy shares similar characteristics with narcissism, such as low levels of empathy, selfishness, and arrogance, and Machiavellianism in features such as callousness, lack of fear, and remorse (McHoskey et al., 1998). However, it is differentiated in that while psychopathy is rooted in psychiatry, with prototypes such as untruthfulness, unreliable, guilelessness, and superficial charm, the theoretical orientation of Machiavellianism hinges on interpersonal power strategies with prototypes on lack of concern with conventional morality and low ideological commitment (see McHoskey et al., 1998). Psychopathic personality in employees has been linked negatively with organisational commitment (Boddy et al., 2010) and positively with counterproductive work behaviour (Boddy, 2014).

Everyday sadism: This is the fourth component added to the dark personality traits and collectively described along with Narcissism, Machiavellianism, and Psychopathy as the Dark Tetrad (Buckels et al., 2013). Everyday sadism is the term used to narrate the subclinical and non-sexual savagery in everyday life. It is further chronicled in the literature as the delight of an individual to be cruel, causing others pain and rejoicing in their misfortune (see Reidy et al., 2011). Sadistic personality has overlapping characteristics with Psychopathy. For example, antisocial behaviour and selfishness, with a desire to punish, control, and bring other people under subjection, thereby injuring their pride and dignity, are evident in everyday sadism and psychopathy (Chabrol et al., 2009). However, research has also shown distinct characteristics of everyday sadism from the dark triad, thereby justifying the expansion of the dark triad to the dark tetrad (Chabrol et al., 2009). In previous research, for example, everyday sadism has been reported to be a predictor of motivation to hurt or destroy other living creatures out of hate (Reidy et al., 2011). Research shows that everyday sadism in employees is positively associated with interpersonal deviance and incivility (Min et al., 2019). Taken together, these dark traits in organisational members should be continuously examined to understand the negative impact they can have on employees' behaviours and well-being and how they might be mitigated.

Factors Associated with Dark Leadership

For dark-side leadership to thrive in organisations, there must be confluence factors that make its functioning possible. This position is well captured in the "toxic triangle," which describes a set of three equal interrelated

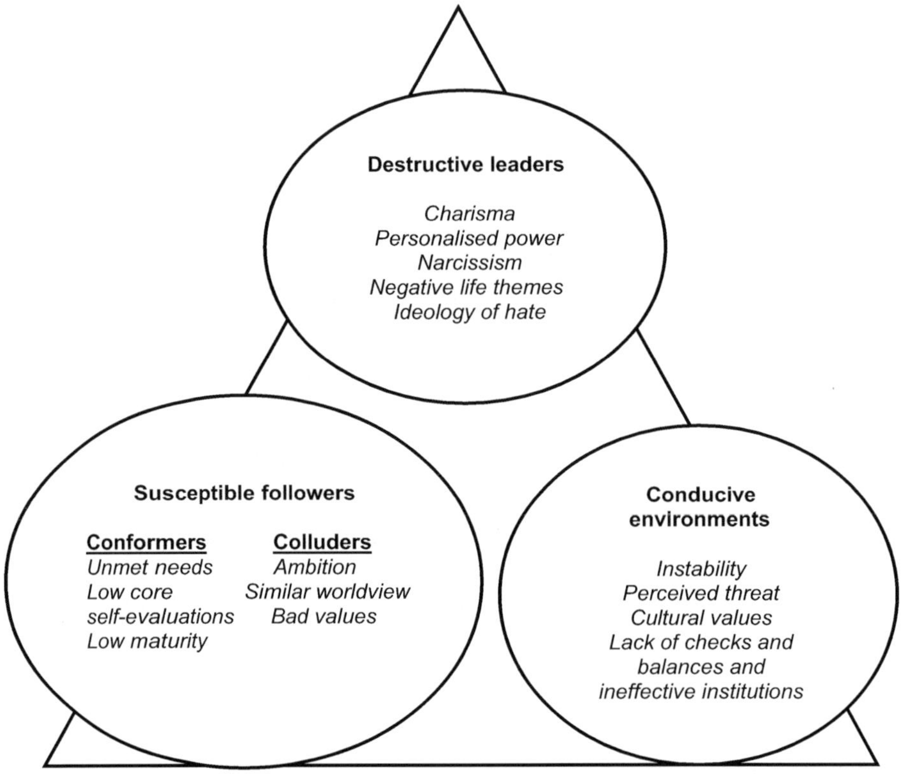

Figure 8.1 The toxic triangle. (Source: Padilla et al., 2007.)

components: destructive leaders, susceptible followers, and a conducive environment, as depicted in Figure 8.1 (Padilla et al., 2007, p. 176).

Destructive leaders: This factor is about the motivation of leaders to lead in a dysfunctional way. It comprises themes such as charisma, narcissism, negative themes of life, personalised use of power, and an ideology of hate (Padilla et al., 2007). These themes are associated with dark leaders who lead in self-serving ways. The disposition of leaders to apply power for personalised gains rather than exercise power for the interest of those being served is a fertile ground for dark leadership in organisations (Conger, 1990; Padilla et al., 2007). Additionally, grandiosity, self-entitlement, and attention seeking, coupled with a previously held destructive image of the world and ideology of hate from childhood hardship or prior bad experiences (Cramer, 2011), confluences to the leader-centric component of dark leadership in organisations (Padilla et al., 2007).

Susceptible followers: For destructive leadership to thrive in organisations, followers usually cooperate with dark leaders in wielding authority for personalised gains. Reasons why followers are unable to resist dark leaders who abuse their authority include the need for the followers to protect their own safety nets, membership needs, and the benefits they get from the dark leaders (Padilla et al., 2007). Interestingly, some followers condone dark leaders ignorantly because they do not understand the vision of the leader or they fear that they might fall out of favour with the leaders (Higgins, 1997). Such followers are called confirmers (Padilla et al., 2007). Similarly, other followers allow dark leaders to thrive without any resistance because they share in the leaders' vision and stand to benefit from the leaders' gains. Such followers are described as colluders (Padilla et al., 2007).

Conducive environment: This is concerned with the organisational context in which dark leadership occurs. The environment is the enabling platform for the interaction of leaders and their followers, which differs from one organisation to another but fundamentally covers four factors, which are "instability, perceived threats, cultural values and absence of checks and balances and institutionalisation" (Padilla et al., 2007, p. 185). Put differently, dark leaders and susceptible followers cannot exclusively entrench dark leadership without a conducive environment and its associated institutional lapses. For example, in times of uncertainty, there are chances for the centralisation of decision-making. This allows the authority to be vested in a leader, who can make unilateral decisions that override institutional controls (Janis & Mann, 1977). Additionally, the prevalence of strong individuals and weak institutionalisation of processes motivates the creation and maintenance of a conducive environment for dark leadership (Hamilton et al., 2000). A culture (national or organisational) that allows leaders to operate unchallenged, where the value system is for followers to adore leaders even when leaders are wrong, is an inherent social system that contributes to the emergence of dark leadership in organisations.

The Revised Leadership Process Model

The revised leadership process model (Tuncdogan et al., 2017) is our theoretical lens for explaining the manifestation of dark leadership in organisations. As shown in Figure 8.2, the model drew from different paradigms on individual differences in leader traits and made three classifications, including physiological, psychological, and background. The physiological difference in traits is based on genetic factors that underlie leadership emergence; for example, physical factors, biological sex/gender, and neurological factors are areas of physiological differences in leader traits as a proximal predictor

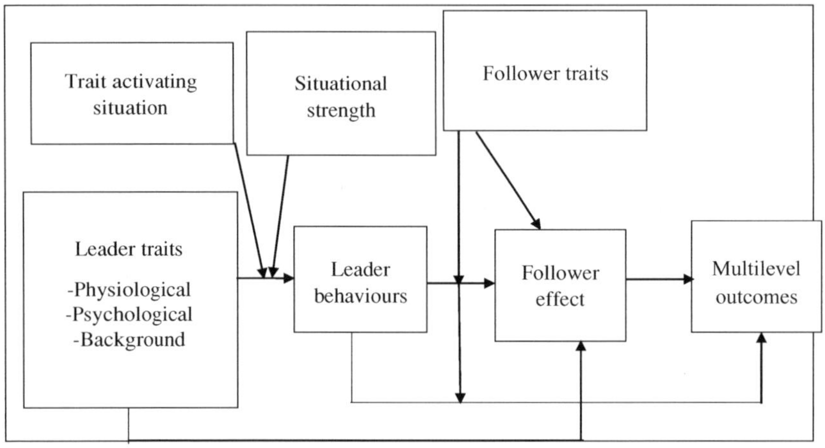

Figure 8.2 The revised leadership process model. (Source: Tuncdogan et al., 2017.)

of leader emergence and behaviour (Tuncdogan et al., 2017). The psychological difference is an important component of leaders' personality traits, predicting a wide range of behaviours, which have been explored in leadership studies, including intelligence, the big-five personality traits, the dark triad personality traits, and self-regulation (e.g., Cavazotte et al., 2012). The personality trait, for example, is explicated in the dark leadership personality triad – narcissism, Machiavellianism, and psychopathy. These dark leadership personality dimensions have been argued to be given legitimacy for the continuity and perpetration of immoral behaviours of leaders at work (Gaur, 2023). Gaur identified both situational and factors associated with followers as a critical trigger. The argument of Gaur on the demonstration of dark leadership behaviour and the revised leadership process model suggests that many factors in the organisation promote the demonstration of dark leadership personality, which, if not controlled, could create a toxic work environment. Last is the background component of leader traits, which includes variables such as culture, age, family, and environment as predictors of leader behaviours (Tuncdogan et al., 2017).

Apart from being indicative of three important elements of leaders' traits, this model highlights three factors in the leader traits and multilevel outcomes process. First, the trait-activating situation (Tett & Burnett, 2003) describes the variability in leader traits, the effect of activated traits on leaders' behaviour, and the extent to which they affect multilevel outcomes (Tuncdogan et al., 2017). Second is situational strength, which is described as the extent to which situational constraints are prevalent in the environment to moderate the effect of leader traits on leaders' behaviour. Put differently, the gravity of the situation determines the extent to which leaders' traits can influence their behaviour, the effect on followers, and multi-level organisational outcomes (Tuncdogan et al., 2017). The third is the follower's trait, such that followers' traits interact with leader traits, leader behaviours and followers' effect to influence multilevel outcomes in organisations. This is consistent with the arguments in the toxic triangle (Padilla et al., 2007), that for dark leadership to occur and thrive in organisations, followers usually play an active role in making it happen. Similarly, the model shows that dark traits are inherent in leaders and followers, and they are activated in the leadership process by the interactions of leaders and followers and situational factors, which can be micro or macro such as a conducive environment, management policies, and national culture and the strengths of such situations (Tett et al., 2021; Tuncdogan et al., 2017).

Toxic Triangle of Dark Leadership: The Case of Pup Enterprise

Pup Enterprises (not real name) is an electronic manufacturing organisation. The enterprise has grown over the years and has recorded tremendous success in its 15 years of operation. As one of the most competitive electronic organisations in the consumer electronic sector in the region, the leaders have the freedom to make decisions and introduce innovations expected to drive growth. Over time, there were several complaints about the leaders' excessive use of power and their untouchable dispositions. Many of the leaders were accused of using their positions to manipulate and disrespect subordinates. The reports and complaints were treated with a sense of avoidance. The organisation was focused on profit maximisation at the expense of ethical behaviour and the well-being of employees.

The organisation seemed to revolve around a charismatic but dark leader, Mr. Smith (not real name). Initially, Mr. Smith's charm and persuasive personality traits helped him climb the corporate ladder swiftly. As Mr. Smith gained power within the organisation, his dark traits became increasingly evident. He exhibited manipulative behaviour, leveraging office politics and deceit to advance his agenda. His narcissistic tendencies prompted him to take credit for his subordinates' work and undermined their contributions. The toxic triangle of dark leadership manifested as susceptible followers within the organisation fell prey to his charisma and manipulation. Employees who questioned his decisions were marginalised, and a culture of fear and distrust permeated the workplace. The conducive environment provided fertile ground for him to exert his destructive leadership, leading to diminished morale and tarnished organisational reputation. The dark leadership practice of Mr. Smith began to reflect in employees' attitudes toward customers and clients.

Lessons for Leaders

It has been substantiated in this chapter that dark leadership personality is manifested in four dimensions – Machiavellianism, narcissism, psychopathy, and everyday sadism. It is interesting to mention that these personalities, despite their negative implications, could unfortunately be promoted by organisational and national cultures. In a work environment where employees are viewed as a means to an end, the tendency for dark leadership practices to thrive is higher. Additionally, dark leadership practices will gain more ground in work structures, conditions, and environments that subjugate, enslave, alienate, and limit employees' voices. These conditions will further strengthen the practice of dark leadership when efforts should be channelled toward mitigating its demonstration. Consequently, managers have the responsibility of creating a work environment where dark leadership practices are reduced to the barest minimum. By creating organisational values where professionalism and respect for persons are highly upheld, the prospects of leaders exhibiting dark leadership characteristics will be significantly limited.

Similarly, national culture can be an antecedent to dark leadership practice, especially in a culture that promotes the dominance of one gender over the other gender, for example, the patriarchal culture of male dominance in leadership. Leaders from such cultures might become dominant, self-driven and many other manifestations associated with dark leadership. Contemporary organisations must design work such that power is not concentrated in the hands of a few, as these could trigger dark leadership attributes, considering the propositions of the toxic triangle. For many leaders, their sociocultural upbringing has influenced their personality, and they grow up in an environment where dominant and oppressive behaviours are tools of survival. Regulating the behaviours of such individuals will demand that an appropriate organisational culture that serves as checks and balances is established.

Our view in this chapter leans towards the proposition from the toxic triangle, specifically the conducive environment element. There might be susceptible employees, but the environment should not be conducive for dark leadership to thrive. Culture, weak institutions, lack of checks and balances, and instability within organisations predispose employees to be led by dark leaders. Managers must ensure that the organisational structure is developed, such that power is decentralised and leaders' dark personalities can be effectively managed.

Conclusion

Dark leadership, if not effectively addressed in organisations, could have negative implications on their success. Unfortunately, organisations too often promote- by employing narcissistic leaders or allowing them to thrive by condoning their destructive behaviours and providing conducive environments for the manifestation of dark leadership. The management of contemporary organisations cannot decide what personality leaders should have, but they can decide which leadership practice is exhibited in the organisation. This outcome can be achieved by strengthening internal institutions and establishing an organisational identity that demonstrates its culture and how it wants people to be treated. Additionally, an understanding that dark leadership can be culturally influenced will help in managing its dynamics appropriately.

References

Arpaci, I., Yalçın, S. B., Baloğlu, M., & Kesici, S. (2018). The moderating effect of gender in the relationship between narcissism and selfie-posting behaviour. *Personality and Individual Differences*, *134*, 71–74.

Boddy, C. R. (2014). Corporate psychopaths, conflict, employee affective well-being and counterproductive work behaviour. *Journal of Business Ethics*, *121*(1), 107–121.

Boddy, C. R., Ladyshewsky, R. K., & Galvin, P. (2010). The influence of corporate psychopaths on corporate social responsibility and organisational commitment to employees. *Journal of Business Ethics*, *97*, 1–19.

Braun, S. (2017). Leader narcissism and outcomes in organisations: A review at multiple levels of analysis and implications for future research. *Frontiers in Psychology*, *8*, 773–782.

Buckels, E., Jones, D., & Paulhus, D. (2013). Behavioural confirmation of everyday sadism. *Psychological Science, 24*, 2201–2209.

Campbell, W. K., & Foster, J. D. (2007). The narcissistic self: Background, an extended agency model, and ongoing controversies. In C. Sedikides & S. Spencer (Eds.), *Frontiers in social psychology: The self* (pp. 115–138). Philadelphia: Psychology Press.

Cavazotte, F., Moreno, V., & Hickmann, M. (2012). Effects of Leader Intelligence, personality and emotional intelligence on transformational leadership and managerial performance. *The Leadership Quarterly, 23*(3), 443–455.

Chabrol, H., Van Leeuwen, N., Rodgers, R., & Séjourné, N. (2009). Contributions of psychopathic, narcissistic, Machiavellian, and sadistic personality traits to juvenile delinquency. *Personality and Individual Differences, 47*, 734–739.

Chatterjee, A., & Hambrick, D. C. (2007). It's all about me: Narcissistic chief executive officers and their effects on company strategy and performance. *Administrative Science Quarterly, 52*(3), 351–386.

Christie, R., & Geis, R. L. (1970). *Studies in machiavellianism*. New York: Academic Press.

Conger, J. (1990). The dark side of leadership. *Organisational Dynamics, 19*, 44–55.

Cramer, P. (2011). Narcissism through the ages: What happens when narcissists grow older? *Journal of Research in Personality, 45*(5), 479–492.

Elbers, A., Kolominski, S., & Blesa Aledo, P. S. (2023). Coping with dark leadership: examination of the impact of psychological capital on the relationship between dark leaders and employees' basic need satisfaction in the workplace. *Administrative Sciences, 13*(4), 96.

Freud, S. (1957/1914). On narcissism: An introduction. In J. Strachey (Ed.), *The standard edition of the complete psychological works of sigmund freud* (Vol. 14, pp. 67–104). London: Hogarth Press,

Gaur, B. (2023). The dark side of leadership. In A. Samad, E. Ahmed, & N. Arora (Eds.), *Global leadership perspectives on industry, society, and government in an era of uncertainty* (pp. 176–201). IGI Global Scientific Publishing. https://doi.org/10.4018/978-1-6684-8257-5.ch011

Hamilton, A., Jay, J., & Madison, J. (2000). *The federalist*. New York: Random House.

Harms, P. D., & Spain, S. M. (2015). Beyond the bright side: Dark personality at work. *Applied Psychology, 64*(1), 15–24.

Higgins, E. T. (1997). Beyond pleasure and pain. *American Psychologist, 52*, 1280–1300.

Hmieleski, K. M., & Cole, M. S. (2023). The contingent effects of intrateam abusive behaviour on team thriving and new venture performance. *Journal of Management, 49*(2), 808–838.

Horney, K. (1950). *Neurosis and human growth: The struggle toward self-realisation*. New York: Norton.

Janis, I., & Mann, L. (1977). *Decision making: A psychological analysis of conflict, choice, and commitment*. New York: Free University Press.

Jones, D. N., & Paulhus, D. L. (2014). Introducing the short dark triad (SD3) a brief measure of dark personality traits. *Assessment, 21*(1), 28–41.

McHoskey, J. W., Worzel, W., & Szyarto, C. (1998). Machiavellianism and psychopathy. *Journal of Personality and Social Psychology, 74*(1), 192–210.

Min, H., Pavisic, I., Howald, N., Highhouse, S., & Zickar, M. J. (2019). A systematic comparison of three sadism measures and their ability to explain workplace mistreatment over and above the dark triad. *Journal of Research in Personality, 82*, 103862.

Muris, P., Merckelbach, H., Otgaar, H., & Meijer, E. (2017). The malevolent side of human nature: A meta-analysis and critical review of the literature on the dark triad (narcissism, Machiavellianism, and psychopathy). *Perspectives on Psychological Science, 12*(2), 183–204.

Ozbilir, T., Day, A., & Catano, V. M. (2015). Perfectionism at work: An investigation of adaptive and maladaptive perfectionism in the workplace among Canadian and Turkish employees. *Applied Psychology: An International Review, 64*(1), 252–280.

Padilla, A., Hogan, R., & Kaiser, R. B. (2007). The toxic triangle: Destructive leaders, susceptible followers and conducive environments. *The Leadership Quarterly, 18*, 176–194. https://doi.org/10.1016/j.leaqua.2007.03.001

Paulhus, D. L. (2014). Toward a taxonomy of dark personalities. *Current Directions in Psychological Science, 23*(6), 421–426.

Paulhus, D. L., & Williams, K. M. (2002). The dark triad of personality: Narcissism, Machiavellianism, and psychopathy. *Journal of Research in Personality, 36*(6), 556–563.

Reidy, D. E., Zeichner, A., & Seibert, L.A., (2011). Unprovoked aggression: Effects of psychopathic traits and sadism. *Journal of Personality, 79*, 75–100.

Schyns, B. (2015). Dark personality in the workplace: Introduction to the special issue. *Applied Psychology: An International Review, 64*(1), 1–14.

Spain, S. M., Harms, P. D., & LeBreton, J. M. (2014). Dark personality at work. *Journal of Organisational Behavior, 35*, 41–60.

Ternes, M., Babin, C., Woodworth, A., & Stephens, S. (2019). Academic misconduct: An examination of its association with the dark triad and antisocial behaviour. *Personality and Individual Differences, 138*, 75–78.

Tett, R. P., & Burnett, D. D. (2003). A personality trait-based interactionist model of job performance. *Journal of Applied Psychology, 88*(3), 500–517.

Tett, R. P., Toich, M. J., & Ozkum, S. B. (2021). Trait activation theory: A review of the literature and applications to five lines of personality dynamics research. *Annual Review of Organisational Psychology and Organisational Behavior, 8*, 199–233.

Tokarev, A., Phillips, A. R., Hughes, D. J., & Irwing, P. (2017). Leader dark traits, workplace bullying, and employee depression: Exploring mediation and the role of the dark core. *Journal of Abnormal Psychology, 126*(7), 911–920.

Tuncdogan, A., Acar, O.A., & Stam, D. (2017). Individual differences as antecedents of leader behaviour: Towards an understanding of multi-level outcomes. *The Leadership Quarterly, 28*(1), 40–64.

Chapter 9

Ethical Behaviour Beyond Convergent Calculative Thinking: From Modern to Meaningful Leadership

Mehrdad Sarhadi

Introduction

Unethical behaviour can lead to a wide range of undesirable consequences, and the scope can be extensive, especially when such behaviour originates from leaders' decisions. Although ethical leadership has been commonly reduced to conforming with mandatory organisational ethical codes, ethical behaviour ought to be driven by voluntary action (Sarhadi & Hasanzadeh, 2022). Ethical codes are commonly used as mandatory laws and requirements, which put structural pressure on individuals. In many instances, leaders reluctantly adopt structural ethics and tolerate psychological pressure to avoid possible punitive measures (Kaptein, 2019; Soltes, 2017; Zhang, 2020). This often happens because there is a distinction between "acting from virtue and acting in conformity to virtue" (Alzola, 2019, p. 26).

In many cases, ethical codes mainly compel leaders to be more creative in hiding their destructive unethical decisions, which can be seen in various types of green-washing and blue-washing behaviours (Yang et al., 2020). For example, some leaders consider stakeholders' engagement as "nothing more than rituals designed to satisfy legal requirements" (Innes & Booher, 2005, p. 419), or they may underestimate costs and overestimate benefits in

 DOI: 10.4324/9781003475262-11

a feasibility study to start a project (Flyvbjerg, 2014). In more complex cases, many corporations allocate over a billion dollars towards lobbying to oppose climate-related regulations (Delmas et al., 2016) and apply sustainability certifications as a protective shield to hide unethical decisions (Whiteman & Cooper, 2016). Therefore, further investigation of structural ethics, such as ethical codes, is necessary (Oladinrin & Ho, 2014).

Several persuasive philosophical arguments assert a lack of ethical reality (Leiter, 2019) and believe "it is ethics itself that is in crisis" (Tajalli & Segal, 2019b, p. 1). Moral behaviour is an evolving process that "can never be fully achieved yet must always be pursued" (Rhodes & Badham, 2018, p. 93). Ethical relativism may challenge managerial frameworks that use ethical codes to put external pressure on guiding individuals' behaviour, reducing morality to a mechanism for enforcing power (Nietzsche 1886/2018). In other words, designing ethical guidelines under predefined convergent principles or theories cannot always be useful because they are not always applicable and cannot provide enough motivation due to contextual complexity and psychological uncertainty. Furthermore, "wrong ethical outcomes can easily be blamed on the inadequacy of the theory" (Tajalli & Segal, 2019a, p. 73). Therefore, unethical leadership not merely originates from ambiguity in definition but also from a lack of moral motivation (Brokerhof et al., 2023). This chapter adopts Heidegger's philosophy to explore these two intertwined challenges that undermine ethical leadership in various cultural contexts.

The rest of this chapter is organised as follows: The second section reveals psychological and voluntary dimensions of ethical leadership at the agency level, beyond social dimensions at the structural level. The third section argues that ethical leadership cannot be limited to convergent frameworks and its divergent aspects should also be acknowledged. The fourth section advocates that the main challenges of ethical leadership in different cultural contexts can be rooted in calculative versus meditative thinking. Modern and meaningful approaches demonstrating the paradoxical nature of ethical leadership are discussed in the fifth section.

Exploring Ethical Leadership at the Agency Level

Structuralists believe that "social elements surrounding a decision often dominate individual character" (Alzola, 2019; Soltes, 2017, p. 460). According to the structuration theory, both social (structural) factors and individual (agentic) factors are critical for explaining human behaviour (Giddens, 1984/1986). Although a structural perspective toward leaders' behaviour can be insightful (Berti et al., 2021), it cannot provide a reliable explanation without considering the complexity of individual factors, which are rooted in discretionary power, attitudes, and psychological drivers (Brokerhof et al., 2023; Kaptein, 2019). For example, "business leaders sometimes donate to charity because they want to increase their prestige," which can create a feeling of power (Kouchaki, 2015; Zhang et al., 2020, p. 80). The importance of emotional dimensions of human behaviour has been stated by postmodern thinkers, highlighting the weaknesses of structures for explaining and encouraging ethical leadership (Baker, 2017; Marchesini, 2017). According to postmodern criticisms, moral behaviour is a context-dependent and subjective phenomenon and cannot be directed by predefined guidelines or codes (Brokerhof et al., 2023). Therefore, current structural strategies for promoting ethical behaviour, such as ethical codes and other types of social pressure, are not useless, but they cannot achieve their predefined goals without considering other connected aspects (Oladinrin & Ho, 2014; Tajalli & Segal, 2019b; Zhang, 2020). Social structures cannot guarantee public benefit (Idowu et al., 2013). On the contrary, as demonstrated by Kouchaki (2015), professional institutions and ethical codes can enhance the likelihood of immoral action.

Furthermore, there is an assumption that if one recognises an action as ethical, then one sincerely behaves accordingly (Leiter, 2019). Moral judgment rarely motivates ethical action (Vasiliou, 2016). For instance, the majority of consumers express their preference to use sustainable products, but sales data show very few are really buying a bit more expensive sustainable products (Sheffi & Blanco, 2018). Furthermore, some ethical decisions that look clear and objective on the surface are proffered because of some unstated unconscious inclinations (Bartels et al., 2009). Therefore, moral judgments include both rational and emotional aspects (Baker, 2017), and it can even be "post-hoc rationalisations of feelings that have an antecedent source" (Leiter, 2019, p. 9). In fact, "there are moralities which are intended to justify their creators before other people" (Nietzsche, 1886, p. 88). Regarding the above reasons, "people are not always aware of the forces that lead them to behave unethically" (Baker, 2017, p. 4). Therefore, ethical thinking includes psychological factors and should be investigated at the agency level (Steyl, 2020).

Convergent versus Divergent Ethical Thinking

Heidegger's ontological investigation in "*Being and Time*" highlights an important distinction between convergent versus divergent thinking (Guilford, 1956; Heidegger, 1927/2010) that can be enlightening for the explanation of ethical behaviour. "Present-at-hand" and "ready-to-hand" are phrases that represent convergent interaction with the world through conscious or unconscious convergent frameworks. Convergent frameworks constrain innovation but facilitate routine ways of behaviour (Sasaki & Ravasi, 2024). On the other hand, "unreadiness-to-hand" represents divergent thinking or innovative interaction with the world beyond convergent mental patterns (Heidegger, 1927/2010). Heidegger believes divergent or deconstructive thinking about a phenomenon and its representative concepts can unravel latent aspects of being beyond established habits, implicit routines, and linguistic mental frameworks, which have been gradually formed by human interaction with the world (Alvarez & Porac, 2020).

Postmodern thinkers believe ethics cannot be based on convergent definitions or fixed guidelines, and it depends on divergent individuals' interpretations and worldviews, as well as unique contextual variables (Bartels et al., 2009; Brokerhof et al., 2023; Leiter, 2019; Nietzsche, 1886/2000; Steyl, 2020). For this reason, defining business ethics has always been challenging. In the same vein, convergent scientific management has been criticised by divergent contingency management (Morgan, 2006). Ethical leadership is a becoming phenomenon with unpredictable agentic dimensions (Brokerhof et al., 2023), which should be innovatively developed within its unique context (Baker, 2017; Marchesini, 2017), instead of freezing within universal rational principles (Barreto, 2023). Therefore, it cannot be completely directed through general pre-established structures or theories that are currently applied in many management guidelines or organisational formal instructions because leaders always have to face unfamiliar aspects alongside familiar aspects (Salovaara et al., 2020). In other words, ethical leadership cannot be considered as objective questions with predefined answers based on convergent guidelines and universal success criteria. Instead, ethical leadership is an ambiguous subjective phenomenon with chaotic and unpredictable connections among contextual factors (Fisher et al., 2021), which requires flexible thinking, creative problem-solving, and moral imagination

(O'Doherty, 2020). Regarding the unpredictable nature of managerial context, "Aristotle's influence in business ethics has mushroomed in recent decades" (Alvarez & Porac, 2020; Steyl, 2020, p. 417).

Calculative versus Meditative Ethical Thinking

The book, "Country Path Conversations", later known as Heidegger's philosophy extends ontological investigation to the calculative versus meditative thinking paradoxical structure. *Gelassenheit* translated as 'releasement,' and *Gestell* often translated as 'enframing' as opposing poles in Heidegger's philosophy. In simple words, the emancipatory potential of meditative thinking warns against the possible threat of calculative thinking (Heidegger, 1995/2010). The second paradoxical structure includes the first paradoxical structure (convergent versus divergent thinking) and develops explanation capacity.

According to Heidegger's philosophy, social and physical environments such as plants, seas, mountains, and even individuals (human resources) implicitly emerge to modern humans as sources of business progress, consumption, and competition. In the same vein, late modern philosophers believe modern structures and instrumental rational order, consciously and unconsciously, give priority to individual identity over collective identity and encourage domination, control, and consumption (Habermas, 1968/2015; Habermas, 1985; Levinas, 1981; Peperzak & Lévinas, 1993). There is a non-synonymous but significant relation between calculative thinking and the 'will to power' concept in Nietzsche's philosophy (Nietzsche, 1886/2000, 1883/2005). Calculative thinking is the basic driver of modern human behaviour in both scientific (modern) and contingency (post-modern) schools of management to develop human control through enforcing scientific and technological order over social and physical environments (Braver, 2009; Parker, 2014).

In his book, "Beyond Good and Evil," Nietzsche revealed the psychological factors of human actions and fundamentally criticised religious and moral beliefs and rational philosophical schools (Leiter, 2019). He distinguished 'master morality' and 'slave morality' as two different approaches toward ethical behaviour (Nietzsche 1886/2018). Master morality highlights power, independence, and nobility, while slave morality highlights empathy, kindness, and sympathy. According to Nietzsche, human behaviour is rooted in the will to power, which invites humans to self-actualisation (Tajalli & Segal,

2019b). Even helping others can be explained by an unconscious inclination to power (Kouchaki, 2015). Kantian and Christian morality are not compatible with human nature, preventing the helper and the one who is helped from self-actualisation and progress because life's challenges are necessary parts of human evolution (Leiter, 2019; Nietzsche, 1883/1995). Therefore, master morality is an unavoidable reality of ethics and cannot be assumed the same as oppression and cruelty. In this regard, "all we need to do is to discover our own particular ethics" (Tajalli & Segal, 2019b, p. 2). Nietzsche believes rational ethical codes cannot achieve their goals of providing practical guidelines simply because they are not consistent with unique contextual factors and human nature.

Calculative ethics can encourage others to resist and promote a destructive cycle (Giacalone & Thompson, 2006). Furthermore, meditative thinking presents a different picture of what Nietzsche called 'slave morality' (Vandyshev, 2015; Odiorne, 1966). Helping others can also be described as the human will to meaning (Park & Jeong, 2016; Wang et al., 2016). According to Levinas, one's infinite responsibility for others, "without waiting for reciprocity" (Levinas, 1995, p. 98; Tajalli & Segal, 2019a), is the radix of a human being (Levinas & Peperzak, 2005). "Morality is not a branch of philosophy, but first philosophy" (Levinas & Lingis, 1969, p. 304). Levinas's account of human ethics has already been emphasised by Dostoevsky (1993/1912, p. 57), who believed that "we are all responsible to all for all," which can lead to a completely new perspective on business ethics (Jørgensen & Boje, 2010).

Meditative thinking can change human relationships within social and natural environments at the ontological level (Braver, 2009; Parker, 2014) and help learners experience a different kind of being in the world (Giacalone & Thompson, 2006; Heidegger, 1995/2010; Parker, 2014). It can be called conscientiousness or mental transformation from an anthropocentric to an ecocentric approach in ethical management (Parks-Leduc et al., 2021). Meditative thinking can motivate ethical behaviour at both conscious and unconscious levels and acknowledges various cultural backgrounds and worldviews (Sarhadi et al., 2021; Tajalli & Segal, 2019b). Although ethical behaviour is assumed to be a completely conscious action, it is under the influence of a wide range of unconscious psychological variables, which reduce individual agency in decisions (Steyl, 2020). Therefore, ethical behaviour not only depends on conscious justification but also needs to be unconsciously motivated (Giacalone & Thompson, 2006; Lee, 2015; Parker, 2014).

From Modern Leadership to Meaningful Leadership

The main problem of unethical leadership originates from the instrumental approach of calculative thinking, which consciously or unconsciously encourages humans to be superior to others (Caradonna, 2014). Although convergent and calculative thinking is unavoidable part of modern leadership and can create various advantages, their dominance over leaders' behaviour can significantly increase the likelihood of unethical actions (Parks-Leduc et al., 2021). Calculative thinking in modern leadership depicts the universe as a source of consumption and encourages humans to extend their dominance by imposing convergent calculative order (Habermas, 1985; Weber & Kalberg, 2013).

From Heidegger's point of view, meditative thinking is critical for meaningful interaction with Being "not because it is complex or abstract, but precisely because it is so near and ubiquitous, so simple and obvious" (Braver, 2009, p. 5; Heidegger, 1927/2010, 1995/2010). The question of Being can appear in different ways (Figal et al., 2020), and "moods put us in touch with beings as a whole in a way that reason cannot" (Braver, 2009, p. 33). Although divergent thinking can serve calculative thinking, it is an inseparable part of meditative thinking for going beyond the current convergent frameworks, which have been shaped by modern calculative thoughts (Giacalone & Thompson, 2006). The unconscious ties together individuals and the conscious world (Phillips, 2017). Habits, calculative structures, instrumental models, and conceptual frameworks are some of the convergent factors that have been merged into the human unconscious and enable someone to interact or even dominate the world, regardless of the arduous and time-consuming conscious process (Dreyfus & Dreyfus, 2005). Nevertheless, Heidegger worries that such a calculative mode of being blinds us to potential divergent meditative experiences outside of them (Braver, 2009, p. 36), which is critical for meaningful experiences, "*unconcealment* of being" and psychological well-being (Braver, 2009; Park & Jeong, 2016).

Leadership is a context-dependent and innovative phenomenon that leads to new ways of interacting with the world. Unexpected experiences can occur along with the repetitive flow of an individual's conscious life (Legrand & Trigg, 2017). However, divergent thinking can serve as calculative thinking. Divergent thinking needs to be supplemented with meditative thinking, which can lead to meaningful leadership. Meaningful leadership encourages leaders to express ethical behaviour and build symbiotic relationships with the environment as part of a co-evolutionary universe rather than a human-centred or top-down relationship, which is prevalent as an erroneous assumption of several definitions of sustainability. Meaningful leadership can be described as a "way of access to being that irremediably withdraws from the manifestation" (Legrand & Trigg, 2017, p. 97), which results in psychological well-being and internal motivation to ethical behaviour (Sarhadi & Hasanzadeh, 2022).

Lessons for Leaders

Based on the above arguments, it can be concluded that rational and law-like ethical codes (structural ethics) cannot define or motivate ethical behaviours (Kaptein, 2019) simply because ethical behaviours are voluntary and personalised innovative actions, which gradually evolve in the face of various psycho-social contextual variables and need to be motivated by in-depth emotions. Although this insight reveals unavoidable situationism, relativism, and sometimes the "meaninglessness of morality itself," moral relativism does not necessarily result in unethical behaviour and can show pure moral intention (Steyl, 2020; Tajalli & Segal, 2019b).

This chapter has presented two paradoxical approaches, which provide better explanations and guidelines for unavoidable relativism in ethical leadership. Modern and meaningful leadership are complementary and inseparable approaches to leadership that represent the paradoxical nature of human behaviour. Modern leadership is an unavoidable part of leadership, which cannot be completely removed, but its dominance can lead to various challenges. Therefore, augmenting meaningful leadership is the most achievable goal, which can lead to psychological well-being and sustainably improve the social environment in organisations. This goal cannot be achieved merely through current convergent frameworks, and it needs to be gradually invented and evolved through innovative ideas in alignment with contextual variables and existing convergent frameworks (Gersel & Johnsen, 2020). In the same vein, ethical behaviour includes both individual and social dimensions; therefore, the desired balance can only occur within the enabling atmosphere of collaboration with other stakeholders for exchanging innovative ideas and meaningful experiences. Leaders need to acknowledge the importance of meditative thinking, practice meaningful decisions, and explore new skills to unleash the meaningful potential of management in a collaborative learning environment.

Conclusion

A critical review of literature from the perspective of philosophical findings showed that the definitions of ethical behaviour depend on individuals' interpretations and worldviews, as well as unique cultural and contextual variables. Furthermore, ethical behaviour is commonly assumed to be motivated consciously, while it is subject to the influence of a wide range of unconscious psychological variables, which can significantly reduce individual agency and moral motivation. This chapter depicted that ethical leadership cannot be completely directed by predefined convergent structures, such as law-like ethical codes, and should also be developed in response to divergent cultural and contextual variables. Ethical behaviour cannot be realised by the current calculative mindset. It can be motivated by meditative thinking, which can create meaningful experiences, internal motivation for ethical behaviour, and psychological well-being.

References

Alvarez, S. A., & Porac, J. (2020). Imagination, indeterminacy, and managerial choice at the limit of knowledge. *Academy of Management Review*, *45*(4), 735–744.

Alzola, M. (2019). Even when no one is watching: The moral psychology of corporate reputation. *Business & Society*, *58*(6), 1267–1301.

Baker, D. F. (2017). Teaching empathy and ethical decision-making in business schools. *Journal of Management Education*, *41*(4), 575–598.

Barreto, I. (2023). Navigating uncharted waters: How executives originate high-quality ideas for strategic responses to unprecedented shocks. *Academy of Management Review*. https://doi.org/10.5465/amr.2022.0035

Bartels, D. M., Bauman, C. W., Skitka, L. J., & Medin, D. L. (2009). *Moral judgment and decision making*. San Diego, CA: Elsevier Academic Press.

Berti, M., Jarvis, W., Nikolova, N., & Pitsis, A. (2021). Embodied phronetic pedagogy: Cultivating ethical and moral capabilities in postgraduate business students. *Academy of Management Learning & Education*, *20*(1), 6–29.

Braver, L. (2009). *Heidegger's later writings: A reader's guide*. Bloomsbury Publishing.

Brokerhof, I. M., Sucher, S. J., Matthijs Bal, P., Hakemulder, F., Jansen, P. G., & Solinger, O. N. (2023). Developing moral muscle in a literature-based business ethics course. *Academy of Management Learning & Education*, *22*(1), 63–87.

Caradonna, J. L. (2014). *Sustainability: A history*. Oxford University Press.

Delmas, M., Lim, J., & Nairn-Birch, N. (2016). Corporate environmental performance and lobbying. *Academy of Management Discoveries*, *2*(2), 175–197.

Dostoevsky, F. (1993/1912). *The grand inquisitor: With related chapters from the brothers Karamazov* (C. Garnett, Trans.). Hackett Publishing Company.

Dreyfus, H. L., & Dreyfus, S. E. (2005). Peripheral vision: Expertise in real-world contexts. *Organisation Studies*, *26*(5), 779–792.

Figal, G., Keiling, T., Yang, G., & D'Angelo, D. (2020). *Paths in Heidegger's later thought*. Indiana University Press.

Fisher, G., Mayer, K., & Morris, S. (2021). From the editors—Phenomenon-based theorising. *Academy of management review*, *46*(4), 631–639.

Flyvbjerg, B. (2014). What you should know about megaprojects and why: An overview. *Project Management Journal*, *45*(2), 6–19.

Gersel, J., & Johnsen, R. (2020). Toward a novel theory of rational managerial deliberation: Stakeholders, ethical values, and corporate governance. *Academy of Management Learning & Education*, *19*(3), 269–288.

Giacalone, R. A., & Thompson, K. R. (2006). Business ethics and social responsibility education: Shifting the worldview. *Academy of Management Learning & Education*, *5*(3), 266–277.

Giddens, A. (1984/1986). *The constitution of society: Outline of the theory of structuration*. University of California Press.

Guilford, J. P. (1956). The structure of intellect. *Psychological Bulletin*, *53*(4), 267.

Habermas, J. (1968/2015). *Knowledge and human interests*. John Wiley & Sons.

Habermas, J. (1985). *The Theory of Communicative Action*. Beacon Press.

Heidegger, M. (1927/2010). *Being and time*. Suny Press.

Heidegger, M. (1995/2010). *Country path conversations*. Indiana University Press.

Idowu, S. O., Capaldi, N., Zu, L., & Gupta, A. D. (2013). *Encyclopedia of corporate social responsibility*. Springer.

Innes, J. E., & Booher, D. E. (2005). Reframing public participation: Strategies for the 21st century. *Planning Theory and Practice*, *5*(4), 419–436.

Jørgensen, K. M., & Boje, D. M. (2010). Resituating narrative and story in business ethics. *Business Ethics: A European Review*, *19*(3), 253–264.

Kaptein, M. (2019). The appearance standard: Criteria and remedies for when a mere appearance of unethical behaviour is morally unacceptable. *Business Ethics: A European Review*, *28*(1), 99–111.

Kouchaki, M. (2015). Professionalism and moral behaviour. *Business & Society*, *54*(3), 376–385.

Lee, S. (2015). A concept analysis of 'meaning in work' and its implications for nursing. *Journal of Advanced Nursing*, *71*(10), 2258–2267.

Legrand, D., & Trigg, D. (2017). *Unconsciousness between phenomenology and psychoanalysis* (Vol. 88). Springer.

Leiter, B. (2019). *Moral psychology with Nietzsche*. Oxford University Press.

Levinas, E. (1981). *Otherwise than being or beyond essence*. Springer Science & Business Media.

Levinas, E. (1995). *Ethics and infinity: Conversations with Philippe Nemo* (R. A. Cohen, Trans.). Duquesne University Press.

Levinas, E., & Lingis, A. (1969). *Totality and infinity: An essay on exteriority*. Duquesne University Press.

Levinas, E., & Peperzak, A. (2005). *To the other: An introduction to the philosophy of Emmanuel Levinas*. Purdue University Press.

Marchesini, R. (2017). *Over the human: Post-humanism and the concept of animal epiphany* (S. D. Sanctis, Trans.). Springer.

Morgan, G. (2006). *Images of organization* (updated edn). Sage.

Nietzsche, F. (1883/1995). *Thus spoke Zarathustra (*Kaufmann, Walter) (Unknown edn). Modern Library.

Nietzsche, F. W. (1883/2005). *Thus spoke Zarathustra: A book for everyone and nobody*. Oxford University Press.

Nietzsche, F. (1886). *enseits von Gut und Böse. Vorspiel einer Philosophie der Zukunft* [Beyond good and evil prelude to a philosophy of the future] (I. Johnston, Trans.). Richer Resources Publications.

Nietzsche, F. (1886/2000). *Beyond good and evil*. Www.BNPublishing.com.

Nietzsche, F. (1886/2018). *Beyond good and evil*. CreateSpace Independent Publishing Platform.

O'Doherty, D. (2020). The Leviathan of rationality: Using film to develop creativity and imagination in management learning and education. *Academy of Management Learning & Education*, *19*(3), 366–384.

Odiorne, G. S. (1966). The management theory jungle and the existential manager. *Academy of Management Journal*, *9*(2), 109.

Oladinrin, T. O., & Ho, C. M.-F. (2014). Strategies for improving codes of ethics implementation in construction organisations. *Project Management Journal*, *45*(5), 15–26.

Park, H. J., & Jeong, D. Y. (2016). Moderation effects of perfectionism and meaning in life on depression. *Personality and Individual Differences*, *98*, 25–29.

Parker, J. (2014). *Critiquing sustainability, changing philosophy*. Routledge.

Parks-Leduc, L., Mulligan, L., & Rutherford, M. A. (2021). Can ethics be taught? Examining the impact of distributed ethical training and individual characteristics on ethical decision-making. *Academy of Management Learning & Education*, *20*(1), 30–49.

Peperzak, A. T., & Lévinas, E. (1993). *To the other: An introduction to the philosophy of Emmanuel Levinas*. Purdue University Press.

Phillips, J. (2017). Merleau-Ponty's nonverbal unconscious. In D. Legrand & D. Trigg (Eds.), *Unconsciousness between phenomenology and psychoanalysis* (pp. 75–92). Springer.

Rhodes, C., & Badham, R. (2018). Ethical irony and the relational leader: Grappling with the infinity of ethics and the finitude of practice. *Business Ethics Quarterly*, *28*(1), 71–98.

Salovaara, P., Savolainen, J., & Ropo, A. (2020). Project is as project does: Emerging microactivities and play ontology. *Project Management Journal*, *51*(1), 49–61.

Sarhadi, M., & Hasanzadeh, S. (2022). A qualitative analysis of unethical behaviours in projects: Insight from moral psychology. *Project Management Journal*, *53*(4), 331–348.

Sarhadi, M., Hasanzadeh, S., & Yousefi, S. (2021). Evolving history of sustainable project: Exploring existential meaning at the agency level. *Journal of Legal Affairs and Dispute Resolution in Engineering and Construction*, *13*(2), 04521003.

Sasaki, I., & Ravasi, D. (2024). Historical consciousness and bounded imagination: How history inspires and constrains innovation in long-lived firms. Academy of Management Discoveries, *10*(1), 59–90.

Sheffi, Y., & Blanco, E. (2018). *Balancing green: When to embrace sustainability in a business (*and when not to). The MIT Press.

Soltes, E. (2017). Teaching versus living: Managerial decision making in the gray. *Journal of Management Education*, *41*(4), 455–468.

Steyl, S. (2020). Aristotelian practical wisdom in business ethics: Two neglected components. *Journal of Business Ethics*, *163*(3), 417–428.

Tajalli, P., & Segal, S. (2019a). Levinas, Weber, and a hybrid framework for business ethics. *Philosophy of Management*, *18*(1), 71–88.

Tajalli, P., & Segal, S. (2019b). A Nietzschean re-evaluation of values as a way of re-imagining business ethics. *Business Ethics: A European Review*, *28*(2), 234–242.

Vandyshev, V. N. (2015). The existential problems of management. *Jagiellonian Journal of Management*, *1*(2), 131–140.

Vasiliou, I. (2016). *Moral motivation a history*. Oxford University Press.

Wang, N., Jiang, D., & Pretorius, L. (2016). Conflict-resolving behaviour of project managers in international projects: A culture-based comparative study. *Technology in Society*, *47*, 140–147.

Weber, M., & Kalberg, S. (2013). *The protestant ethic and the spirit of capitalism*. Routledge.

Whiteman, G., & Cooper, W. H. (2016). Decoupling rape. *Academy of Management Discoveries*, *2*(2), 115–154.

Yang, Z., Nguyen, T. T. H., Nguyen, H. N., Nguyen, T. T. N., & Cao, T. T. (2020). Greenwashing behaviours. Causes, taxonomy and consequences based on a systematic literature review. *Journal of Business Economics and Management*, *21*(5), 1486–1507.

Zhang, S. (2020). Workplace spirituality and unethical pro-organizational behaviour: The mediating effect of job satisfaction. *Journal of Business Ethics*, *161*(3), 687–705.

Zhang, G., Zhong, J., & Ozer, M. (2020). Status threat and ethical leadership: A power-dependence perspective. *Journal of Business Ethics*, *161*(3), 665–685.

Chapter 10

Leadership: Disruption and Influence

Lisa C. Barefield

Introduction

We can all recognise the unprecedented challenges the pandemic created and how the unknown environment caused individuals and organisations to undergo dynamic transformations. During the pandemic, organisations needed to recognise ways to survive, encouraging individuals to identify opportunities to achieve business efficiencies and successes (Nassif, Hackett, & Wang, 2021). However, this also facilitated the realisation of their personal objectives and agendas in the aftermath (Boonstra, 2022). This led organisations to develop leadership strategies aimed at increasing influence over employees, an implication of the work-from-home regulation the government had issued as part of the United Kingdom COVID rules. These sudden and new way of working quickly became adopted by employees and understandably led to a "preferred method of working" for many. The post-pandemic landscape and working environments were changed forever, and organisations were forced to acknowledge that employees had identified new priorities and expectations as they strived for work-life balance. This shift meant that working cultures and environments evolved, and organisations needed to be seen to support the employee's post-pandemic mindsets. Organisations and their leaders recognised they needed to move towards more transformational leadership styles, identifying the benefits of two-way communication, idea generation, and the creation of cultures in

 DOI: 10.4324/9781003475262-12

which collaboration and supportive networks could be encouraged (Bass & Steidlmeier, 1999). However, this created the potential for the "darker side" of leadership to grow and build traction. The new pandemic working cultures allowed for coercive and manipulative characteristics to be exhibited by leaders on many levels. This ultimately led to an increase in the darker leadership personality traits which mitigates the creative and innovative elements within work environments. Leaders with a predisposition towards a darker approach achieve their own self-serving goals through unethical methods. It is important to consider the key aspects that drive the dynamics of leadership in the work environment. Specifically, how transformational leadership influences employees and how the dark side of leadership can evolve. The chapter explores the strengths and weaknesses of transformational leadership, assessing its morality and the potential for misuse. To achieve this, a case study is provided to reflect the practicalities of the chapter.

Pandemic Partying and Misleading the House: A Case Study

On 15th June 2023, the House of Commons published a report titled "Conduct of Rt Hon Boris Johnson" (Committee of Privileges, 2023). This episode has become more commonly known as "Partygate", a political scandal about the gatherings at No.10 Downing Street during the 2020 pandemic. We can probably all remember the public health restrictions that prohibited most gatherings during this time. The report "Matter referred on 21 April 2022: Final Report" conducted by the Committee of Privileges with the authority of the House of Commons reviewed several of the gatherings held at No.10 Downing Street, in which fixed penalty notices were issued by police. Importantly, the inquiry specifically considered the leader's explanation on the floor of the House, as captured in the report "Oral evidence: Matter referred on 21 April 2022: Conduct of Rt Hon Boris Johnson MP, HC564" (Committee of Privileges, 2023). This report which includes the "Explanation of witness", reviewed the legality of activities at these gatherings (House of Commons Committee of Privileges, 2023b). It also assessed the leader's conduct afterward, as highlighted in the report titled "Matter referred on 21 April 2022: Co-ordinated Campaign of Interference in the Work of the Privileges Committee" and whether this interference amounted to contempt (House of Commons Committee of Privileges, 2023). In the report issued on the 15th of June 2023, the committee interestingly mentioned the importance of all "members acting with integrity". The report also clearly stated it was not about examining "the rights and wrongs of the COVID rules" but that its scope was to investigate whether the leader told the truth. The committee concluded that the leader had misled the House, deliberately. With the outcome of the inquiry sanctioning a "suspension from the service of the House for 90 days". However, the leader had resigned by this point which rendered this outcome impossible to impose. The post-pandemic landscape enabled some leaders to use their leadership positions and charismatic personalities to manipulate the culture and ignore codes of behaviour (Eisenbeiß & Boerner, 2013). The report of the Privileges Committee identified a "wider culture of not adhering to the rules," specifically during the pandemic, supporting the idea that standard codes of practice and behaviour were being manipulated. The report stated that the leader had "personal knowledge of the breaches in rules" and was found to have conveniently taken a "flexible interpretation of the rules of gathering". At the time, there were strict regulations around social distancing considering the potentially harmful impact on well-being (House of Commons Committee of Privileges, 2023a).

Transformative Mindsets: The Morality of Leadership

The pandemic influenced stakeholder salience, specifically the employee transformative mindset. It prompted organisational leaders to develop dynamic strategies to maintain influence on employees dealing with significant workplace disruptions (Kellerman, 2019). These leadership strategies entailed flexible working practices to align with employees' needs and facilitate integral work-life balance processes (Ali, Ferdous, & French, 2023). This leads to questioning the morality of leadership, the importance of the "moral character of the leader", and their ethical values. These dimensions are embedded within the leader and the moral processes that define the collective choices and actions they engage in (Bass & Steidlmeier, 1999). The increase in transformative mindsets amongst employees created the opportunity for mutually beneficial interactions within this leader-employee relationship. However, it is worth noting that leaders will seek to identify and pursue their dynamic transformations, which do not always align with the employees' expectations. In fact, in some instances, leaders will actively seek to disrupt as a veritable means to accelerate employee influence

(Koutsopoulos, Henkel, & Stirna, 2021). Consequently, instability and cultural values are being tested and, if poorly managed, will culminate in negative employee outcomes.

The toxic triangle model of dark leadership highlights five critical factors: charisma, personalised use of power, narcissism, negative life themes, and a negative ideology (Padilla, Hogan, & Kaiser, 2007). A multiple cross-case/cross-nation comparative analysis (MCCA) reviewed how destructive and disruptive leadership is perceived (Patel, Hamlin, & Louis, 2022). It concluded that these five factors are linked to ineffective management practices, highlighting that it is not just conspicuous "bad" behaviour but also less conspicuous "poor" behaviour that creates negative perceptions and disruptive work environments. Reviewing the environment in our case study it was particularly interesting to examine the quotes from employees. These employees felt the need to "follow the workplace culture" (House of Commons Committee of Privileges, 2023a). The report identified that senior leaders led a disruptive culture in which personalised use of power culminated in it being impossible for many employees to express concerns or criticise the practice of gathering during the pandemic. It was quoted in the report as potentially being "career-damaging criticism". The report concluded the behaviour of the leader was "reckless", enabling the creation of a culture at No.10 that did not adhere to any rules. The report presented evidence from a junior official who stated that the leaders at No.10 did not follow the same rules that they had instructed the rest of the country to follow.

Transformational Leadership: A Dark Side

One important element of the transformational leadership style is charisma, which is a powerful tool for leaders to inspire and unify teams to foster growth and empower individuals (Northouse, 2018; Schattke & Marion-Jetten, 2022). Characteristics and behaviours include dominance, a desire to influence, self-confidence, and strong self-values (House, 1977). The dark elements of this leadership style may include narcissism, controlling tendencies, arrogance, selfishness, and a lack of empathy. These can result in exploitative influence over employees, also known as unethical pro-organisational behaviour (UPOB) (Basaad, Bajaba, & Basahal, 2023). Similar to the toxic triangle, the negative characteristics of transformational leaders can also be manifested by destructive leaders or pseudo-transformational leaders (Bass & Steidlmeier, 1999; Conger, 1990). A meta-analysis conducted by Schyns and

Schilling (2013) found a strong relationship between destructive leadership traits and negative attitudes of employees towards their jobs, correlating the experience of dark leadership with occupational stress. This toxic triangle of destructive leadership, susceptible employees, and a conducive environment can result in emptiness and alienation and can subsequently lead to unethical and negative outcomes. These can typically occur with little or no reflection of the impact on others, especially those employees who are directly targeted (Northouse, 2018). Paulhus and Williams (2002) introduced the dark triad model, and in this model, they define "dark personalities" which are narcissism, Machiavellianism, psychopathy, and recently added sadism (Mathieu, 2021). These leadership personalities were found to be associated with unethical and counterproductive behaviours, which result in low levels of employee satisfaction, motivation, and commitment.

The strong relationship between transformational leadership and dark leadership is apparent. Schattke and Marion-Jetten (2022) compared transformational leadership and the dark leadership triad framework and found that the latter shares characteristics with the dark triad. The research showed that transformational leadership could easily be misused, especially as it is centred on satisfying an individual's desire for power, whereas a principled transformational leader will seek pro-social outcomes (Lacerenza, Reyes, Marlkow, & Salas, 2017). Applying this to the case study, it was established in the final report in June 2023 that several of the gatherings at the height of the pandemic, including the one held on the 13th of November 2020, showed a disparity between what the public was being told to do and what was occurring during these gatherings. At this point in the pandemic, the government was issuing rules around social distancing at a minimum of two meters, which was justified as appropriate for public health. The report highlights that these same leaders felt "staff morale" was a legitimate reason or "a licence for [the leader's] conveniently flexible interpretation of the rules on gatherings or guidance on social distancing" (House of Commons Committee of Privileges, 2023a). This continued behaviour and disregard for the COVID rules was further evidenced by a gathering just 2 weeks later. The report quotes that the leader joked during this very event saying, "it was probably the most unsocially distanced gathering in the UK right now" (House of Commons Committee of Privileges, 2023b). This report reflects how the employees complied with the unethical directive of the leadership and the senior members of the team, suggesting that the leader was overseeing a culture that was "lackadaisical in observing the rules and guidance" (House of Commons Committee of Privileges, 2023b).

The Dark Side: Risks to Employee Welfare

Transformational leadership is regularly associated with an increase in emotional exhaustion from the unyielding, continual cycle of responsibility to achieve organisational success. This opens the potential for leaders to tend to the dark side of leadership which can lead to detrimental effects (Szu-Han, Scott, & Matta, 2019). Leaders can act, consciously or unconsciously, in bad faith (Sarter, 1992), and disrupt and trample over others to achieve their own goals (Bass & Steidlmeier, 1999). Their disruptive and manipulative approach includes unethical behaviour, drawing attention to themselves whilst being inconsistent and unreliable. They attain value congruence through "sharing unrealistic, unattainable and exploitative expectations" including the abuse of power. This style of leadership creates ambiguity within the wider organisational expectations or business goals, and this allows the leader to act in a silo mode creating a negative environment and outcomes (Milosevic, Maric, & Loncar, 2019). Dark leaders enact self-serving values to the point of narcissism, actively discouraging creative thoughts and innovative ideas that challenge their own thinking. They will compromise standards through exploitation and unreasonable demands, threatening the well-being and welfare of their employees (Christie, Barling, & Turner, 2011). The increase in the dark side of transformational leadership in the post-pandemic environment indicates that organisations should actively mitigate the negative impact on the well-being of employees (Octavian, 2023). The concluding section of the report by the House of Commons Committee of Privileges (2023a) states how the leaders repeatedly urged the public to follow the pandemic rules and guidance yet attended the "work events". These gatherings were in contempt of the very justifications, rules and guidance that were issued.

Lessons for Leaders

The pandemic created a disruption that many were unprepared for. This period was characterised by enormous stresses and strains of meeting targets to ensure business success, creating varied opportunities for the manifestation of dark leadership. So, what can we learn and do differently? For leaders who tend towards the dark side, it is important to understand that increased pressures can negatively impact brighter leadership traits. It is important to understand that everyone has a dark side to some degree and acknowledging this is a first step to initiating the necessary interventions. This process can be done by reflecting on what influences the emergence of dark leadership traits. Finally, gaining peer feedback will facilitate the understanding of how leadership style is perceived and how it affects others. By developing self-awareness, leaders can counter negative traits and develop behaviours that promote a positive approach characterised by empathy, compassion, and respect.

Conclusion

Organisations must foster ethical and empathetic cultures, creating brighter, more productive, engaged environments. This will enable leaders and employees to be collectively more supportive and hold high moral standards which will result in dynamic and innovative landscapes. In this chapter, we explored how a disruptive leadership style can impact employees' well-being negatively and ultimately affect organisational effectiveness. The brighter side of leadership can be cultivated by encouraging teams to be reflective, self-aware, thoughtful, compassionate, and observant. Encouraging a willingness at all team levels to learn, grow, understand, and connect with others as well as themselves will help individuals evaluate situations, make decisions, and maintain self-control. Finally, the bright side of leadership will improve internal and external perceptions of the leader, the team, and its individuals and invigorate the organisational environment.

References

Ali, M., Ferdous, T., & French, E. (2023). Use of flexible work practices and employee outcomes: The role of work-life balance and employee age. *Journal of Management and Organisation*, *29*(5), 833–853.

Basaad, S., Bajaba, S., & Basahal, A. (2023). Uncovering the dark side of leadership: How exploitative leaders fuel unethical pro-organizational behaviour through moral disengagement. *Cogent Business and Management*, *10*(2), 2233775. https://doi.org/10.1080/23311975.2023.2233775

Bass, B. M., & Steidlmeier, P. (1999). Ethics, character, and authentic transformational leadership behaviour. *Leadership Quarterly*, *10*(2), 181–217. https://doi.org/10.1016/S1048-9843(99)00016-8

Boonstra, J. (2022). Reflections: From planned change to playful transformations. Retrieved January 20, 2023, from https://www-tandfonline-com.ezproxy.tees.ac.uk/doi/full/10.1080/14697017.2022.2151149

Christie, A., Barling, J., & Turner, N. (2011). Pseudo-transformational leadership: Model specification and outcomes. *Journal of Applied Social Psychology, 41*(12), 2943–2984.

Committee of Privileges. (2023). Matter referred on 21 April 2022 (conduct of Rt Hon Boris Johnson): Final report – Report summary. Retrieved from UK Parliament: https://publications.parliament.uk/pa/cm5803/cmselect/cmprivi/564/summary.html#

Conger, J. (1990). The dark side of leadership. *Organisational Dynamics, 19*, 44–55.

Eisenbeiß, S. A., & Boerner, S. (2013). A double-edged sword: Transformational leadership and individual creativity. *British Journal of Management, 24*, 54–68.

House, R. J. (1977). A 1976 theory of charismatic leadership. In: J. G. Hunt & L. L. Larson (Eds.), *Leadership: The Cutting Edge* (pp. 189–207). Carbondale, IL: Southern Illinois University Press. https://www.mendeley.com/catalogue/1976-theory-charismatic-leadership-working-paper-series-7606/

House of Commons Committee of Privileges. (2023a). Matter referred on 21 April 2022: Co-ordinated campaign of interference in the work of the privileges committee. https://committees.parliament.uk/publications/40679/documents/198237/default/

House of Commons Committee of Privileges. (2023b). Matter referred on 21 April 2022 (conduct of Rt Hon Boris Johnson): Final report – Report summary. https://committees.parliament.uk/publications/40412/documents/197897/default/

House of Commons Committee of Privileges. (2023c). Oral evidence: Matter referred on 21 April 2022: Conduct of rt hon boris johnson mp, hc 564. Retrieved May 2024, from https://committees.parliament.uk/oralevidence/12878/pdf/

Kellerman, B. (2019). The future of followership. *Strategy & Leadership, 47*(5), 42–46.

Koutsopoulos, G., Henkel, M., & Stirna, J. (2021). An analysis of capability meta-models for expressing dynamic business transformation. *Software and System Modelling, 20*(1), 147–174.

Lacerenza, C. N., Reyes, D. L., Marlkow, S. L., & Salas, E. (2017). Leadership training design, delivery, and implementation: A meta-analysis. *The Journal of Applied Psychology, 102*(12), 1686–1718.

Mathieu, C. (2021). *Dark personalities in the workplace*. San Diego: Elsevier Science & Technology.

Milosevic, I., Maric, S., & Loncar, D. (2019). Defeating the toxic boss: The nature of toxic leadership and the role of followers. *Journal of Leadership & Organizational Studies, 27*(2), 117–137.

Nassif, A. G., Hackett, R., & Wang, G. (2021). Ethical, virtuous, and charismatic leadership: An examination of differential relationships with follower and leader outcomes. *Journal of Business Ethics, 172*(3), 581–603. https://doi.org/10.1007/s10551-020-04491-8

Northouse, P. G. (2018). *Leadership: Theory & practice*. United Kingdom: SAGA.

Octavian, S. M. (2023). About the impact and effects of toxic leadership on employees and organizations. *European Review of Applied Sociology, 16*(27), 87–93.

Padilla, A., Hogan, R., & Kaiser, R. B. (2007). The toxic triangle: Destructive leaders, susceptible followers, and conducive environments. *The Leadership Quarterly, 18*, 176–194.

Patel, T., Hamlin, R. G., & Louis, D. (2022). Toward a generic framework of perceived negative manager/leader behaviour: A comparative study across nations and private sector industries. *European Management Review, 19*, 608–624.

Paulhus, D. L., & William, K. M. (2002). The dark triad of personality: Narcissism, Machiavellianism, and psychopathy. *Journal of Research in Personality, 36*(6), 556–563.

Sarter, J. P. (1992). *Being and nothingness: A phenomenological essay on ontology*. New York: Washington Square Press.

Schattke, K., & Marion-Jetten, A. S. (2022). Distinguishing the explicit power motives - Relations with dark personality traits, work behaviour, and leadership styles. *Zeitschrift für Psychologie, 230*(4), 290–299. https://doi.org/10.1027/2151-2604/a000481

Schyns, B., & Schilling, J. (2013). How bad are the effects of bad leaders - A meta-analysis of destructive leadership and its outcomes. *The Leadership Quarterly, 24*, 138–158.

Szu-Han, L., Scott, B. A., & Matta, F. K. (2019). The dark side of transformational leader behaviours for leaders themselves: A conservation of resources perspective. *Academy of Management Journal, 62*(5), 1556–1582.

THE CONTEXT OF DARK LEADERSHIP

III

Chapter 11

Dark Triad and Leadership: A Perspective on the Causes and Consequences in Family Business Environments

José Ricardo Andrade

Introduction

The term "dark triad" is used in psychology to describe a trio of personality traits that are considered evil and socially aversive. These traits are narcissism, Machiavellianism, and psychopathy, and they can influence the performance of different types of organisations. In the case of family businesses, they are typically characterised by the existence of a relationship of dominance since its members are the founders and owners of the company. A common feature of family businesses is a strong bond between management and employees, creating a closer working relationship and a unique corporate culture. For this reason, these companies seek to maintain strategies that allow for the continuity of family domination, combining different management trajectories. Existing literature also suggests that the kinship relationship between top managers in family businesses, relative to other types of companies confers a competitive advantage in terms of strategy (Kraiczy, Hack, & Kellermanns, 2015).

DOI: 10.4324/9781003475262-14

It is well known that leadership has a direct and positive influence on performance, culture, and the work environment (Scheepers & Storm, 2019; Srour, Shefer, & Carmeli, 2022; Andrade et al., 2020; Andrade, 2024; Men & Yue, 2019; Nakamura & Milner; 2023; Santos et al., 2021). This influence can also be observed at the level of innovation (Wei, Zhou, & Wang, 2023), strategy (Jansen, Vera, & Crossan, 2009), and the way it influences organisational culture (McDonough, 2011), as well work processes (Chang, 2016). Patiar and Wang (2020) and Oakland (2011) have also shown that effective leadership can harmonise behaviours, internal processes, and performance, and transform organisations as well as align behaviours with corporate values (Engelen, Gupta, Strenger, & Brettel, 2015). However, leadership in organisations is not always positive and effective when it comes to developing organisational strategies. The literature suggests that a negative view of leadership, associated with a set of harmful behaviours have a negative impact on organisations (Octavian, 2023). In addition, the development of stress and mental health situations, low confidence or reduced productivity, and low performance have been identified as consequences of the "dark side" of leadership (Octavian, 2023; Ofei, Poku, Paarima, Barnes, & Kwashie, 2023).

This chapter addresses the impact of dark triad traits on family business leadership, family relationships, and overall company performance. Specific challenges of these businesses are examined and opportunities to mitigate negative impacts and strengthen interpersonal relationships are discussed. The chapter contributes to the existing literature by critically identifying and synthesising the relationships that emerge in the literature on how dark triad traits manifest in family business leaders.

Dark Triad: Concepts and Components

The dark triad is a set of three personality traits that are generally considered socially aversive: narcissism, Machiavellianism, and psychopathy. These traits, although distinct, have been associated with extreme egocentrism, a lack of empathy, a propensity to exploit others, and unethical and undesirable behaviours (Mutschmann, Hasso, & Pelster, 2022). Research into the personality of leaders and managers in organisations has been a focus of study, with particular attention to the less positive aspects of personality in the context of SMEs (Cesinger, Gundolf, Hughes, Khedhaouria, & Montani, 2023). The existing literature indicates that certain characteristics and behaviours associated with the dark triad traits influence the performance of SMEs (Hambrick & Mason, 1984). Indeed, the "dark side" of leadership traits in family businesses can also have profoundly negative consequences for the company, including low employee morale, high turnover, family conflicts, and even business failure (Mathieu, Neumann, Hare, & Babiak, 2014).

The study of psychopathy in organisations is relatively recent, especially considering the business implications of the phenomenon. According to Mathieu et al. (2014), psychopathy is a construct defined around a set of characteristics that includes irresponsibility, impulsiveness, feelings of grandiosity, lack of empathy, or egocentrism and involves psychological conditions that cause suffering or dysfunction for the individual. Leaders who display psychopathological traits demonstrate behaviours and characteristics that can have negative implications for the organisation and the teams they lead. Hogan and Hogan (2001) argue that some of the problems observed in companies, particularly concerning absenteeism, lack of motivation, and employee dissatisfaction, are attributable to certain personality dysfunctions of their managers.

The narcissism personality trait is characterised by excessive self-love, self-centredness, and a constant need for admiration (Bader et al., 2021; Octavian, 2023). In organisations, this trait can manifest itself in different ways, often with negative consequences for the work environment and collective performance. The narcissistic leader displays tendencies related to their image and personal success. They are often extremely charismatic, and persuasive. They win over followers and inspire confidence, which can have a detrimental effect on the team or the organisation (Ofei et al., 2023). The narcissistic personality is characterised by a feeling of dominance and superiority, self-importance, and a deep need for admiration and praise. Those with narcissistic traits may be manipulative, demanding, and insensitive to the needs and feelings of others. By fostering an environment of internal competition and mistrust, a narcissistic leader may attempt to manipulate situations to ensure that they take credit for everyone's successes and avoid responsibility for failures.

Another aspect of narcissism in organisations is the tendency to make impulsive and risky decisions in pursuit of personal glory without adequately considering the risks and consequences for the organisation as a whole (Mutschmann et al., 2022). This behaviour can have a negative impact on the stability and success of the organisation (Cesinger et al., 2023). A narcissistic leader may monopolise conversations in meetings, thereby devaluing the contributions of other team members. Alternatively, they may display ostentatious behaviour on social media, constantly seeking validation and approval (Bader et al., 2021). In essence, the narcissistic leader's lack of empathy and insensitivity manifests in a pattern of self-centered and manipulative behaviour in which personal interests and the search for admiration are placed above the needs and feelings of others.

The Machiavellian personality is typified by the utilisation of manipulation and deception strategies to achieve personal goals. Those with Machiavellian traits are characterised by a calculated, cunning demeanour and a tendency towards a detached, rational approach to interpersonal relationships (Hughes, 2022). In the workplace, these behaviours can result in a breakdown of trust and collaboration. However, these individuals often demonstrate effectiveness in achieving immediate results. This type of personality trait exerts a significant and often negative influence on organisational environments. The characteristics of manipulation, strategic calculation, cynicism and a lack of moral principles can have a complex impact on different areas of the organisation. The influence of this personality trait on organisations can include the development of a climate of mistrust, which can lead to individuals being suspicious of each other and a lack of team collaboration. This can also affect interpersonal relationships, group motivation, decision-making capacity, conflicts, and instability. Alternatively, it can result in reduced productivity and a negative impact on the company's reputation and image.

The existing literature indicates the existence of enabling conditions that facilitate the action of these leaders' personalities, although it also presents challenges for organisations. These include the context, the company culture, poor reward systems, and also the characteristics of employees that ultimately help to understand leadership in companies (Hughes, 2022). Additionally, several organisational attributes can facilitate the actions of individuals with Machiavellian personality traits. These include a lack of transparency in decision-making processes, which allows individuals displaying such behaviours to manipulate information and situations without being detected. Another attribute is a high level of internal competition, which allows individuals with this personality type to employ unethical and manipulative strategies to gain an advantage over their colleagues. Other structural, cultural, or contextual conditions can act as facilitators of the actions of individuals with a Machiavellian personality. These conditions include centralised hierarchical organisational structures where power is concentrated; a lack of supervision and control; ambiguous or weak organisational cultures, or organisational environments with few resources or opportunities for recognition or promotion.

Leadership and Dark Triad in Family Businesses

It is acknowledged that family businesses exhibit distinctive characteristics, shaped by family dynamics, historical context, and shared values (Yang, Li, Stanley, Kellermanns, & Li, 2020). These companies can be defined as organisations where control and management are vested in members of the same family. One of the defining characteristics of family businesses is the interconnection between family life and the business. This interconnection is characterised by the strong influence of family values on the company's organisational culture, which often reflects traditions, loyalties, and family dynamics (Yang et al., 2020). In this context, leaders in family businesses often occupy dual roles as family heads and business leaders (Fries et al., 2021). The transition of leadership in family businesses frequently presents a challenge, as it frequently involves complex emotional and political issues, such as the choice between family and non-family members for key positions (Yang et al., 2020). In formal governance structures, such as boards of directors, there is often a combination of family and non-family members (Gedajlovic, Lubatkin, & Schulze, 2004). In these contexts, trust is often greater among family members, which can facilitate collaboration. However, this can also result in greater resistance to change (Bargoni, Alon, & Ferraris, 2023; Gedajlovic et al., 2004).

The existing literature indicates that instances of overlapping roles (such as that of a leader and a family member) can give rise to conflicts of interest. In such cases, business decisions can be influenced by family considerations, emotional ties, and personal considerations, or affected by the needs of the company, particularly concerning decisions on the distribution of profits and their impact on the family's expected income (Smith, Nordqvist, De Massis, & Miller, 2021). Another factor to consider is the potential for resistance to change and the difficulty in adopting new practices inconsistent with traditional family values (Spagnoli, Manuti, Buono, & Ghislieri, 2021). In this context, governance can be impeded by family conflicts and the difficulty of balancing family interests with those of the business (Mathieu et al., 2014). These aspects can present considerable challenges for leadership in the context of family businesses, as conflicts between family members can have a deleterious impact on decision-making and organisational harmony (Mutschmann et al., 2022). Family businesses can be reluctant to embrace change, particularly when new practices challenge traditional ways of working (Spagnoli et al., 2021). Conversely, members of family businesses frequently demonstrate a high degree of loyalty and commitment to the company (McLarty & Holt, 2019).

Family businesses are more likely to focus on long-term goals rather than immediate gains (Spagnoli et al., 2021). The leaner structure and proximity of managers to the business can allow for faster and more flexible decision-making. The transfer of knowledge and experience from generation to generation can be equally effective in family businesses (Waldkirch, Nordqvist, & Melin, 2018). The context of family businesses provides an interesting framework for examining the influence of dark triad traits on the behaviour of family leaders and their interactions with family members and employees. Some aspects of this influence are suggested in the literature, namely at the level of succession challenges, impact on family ties, culture and tradition, succession, or trust and loyalty. The succession process in family businesses can provide fertile ground for power struggles, manipulation, and antisocial behaviour, particularly if heirs or leadership candidates exhibit dark triad traits. The influence of the dark triad on organisational culture can be observed in the negative impact it has on corporate culture, promoting unfair competition, distrust, and a lack of cooperation. The literature also suggests that leaders in family businesses often have strong family ties with team members, which can facilitate communication and build trust. However, these family ties can also complicate power and authority relationships, create conflicts of interest, and make it difficult to separate family and business matters.

In family businesses, decision-making is often more agile and flexible, as leaders have greater autonomy and freedom to implement their visions without the bureaucracy associated with large corporations. Autocratic decision-making can be detrimental if family leaders do not seek external advice or refuse to consider alternative perspectives, limiting innovation and company growth.

It should be noted that family businesses offer the opportunity to integrate family and professional life, allowing leaders to share common values and goals with their loved ones. The challenge of balancing family and business interests is significant, particularly when family issues impede the efficient and effective operation of the company, or vice versa.

Narcissistic family leaders may prioritie their own self-image and personal status above the interests of the company, making decisions that seek only to increase their fame or recognition rather than promote the company's sustainable success. They may even prefer family members who admire or blindly obey them, instead of promoting a culture of meritocracy. Furthermore, their lack of empathy can result in unequal and insensitive treatment of workers. In contrast, Machiavellian family leaders can be highly manipulative and strategic in their leadership approaches, using subterfuge and power plays to achieve their personal goals, often to the detriment of the interests of the company and the team. They may attempt to control and manipulate family members and workers to consolidate their power and influence within the company. Such a situation can give rise to an atmosphere of distrust and competition among employees. Individuals with psychopathic traits may also display impulsive and antisocial behaviours, making risky and harmful decisions for the company without considering the long-term consequences. Such individuals may exhibit irresponsible behaviour, including fraud and financial manipulation, and engage in abusive and manipulative interactions with others.

Causes and Consequences of the Dark Triad in Family Business Leadership

The combination of genetic predispositions and influences from the family environment may contribute to the development of dark triad traits in family business leaders (Blonigen, Carlson, Krueger, & Patrick, 2003; Vernon, Villani, Vickers, & Harris, 2008). These traits can significantly influence the way these leaders conduct their business, affecting organisational culture and business strategies. The existing literature indicates that narcissism has a significant genetic basis. For instance, the study by Szücs et al. (2020) demonstrates that specific genetic predispositions can result in heightened self-perception and a persistent need for admiration, which are common characteristics observed in narcissists. Conversely, the literature also asserts that growing up in an environment where admiration and validation are frequently offered without limitations can foster narcissistic traits. Brummelman et al. (2015) investigated the potential influence of parental socialisation on the development of narcissism in children. The results indicated that overvaluation by parents may contribute to the emergence of narcissistic traits. Children of business leaders who are consistently praised and treated as special may develop an exaggerated sense of self-importance, exhibiting a persistent need for recognition and validation, which may influence their decisions and professional relationships.

The hypothesis that the predisposition to manipulate and exploit others may have a genetic basis, as well as being favoured by family environments where manipulation and internal politics are common, has been put forth. The study by Ferencz et al. (2023), which used a sample of twins, found evidence that Machiavellian traits have a significant genetic basis. In turn, the study by Vernon et al. (2008) examined the relationship between personality traits and empathy deficits. The authors highlight that family environments characterised by low empathy and high manipulation can contribute to the development of Machiavellian traits. In an organisational context, individuals with Machiavellian traits may be more prone to Machiavellian behaviour, be strategic and calculating, and their actions may be seen as deceptive and unethical.

The literature indicates that psychopathic traits, including emotional insensitivity and impulsivity, are also genetically influenced. However, the literature also suggests that this pattern can be developed in dysfunctional family environments, where insensitivity and a lack of empathy are common and may contribute to the development of psychopathic traits. Exposure to intense family conflict and a lack of emotional support can shape detached and insensitive behaviour. The study by Blonigen et al. (2003) investigated the heritability of psychopathic traits using a sample of twins. The results indicated a strong genetic influence on the manifestation of these traits. Conversely, the study by Lynam, Caspi, Moffitt, Loeber, and Stouthamer-Loeber (2007) examined the influence of family factors on the development of psychopathic traits. The findings demonstrated a correlation between exposure to dysfunctional family environments, including emotional and physical abuse, and the manifestation of psychopathic traits in adulthood.

It is well documented that family business leaders are subject to a multitude of pressures and expectations that can influence the emergence of dark triad traits (O'Boyle, Forsyth, Banks, & McDaniel, 2012). With regard to pressures and expectations, the leader of a family business must maintain the family legacy at the level of the family business's reputation. This legacy is often constructed by previous generations and can result in the emergence of narcissistic traits in leaders who prioritise their image and prestige (Kets de Vries, 1993). Conversely, family leaders frequently encounter the expectation of attaining and maintaining high levels of performance and success, both on behalf of the family and of employees. This can give rise to Machiavellian behaviours, characterised by the use of manipulation and strategy to achieve objectives (Stewart & Hitt, 2012). In family business environments, leaders are frequently required to make challenging decisions that can impact the company's financial stability and the well-being of employees (García-Álvarez & López-Sintas, 2001). These circumstances can foster psychopathic traits, such as a lack of empathy and an inability to recognise the needs of others (Carr, Vardaman, Marler, McLarty, & Blettner, 2021). In the context of family businesses, the necessity to navigate conflicts between family members regarding the direction of the company, roles, and responsibilities is a common occurrence. This can give rise to the development of Machiavellian and psychopathic traits, characterised by the utilisation of manipulation and cold strategies to mediate and resolve disputes (Ferencz et al., 2023; Mathieu et al., 2014).

The presence of narcissism, Machiavellianism, and psychopathy traits have a significant and generally negative impact on family and business relationships, organisational performance, and the work climate. These traits generate conflicts, tensions, manipulative behaviours, distrust, and a lack of empathy and support. In family relationships, psychopathic traits can create a culture of fear and intimidation within the company, where workers are afraid of reprisals. Machiavellian traits can be observed in individuals who engage in manipulation and intrigue to maintain power and control, thereby undermining collaboration and trust between employees. Narcissistic traits can lead to excessive self-evaluation and disregard for the contributions of others, which can demotivate workers. The consequences of the actions of these traits in family business environments can be evidenced in egocentric decision-making, where the leader prioritises his image and success over the interests of the company. This is exemplified by the focus on short-term results, where the focus on gains for profit is evident. The manipulation of employees, the neglect of long-term sustainability, and the lack of empathy and involvement are all factors that contribute to the decline of family businesses.

A reflection on the presence of the dark triad traits – psychopathy, Machiavellianism, and narcissism – in the leadership of small and medium-sized family businesses (SMEs) leads us to consider the profound and multifaceted effects on organisational culture and employee well-being. In a family environment, where trust and collaboration are fundamental, such characteristics can create tensions, undermine interpersonal relationships, and destabilise the organisational structure. The dominance of these traits can create a toxic work environment, resulting in high levels of stress, low morale, and high employee turnover, negatively affecting the company's overall performance. The recognition and mitigation of the impacts of dark triad traits on leadership are essential for fostering a healthy work environment and ensuring the sustainability of family-owned small and medium-sized enterprises (SMEs). Strategies for leadership development that prioritise empathy, transparency, and collaboration can serve as effective countermeasures against the adverse effects of these traits. Furthermore, the implementation of governance practices that promote responsibility and active involvement from all family members can bolster organisational culture and enhance business performance. Therefore, it is crucial to acknowledge and confront the influence of the Dark Triad to convert potential weaknesses into opportunities for growth, ultimately nurturing a positive and enduring organisational culture.

Lessons for Leaders: Strategies for Dealing with the Dark Triad in Family Business Leadership

To effectively address the dark triad in family business leadership, it is essential to implement a comprehensive approach that integrates several different elements. These include education, effective governance, leadership development, fostering a positive organisational culture, and supporting employees to mitigate the adverse effects of personality traits associated with the dark triad and promote a healthy and productive work environment. Consequently, the prevention of such individuals commences during the recruitment and selection process. The utilisation of psychometric tools and personality assessments can assist in the identification of candidates exhibiting dark triad traits (Paulhus & Williams, 2002). Furthermore, structured interviews that delve deeply into past behaviour in leadership and teamwork contexts can also be employed. Similarly, it is important to emphasise the necessity of fostering an organisational culture that prioritises transparency, ethics, and respect. These values can serve to mitigate the impact of leaders with dark triad traits (Cameron & Quinn, 2006). Furthermore, the promotion of leaders who exemplify positive behaviours and align with the company's values can serve as a model for others to emulate. Celebrating these examples of positive leadership can encourage an environment where dark triad traits are less likely to flourish. One factor is the existence of a robust and delineated culture that serves as a behavioural guide for all members of the company, thereby making it challenging for manipulative and unethical behaviours to flourish.

The literature also suggests a set of control and monitoring tools, including training and personal development, the implementation of clear policies and procedures, and the existence of family governance structures that support decisions. Thus, investing in leadership development programmes can help shape leaders' behaviour and mitigate unwanted traits (Day & Harrison, 2007). Providing training in emotional intelligence, business ethics, and communication skills can be particularly effective (London, 2003). The establishment of transparent policies and procedures for decision-making, conflict resolution, and corporate governance can serve to mitigate the deleterious effects of leaders exhibiting traits associated with the dark triad (Kolb & Putnam, 1992). Well-defined policies ensure that members of the company are aware of the expectations and limitations of acceptable conduct. In family businesses, governance presents a challenge due to the overlap between family and business interests (Davis, Hampton, & Lansberg, 1997). The establishment of a governance structure comprising advisory or steering boards comprising external members can facilitate the introduction of objectivity and impartiality into business decisions. The presence of external members can serve as a counterbalance to the negative influences of those exhibiting traits associated with the dark triad.

Conclusion

This chapter is an in-depth exploration of the dark triad, comprising narcissism, Machiavellianism, and psychopathy. It examines the impact of these traits on the leadership of family businesses. Narcissism is typified by inflated self-esteem and the craving for admiration, while Machiavellianism is characterised by strategic manipulation and emotional detachment. Psychopathy involves impulsivity and a lack of empathy. The presence of these traits in family business leadership can lead to both advantageous and disadvantageous outcomes. Family business leaders with dark triad characteristics may initially exhibit a strong sense of purpose and determination, which can propel the company forward in times of crises or stagnation. However, these same traits can also lead to manipulative practices, a lack of consideration for other family members, and impulsive decisions, which can compromise family cohesion and the long-term sustainability of the company.

The causes of the dark triad in the leadership of family businesses are numerous and complex. These include the influence of family dynamics, the necessity to maintain control and succession, and the need to survive in competitive environments. The consequences of this phenomenon can range from innovation and business growth to intense family conflicts, ethically questionable decisions, and, in extreme cases, the dissolution of the company. To effectively manage the dark triad in family business leadership, the chapter recommends implementing several key strategies. These include establishing transparent governance policies, cultivating an organisational culture anchored on ethical values, and conducting comprehensive psychological assessments during succession processes. Furthermore, it is crucial to invest in developing leadership skills that prioritise empathy, transparency, and collaboration. Seeking assistance from external consultants and professional mediation can also play a crucial role in managing conflicts and projecting the best interests of the company and the family. By comprehensively addressing the elements of the dark triad, it is possible to alleviate its adverse effects and promote a more balanced and sustainable leadership approach in family businesses.

References

Andrade, J. R. (2024). Empathy, communication skills, and emotions : a reflection through the organisational perspective. In M. D. D. Sharma & B. Bhardwaj (Eds.), *Leveraging AI and Emotional Intelligence in Contemporary Business Organizations* (pp. 23–42). IGI Global. https://doi.org/10.4018/979-8-3693-1902-4.ch002

Andrade, J., Franco, M., & Mendes, L. (2020). Technological capacity and organisational ambidexterity: the moderating role of environmental dynamism on Portuguese technological SMEs. *Review of Managerial Science, 15*, 2111–2136. https://doi.org/10.1007/s11846-020-00416-x

Bader, M., Hartung, J., Hilbig, B. E., Zettler, I., Moshagen, M., & Wilhelm, O. (2021). Themes of the dark core of personality. *Psychological Assessment, 33*, 511–525. https://doi.org/10.1037/pas0001006

Bargoni, A., Alon, I., & Ferraris, A. (2023). A systematic review of family business and consumer behaviour. *Journal of Business Research, 158*(June 2022), 113698. https://doi.org/10.1016/j.jbusres.2023.113698

Blonigen, D. M., Carlson, S. R., Krueger, R. F., & Patrick, C. J. (2003). A twin study of self-reported psychopathic personality traits. *Personality and Individual Differences, 35*(1), 179–197. https://doi.org/10.1016/S0191-8869(02)00184-8

Brummelman, E., Thomaes, S., Nelemans, S. A., De Castro, B. O., Overbeek, G., & Bushman, B. J. (2015). Origins of narcissism in children. *Proceedings of the National Academy of Sciences of the United States of America, 112*(12), 3659–3662. https://doi.org/10.1073/pnas.1420870112

Cameron, K. S., & Quinn, R. E. (2006). *Diagnosing and Changing Organizational Culture: Based on the Competing Values Framework.* John Wiley & Sons.

Carr, J. C., Vardaman, J. M., Marler, L. E., McLarty, B. D., & Blettner, D. (2021). Psychological antecedents of decision comprehensiveness and their relationship to decision quality and performance in family firms: an upper echelons perspective. *Family Business Review, 34*(1), 33–47. https://doi.org/10.1177/0894486520917774

Cesinger, B., Gundolf, K., Hughes, M., Khedhaouria, A., & Montani, F. (2023). The bright and dark sides of the dark triad traits among senior managers: effects on organizational commitment. *Review of Managerial Science, 17*, 1731–1763. https://doi.org/10.1007/s11846-022-00571-3

Chang, Y.-Y. (2016). High-performance work systems, joint impact of transformational leadership, an empowerment climate and organisational ambidexterity: Cross level evidence. *Journal of Organizational Change Management, 29*, 424-444. https://doi.org/10.1108/JOCM-09-2015-0150

Davis, J. A., Hampton, M. M., & Lansberg, I. (1997). *Generation to Generation: Life Cycles of the Family Business*. Harvard Business Press.

Day, D. V., & Harrison, M. M. (2007). A multilevel, identity-based approach to leadership development. *Human Resource Management Review, 17*(4), 360–373. https://doi.org/10.1016/j.hrmr.2007.08.007

Engelen, A., Gupta, V., Strenger, L., & Brettel, M. (2015). Entrepreneurial Orientation, firm performance, and the moderating role of transformational leadership behaviors. *Journal of Management, 41*(4), 1069–1097. https://doi.org/10.1177/0149206312455244

Ferencz, T., Láng, A., Kocsor, F., Kozma, L., Babós, A., & Gyuris, P. (2023). Sibling relationship quality and parental rearing style influence the development of dark triad traits. *Current Psychology, 42*(28), 24764–24781. https://doi.org/10.1007/s12144-022-03506-z

Fries, A., Kammerlander, N., & Leitterstorf, M. (2021). Leadership styles and leadership behaviors in family firms: a systematic literature review. *Journal of Family Business Strategy, 12*(1), 100374. https://doi.org/10.1016/j.jfbs.2020.100374

García-Álvarez, E., & López-Sintas, J. (2001). A taxonomy of founders based on values: the root of family business heterogeneity. *Family Business Review, 14*(3), 209–230. https://doi.org/10.1111/j.1741-6248.2001.00209.x

Gedajlovic, E., Lubatkin, M. H., & Schulze, W. S. (2004). Crossing the threshold from founder management to professional management: a governance perspective. *Journal of Management Studies, 41*(5), 899–912. https://doi.org/10.1111/j.1467-6486.2004.00459.x

Hambrick, D. C., & Mason, P. A. (1984). Upper echelons: the organization as a reflection of its top managers. *Academy of Management Review, 9*(2), 193–206.

Hogan, R., & Hogan, J. (2001). Assessing leadership: a view from the dark side. *International Journal of Selection and Assessment, 9*(1–2), 40–51. https://doi.org/10.1111/1468-2389.00162

Hughes, B. C. (2022). Examining toxic leadership: an integrated framework for organizational recovery. *Journal of Behavioral and Applied Management, 22*(3), 309–344.

Jansen, J. J. P., Vera, D., & Crossan, M. (2009). Strategic leadership for exploration and exploitation: the moderating role of environmental dynamism. *Leadership Quarterly, 20*(1), 5–18. https://doi.org/10.1016/j.leaqua.2008.11.008

Kets de Vries, M. F. R. (1993). The dynamics of family-controlled firms: the good and the bad news. *Organizational Dynamics, 21*(3), 59–71.

Kolb, D. M., & Putnam, L. L. (1992). The multiple faces of conflict in organizations. *Journal of Organizational Behavior, 13*(3), 311–324. https://doi.org/10.1002/job.4030130313

Kraiczy, N. D., Hack, A., & Kellermanns, F. W. (2015). What makes a family firm innovative? CEO risk-taking propensity and the organizational context of family firms. *Journal of Product Innovation Management, 32*(3), 334–348. https://doi.org/10.1111/jpim.12203

London, M. (2003). *Job Feedback: Giving, Seeking, and Using Feedback for Performance Improvement.* Psychology Press.

Lynam, D. R., Caspi, A., Moffitt, T. E., Loeber, R., & Stouthamer-Loeber, M. (2007). Longitudinal evidence that psychopathy scores in early adolescence predict adult psychopathy. *Journal of Abnormal Psychology, 116*(1), 155–165. https://doi.org/10.1037/0021-843X.116.1.155

Mathieu, C., Neumann, C. S., Hare, R. D., & Babiak, P. (2014). A dark side of leadership: corporate psychopathy and its influence on employee well-being and job satisfaction. *Personality and Individual Differences, 59*, 83–88. https://doi.org/10.1016/j.paid.2013.11.010

McDonough, E. F. (2011). Investigating the role of leadership and organizational culture in fostering innovation ambidexterity. *IEEE Transactions on Engineering Management, 58*(3), 497–509. https://doi.org/10.1109/TEM.2010.2092781

McLarty, B. D., & Holt, D. T. (2019). A bright side to family firms: how socioemotional wealth importance affects dark traits–job performance relationships. *Family Business Review, 32*(4), 378–395. https://doi.org/10.1177/0894486519888397

Men, L. R., & Yue, C. A. (2019). Creating a positive emotional culture: effect of internal communication and impact on employee supportive behaviors. *Public Relations Review, 45*(3), 101764. https://doi.org/10.1016/j.pubrev.2019.03.001

Mutschmann, M., Hasso, T., & Pelster, M. (2022). Dark triad managerial personality and financial reporting manipulation. *Journal of Business Ethics, 181*(3), 763–788. https://doi.org/10.1007/s10551-021-04959-1

Nakamura, Y. T., & Milner, J. (2023). Inclusive leadership via empathic communication. *Organizational Dynamics, 52*(1), 100957. https://doi.org/10.1016/j.orgdyn.2023.100957

O'Boyle, E. H., Forsyth, D. R., Banks, G. C., & McDaniel, M. A. (2012). A meta-analysis of the dark triad and work behavior: a social exchange perspective. *Journal of Applied Psychology, 97*(3), 557–579. https://doi.org/10.1037/a0025679

Oakland, J. S. (2011). Leadership and policy deployment: the backbone of TQM. *Total Quality Management & Business Excellence, 22*(5), 517–534.

Octavian, S. M. (2023). About the impact and effects of toxic leadership on employees and organizations. *European Review Of Applied Sociology, 16*(27), 87–93. https://doi.org/10.2478/eras-2023-0012

Ofei, A. M. A., Poku, C. A., Paarima, Y., Barnes, T., & Kwashie, A. A. (2023). Toxic leadership behaviour of nurse managers and turnover intentions: the mediating role of job satisfaction. *BMC Nursing*, *22*(1), 1–11. https://doi.org/10.1186/s12912-023-01539-8

Patiar, A., & Wang, Y. (2020). Managers' leadership, compensation and benefits, and departments' performance: evidence from upscale hotels in Australia: leadership, compensation and performance. *Journal of Hospitality and Tourism Management*, *42*(November 2019), 29–39. https://doi.org/10.1016/j.jhtm.2019.11.005

Paulhus, D. L., & Williams, K. M. (2002). The dark triad of personality: narcissism, Machiavellianism, and psychopathy. *Journal of Research in Personality*, *36*(6), 556–563. https://doi.org/10.1007/978-3-319-98446-9_43

Santos, G., Sá, J. C., Félix, M. J., Barreto, L., Carvalho, F., Doiro, M., … Stefanović, M. (2021). New needed quality management skills for quality managers 4.0. *Sustainability (Switzerland)*, *13*(11), 1–22. https://doi.org/10.3390/su13116149

Scheepers, C. B., & Storm, C. P. (2019). Authentic leadership's influence on ambidexterity with mediators in the South African context. *European Business Review*, *31*(3), 352–378. https://doi.org/10.1108/EBR-11-2017-0207

Smith, C., Nordqvist, M., De Massis, A., & Miller, D. (2021). When so much is at stake: understanding organizational brinkmanship in family business. *Journal of Family Business Strategy*, *12*(4), 100425. https://doi.org/10.1016/j.jfbs.2021.100425

Spagnoli, P., Manuti, A., Buono, C., & Ghislieri, C. (2021). The good, the bad and the blend: the strategic role of the "middle leadership" in work-family/life dynamics during remote working. *Behavioral Sciences*, *11*(8), 112. https://doi.org/10.3390/bs11080112

Srour, Y., Shefer, N., & Carmeli, A. (2022). Positive Chair-CEO work relationships: micro-relational foundations of organisational capabilities. *Long Range Planning*, *55*(3), 102124. https://doi.org/10.1016/j.lrp.2021.102124

Stewart, A., & Hitt, M. A. (2012). Why can't a family business be more like a non-family business? Modes of professionalisation in family firms. *Management Faculty Research and Publications*, *155*. Retrieved from https://epublications.marquette.edu/mgmt_fac

Szücs, A., Szanto, K., Adalbert, J., Wright, A. G. C., Clark, L., & Dombrovski, A. Y. (2020). Status, rivalry and admiration-seeking in narcissism and depression: a behavioral study. *PLoS ONE*, *15*(12 December), 1–17. https://doi.org/10.1371/journal.pone.0243588

Vernon, P. A., Villani, V. C., Vickers, L. C., & Harris, J. A. (2008). A behavioral genetic investigation of the dark triad and the big 5. *Personality and Individual Differences*, *44*(2), 445–452. https://doi.org/10.1016/j.paid.2007.09.007

Waldkirch, M., Nordqvist, M., & Melin, L. (2018). CEO turnover in family firms: how social exchange relationships influence whether a non-family CEO stays or leaves. *Human Resource Management Review*, *28*(1), 56–67. https://doi.org/10.1016/j.hrmr.2017.05.006

Wei, W., Zhou, Y., & Wang, D. (2023). Learning to integrate conflicts: paradoxical leadership fosters team innovation. *Journal of Business Research*, *165*(May), 114076. https://doi.org/10.1016/j.jbusres.2023.114076

Yang, X., Li, J., Stanley, L. J., Kellermanns, F. W., & Li, X. (2020). How family firm characteristics affect internationalization of Chinese family SMEs. *Asia Pacific Journal of Management*, *37*(2), 417–448. https://doi.org/10.1007/s10490-018-9579-7

Chapter 12

Bending the Rules of the Game: Dark Entrepreneurship in a Capitalist System

Gbemisola Ogbolu and Suzanne Hague

Introduction

In the grand theatre of capitalism, entrepreneurs are often celebrated for their innovation and risk-taking. While the system enables profit creation and exploitation (Leary, 2019), the relentless pursuit of profit can push some towards unethical ventures, blurring the lines between innovation and exploitation. Knight (2013) suggests that entrepreneurs, as calculated risk-takers, may often navigate murky waters in their quest for success. Understanding dark entrepreneurship as a byproduct of the capitalist drive for profit necessitates examining specific factors within this system that encourage unethical behaviours. Safran and Ozdemirci (2020) argue that dark entrepreneurial activities are incentivised by an economic environment that rewards short-term gains over long-term stability and ethics. Schmidtz (2013) describes a regulatory landscape where parasitic behaviour can be more lucrative than genuine productivity. Cooke (2020) adds that the allure of rapid innovation and market dominance can lead entrepreneurs to rationalise questionable practices under the guise of disrupting traditional industries and driving progress. These factors create a fertile ground for dark entrepreneurship, exploiting systemic vulnerabilities to their advantage, often at significant social costs. The impacts of such practices are widespread,

DOI: 10.4324/9781003475262-15

affecting economic equity and diminishing trust in the business sector. Grant (2014) contrasts 'givers', who create trusting networks, with 'takers', who extract maximum personal benefit at the expense of others. There is also potential for substantial innovation through ventures that initially push ethical boundaries. Addressing these challenges requires reforms in legal frameworks and fostering a culture where ethical conduct is rewarded within capitalist enterprises. John D. Rockefeller, for instance, used his wealth to address social problems (Shaw et al., 2011), though Abrahamson (2013) notes that such actions can have political connotations affecting policy and regulation.

This chapter primarily focuses on the push factors within capitalism that breed dark entrepreneurship. While some may be attracted by ambition to build something new (pull factor), the harsh realities of the capitalist system often force individuals to navigate market fringes, making dark ventures seem like a viable path to survival or economic advancement. Saunders-Hastings (2021) discusses 'dirty money', explaining how ill-gotten gains are often used to create better situations or societies. High unemployment, limited resources, intense competition, and lax enforcement create an environment where ethical considerations are sidelined in the scramble for success. Within dark entrepreneurship, a spectrum exists; some ventures are purely exploitative, while others might possess innovative potential despite adopting unorthodox methods (Pidduck & Tucker, 2022).

This chapter reflects on the activities of the *National Agency for Food and Drug Administration and Control (hereon referred to as NAFDAC)* in combating unethical practices in Nigeria's food and drug market. It explores the importance of adopting a culture of ethical business conduct and the need to promote an equitable playing field that mitigates the push factors toward dark entrepreneurship. It proposes potential solutions for change and discusses the necessity of systemic reforms.

Dark Entrepreneurship: Definition and Characteristics

Entrepreneurship is a transdisciplinary field with a rich history. Originating from Latin in the 1700s and entering the English lexicon in the 19th century, the term's roots can be traced to scholars like Cantillon (Redlich, 1949). Early approaches have been criticised for not addressing the micro aspects of entrepreneurship—when, why, and how it occurs (Fitz-Koch et al., 2018). Its modern resurgence aligns with changing social perceptions, economic evolution, and the importance of innovation in a globalised world. This prominence is evident in the extensive international research on entrepreneurship, the economy, and innovation (Kiss et al., 2012).

Whilst research continues to flourish, a lesser-known aspect of entrepreneurship is "the dark side," where individuals engage in destructive business practices for personal gain, causing significant harm. Sorensen and Sharkey (2014) note that society often fails to foresee the relationship between entrepreneurs and their actions. Wilson and Stokes (2006) highlight the difference between the behaviour of entrepreneurs and the process of entrepreneurship. Thus, defining dark entrepreneurship and understanding its motivations presents a valuable research opportunity.

The concept of entrepreneurship is continually evolving to reflect changing social and economic landscapes (Bruton, Ahlstrom, & Li, 2010). Entrepreneurship involves identifying opportunities and initiating the creation of new products or services. Schumpeter (1885–1950) is often credited as the first economist to emphasise the role of entrepreneurship in economic development. Schumpeter highlighted the importance of individual entrepreneurs who innovate by introducing new production methods, products, and organisational forms (Schumpeter, 1942). Entrepreneurs, with their vision, risk tolerance, and resourcefulness, drive economic growth and innovation (Ireland, Hitt, & Sirmon, 2003). However, the pursuit of profit can sometimes lead entrepreneurs down a darker path. Dark entrepreneurship refers to unethical business practices aimed at short-term gain, including selling counterfeit products, engaging in deceptive marketing, or exploiting regulatory loopholes (Theoharakis, Voliotis, & Pollack, 2021). While generating profit is a natural part of business, entrepreneurship should ideally provide broader benefits beyond financial gain. The sociological approach to entrepreneurship links economic and social contexts, showing how innovation and positive change are essential aspects of its impact (Martinez-Martinez, 2022). Despite this, a growing emphasis on materialism and consumerism can overshadow positive aspects. The focus on quick profits and the ease of acquiring financial resources in some cases have led to an increase in dark entrepreneurship. Individuals motivated by a desire for quick wealth and ethical disregard are drawn to this path, which can diminish society's overall productive capacity as more people turn to illegal or unethical wealth acquisition methods.

The challenge lies in promoting entrepreneurship that fosters innovation and economic growth while adhering to ethical principles. This requires creating an environment that rewards responsible business practices, discourages dark entrepreneurship, and emphasises the long-term social and economic benefits of ethical conduct. Entrepreneurship should balance risk-taking with ethical behaviour, ensuring that innovation leads to positive change rather than exploitation or harm. Thus, entrepreneurship should not be solely about making money but also about creating value for individuals and society.

Duality of Entrepreneurship towards Innovation and Exploitation

The popular image of the entrepreneur is a heroic, often maverick individual, characterised by a drive to accumulate personal fortune with a groundbreaking idea and driven by the relentless pursuit of success (Bishop & Green, 2008). This narrative, while inspiring, paints an incomplete picture. Entrepreneurship exists on a spectrum, fuelled by both ambition and necessity, with the potential for both innovation and exploitation. We explore the various forces that motivate individuals to embark on the entrepreneurial journey, focusing on the contrasting pull and push factors and the potential for ethical grey areas that can lead to dark entrepreneurship.

Pull Factors and Opportunity

Entrepreneurship is about identifying and seizing opportunities. This pull towards innovation is often driven by a combination of factors. Some entrepreneurs are motivated by a strong desire for achievement and a burning ambition to build something new and impactful (Sorensen & Sharkey, 2014). Others are drawn to the potential for financial independence and the ability to control their destiny. Additionally, some individuals possess a natural inclination for creativity and innovation, constantly seeking solutions to problems and identifying unmet needs in the market (Koellinger, 2008). These pull factors, often referred to as opportunity-based entrepreneurship create a fertile ground for ideas and ventures.

Push Factors and Necessity

Not all entrepreneurs are driven by ambition and opportunity. For many, particularly those facing economic constraints or limited opportunities, entrepreneurship becomes a matter of necessity (Morris et al., 2023). This push factor, often referred to as necessity-based entrepreneurship (Tipu, 2016), can be fuelled by high unemployment. When traditional job opportunities are scarce, individuals may turn to entrepreneurship as a means of self-employment and income generation. Also, individuals with limited access to capital, education, or training may find entrepreneurship to be the only viable path to economic advancement. Finally, systemic inequalities can limit upward mobility for certain groups, pushing them towards entrepreneurial ventures to overcome these barriers. Entrepreneurship driven by necessity can be a powerful force for economic empowerment. However, it can also lead to a peculiar set of challenges. Necessity entrepreneurs might lack the resources, skills, or market knowledge to build sustainable ventures (Morris et al., 2023). This pressure to survive may lead them to compromise on ethical considerations or take shortcuts, blurring the lines between legitimate business practices and dark entrepreneurship.

The Dark Side of Innovation

The dark side is commonly used as a synonym for evil, dangerous, and harmful. Dark entrepreneurship can be motivated by a complex interplay of pull and push factors. While some are driven by pure greed and the allure of easy money, others may leverage dark entrepreneurship to escape poverty or secure their livelihood. This aligns with the moral disengagement theory, where individuals find justification to defend their immoral behaviour (Qin et al., 2022). The methods employed by dark entrepreneurs can vary widely. They may engage in activities like producing and selling counterfeit goods ranging from fake medication to luxury items; market manipulation which may involve creating artificial scarcity, price fixing, or misleading advertising practices to gain an unfair advantage; and exploiting loopholes in unregulated sectors to engage in unethical practices. The consequences of dark entrepreneurship are far-reaching. Consumers are directly harmed by fake products and unfair market practices. It erodes trust in legitimate businesses and weakens the overall market infrastructure. Furthermore, it can exacerbate existing social inequalities by disproportionately impacting lower-income consumers who may be more susceptible to predatory pricing or unaware of the dangers of counterfeit products.

The relationship between entrepreneurship and dark entrepreneurship is complex. While some dark ventures are purely exploitative, others might possess the potential for disruptive innovation. For instance, in pushing the competitive edge, some dark entrepreneurs may stretch the boundaries of creativity and innovation, which could later be adopted and legitimised within the broader market. However, it is crucial to distinguish between genuine innovation and mere cutting corners at the expense of consumer safety and ethical business practices (Zadek, 1998).

The Capitalist Imperative and the Unequal Playing Field

Several theoretical frameworks can be used to understand dark entrepreneurship within a capitalist system. For instance, institutional theory suggests that weak institutions and regulations create opportunities for dark entrepreneurship. When enforcement mechanisms are lax or unclear, individuals are more likely to exploit loopholes and engage in unethical practices (Bruton et al., 2010). In countries with weak intellectual property laws, the protection of business interests may be compromised. Conversely, the strain theory focuses on the concept of anomie, a state of normlessness where traditional goals (e.g., financial success) are emphasised, but legitimate means of achieving them are limited (Agnew, 2006). In a capitalist system, social pressure to achieve wealth can be immense. When legitimate avenues for success are unavailable, especially for those facing social and economic marginalisation, individuals may resort to dark entrepreneurship to bridge the gap between their aspirations and reality. Similarly, the dark triad describes three personality characteristics (narcissism, psychopathy, and Machiavellianism) that may impact entrepreneurial intention and behaviour.

With its ethos of competition and relentless pursuit of profit, capitalism is often hailed as the engine of economic progress. Yet, beneath the gleaming narrative lies a shadow: the inherent inequalities woven into the very fabric of the system. There is often a constant pressure to maximise profit within a capitalist framework which can create an uneven playing field that pushes individuals towards the fringes of the market, fostering the rise of dark entrepreneurship (Appleby, 2011). Access to capital, the lifeblood of any venture, is a major hurdle for new businesses. Traditional financial institutions view them as high-risk and are hesitant to invest, leaving individuals from low-income backgrounds struggling to secure initial resources (Ogbolu, 2021). Additionally, navigating the labyrinthine regulatory system further disadvantages smaller businesses. Established companies, with their legal teams, have a clear advantage in traversing these bureaucratic hurdles. Moreover, market fragmentation and information asymmetry further tilt the scales. Large corporations benefit from economies of scale and brand recognition, dominating certain market segments. Smaller players struggle to compete due to limited marketing budgets and difficulty reaching a wider audience.

The pressure to succeed within this uneven playing field can force individuals towards desperate measures. For those facing limited opportunities or struggling to make ends meet, entrepreneurship becomes a matter of survival, not simply ambition. This creates fertile ground for dark entrepreneurship, as individuals engage in unethical practices to achieve financial success on a playing field already stacked against them. Scholars argue that inherent inequalities within capitalism create a system rigged in favour of the wealthy and powerful (Reich, 2020; Stiglitz, 2019). This unequal playing field pushes individuals towards the fringes of the market, incentivising some to engage in dark entrepreneurial practices. For instance, limited access to capital can force aspiring entrepreneurs to turn to loan sharks with predatory interest rates, creating a cycle of debt that makes ethical business practices seem unsustainable. This situation exemplifies the desperation that can fuel dark entrepreneurship. Individuals trapped in such a cycle might resort to selling counterfeit goods or engaging in other unethical activities simply to make ends meet and service their crushing debt burdens.

A Glimpse into Dark Entrepreneurship

In December 2023, NAFDAC conducted a raid in a popular market in Eastern Nigeria, uncovering a large-scale operation selling counterfeit wines, soft drinks, and medications (Ugwu, 2023). The agency found recycled bottles, dubious colourings, sweeteners, and unknown chemicals being used, raising serious safety concerns. The volume of seized products, estimated at over 1,500 cartons with a street value of approximately $1.7 million, underscores the scale and motivation behind dark enterprises. While counterfeit wines and soft drinks pose significant concerns regarding consumer safety due to potential contamination, the presence of fake medications raises an even more alarming issue. Counterfeit medicines can be ineffective, contain the wrong dosage, or be laced with harmful substances, potentially leading to serious health complications and even death. As in many developing countries, Nigeria's healthcare system already faces a myriad of challenges, the proliferation of fake medication further complicates this situation.

This case study exemplifies the complex interplay of factors that contribute to the rise of dark entrepreneurship. Push factors, often driven by necessity, likely played a significant role (Morris et al., 2023). Nigeria contends with high unemployment rates, particularly among young people (Adesina, 2013). Limited access to capital and formal employment opportunities can push individuals towards the outer fringe of the market, making dark enterprises seem like a viable, albeit risky, option for survival. Furthermore, weak regulatory frameworks and lax enforcement create an environment where dark entrepreneurs can operate with relative impunity. The scope of the raid highlights the urgency for strengthened institutions and stricter enforcement mechanisms to deter such illegal activities. Pull factors, driven by greed and the lure of easy money as mentioned above, also play a pivotal role. The potential for significant financial gain, especially considering the high volume of counterfeit products in this case, can be a powerful motivation.

The NAFDAC raid is a crucial step towards curbing dark entrepreneurship. However, it represents only a single intervention within a larger systemic issue. Addressing the root causes of this phenomenon requires a multi-faceted and multi-agency approach. First, strengthening regulatory frameworks and empowering enforcement agencies with adequate resources is crucial. Increased inspections and stricter penalties for the perpetrators who produce and sell counterfeit goods, coupled with improved public awareness campaigns about the dangers of fake products are also essential. Likewise, fostering a culture of ethical business practice is fundamental to improving the overall business climate of the country. Education programs and incentives for aspiring entrepreneurs, which emphasise ethical sourcing, production processes, and responsible marketing, can help create a new generation of entrepreneurs who prioritise sustainability, social value, and consumer safety. Moreover, addressing the socio-economic factors that push individuals towards dark entrepreneurship as a last resort is vital. This includes initiatives to create more employment opportunities, improve access to capital, and provide continuous training and development. Nations facing similar challenges need to work towards creating a more sustainable and ethical entrepreneurial ecosystem. Dark entrepreneurship harms consumers, erodes trust in legitimate businesses, and weakens the overall market economy. Such practices exacerbate social inequalities by disproportionately impacting lower-income consumers who are more susceptible to predatory pricing or unaware of the dangers of counterfeit products.

Lessons for Leaders

Leaders across various sectors must confront the complex phenomenon of dark entrepreneurship. Recognising both push and pull factors is a crucial first step for leaders to develop effective solutions. Addressing dark entrepreneurship requires a multi-pronged approach. Strengthening regulatory frameworks is essential and policymakers should prioritise creating robust legal systems that deter unethical practices. For instance, increased funding for regulatory bodies and stricter penalties for violations can serve as a deterrent. Additionally, consolidating the process for reporting suspected dark entrepreneurial activities can empower individuals to come forward (Manesh et al., 2024). Business leaders also have a significant role to play by implementing clear and comprehensive codes of conduct. Training programs on ethical sourcing, production, and marketing equip employees to identify and avoid unethical behaviour. Partnering with NGOs or academic institutions to develop educational resources on ethical entrepreneurship can foster a new generation of business owners. Additionally, cultivating a culture of transparency and accountability across sectors is essential. Collaborating with media and industry associations to raise awareness about the dangers of dark entrepreneurship can further shift mindsets towards ethical conduct. It is equally important to address the underlying socio-economic factors that push individuals towards the fringes of the market. Policymakers can create more employment opportunities, particularly for young people, through job training programs or subsidies for businesses that hire young workers. Investing in vocational training and skills development will equip individuals with marketable skills, making them less susceptible to dark entrepreneurship. Strengthening social safety nets provides a safety cushion for those struggling financially, reducing the pressure to resort to desperate measures.

Finally, the fight against dark entrepreneurship cannot be won by a single entity. Effective solutions require collaboration across different sectors. Leaders can establish multi-stakeholder forums that bring together policymakers, regulators, business leaders, and academic experts to develop comprehensive strategies. Encouraging information sharing, fostering a culture of financial disclosure, and developing joint initiatives that address the social, economic, and regulatory aspects of dark entrepreneurship are all crucial steps toward a more ethical and sustainable business landscape.

Conclusion

This chapter examined the conceptualisations, motivations, and consequences of dark entrepreneurship within a capitalist system. The case study discussed represents the dangers of unethical business practices, particularly the life-threatening risks of counterfeit products. We offer practical lessons for policymakers, regulators, business executives, and SMEs on the importance of developing effective interventions to create a more ethical marketplace. Entrepreneurship is a powerful force that can drive economic growth and innovation. However, there is a dark side to it. By taking proactive measures to address its root causes, leaders can foster a more sustainable and ethical entrepreneurial ecosystem. This approach empowers individuals to pursue legitimate ventures that benefit themselves, their communities, and broader society. Ultimately, the future of entrepreneurship rests in the hands of leaders who will navigate its duality, promoting innovation alongside ethical conduct to create a more positive and responsible marketplace for all.

References

Abrahamson, E. (2013). Beyond charity: A century of philanthropy innovation. The Rockefeller Foundation. https://www.rockefellerfoundation.org/reports/beyond-charity-a-century-of-philanthropy-innovation/

Adesina, O. S. (2013). Unemployment and security challenges in Nigeria. *International Journal of Humanities and Social Science*, *3*(7), 146–156.

Agnew, R. (2006). *Pressured into crime: An overview of general strain theory*. Roxbury Publishing.

Appleby, J. (2011). *The relentless revolution: A history of capitalism*. W.W. Norton & Company.

Bishop, M., & Green, M. (2008) *Philanthrocapitalism: How the rich can save the world*. Bloomberg Press.

Bruton, G. D., Ahlstrom, D., & Li, H. L. (2010). Institutional theory and entrepreneurship: Where are we now and where do we need to move in the future? *Entrepreneurship Theory and Practice*, *34*(3), 421–440. https://doi.org/10.1111/j.1540-6520.2010.00390.x

Cooke, P. (2020). Dark entrepreneurship, the 'dark triad' and its potential 'light triad' realisation in 'green entrepreneurship'. *Urban Science*, *4*(4), 45.

Fitz-Koch, S., Nordqvist, M., Carter, S., & Hunter, E. (2018). Entrepreneurship in the agricultural sector: A literature review and future research opportunities. *Entrepreneurship Theory and Practice*, *42*(1), 129–166.

Grant, A. (2014). *Give and take*. Weidenfeld & Nicholson.

Ireland, R. D., Hitt, M. A., & Sirmon, D. G. (2003). A model of strategic entrepreneurship: The construct and its dimensions. *Journal of Management*, *29*(6), 963–989. https://doi.org/10.1016/S0149-2063_03_00086-2

Kiss, A. N., Danis. W. M., & Cavusgil, S. T. (2012). International entrepreneurship research in emerging economies: A critical review and research agenda. *Journal of Business Venturing*, *27*(2), 266–290.

Knight, F. H. (2013). *Risk, uncertainty and profit*. Vernon Press.

Koellinger, P. (2008). Why are some entrepreneurs more innovative than others? *Small Business Economics*, *31*, 21–37. https://doi.org/10.1007/s11187-008-9107-0

Leary, J. P. (2019). *Keywords: The new language of capitalism*. Haymarket Books.

Manesh, M., Tavakoli, A., Oyewunmi, A. E., & Pillay, S. (2024). Ethical decision-making in East Africa: Predictors of whistleblowing intention. *Society and Business Review*, *19*(3), 424–454. https://doi.org/10.1108/SBR-03-2022-0067

Martinez-Martinez, S. L. (2022). Entrepreneurship as a multidisciplinary phenomenon: Culture and individual perceptions in business creation. *Academia Revista Latinoamericana de Administración*, *35*(4), 537–565.

Morris, S., Carlos, C., Kistruck, G. M., Lount, R. B. Jr., & Thomas, T. E. (2023). The impact of growth mindset training on entrepreneurial action among necessity entrepreneurs: Evidence from a randomized control trial. *Strategic Entrepreneurship Journal, 17*(3), 671–692.

Ogbolu, G. (2021). *The impact of entrepreneurial orientation on SMEs' performance in Nigeria: The moderating role played by entrepreneurial ecosystems.* University of Northumbria.

Pidduck, R. J., & Tucker, R. (2022). Meaningful heterodoxies: Advancing entrepreneurship through engagement with unorthodox phenomena. *Journal of Business Venturing Insights, 18*, e00319.

Qin, X., Shepherd, D. A., Lin, D., Xie, S., Liang, X., & Lin, S., 2022. The dark side of entrepreneurs' creativity: Investigating how and when entrepreneurs' creativity increases the favourability of potential opportunities that harm nature. *Entrepreneurship Theory and Practice, 46*(4), 857–883.

Redlich, F., 1949. The origin of the concepts of "entrepreneur" and "creative entrepreneur". *Explorations in Entrepreneurial History, 1*(2), 1–7.

Reich, R. B. (2020). *The system: Who rigged it, how we fix it.* Vintage.

Safran, B., & Ozdemirci, A. (2020). The dark or bright side of entrepreneurs' social capital: Effects on creativity and innovation. *Business Management and Strategy, 11*(1), 17.

Saunders-Hastings, E. (2021). Send back the bloodstained money: Frederick Douglas on tainted gifts. *American Political Science Review, 115*(3), 729–741.

Schmidtz, D. (2013). Adam Smith on the dark side of capitalism. *Georgetown Journal of Law & Public Policy, 11*, 371.

Schumpeter, J. A. (1942). *Capitalism, Socialism and Democracy.* New YorK: Harper & Row.

Shaw, E., Gordon, J., Harvey, C., & Maclean, M. (2011). Exploring contemporary entrepreneurial philanthropy. *International Small Business Journal, 31*(5), 580–599.

Sorensen, J. B., & Sharkey, A. J. (2014). Entrepreneurship as a mobility process. *American Sociological Review, 79*(2), 328–349.

Stiglitz, J. E. (2019). *People, power, and profits: Progressive capitalism for an age of discontent.* Penguin Books Ltd.

Theoharakis, V., Voliotis, S. & Pollack, J. M. (2021). Going down the slippery slope of legitimacy lies in early-stage ventures: The role of moral disengagement. *Journal of Business Ethics, 172*, 673–690. https://doi.org/10.1007/s10551-020-04508-2

Tipu, S. A. A. (2016). Comparing the behaviour of opportunity and necessity driven entrepreneurs. *International Journal of Entrepreneurship and Small Business, 27*, 84. https://doi.org/10.1504/IJESB.2016.073359

Ugwu, C. (2023). NAFDAC destroys fake wines in Abia, shuts market. https://www.premiumtimesng.com/news/top-news/652455-nafdac-destroys-fake-wines-in-abia-shuts-market.html?tztc=1

Wilson, N., & Stokes, D. (2006). *Enterprise education: The road less travelled.* National Council for Graduate Entrepreneurship (NCGE).

Zadek, S. (1998). Balancing performance, ethics, and accountability. *Journal of Business Ethics, 17*(13), 1421–1442.

Chapter 13

Voluntary Veils and Community Camouflage: Finding Darkness in the United Kingdom's Voluntary, Community and Social Enterprise Sector

Jennifer Hagan and Lucy Philipson

Introduction

When people hear the terms 'voluntary', 'non-profit', 'charity', and 'volunteer,' the connotations are unavoidable. While extensive research has shown we cannot realistically consider individuals who participate in such activity as entirely selfless (Bussell & Forbes, 2002; Hagan, 2014) or as 'angelic humanitarians' (Smith, 1983), still 40 years later, studies found that the general perception is that volunteers as warmer, more generous and friendlier than paid employees, identifying pro-social traits including competence, and altruism as core motives for their actions (Peiffer et al., 2020). As these individuals constitute the majority of organisations in the VCSE, including many of its leaders, the perception is expected to permeate to the organisational level. Aaker et al. (2010) found public perception of non-profit organisations as 'warm', proposing that perceptions of an

DOI: 10.4324/9781003475262-16

organisation depend on whether they are profit-making or not. However, Tavanti and Tait (2021) state that the sector is subject to darkness just as any other is, perhaps more so. Despite these engendering conflicts, the growth in the VCSE in terms of scale and diversity in the UK, and the rapid growth of the dark leadership research, there is little investigation into VCSE leadership: who leads, why, what they do, and how does the context impact these variables?

Three suggestions we make here challenge assumptions on three 'levels', proposing that the sector may engender dark leadership through:

i. There is an increased opportunity to hide or disguise unethical motives and behaviours than in other sector contexts.
ii. The legitimisation of dark actions and behaviours through a pro-organisational behaviour lens i.e., 'for the good of the beneficiaries and organisation'.
iii. Influence/jurisdiction regarding ethical standards not applied equitably across sectors, leaving the VCSE exposed.

The above may be fostered through different levels of leadership and stages of relationships between organisations and individuals, from an initial motivation to entrenched cultures, and it may exist at conscious or subconscious levels.

These three suggestions above are linked to exploitative and destructive leadership in the UK VCSE and can, unfortunately, be explored through tabloid headlines and high-profile investigation reports as much as academic literature. Nonetheless, there is a need for greater primary research. We know charities are often used as a front for nefarious activities, setting up nonprofit vehicles to funnel or siphon funds available only to such organisations (Charity Commission, 2019a) and using such funds for other purposes. According to the Charity Commission (2019b, p. 1), "relatively little is known about the nature and extent of charity fraud, resulting in vulnerabilities", and overall investigations of charity wrongdoing, specifically into safeguarding issues, increased by 144% from 2017 to 2018. On a surface level, it may seem unsurprising that the sector offers camouflage perhaps attracting those with dark intentions, but our interest is deeper than this. We examine the commonalities between what has been revealed very publicly about the VCSEs 'dark corners', and the darkness, which is much more subtle, yet even endemic, both extremes representative of the uniquely powerful factors of this fascinating context.

Context-Dependent Dark Leadership?

In 2015, *The Journal of Business Ethics* published Boddy's fascinating longitudinal study of a UK charity CEO as a 'corporate psychopath' with outcomes of bullying, staff withdrawal, and turnover, and understandably, as a result, organisational decline in revenue, creativity, and innovation. Interestingly, though, these outcomes were produced through leadership, which was described as at times 'conceptually and intellectually absent' rather than just actively negative, leaving employees 'aimless'. The focus on the individual rather than the context is interesting, alongside assertions that there is a context deficit in what we know about leadership, which Johns (2024) attributes as a manifestation of our romantic views of leadership. This begs the question given our romantic perceptions of the VCSE and those involved in it – surely an understanding of leaders and context here is even more important?

Psychopaths are generally assumed to be those who act without conscience, constituting approximately 1% of the population (Stout, 2005). This percentage has been repeatedly found to be higher in leadership positions (Vergauwe et al., 2021) and higher in certain types of organisations. Expectedly such contexts are those in which money and power are evidently 'available' to those individuals, more expected in the for-profit sector. However, research in organisations in the non-profit, charitable sector is extremely limited by comparison; the evidence of dark leadership is not here simply because it has not been looked for. In fact, dark leadership research significantly favours the exploration of individuals rather than context to understand this phenomenon. Where context is explored it is usually in a cultural or geographical sense rather than sector or purpose.

While the VCSE may appear to be less financially rewarding as it is generally considered 'third' by name and nature, when it comes to power, a consideration of the exploitative and destructive leadership seen over recent years could turn this view on its head almost entirely. In a context where purposes are supposedly entirely for the benefit of the planet and its inhabitants, usually the most vulnerable, there is a readily available 'veil' for leaders seeking to protect or hide their own agendas. In a very similar way to discussions of greenwashing by corporates associating themselves with charitable organisations to enhance, reduce, or disguise perceptions of their core activities, individuals with dark intentions may gravitate towards the sector for these same benefits. Tavanti and Tait (2021) saw the uniqueness of this context linked to dark leadership, developing a theoretical model of nonprofit-specific toxic leadership, noting the influence of destructive leaders, susceptible followers, and conducive environments creating a 'toxic triangle'. They highlight a 'mission impossible' facing most non-profits amid an incredibly complex, challenging, and changing landscape making them vulnerable to leadership abuse. Tavanti and Tait (2021) discuss the impacts on public trust, and although the high-profile examples discussed here connect to that, our interest is in tying these examples together to suggest that the UK VCSE is just as subject to dark leadership, and its implications as for-profit organisations and its unique context makes it more so.

Context-dependent leadership was borne out of a limitation in leadership theory: a focus on the individual, their traits, styles, and actions. Recognition that leadership does not occur in a vacuum (House & Aditya, 1997; Porter & McLaughlin, 2006) has increasingly focused on a range of contextual factors and types, from task and culture to the meso-economic, with purpose-specific sector and industry range being broadened all the time to highlight distinctive places for leaders. Over time, the issue of context went off the boil, and in the early 21st century, a call was again made to recognise its importance for leadership (Porter & McLaughlin, 2006).

Yet, a deficit remains. What has not happened is adequate recognition of the importance of context in dark leadership literature, despite its huge surge in popularity for publication. It has been argued by dark leadership researchers, in education particularly, that context remains in the shadows of leadership study (Hallinger, 2018). The most common knowledge sought and gained in context-focused leadership research is of the role of context as a moderator between leadership styles and outcomes, and Johns (2024) reminds us that a simple misfit between context and leader can make good leadership turn bad. Dark leadership can be a result of context in the sense of poor contextual fit (Ziegert et al., 2021) but what about when it is a 'good' fit? We see arguments that leadership roles offer psychopaths opportunities to be their 'dark selves', so why not contexts? Here we take on one of Johns' (2024) recommendations to highlight the importance of context in dark leadership, looking at the unique qualities of the UK VCSE.

Events, Behaviour and Change: Dark Times in the UK VCSE

To better understand the relationship between context and dark leadership, we focus on three factors that often work together in times of crisis: events, behaviour, and change. Olive Cooke is a name that should be known by anyone remotely connected to UK fundraising. She was a humanitarian; she was financially abused and was responsible for probably the most significant sector-wide change seen by the VCSE. In terms of events, behaviour, and change, things don't get much bigger for leaders in this context or much darker. Olive was hounded by charitable organisations and their affiliates who shared, misused, bought, and sold the details of so many vulnerable people like her until she sadly took her own life in 2015, aged 92. Leader responses from the sector were shockingly absent, and a wide range of unethical, unlawful, and at times illegal practices were revealed to have been continuing across organisations large and small for many years as part of a culture in which these actions were commonplace and considered acceptable.

Recognised in the highly critical *Etherington Inquiry* of 2016, the Olive Cooke affair sparked understandable mistrust in charities, but also much stronger data regulation, a new monitoring body, and efforts to focus on donor experience through a Commission. A total of 18 key recommendations were made by Etherington and 25 made in the Donor Commission, but it is argued we have not come far enough at all several years on (Sargeant, 2021). Although there has been a change in this event, the behaviours which caused it were undoubtedly emblematic of dark leadership in a context that had a twist: its behaviours were less governed, perceived differently, and somewhat legitimised, because of where it was happening. The sad reality is Olive Cooke is not the first or only headline-grabbing example of how dark leadership in the VCSE has been allowed to continue.

The exploitation of the vulnerable was seen in a very different form in Haiti. This was exhibited by leaders of the UK-based charity, Oxfam in 2019 after an almost ten-year cover-up of sexual abuse by the organisation. At least 222,500 people were killed by the catastrophic earthquake in Haiti in 2010, 300,000 were injured and 1.3 million were displaced. Members of Oxfam's humanitarian aid staff and volunteers at the senior level were found to have sexually abused young children. Disturbingly, the England and Wales Charity Commission CEO commented after the full independent investigation in 2019 that, "what went wrong in Haiti did not happen in isolation" (Stephenson cited by BBC Online, 11/6/2019). Stephenson confidently noted that "over a period of years, Oxfam's internal culture tolerated poor behaviour, and at times lost sight of the values it stands for", highlighting that seniority in the organisation had influenced the level of disciplinary action, which the charity's Chair of trustees acknowledged as a "terrible abuse of power" (Thomson cited by BBC online 11/6/2019). Tavanti and Tait (2021) consider the Oxfam case and argue that it exemplifies "all the trajectories of nonprofit toxic leadership behaviours" (p. 12):

i. Senior leadership demonstrated a lack of safeguarding for their most vulnerable stakeholders, violating Oxfam's mission.
ii. Staff and volunteers (including those working closely with the director) failed to properly report violations.
iii. Regulatory policy and monitoring mechanisms were inadequate, enabling and legitimising delayed responses.

Here, we can see dark leadership both through the absence of leadership and through exploitation as found by Boddy within the VCSE (2015).

The case of Kids Company is more complex in terms of dark leadership. Allegations made in 2015 against former founder and CEO Camila Batmanghelidjh and seven former trustees led to the charity's collapse. However, after a lengthy court case, these allegations of failure to operate the charity "on a proper and financially sustainable basis" (Butler in The Guardian 12/2/2021) were thrown out. While courts agreed these individuals were not to blame for the charity's failure as depicted and that they should not be banned from holding such powerful positions, questions about their leadership, and others, still abound. The judge in 2019 reflected on the charity's financial operations as risky, and in previous reports, there are references to an "extraordinary catalogue of failures of governance and control", negligent trustees, and an "unaccountable and dominant" CEO, creating an organisation which did not make decisions as it should (Public Administration & Constitutional Affairs Committee, 2016).

The unethical issues of leadership here demonstrate another key factor of context in the VCSE - the critical position of funding stakeholders. Over its operation, Kids Company received millions of pounds in central government grants, which were spent without any robust evidence of output or outcomes (Public Administration & Constitutional Affairs Committee, 2016). The charity had a range of high-level figures as public supporters and trustees, in government and the media, with Batmanghelidjh, the CEO, as a celebrity figurehead. The decision-making of the CEO may have at times been questioned, but part of the culture of risk was perpetuated by the charity's network, the investigation found. Dark leadership rarely considers actions beyond organisational 'walls', but to investigate this fully appreciative of the unique context of the VCSE, key stakeholders must be considered as leaders too. The element of risk associated with the charity's finances and associated decision-making is of note as characteristic of dark leadership.

All these examples compromised the individuals the organisations – and their people - supposedly existed to serve in different ways. The exploitative and destructive actions which took place in Haiti were not 'pro-organisational', but those in the case of Olive Cook and Kids Company illustrate behaviours that worked actively against their purposes and for them at the same time, predominantly around financial sustainability. Undoubtedly, thousands of supporters like Olive Cooke will have been abused into anxiety, depression, and in some horrific cases like hers, self-harm. Haiti survivors were sexually abused, and thousands of young people were at risk of being unsupported by Kids Company because their operation model was demand-led without the strength required to be sustainable. In all three cases, there was a sense of leaders being 'untouchable', whether through ignorance and hierarchy, arrogance, and others' negligence, stretching of the law to its limits, or keeping high-level company that sought to perpetuate and legitimise exploitative, destructive behaviours. While it is difficult to argue that individual leaders or the context are entirely at 'fault' here, the irresponsible and exploitative behaviours, particularly around risk-taking in all these examples demonstrate that across very different missions, locations, structures, and organisations, dark leadership was found to be in so many places in so many guises, at the same time.

Darkness Deeper in the Shadows

The extreme examples of abuse above are no doubt shocking, but the VCSE veil of ethics and 'light' over the darkness of certain leaders needs to be examined further. At the coalface, away from the boardroom, decisions are made that reveal a darkness that is undoubtedly exploitative, toxic, and destructive. We are talking about two different kinds of dark leadership here, and not just at senior levels: those who are attracted to the sector because of the coverage they can receive and those who become part of an existing culture. Lian et al. (2016) found that in for-profit organisations, unethical pro-organisational behaviour (UPOB), as opposed to unethical pro-self-behaviour in leaders, led to moral disengagement in employees, in turn increasing their likelihood to behave unethically. Umphresset al.'s seminal work on UPOB (2010) originally argued that this is likely to lead to behaviours that do not benefit the organisation and may even destroy it. Later, Lian et al. (2022) found that as employees learn from leader engagement in UPOB, they not only engage in UPOB but further unethical self-interested behaviours harmful to organisations. Employees were found to be more likely to commit unethical acts when observing leaders engaging in UPOB. Surely, this gives rise to the suggestion that where UPOB may more likely exist within non-profits, such darkness in leadership could be more prevalent, and even have the highest implications.

Another unique aspect of the VCSE context is the trend for a positive value-based role and strong organisational identification, juxtaposed against lower-than-average wages, great difficulty in recruitment, and insecurity of short-term contracts. There is a greater acceptance of unpaid overtime, possibly due to the voluntary, and non, almost anti-economic underpinnings of the sector. So much of this is seemingly not in an individual's self-interest. These factors could encourage UPOB to an individual's detriment leading to fatigue, dissatisfaction, and burnout, while they could also be entirely self-serving in attempting to combat themselves. Mishra et al. (2022) note that employees who fear job loss may perform UPOB in the hope of acceptance in the organisation (see also Ghosh, 2017). Strong identification with an organisation's charitable purpose is likely to further lead some to engage in UPOB to improve their position as well as help the organisation (Lee et al., 2019).

Umphress and Bingham (2011) note that UPOB presents an inherent conflict between the performance of an organisation and its ethical ideals. This potential reality could be 'easier to take' in contexts where profit, competition, and materiality are the core of the organisation (in terms of the sale of products, tangible goods, or experiences) or of course, where no ethical ideals are identified. When an organisation is entirely founded upon charitable goals, the very idea of UPOB existing seems absurd, almost impossible, yet those within it face additional challenges, both personally and in their roles, and perhaps there is a sense of greater invisibility and protection for unethical self-interested behaviours. These types of destructive leadership styles typically involve prioritising objectives at odds with those of the company and/or detrimental to the people who follow them (Bajaba et al., 2022). Exploitative leadership has yet to receive much-needed research despite its prevalence and importance (Schmid et al., 2017) in organisations where behaviour is at odds with the objectives of an organisation. In the VCSE, where these behaviours often occur perfectly (at least immediately) in line with the organisational objectives, there is potentially a melting pot.

Many effects of exploitative leadership have been identified in a range of industry contexts from tourism and sport to education, including knowledge sharing (Wang et al., 2023), workplace deviance (Lyu et al., 2023), absenteeism (Akhtar et al., 2022) and job strain (Bajaba et al., 2022). There are arguments to suggest mediating factors against the potential negative impact of exploitative leadership. Bajaba et al. (2022) suggest employees' proactive personalities mediate positively against these forms of leadership behaviour, reducing effectiveness, such as job strain. This links to instances where dark leadership leads to evidenced dissatisfaction in employees (Brouwers and Paltu, 2020) and volunteers and places much emphasis on the role and actions of designated leaders. However, something rarely touched upon again is where followers become accepting and part of a culture of dark operations of an organisation.

The framework by de Bruin Cardoso et al. (2024) on the influences of moral superiority, naivety, and justification is focused on the wider sectoral definition of non-government organisations but brilliantly identifies the key factors uniquely associated with such organisations (into which the VCSE falls) which lead to unethical behaviours at all levels. Their international exploratory findings suggest behaviours across organisational activities which would be described as corrupt, discriminatory, exploitative, and illegal, are far more commonplace than perceived, giving significant weight to an 'NGO Halo Effect'. A key aspect of their proposed framework identifies a connection between the voluntary nature of that sector, the perception that people within it are inherently 'good' and moral naivety, alongside beliefs that bending traditional rules is often morally justified because of the cause at the heart of the organisation. de Bruin Cardoso et al. (2024) argue that in such organisations, the import of the mission is elevated; thereby, the ends justify the means. One powerful quote from an interviewer indicates the potential connotations of this:

> We are not married to how we do it, we're married to the problem we're solving. If we found out tomorrow that giving hot dogs to children is more effective for [the mission of] religious freedom, then we'll sell hot dogs.
>
> *de Bruin Cardoso (2024, p.10, Interview 31)*

de Bruin Cardoso et al. (2024) found that in many NGO organisations, moral naivety, coupled with moral justification related to mission, meant a lack of policy, training, and lack of attention to it, quoting trust at 'face value' from staff. The perception of an organisation's people as inherently good, the likelihood that monitoring of behaviours and general ethical risk awareness is lower, becomes more likely too. The VCSE begins to look like a potential context not only attractive to dark leaders because it offers some concealment but also one at higher risk of compromise in every sense because of deep-seated internal beliefs, norms, and cultures based upon the very premise of morality and benevolence.

The Regulation of VCSE

It is concerning that despite the evident 'reach' of dark actions and attitudes in the examples above, there are continuing regulatory inconsistencies and omissions. While the cases of wrongdoing and harm in UK charities rose significantly from 2017 to 2018 (Charity Commission, 2019b), the annual data collection was halted in 2019 and closed formally in 2022. The Charity Commission serves all registered charities in England and Wales, while Scotland is regulated by the Office of the Scottish Charity Regulator (OSCR). In April 2024, OSCR launched a consultation to establish the purpose and parameters for a review of the organisation (OSCR, 2024). The review followed a consultation on Scottish Charity Law published in 2019 which saw many respondents agree that the criteria for disqualification and removal of charity trustees be extended to match the criteria in England and Wales. One of the 11 sections specifically focussed on ensuring that "a disbarred trustee of one charity was not able to take up a leadership role within another charity" (The Scottish Government, 2019, p. 6).

We have discussed VCSE leaders in a broad sense so far, but trustees are absolutely at the centre of this when we consider the average organisational vehicle and traditional hierarchical setup. The voluntary position of trustee boards can result in a lack of diversity, as with UK volunteering in general (Dean, 2022), the lived experience of charity recipients, and significant inequality. Willow (2023) notes that "boards remain on average majority wealthy, older, white, male and middle class. Diversity standards mean we are trying to tweak a fundamentally unequal structure". While attaining diversity is a moral imperative, we know workplace diversity leads to creativity and innovation; it can provide strategic advantage and is positively linked to organisational performance, found specifically in the nonprofit sector (Weisinger et al., 2016). A lack of diversity is naturally conducive to all the unfortunate opposites, but when considering the events and behaviours described above, we need to consider the links to entrenched cultures, lack of will/confidence to challenge, and a combination of similar attitudes and values. The advice of regulatory bodies on diversity and best management practices is widely available, but the civic core persists, and there is more they could do to stimulate diversity and utilising their powers in this space.

It does, however, remain a concern that Trustees are volunteers, often referred to as non-executive directors, who may or may not have legal responsibility for the financial solvency/sustainability of the organisation depending upon the charity vehicle used for its setup (social enterprise, inc. charity, CIC, etc.). Spear et al. (2007) propose the approaches taken by charity boards can be viewed within four perspective models, two of which – focused on stakeholders and partnerships - not only represent approaches strongly encouraged from all angles upon the VCSE but also result in reduced scrutiny of detail or internal supervision.

This further emphasises the fact that the charity hierarchy formation remains flawed, in that these trustee volunteers are seen by the Charity Commission as "custodians of their charities...publicly accountable and have responsibilities and duties to safeguard their charity and its beneficiaries" (2015, p.3). Despite the significant responsibility, Dent (2014) notes that "a remarkable consensus of experts on nonprofits agree that their governance is generally abysmal, considerably worse than that of for-profit corporations" (p. 93). This argument is founded upon the theory that, unlike corporate boards, held to account by shareholders; nonprofit boards are "legally self-perpetuating". This lack of consistent and clear regulation has been seen to create an environment where dark leadership can perpetuate. The traditional hierarchy of the VCSE can enable an environment where leadership approaches and decisions go unchallenged and are far from inclusive or collaborative. Opposing views as to where the power of decision-making and leadership lies are evident. Dent (2014) argues that trustees are "ill-informed, quarrelsome, clueless about their proper role and dominated by the CEO" (p. 93), while leadership powers are held predominantly by the CEO because uncertain directors "know nothing more than the CEO deigns to divulge" and are therefore "unlikely to even ask pointed questions, much less to challenge the CEO" (p. 110). In contrast, Willow (2023) states that:

> Many trustees struggle with their role, overstep, breach charity rules, or otherwise behave inappropriately. Bullying is rife – I can't count how many CEOs I know who have been bullied by trustees while the rest of the board does nothing.

Although these authors disagree with where the power lies, there is consensus in the belief that trustees lack awareness of their responsibilities, which perpetuates an environment where dark leadership can thrive, be it through bullying or fear, ignorance or acceptance. There is a further argument that the distance between trustee boards and operational staff, even from the CEO, may result in a lack of knowledge of what is 'really going on', or perhaps an opportunity to claim this as we so often see in for-profit scandals between the top and bottom of traditional hierarchies. The lonely CEO swiftly goes from fable to reality. This points to a potential root of dark leadership in this context, within the structure and hierarchy of the organisation, likely where the greatest emphasis is on regulation, outside-in and inside-out. An article published by the British Overseas NGOs for Development (BOND), an international charity network, examined the increased use of non-disclosure agreements (NDAs) in the charity sector to workplace harassment and discrimination, two extremely dark concepts. The article quoted a charity sector employee who stated - "if you are brave enough to make a formal complaint and put your head above the parapet, you have sealed your fate and most likely the end of your career at the charity" (Bheeroo, 2020). This culture of fear and lack of accountability would appear contradictory to the very nature of the sector, and yet organisations are more frequently using NDAs in everyday human resource practices.

While their focus was on the USA, Tavanti and Tait (2021) use examples that stretch to the UK to suggest there are systemic and organisational factors leading to a weaker regulatory environment surrounding non-profits. They argue that the wider systemic environment allows destructive leadership to occur, but further, there is a 'toxic triangle' of non-profit leadership that responds to susceptible followers combined with destructive leaders. Susceptible followers may have unmet needs or insecurity, which they feel require tactics of self-preservation that could involve UPOB or unethical self-interested behaviours in the face of low-paid short-term contracts, the norm across the sector. The focus of Tavanti and Tait (2021), however, is on leaders who are explicitly destructive to the organisation, rather than those engaging in UPOB. In situations where the three elements of the 'toxic triangle' are present, leaders in the VCSE may be more likely to engage in UPOB (as well as unethical self-interested behaviour), and the fact that this makes the implications potentially much less visible, must be acknowledged.

Not only are there inconsistencies in VCSE regulation, but also in the opportunities available to them to demonstrate ethical leadership and operations. Several regulations and external bodies have been set up in the last decade, particularly to encourage – and offer the benefits of – ethical, responsible decision-making in the for-profit world. The B Lab was founded in the USA in 2006 with a vision to make businesses a force for good, awarding certification to those who meet verified standards of social and environmental impact, commit to transparency requirements, and are legally accountable to all stakeholders (B-Corp, 2024). Amongst the assessment criteria are five key impact areas: governance, workers, community, environment, and customers. B-Corp is itself a non-profit, but non-profits are excluded from the process since they do not trade to earn income (B-Corp, 2024). Considering their fundamental purposes and recent scandals on top of this, with the rise of ESG and increasing pressure on corporate organisations to prove their CSR policies are not simply rhetoric or greenwashing, it is unusual that charities are excluded from this process. One might argue that regulations are in place, but research and reviews would suggest that these are insufficient. It is also, in line with the research on UPOB and context-dependent factors noted above, fair to suggest that perhaps the very fact that VCSE organisations have charitable purposes at their 'core' creates a perception that such additional expectations are unnecessary and that best practice is seen as a given.

However, we know from the stories above that this is simply not the case, and even in the case of Kid's Company where the charity's leader was exonerated from all charges, an additional monitoring/evaluation process could have been a critical lifeline to the organisation and its prior beneficiaries in recent years of investigation. Clearly, in that example, the investigative process and procedures even with such a public scandal and previous damning reports, were not of a standard to identify what was actually happening.

Lessons for Leaders

When considering what leaders can (and should) learn from the situations above it may appear simple: place the mission and beneficiaries at the heart of every action and decision. But in a context where pro-organisational behaviour can often be unethical, where there is a significant lack of diversity to challenge norms, and where those with naturally dark tendencies can hide their pursuits, it is certainly not simple. We can return to a simple question supposedly (and partly) answered by academic research noted at the start of this chapter to help us get somewhere though: are those involved in the VCSE inherently more ethical or selfless in their work? Much research has been done to show volunteers cannot be thought of in this way, and scandals have shown we absolutely should not assume VCSE organisations are more positive than any other in terms of their ethical standards of decision-making, but we continue to do so. We must raise awareness of the contextual factors surrounding the VCSE to highlight that these perceptions are just as risky as some of the behaviours we have seen over the past decade in the UK. VCSE leaders at all levels need greater awareness of the context they are working in, and in many ways, they need to work against it rather than rest on the laurels of the sector.

Those leaders with a penchant for the dark side will always be attracted to contexts that allow them to behave badly, but these are in the minority. The emphasis on stakeholders and partnerships may be seen as one which enables a lack of scrutiny, but it can also be utilised to bring in the advantages of a diversity of perspectives. If those VCSE leaders, in the vast majority who have a strong moral compass, can recognise the potential in this, they can bring in perspectives to begin to break down any negative cultures of exploitative or destructive behaviour, possibly through UPOB. This could be through the trustee board, closing the gap between those members, the operational staff of the organisation, and the full range of stakeholders (including beneficiaries) all at once. Leaders within regulation across the Charity Commission and OSCR could play their part in this, initially simply collecting annual data on diversity at the board level, as well as continuing to ensure parity between both of their operations to ensure the UK VCSE has a more level playing field.

Ultimately, leaders in this sector need to look deeper at their environment, their supporters, and themselves alongside the mission, taking a grass-root approach from the inside as well as the outside.

Conclusion

In terms of context, it seems the UK VCSE faces a myriad of situations that could lead to UPOB in general at a greater level than its for-profit counterpart organisations, but primarily the purposes and perceptions of the sector may attract and/or create dark leadership since regulation and monitoring expectations are limited, and there is a lack of diversity. In the major scandals discussed in this chapter, the events themselves were very recent, and implications are still ongoing, yet our understanding and approaches to this form of behaviour and decision-making still have not caught up. These were not scandals linked to single or small organisations. The Charity Commission admitted that in certain cases things were not isolated, and as shown by the latest reports on charity wrongdoing, cases of mismanagement have taken a steep rise in recent years. There is a significant need for better understanding and awareness of the risks around our perceptions of the UK VCSE and greater parity in external involvement, whether through regulation or opportunities for improvement.

References

Aaker, J., Vohs, K. D., & Mogilner, C. (2010). Nonprofits are seen as warm and for-profits as competent: Firm stereotypes matter. *Journal of Consumer Research*, *37*(2), 224–237.

Akhtar, M. W., Huo, C., Syed, F., Safdar, M. A., Rasool, A., Husnain, M., Awais, M., & Sajjad, M. S. (2022). Carrot and stick approach: The exploitative leadership and absenteeism in education sector. *Frontiers in Psychology*, *13*, 890064. https://doi.org/10.3389/fpsyg.2022.890064

Bajaba, S., Bajaba, A., & Fuller, B. (2022). Enduring exploitative leaders at work: The buffering role of proactive personality on employee job strain. *Organization Management Journal*, *19*(2), 60–71.

B-Corp. (2024). How did the B-Corp movement start? Available at: https://www.bcorporation.net/en-us/faqs/how-did-b-corp-movement-start/#:~:text=FAQs-,How%20did%20the%20B%20Corp%20movement%20start%3F,Corps%20were%20certified%20in%202007

BBC Online. (2019). *Oxfam criticised over Haiti sex claims*. British Broadcasting Corporation.

Bheeroo, L. (2020). Silenced by unethical gag orders or protected by confidentiality agreements: Should the charity sector use NDAs? Available at: https://www.bond.org.uk/news/2020/11/silenced-by-unethical-gag-orders-or-protected-by-confidentiality-agreements-should-the/

Boddy, C. R. (2015). Psychopathic leadership: A case study of a corporate psychopath CEO. *Journal of Business Ethics*, *145*, 141–156.

Brouwers, M., & Paltu, A. (2020). Toxic leadership: Effects on job satisfaction, commitment, turnover intention and organisational culture within the South African manufacturing industry. *SA Journal of Human Resource Management*, 18(1), 1–11.

Bussell, H., & Forbes, D. (2002). Understanding the volunteer market: The what, where, who and why of volunteering. *International Journal of Nonprofit and Voluntary Sector Marketing*, *7*(3), 244–257.

Butler, P. (2021). Mismanagement claims against Kids Company founder thrown out. *Guardian*. Available at: https://www.theguardian.com/uk-news/2021/feb/12/mismanagement-claims-kids-company-founder-thrown-out-camila-batmanghelidjh. Accessed 30 May 2024.

Charity Commission. (2015). *Charity fundraising: A guide to trustee duties*. Charity Commission for England and Wales.

Charity Commission. (2019a). *Preventing charity fraud: Insights and action*. Fraud Advisory Team, Charity Commission for England and Wales.

Charity Commission. (2019b). *Dealing with wrongdoing and harm*. Charity Commission for England and Wales.

de Bruin Cardoso, I., Russell, A. R., Kaptein, M., & Meijs, L. (2024). How moral goodness drives unethical behaviour: Empirical evidence for the NGO halo effect. *Nonprofit and Voluntary Sector Quarterly*, *53*(3), 589–614. https://doi.org/10.1177/08997640231179751

Dean, J. (2022). Informal volunteering, inequality, and illegitimacy. *Nonprofit and Voluntary Sector Quarterly*, *51*(3), 527–544.

Dent, G. W. (2014). Corporate governance without shareholders: A cautionary lesson from non-profit organizations. *The Delaware Journal of Corporate Law*, *39*(1), 93.

Ghosh, S. K. (2017). The direct and interactive effects of job insecurity and job embeddedness on unethical pro-organizational behaviour. *Personnel Review*, *46*(6), 1182–1198.

Hagan, J. (2014). The sustainability of cultural heritage tourism volunteering. PhD Thesis. Submitted to Teesside University Business School.

Hallinger, P. (2018). Bringing context out of the shadows of leadership. *Educational Management Administration and Leadership*, *46*(1), 5–24.

House, R. J., & Aditya, R. N. (1997). The social scientific study of leadership: Quo vadis? *Journal of Management*, *23*(3), 409–473.

Johns, G. (2024). The context deficit in leadership research. *The Leadership Quarterly*, *35*(1), 101755.

Lee, A., Schwarz, G., Newman, A., & Legood, A. (2019). Investigating when and why psychological entitlement predicts unethical pro-organizational behaviour. *Journal of Business Ethics*, *154*(1), 109–126.

Lian, H., Huai, M., Farh, J. L., Huang, J. C., & Chao, M. M. (2016). Leader UPB and employee unethical conduct: A moral disengagement perspective. *Academy of Management Proceedings*, *2016*(1), 13478.

Lian, H., Huai, M., Farh, J.-L., Huang, J.-C., Lee, C., & Chao, M. M. (2022). Leader unethical pro-organizational behaviour and employee unethical conduct: Social learning of moral disengagement as a behavioural principle. *Journal of Management*, *48*(2), 350–379.

Lyu, Y., Wu, L.Z., Ye, Y., Kwong Kwan, H., & Chen, Y. (2023). Rebellion under exploitation: How and when exploitative leadership evokes employees' workplace deviance. *Journal of Business Ethics*, *185*, 483–498.

Mishra, M., Ghosh, K., & Sharma, D. (2022). Unethical pro-organizational behaviour: A systematic review and future research agenda. *Journal of Business Ethics*, *179*(1), 63–87.

Office of the Scottish Charity Regulator. (2024a). Scottish Ministers test demand for review of key aspects of charity law. Available at: https://consult.gov.scot/third-sector/review-of-charity-regulation/. Accessed 19 May 2024.

Peiffer, M., Villotti, P., Vantilborgh, T., & Desmette, D. (2020). Stereotypes of volunteers and nonprofit organizations' professionalization: A two-study article. *Non-Profit Management and Leadership*, *31*(2), 355–372.

Porter, L. W., & McLaughlin, G. B. (2006). Leadership and the organizational context: Like the weather? *The Leadership Quarterly*, *17*(6), 559–576.

Public Administration and Constitutional Affairs Committee. (2016). *The collapse of Kids Company: Extraordinary catalogue of failures*. UK Parliament Committees.

Sargeant, A. (2021). Olive Cooke: Five years' on – what have we learned, and how can the sector move forward? Institute for Sustainable Philanthropy online. Available at: https://www.philanthropy-institute.org.uk/blog/olive-cooke-five-years-on-what-have-we-learned-and-how-can-the-sector-move-forward

Schmid, E., Verdorfer, A. P., & Peus, C. (2017). Shedding light on leaders' self-interest: Theory and measurement of exploitative leadership. *Journal of Management*, *45*(4), 1401–1433.

Smith, D. H. (1983). Altruism, volunteers, and volunteerism. *Journal of Voluntary Action Research*, *12*, 21–36.

Spear, R., Cornforth, C., & Aiken, M. (2007). *For love and money: Governance and social enterprise*. National Council for Voluntary Organisations.

Stout, M. (2005). *The Sociopath next door*. Broadway Books, pp. 94–95.

Tavanti, M., & Tait, A. (2021). The dark side of nonprofit leadership: cases, causes, and consequences in Camgöz, In S. M. Camgöz and Ö. T. Ekmekci (Eds.), *Destructive leadership and management hypocrisy*. Emerald Publishing Limited, pp. 255–279.

The Scottish Government. (2019). Analysis of consultation on Scottish Charity Law. Available at: https://www.gov.scot/publications/analysis-consultation-scottish-charity-law/

Umphress, E. E., & Bingham, J. B. (2011). When employees do bad things for good reasons: Examining unethical pro-organizational behaviours. *Organisation Science*, *22*(3), 621–640.

Umphress, E. E., Bingham, J. B., & Mitchell, M. S. (2010). Unethical behaviour in the name of the company: The moderating effect of organizational identification and positive reciprocity beliefs on unethical pro-organizational behaviour. *Journal of Applied Psychology*, *95*(4), 769.

Vergauwe, J., Hofmans, J., Wille, B., Decuyper, M., & De Fruyt, F. (2021). Psychopathy and leadership effectiveness: Conceptualizing and testing three models of successful psychopathy. *The Leadership Quarterly*, *32*(6), 101536. https://doi.org/10.1016/j.leaqua.2021.101536

Wang, C., Zhang, Y., & Feng, J. (2023). Is it fair? How and when exploitative leadership impacts employees' knowledge sharing. *Management Decision*, *61*(11), 3295–3315.

Weisinger, J. Y., Borges-Méndez, R., & Milofsky, C. (2016). Diversity in the nonprofit and voluntary sector. *Nonprofit and Voluntary Sector Quarterly*, *45*(1_suppl), 3S–27S. https://doi.org/10.1177/0899764015613568

Willow, F. (2023). The charity sector structure is broken. Available at: https://www.gettingonboard.org/post/the-charity-sector-structure-is-broken. Accessed 19 May 2024.

Ziegert, J. C., Mayer, D. M., Piccolo, R. F., & Graham, K. A. (2021). Collectivistic leadership in context: An examination of how and when collective charismatic leadership relates to unit functioning. *Journal of Leadership and Organisational Studies*, *28*(2), 112–136.

Chapter 14

The Dark Side: A Philosophical Analysis of Leadership in Nigeria's Arts and Entertainment

Olamilekan "Laycon" Agbeleshe

Introduction

Since leadership has so many different meanings to different people, it is important to conceptualise leadership based on the characteristics that are consistent with its many definitions and explanations, and this can be summed up thus, the goal of leadership is to influence and guide others to achieve goals that would be impossible for them to achieve on their own. Yukl (2013) defines leadership as the process of influencing others to understand and agree on what needs to be done and how to do it. Leadership is the human factor that binds a group together and motivates it towards specific goals (Sabir, 2017). Leaders are frequently referred to as guides and visionaries, which implies that a leader not only has the authority to influence and act in difficult situations but is also responsible for determining a group's or organisation's trajectory (Raula, 2016).

Leadership is frequently associated with positive characteristics such as vision, inspiration, and guidance. However, there is another side to leadership that is less discussed but just as important. The destructive or counter-productive forms of leadership have received considerably less attention,

DOI: 10.4324/9781003475262-17

than those associated with more positive outcomes (Harris & Jones, 2018). The dark side of leadership is an ongoing pattern of behaviour exhibited by a leader that results in negative outcomes based on the interactions between the leader, follower, and the environment (Oyewunmi et al., 2024). This is when a leader's abuse of power and self-interest undermines organisational goals, morale, and follower satisfaction. The deprivation of good leadership, to put it simply, is the dark side of leadership, and it happens when those in positions of authority misuse their influence, put their interests ahead of those of their followers, or act in an unethical or harmful manner.

It encompasses a range of negative behaviours and attributes that can have profound implications for individuals, organisations, and society. Dark traits in leaders will lead to the abuse of power, unethical behaviour, and toxic behaviours manifested in different contexts. For example, a business CEO who abuses and belittles staff while prioritising profit over employee well-being is a toxic leader with dark leadership characteristics. Another manifestation of dark leadership is when a leader's mission is tailored to fulfil their own needs, and they are more concerned with maximising opportunities for personal dominance. Examples of these are, political leaders misusing their positions for personal benefit, corporate executives indulging in financial misconduct, or religious leaders exploiting their followers for control. Leaders have the discretion to engage in either group or self-serving actions (Mumford & Connelly, 1991). What then influences or causes dark side behaviours in leaders? Are they innately terrible, or do they become bad through their experiences? In essence, are terrible leaders indicative of a bad society? Can the argument of nature or nurture also play a role in determining how a leader becomes good or bad? Is it bad people that become bad leaders and if so, are they aware of it, and can it be changed? Another factor to consider is whether a person's good qualities indicate that they will become a good leader and vice versa. Furthermore, is the dark side leader always an unpopular leader?

Moral and ethical values impact our perspectives of leadership. Hence, from a philosophical standpoint, the dark side of leadership is characterised by ethical frameworks such as consequentialism, deontology, and virtue ethics. These three ethical theories agree that being in a position of authority and influence over others entails some degree of power, and using that power ethically requires leaders to behave honourably, fairly, and with regard to the welfare of their followers. Leaders break the moral confidence entrusted to them and transgress basic ethical norms when they abuse their position of authority or put their personal interests ahead of those of their followers (Wood, 2019). These theories argue that leaders are to be judged based on the morals and the ethical values underpinning their actions and decisions. Plato and Aristotle state that leaders who are morally upright, virtuous, humble, ethically pure, and dedicated to the greater good may be more likely to act justly, compassionately, and without succumbing to the allure of power (Kodish, 2006). According to them, those who aspire to be leaders must have moral qualities that prevent them from being corrupt. Essentially, a leader can only manifest a dark side if they lack moral integrity or virtue.

According to Bowman and West (2007), when given complete control, even people with originally impeccable morals might be corrupted because they lose sight of obligations and responsibilities. The power and authority that comes with being a leader taint them, and when this power is not restrained, a leader's dark side comes to the fore. In addition, people who rise to positions of responsibility could feel pressured to misuse their influence to further their interests or hold on to their positions of authority (Stangor et al., 2014). This is a Machiavellian school of thought because to stay in power, leaders adopt immoral methods that include deceit, manipulation, and even cruelty. This viewpoint supports the idea that a leader's dark side is revealed by their authority or influence. Foucault's analysis of contemporary society and power structures sheds more light on this side of leadership. He believed that organisations and control structures, such as jails, schools, and bureaucracies, can influence people and shape their conduct. As such, they can determine whether a leader becomes good or bad (Harter, 2016). This implies that a bad society can bring forth the dark side of a leader and vice versa. If the society is bad, the dark side of leadership can be traced to the institutions within the society.

Sartre's existentialist philosophy places a strong emphasis on individual freedom, responsibility, and authenticity, and these ideas suggest that people are ultimately in charge of their decisions and acts, independent of other forces at play or cultural norms (Reynolds & Pierre-Jean, 2022). This position asserts that leaders ultimately have the power to choose whether they become unethical or not, and they are only susceptible to influence if they voluntarily allow it. Another school of thought is that leaders must learn to control their dark side because history has proven that man, by nature has an inherent dark side. This is why according to Rousseau, there should be procedures in place to hold leaders responsible for their actions as part of the social contract between them and their followers (The Editors of Encyclopaedia Britannica, 2024). Therefore, followers should be informed and involved in the leadership process to hold leaders accountable through scrutiny and other processes (Warner, 2001).

The emergence of dark leadership is a question that is strongly tied to ideas of morality, ethics, authority, and power. Depending on individual ethical orientation, there will always be divergent views on what makes a good leader. This suggests that there are a variety of reasons why a leader could be perceived as dark, and from the leaders' point of view, this might be justified by prior experiences and the pressures of their current objectives. What we can conclude is that there are complex dynamics that contribute to the dark side of leadership, and as demonstrated by philosophical references, dark leaders may not agree that they are dark, they believe in a cause, and they justify every action and decision that they make to achieve that cause.

Nigeria's Arts and Entertainment: An Overview

All facets of society and human existence involve leadership. Since other sectors are seemingly dominated by analytical, rational, and well-organised thoughts and actions, this chapter focuses on leadership in the arts and entertainment industry. This industry is extremely important, both economically and culturally, and it has an impact on almost every facet of society. Although it is characterised by enormous prospects and significant uncertainty, it is constantly evolving due to emerging technologies, new business strategies, and increasing markets. As the industry an array of changes, there is a demand for effective leaders who can manage and leverage change on multiple levels. Beneath the glamour of the entertainment industry is a battlefield of egos, power struggles, and aspirations that not only alter people's lives but also shape the industry's future. From the actors, musicians, and managers to the label executives, producers, and the people behind the scenes, there is a quest for influence, control, and power. This pursuit of power overrides the pursuit of artistic brilliance and greatness and, in the end, degrades art and creativity to the status of mere pieces on the business chessboard. Understanding the concept of leadership in Nigeria's entertainment sector requires a knowledge of the industry's unique challenges and opportunities. While there has been immense growth, and incredible strides in music, film, fashion, and other creative fields, with Nigerian artists gaining international recognition and the culture influencing global trends, it is crucial to identify the industry's challenges.

Piracy and copyright infringement remain a huge danger to the industry, depriving content creators of their legitimate earnings and deterring investment in new projects. Furthermore, inadequate infrastructure, such as a lack of production facilities means that there is no direct performance revenue going back into the industry. In addition, the lack of local investments and capital impedes not just the quality and scope of productions but also the means to effectively market the content, especially for independent creators. To address these challenges and build a sustainable structure for Nigeria's entertainment industry, adequate and responsible leaders, as well as entertainment regulatory bodies such as the Nigerian Copyright Commission (NCC), Collecting Society of Nigeria (COSON), PMAN (Performing Musician's Association of Nigeria), Actors' Guild of Nigeria (AGN), Bank of Industry (BOI), and others, are required to step up and play their roles.

From observing and being a part of Nigeria's entertainment industry, I opine that the type of leadership practised by the regulatory and professional organisations mentioned is structural. These are organisations that entertainment practitioners or intending practitioners can join and identify with. They are legally recognised and charged with the responsibility of combating piracy, providing and promoting legal alternatives for accessing entertainment content, advocating for government policies that prioritise infrastructure development within the entertainment sector, and establishing dedicated funding mechanisms tailored to the needs of the industry, such as grants, loans, and venture capital funds. It is expected that these entities and organisations will work together with creative individuals, stakeholders, governmental bodies, industry associations, and consumers to devise and execute strategies that will enable Nigeria's entertainment sector to realise its full potential and solidify its standing as a worldwide cultural superpower. The decision-makers of structural leadership often comprise retired creatives and individuals appointed by the government.

Individual leadership is another style of leadership that exists in Nigeria's entertainment industry. This is the most common form of leadership seen among creatives and talents. It is an undocumented leadership style that involves apprenticeship and mentorship. There is no explicit agreement between the leader and the follower; it often occurs during the process of creating or the process of creative development. Relationships between music producers, label executives, and artistes, as well as movie directors, producers, and actors, provide examples of this. Although the business component of the industry requires a legally binding document to define the terms of the partnership on paper, creatives frequently share a bond that is stronger than a legal document. While the label executive, producer, and artiste must sign contracts before the release of music, their relationship and bond often extend beyond the contract. The artiste may regard the label executive or label owner as a mentor and a leader. This is comparable to how new artistes look up to and interact with established artistes in the industry. This same dynamic can be seen in the film industry, where emerging actors, producers, and directors look up to their established colleagues. Individual leadership is thus more personal, and the parties engaged have a greater emotional investment in it. The followers or apprentices attach their growth and success in the industry to the lessons, experiences, and connections they gain from their leaders and mentors and, as such, feel indebted to them. The leaders also believe that without their support, the apprentices would not have accomplished their goals, making them deserving of credit and respect. These perspectives birthed the concepts of "godfatherism", "gatekeepers" and "gatekeeping" in Nigeria's entertainment industry.

Dark Side of Leadership in Nigeria's Arts and Entertainment: An Insider's Reflection

There are many examples of leaders in Nigeria's arts and entertainment acting unethically or exploitatively, maintaining power disparities, and putting their own interests ahead of the welfare of artistes and creatives, and I have experienced my fair share. Having worked tirelessly to break into the entertainment industry, I discovered that there is a dark side that lurks beneath the surface of fame. I discovered and witnessed that behind the scenes, there are people wielding power and influence through manipulation, exploitation, and intimidation, thriving on the fear of victims. These dark leaders frequently use their positions to exercise control over others, exploiting their weaknesses and taking advantage of their ignorance and innocence. I have witnessed talented artistes and aspiring creatives fall victim to these predators, their dreams shattered and spirits crushed by deceit.

Nigeria has a strong power distance culture, with hierarchical systems and a significant respect for authority. This cultural norm is manifested in the music industry, where established personalities exert enormous power over emerging artists. The "godfathers" or "gatekeepers," have control over the industry's resources, opportunities, and networks. As a result, aspiring artistes may find themselves negotiating a world in which success is often dependent on gaining the acceptance of these powerful persons. The concepts of godfatherism and gatekeepers in Nigeria's entertainment business are inextricably linked, indicating the industry's hierarchical and often opaque power dynamics. Godfatherism is a system in which prominent individuals, such as industry veterans or decision-makers, have tremendous control and influence over the opportunities and career trajectories of emerging artistes. These godfathers or "big men" as they are frequently referred to, use their connections, resources, and clout to influence the careers of emerging artists, actors, filmmakers, and other industry professionals. Gatekeepers, on the other hand, are individuals or organisations in charge of controlling access to industry opportunities, resources, and networks. Record labels, film production companies, talent agencies, media outlets, and industry groups or regulatory bodies are some examples of gatekeepers.

Godfatherism and gatekeeping are two sides of the same coin, with advantages as well as disadvantages. While godfatherism and gatekeepers can positively influence emerging talents and provide them with platforms for opportunities and exposure, I have witnessed them take an exploitative and manipulating form. Leaders use their influence to obtain favours, loyalty, or financial advantage, exploiting their role in shaping the landscape of the entertainment industry by determining which artistes or projects receive exposure, funding, distribution, and other forms of support. I have encountered people without connections or networks restricted from career opportunities, regardless of their talent or potential. I have concluded that as long as the practice of godfatherism and gatekeeping continue, innovation and creativity will be hindered because new voices and talents will struggle to break through the established barriers.

The Nigerian movie industry, popularly known as *Nollywood,* is one of the world's largest and most vibrant. Nollywood has evolved as a cultural powerhouse with global influence as a result of technology improvements, entrepreneurial drive, and cultural resonance. It is well-known for its prolific output, diversified storytelling, and grassroots filmmaking method. In Nollywood, the power that movie producers and directors possess over actors, actresses, and even crew members is great, as they frequently force them to sign restrictive contracts, put them in unfavourable working conditions, and subject them to harassment. I had a conversation with a prominent actor in *Nollywood,* and he said, "*being a good leader in Nollywood is an anomaly*". This is because actors and crew personnel frequently endured difficult working conditions, inadequate compensation, and disregard for their comfort and rights. Several actors and actresses have been banned from major awards and movie roles for speaking out against exploitation, favouritism, and harassment in the industry. Meredith Williams (not real name), a well-known Nollywood actress, recounts how she nearly quit the film industry due to sexual harassment. She described how, despite being cast in a film for her talent, a producer made sexual overtures to her after auditions. Another actress, Joyce James (not real name), also disclosed in an interview that she was sexually harassed by a notable filmmaker early in her career. She described how the filmmaker made unwelcome advances and proposed roles in exchange for sexual favours.

Here is a story from a film producer. He is allocated a limited amount to shoot a high-budget movie and is expected to finish in a time frame that is unachievable. For him, the tight budget and the stressful working environment will justify the behaviour he exhibits with actors and crew members while the film is being made. However, to the cast and crew members, he has exhibited the traits of a bad leader. A similar story was told by record label executives concerning the expenses they bore while trying to build the artiste who is accusing them of being partial. From the standpoint of these leaders, they are attempting to attain their goals and objectives but are inconsiderate of others. It is crucial to note, nevertheless, that in numerous cases, the same label owner or movie producer who is viewed negatively by individual A may be viewed positively by individual B.

One of the most devastating elements of dark leadership in the entertainment industry is that it operates in the shadows. Behind closed doors, deals are struck, alliances are formed, and rivalries boil. Those who dare to speak up or challenge the status quo face retaliation and ostracism, thereby restricting criticism and creating a culture of fear and distrust. The connection between record labels, music executives, and the musicians they sign is another illustration of how a leader-follower dynamic may go sour in the entertainment industry. Documented trends of exploitation and abuse show that managers and record labels are frequently subject musicians to predatory behaviour, financial manipulation, and unjust contracts.

Nigeria's music industry is a thriving and diverse sector that has achieved international attention for its rich cultural heritage, unique sounds, and dynamic artistes. The music landscape is broad, encompassing genres and styles that represent the country's diversity and creative spirit. From Afrobeat to Afrobeats, Highlife to Hip Hop, Nigerian music, is rooted in ancient rhythms and imbued with contemporary influences that have evolved over the decades, influencing the soundtracks of everyday life for millions of people in the country and around the world. Historically, the Nigerian music industry is rife with incidences of breach of contracts and exploitative arrangements. Several artistes have fallen prey to intellectual property theft and lopsided reward systems, which have culminated in unrealised potential. There are numerous stories of artistes falling out with their labels, accusing them of exploitation through unfair contracts, financial manipulation, and lack of transparency. A while back, a popular artiste accused his label of unfair treatment and isolation despite existing contractual obligations.

The label owners also accused the artiste of being disloyal and uncommitted despite the heavy investments made to promote him and his music. Another artiste, Flappy J (not real name), accused a music executive and label manager of abuse and financial exploitation. Flappy J claimed that the manager violated contractual obligations, withheld his pay, and treated him unfairly.

I have witnessed the toll that dark leadership exacts on the mental and emotional well-being of those who are caught in its grip. The pressure to succeed becomes suffocating, and the line between ambition and desperation becomes blurred. Despite the darkness, there are hints of optimism. I have seen and encountered folks who refuse to sacrifice their integrity and convictions, disruptors who dare to confront the status quo and speak truth to power. Just recently, many artistes have started speaking out and making efforts to maintain creative freedom and earn appropriate compensation for their work, emphasising the power disparities that exist in the music business as a result of dark-side leadership. In my journey through Nigeria's entertainment industry, I have encountered the darkest levels of leadership, where power is wielded as a weapon and ambition has no bounds. But I have also witnessed the resolve and courage of people who refuse to be intimidated by fear, fighting for justice and fairness in an industry riddled with deceit and exploitation. I recently dealt with a prominent figure in the music industry. Previously, I had heard from certain musicians who had left his label that he had a darker side. However, I experienced a different side of him in our dealings, and if you ask me, he does not have a dark side. My experience validates the initial argument that dark leadership could also be an unpopular leader. Furthermore, my experience has shown me that the dark side of the entertainment industry is not restricted to the leaders alone. Actors, and artistes, practically everyone in the business has a dark side that reveals itself in their interactions with others. This supports the view that individuals can show dark leadership traits without being a leader; the position of leadership simply provides them with the power and authority to do so openly while justifying it with the pressure and duties that come with being a leader.

Lessons for Leaders

It is pertinent to understand that the concept of dark-side leadership is multifaceted, and there are different explanations for its existence. However, the consistent phenomenon is that a leader is chosen to lead and influence decisions for a greater goal, not to satisfy themselves. This is why leaders need to understand their role and what the bigger goal is outside their personal ambitions. Although facing and addressing one's inadequacies might be difficult, leaders must practise self-awareness and honest self-reflection. Leaders need to reflect on their actions, intentions, and influence on others to identify any tendencies towards abuse, exploitation, or manipulation. Furthermore, it is pertinent that leaders understand the effects of the dark side that they manifest and how it affects their team, their organisation, and the industry as a whole.

Because the arts and entertainment industry play a huge role in shaping the values and norms in society, incidents of mistreatment, exploitation, or unethical conduct may have wider social effects, strengthening negative stereotypes, sustaining inequalities, and fostering an atmosphere of impunity. Furthermore, when artistes or creatives keep experiencing exploitation and harassment, the motivation to produce their best work reduces, and this affects the output and quality of content while diminishing audience engagement and satisfaction. Again, there may be a loss of diversity and talent pool in the arts and entertainment industry as a result of the negative aspects of leadership driving creative people away. As we have seen multiple times, creatives who are subjected to mistreatment or exploitation may decide to quit the business entirely in search of more welcoming and equal settings. The exodus of talent may rob the industry of important viewpoints and contributions.

While the pursuit of fame and fortune can amplify existing issues and tempt people to compromise their values, there are deeper systemic factors at work that fuel unethical behaviour and toxic leadership. Intense competition for limited opportunities and recognition creates situations in which people employ unethical measures to obtain a competitive advantage, such as sabotaging competition or exploiting vulnerable newcomers. In a culture that sometimes glorifies money and status, people may feel pressured to project a specific image of success at any cost, even if it means sacrificing their integrity or exploiting others. The potential for reputational harm to both the individuals and the industry at large is a drawback of the dark side of leadership in the entertainment business. Herein lies the lessons for the leaders and the industry as a whole because preventing these effects requires leaders to regulate themselves. Addressing and proffering solutions to the dark side of leadership should be a collective effort. Organisations involved in the arts and entertainment industry should incorporate ethical leadership as the foundation of their culture and processes.

Conclusion

In an ideal world, leaders ought to be able to achieve their goals and targets while also ensuring the happiness of followers or at least the majority of followers. However, the world we live in is far from ideal. In a world where most decisions and views are formed and easily influenced by emotions rather than reasoning, leaders should strike a balance between logic and emotions, as this plays an important role in determining the type of leader they are and how others see them. While most organisations evaluate leaders based on targets and goal achievement, it is pertinent that leaders in arts and entertainment, as well as in other sectors, adopt an inclusive approach that mainstreams the opinions, interests, and well-being of their followers.

References

Bowman, J. S., & West, J. P. (2007). Lord Acton and employment doctrines: absolute power and the spread of at-will employment. *Journal of Business Ethics, 74*(2), 119–130. https://www.jstor.org/stable/25075451

Harris, A., & Jones, M. (2018). The dark side of leadership and management. *School of Leadership & Management, 38*(5), 475–477. https://doi.org/10.1080/13632434.2018.1509276

Harter, N. W. (2016). *Foucault on leadership: The leader as subject.* Routledge/Taylor & Francis Group. https://psycnet.apa.org/record/2016-22657-000

Kodish, S. (2006). The paradoxes of leadership: the contribution of Aristotle. *Leadership, 2*(4), 451–468. https://doi.org/10.1177/1742715006069175

Mumford, M. D., & Connelly, M. S. (1991). Leaders as creators: leader performance and problem-solving in ill-defined domains. *The Leadership Quarterly, 2*(4), 289–315. https://doi.org/10.1016/1048-9843(91) 90017-V

Oyewunmi, A. E., Adedeji, O., & Adegbuyi, A. (2024). Spiritual intelligence in the workplace: is there a dark side? *Journal of Organizational Change Management, 37*(4), 704–716. https://doi.org/10.1108/JOCM-06-2023-0255

Raula, K. (2016). The role of a leader in a creative entertainment company - Case: Universal Music Finland. Bachelor's Thesis Degree Programme in International Business. https://typeset.io/pdf/the-role-of-a-leader-in-a-creative-entertainment-company-43dcww2agj.pdf

Reynolds, J., & Pierre-Jean, R. (2022). Jean-Paul Sartre. In E. N. Zalta (Ed.), *The Stanford encyclopedia of philosophy* (Summer edition), https://plato.stanford.edu/archives/sum2022/entries/sartre/

Sabir, A. (2017). A leader: one who knows the way, goes the way and shows the way. *European Business & Management, 3*(5), 82–85.

Stangor, C., Jhangiani, R., & Tarry, H. (2014). *Principles of social psychology* (1st international edition). BC Open Textbook Project, & Open Textbook Library. https://open.umn.edu/opentextbooks/textbooks/74

The Editors of Encyclopaedia Britannica. (2024). *Social contract*. Encyclopaedia Britannica. https://www. britannica.com/topic/social-contract

Warner, B. E. (2001). John Stuart Mill's theory of bureaucracy within representative government: balancing competence and participation. *Public Administration Review, 61*(4), 403–413. https://www.jstor.org/stable/977502

Wood, N. (2019). *Virtue rediscovered: deontology, consequentialism, and virtue ethics in the contemporary moral landscape*. Rowman & Littlefield.

Yukl, G. A. (2013.). *Leadership in organizations* (3rd edition). Pearson Custom Publishing. https://www. academia.edu/42939920/Leadership_in_Organizations_Global_Edition

Chapter 15

Does Culture Influence Dark Leadership Manifestation? A Hofstede Exploration of Nigeria

Ogechi Adeola, Obinna Muogboh,
Isaiah Adisa, and Bernadine Bukomeko

Introduction

The identification of the dark leadership triad by Paulhus and Williams in 2002 has spurred extensive research into the formation of leadership personalities, along with the implications for followers and organisations. The triad—comprising narcissism, Machiavellianism, and psychopathy—has been examined in numerous studies, underscoring its impact on both individuals and organisations (Paulhus & Williams, 2002). Narcissism is characterised by self-importance, a lack of empathy, and an excessive need for admiration (Paulhus & Williams, 2002). Machiavellianism, on the other hand, is defined by self-interest and a willingness to erode moral standards in the pursuit of personal goals (Paulhus & Williams, 2002). The final element of the triad, psychopathy, is marked by impulsivity, shallow emotions, and little to no remorse. Volmer et al. (2016) identified both the bright and dark sides of these leadership personalities. However, while some attention has been given to managing the manifestation of these traits, it remains an under-explored area (Schyns et al., 2022). Much of the current literature on dark

DOI: 10.4324/9781003475262-18

leadership is focused on how these traits manifest, seeking to understand the factors that contribute to their development and the role that culture plays (Oyewunmi & Oyewunmi, 2022; Nuzulia & Why, 2020).

In societies with high power distance, subordinates often refrain from reporting abusive supervisory behaviour due to fear of their leaders. This aligns with Hofstede's cultural dimension theory, which suggests that societies have dominant cultural characteristics that influence individual behaviour. While some research findings (e.g., Oyewunmi & Oyewunmi, 2022) address subordinates' responses, they do not comprehensively examine the abusive tendencies of supervisors—an aspect closely associated with Machiavellianism in dark leadership (Wisse & Sleebos, 2016). Consequently, in contexts marked by high power distance, there is the potential for the manifestation of dark leadership, underscoring the necessity for further exploration. The significance of culture as an influential factor in shaping individual personality and behaviour cannot be overstated. Considering the arguments within contexts characterised by high power distance and individualism, this chapter evaluates the extent to which the dominance of Hofstede's cultural dimensions—power distance and individualism—acts as a catalyst for dark leadership personalities. The argument of this chapter is derived from Hofstede's cultural dimensions, suggesting that the most dominant orientation in a culturally sensitive nation will influence leadership attributes. The chapter proposes recommendations for mitigating dark leadership manifestations, such as the abuse of subordinates attributable to excessive power and dominance.

The Dark Leadership Triad

The dark triad proposed by Paulhus and Williams (2002) identifies traits that do not conform with the basic tenets of good and ethical leadership (Ciulla, 2020). Leadership transcends position, authority or whether the expected organisational result is achieved. That is, leadership should not be solely about achieving milestones, but also about how it is achieved. Is it done ethically? Is human dignity ensured in the process of influencing and leading people to achieve the desired outcomes? These are important questions that must be answered. This school of thought negates the concept of dark leadership, which revolves around a self-centered leadership personality that breaks the rules and norms, and disregards standard processes.

Three dimensions of personality traits identified by Paulhus and Williams (2002) are narcissism, Machiavellianism, and psychopathy. Narcissism, characterised by an inflated sense of self-importance and a constant need for admiration, can lead to self-centred and manipulative leadership behaviours. Leaders' high in narcissism may exploit others for their own gain and lack empathy. This can result in toxic work environments, decreased morale, and reduced productivity. On the other hand, Machiavellianism is a leadership personality that portrays the dark aspects of leadership associated with highly exploitative practices and the adoption of processes that contradict acceptable norms. The last of the triad is psychopathy. Psychopathy is a leadership trait wherein the leader is characterised by a lack of self-control, weakened regulation, and high impulsivity.

The personalities have gained interest in practice and in literature because of their multiplier effects. For instance, people with a high level of impulsivity have been associated with risky behaviours, engagement in arguments, and hasty decision-making. Identifying leaders with these personality disorders could help organisations manage workplace tension and improve organisational effectiveness. However, some literature has emphasised that these personalities have their bright side, especially in circumstances where the end is the most important consideration. The argument here is that the outcome of a leadership process is of no importance if leaders act inhumanely and treat subordinates inappropriately. The interplay of these dark traits can create a highly challenging and toxic leadership environment, adversely affecting the employees as well as the organisational culture and performance. However, it is important to note that individuals may exhibit varying degrees of these traits, and not all leaders who demonstrate some of these characteristics are inherently toxic or destructive.

Identifying the implications of culture on the development of these leadership personalities could help organisations develop cultures that will limit the manifestation of negative or dark traits. Culture influences individuals' worldviews, attitudes, and actions. Therefore, understanding the dominant cultural elements in societies and their implications for the formation of dark leadership can help multinational organisations adapt to different contexts. Hence, we use Hofstede's national cultural dimensions to explore how a society's dominant cultural orientation may influence the manifestation of dark leadership traits.

Culture and the Hofstede Theory

Culture is a complex and multifaceted concept encompassing a particular group of people's beliefs, values, norms, customs, and traditions (Johnson et al., 2011). It plays a significant role in shaping societies, influencing individual behaviours, and understanding cultural dimensions, especially how they define our daily living practices. Geert Hofstede, a renowned social psychologist, developed the Cultural Dimensions theory in 1980 to provide a framework for understanding cultural differences across different countries. This theory has been widely used in various fields, including business, sociology, and psychology, to analyse the impact of culture on behaviours, attitudes, and values (Hofstede, 1998). In this chapter, the theory is adopted to explain the likelihood that the dominance of certain cultural orientations could influence the manifestation of dark leadership behaviours.

The Cultural Dimensions theory identifies six dimensions of national cultures, each of which reflects a range of values and behaviours commonly observed in different societies. These dimensions are power distance, individualism vs. collectivism, masculinity vs. femininity, uncertainty avoidance, long-term vs. short-term orientation, and indulgence vs. restraint (Hofstede, 1998). According to Hofstede, power distance refers to the extent to which less powerful members of a society accept and expect that power is distributed unequally (Puni & Anlesinya, 2017; Oyewunmi et al., 2018). In cultures with high power distance, hierarchy, and authority are valued, and individuals may feel more comfortable with a significant power gap between those in authority and themselves. In contrast, cultures with low power distance emphasise equality and may encourage more participative decision-making processes. This indicates that in nations, communities, and societies where power distance is high, inequality will be high, likewise, the centrality of power. The second cultural dimension proposed is individualism versus collectivism, which pertains to the degree of interdependence a society maintains among its members (Nguyen et al., 2010). Individualistic cultures prioritise personal goals and autonomy, while collectivist cultures emphasise group harmony and prioritise the needs of the community over the individual (Nguyen et al., 2010).

The third dimension is masculinity versus femininity, which describes the distribution of emotional roles between the genders within a society (Spence & Buckner, 1995). Masculine cultures tend to exhibit assertive and competitive traits, while feminine cultures prioritise nurturing and cooperation. The fourth cultural dimension proposed by Hofstede is uncertainty avoidance which relates to the extent to which a society tolerates ambiguity and uncertainty (Hofstede, 2011). Cultures with high uncertainty avoidance have strict rules and exhibit a low tolerance for risk, while those with low uncertainty avoidance are more open to change and innovation. The fifth dimension is long-term versus short-term orientation, and this refers to a society's time horizon in relation to values and behaviours (Hofstede, 2011).

Cultures with a long-term orientation tend to prioritise future rewards and sustainable practices, while those with a short-term orientation focus on immediate gratification and tradition. Finally, the dimension of indulgence versus restraint measures reflects the extent to which society permits free gratification of basic and natural human desires (Hofstede, 2011). Cultures with high indulgence tend to embrace the enjoyment of life and maintain a positive outlook. In contrast, those with high restraint tend to exhibit a more controlled approach to life and are more conservative in expressing emotions.

Unlocking the essence of Hofstede's Cultural Dimensions theory is essential for individuals and businesses operating in a global context (Srivastava et al., 2020). By leveraging the cultural values associated with different dimensions, organisations can effectively adapt their strategies, communication styles, and management practices to engage with diverse cultures. Moreover, this framework facilitates cross-cultural understanding, enhances teamwork, and promotes effective collaboration. Hofstede's cultural dimensions theory provides valuable insights into the impact of culture on societies and individuals. Thus, by recognising and respecting cultural differences, individuals and organisations can build stronger relationships, promote mutual respect, and achieve success in today's interconnected and culturally diverse world.

Culture and Dark Leadership

Several research outcomes have shown that culture affects personality formation (e.g., Carlson et al., 2004; Côté & Levine, 2014). However, the dimension to which it influences dark leadership personality has received less attention (e.g., Nuzulia & Why, 2020; Ma et al., 2021; Tiwari & Jha, 2022). Some of the findings from these studies allude to the fact that culture at both micro and macro levels can further influence the manifestation of a dark leadership personality. For instance, Tiwari and Jha (2022) found significant narcissistic traits in an environment characterised by a toxic work culture. The authors emphasised that a narcissistic leader promotes abusive supervision and enhances a toxic work culture. In their study, Nuzulia and Why (2020) sampled teachers and principals in Indonesia. Indonesia was identified as a nation with a collectivist culture, and the authors found that narcissism is a prevalent positive factor in leadership role occupancy and hiring decisions. The study indicates that narcissism thrives in societies with collectivist orientation, challenging previous studies that associated narcissism with negative job outcomes.

Furthermore, Ma et al. (2021) also presented arguments in favour of the positive aspects of dark personality traits, although they noted that the mode of the manifestation could vary across cultures. Their research, which focused on China and the USA - two countries with different cultural backgrounds- revealed that Machiavellianism was perceived more positively in China than in the United States. On the other hand, narcissism appeared to demonstrate a relatively more positive association in the United States than in China, as it was found to be more closely linked to proactive behaviour and job engagement and less closely linked to fatigue and disinterest at work in the United States than in China. The findings from Ma et al. (2021) indicate the importance of culture in the manifestation of the personality triad. Therefore, it is plausible that different strands of cultural dominance would influence the expression of identifiable dark leadership personalities. Importantly, extant literature has indicated that culture impacts relational outcomes, including dark leadership personalities. The interrogation of this dimension, especially in the context of Africa, has not gained much attention.

The Context of Africa and the Case of Nigeria

Despite Africa being a multicultural continent of 54 nations, understanding the influence of culture on both dark leadership formation and implications on organisations has received limited attention. Focus has been mostly given to toxic organisational leadership in different sectors (Abdulai, 2021). This is not to suggest that the attention of researchers and practitioners has not been drawn to demonstrating dark leadership personality traits in Africa. For instance, Adewale (2020) developed a model of virtuous leadership in Africa and suggested that a leader's ethical practices will also inform the follower's ethical behaviours. Adewale noted that followers are also indoctrinated into unethical practices when leaders exhibit dark leadership behaviours. The author's findings suggest that leaders' ethical and moral values are important in determining the ethical behaviours of followers.

Toxic leadership is a significant issue often associated with dark leadership personalities. Abdulai (2021) demonstrated that certain cultural factors contribute to toxic organisational leadership in Sub-Saharan Africa. The research highlights clientelism, insufficient leadership education, the tradition of respecting elders, and a cultural reluctance to criticise leaders as key contributors to toxic leadership in Ghana. Considering these findings, the study strongly recommends that leaders be constructively criticised by their followers to help improve their leadership skills. Essentially, when the prevailing culture suggests that leaders are untouchable, it promotes an environment conducive to dark leadership personalities.

Empirical studies on dark leadership in Africa are limited; however, using Hofstede's Cultural Dimension theory as a framework, it is possible to determine the dominant cultural orientation in Africa and predict its likely impact on leadership personalities. Hofstede posited that a society's dominant cultural orientation shapes its social behaviours and structures, influencing interpersonal relationships. Aside from Abdulai (2021), who did not specify the most dominant cultural orientation in Africa, previous studies (Tiwari & Jha, 2022; Nuzulia & Why, 2020; Ma et al., 2021) focused on cultural dominance in countries outside Africa and how this affects dark personality traits in workplace relationships. In this chapter, Nigeria is used as a case example for Africa.

Nigeria is considered in this context because it is the most populous nation on the continent, with over 250 ethnic groups (National Bureau of Statistics [NBS], 2018). Highlighting the dominant cultural traits in Nigeria and their likely implications for the formation and behaviour of dark leadership could help mitigate negative outcomes and promote more positive leadership qualities. Adeola et al. (2020) indicated that Hofstede's cultural dimensions are applicable to explain relationship dynamics in Africa, particularly in Nigeria, especially in the context of customer service experience management. Bustamante and Ogunyemi (2021) further described Nigeria's most dominant cultural orientations as masculine, hierarchical (high power distance), indulgent, and community-oriented. These descriptions align with Hofstede's cultural theory. The submission is that the country demonstrates a dominant masculine orientation (masculinity vs. femininity), hierarchical orientation (high power distance), indulgence, and community (individualism vs. collectivism). Table 15.1 further explains these dimensions and their implications.

These cultural nuances have implications for the manifestation of dark leadership in Nigeria (Oyewunmi et al., 2021). Wisse and Sleebos (2016) found that in contexts where power distance is dominant, dark leadership styles such as Machiavellianism and abusive supervision are likely to manifest. It also found that power culture moderates the effect of paranoid and passive-aggressive leadership on ethical climate. This was also corroborated by Oyewunmi and Oyewunmi (2022), who alluded to the fact that abusive supervisors thrive more, and their activities are further amplified because of the excessive respect given to them by their subordinates and the emphasis on hierarchy.

TABLE 15.1 Key Cultural Dimensions and Their Implications in Nigeria

Dominant Culture in Nigeria	*Implications*
High masculinity	• Values competition and assertiveness • Upholds traditional masculine systems and roles • Promotes male dominance
High power distance	• Emphasises respect for authority • Values hierarchy and hierarchical structures • Concentration of power; high inequality
High indulgence	• Highly hedonistic • Encourages extravagant lifestyles • Associated with a preference for less regulated economic policies, spending more than saving
High collectivism	• Predominance of the "We" over the "I" concept • Emphasis on group goals and well-being • Values relationships and loyalty • Prioritises communal living

Source: Adapted from Bustamante and Ogunyemi (2021).

Considering the findings from the extant literature, in high power distance contexts such as Nigeria—where excessive respect for hierarchy, concentration of power, and high inequality prevail—there is a strong likelihood that dark personality traits like Machiavellianism will thrive. Behaviours, such as the abuse of subordinates by leaders, cutting corners, and engaging in unethical practices are likely to be more prevalent. Subordinates in highly collectivist environments often refrain from reporting or challenging abusive supervisors (Oyewunmi & Oyewunmi, 2022). This reluctance stems from their perception of the leader as a member of their community who may act ethically in the future. As a result, abuse is likely to persist and go unreported in Nigeria, given the dominance of power distance and collectivism in its culture.

Nigeria's cultural orientation tends to promote inequality in this regard and elevate leaders to a near-deified status. In such a society, dark leadership traits like Machiavellianism are likely to persist. When power is highly concentrated and not diffused in a society that places excessive respect on authority figures, the tendency for misuse and abuse of power becomes significant. Additionally, cultures with a high collectivist orientation often encourage individuals to protect themselves and support those engaging in unethical behaviour, rather than challenge or reject them. Nigeria's high ranking in power distance and collectivist culture (Adeola et al., 2020) may thus contribute to strained leader-follower dynamics and an increased potential for dark leadership traits to be in place or to emerge. Implementing measures to limit and regulate the powers of leaders in such contexts is imperative to fostering ethical leadership and healthy leader-subordinate relationships.

Lessons for Leaders

Nigeria, as a case context, is fit for recommendation to other African nations because of the huge number of ethnic groups (more than 250) and the country's population —more than 200 million. It is most probable, owing to established cultural affinities and socioeconomic structures, that most African countries rank high on power distance and collectivism. Hence, specific lessons are stated, considering the importance of mitigating aggravated abusive behaviour associated with Machiavellianism and power distance in Hofstede's cultural dimensions.

First, managers must put in place measures to limit the concentration of power, this will curtail the abuse of leadership positions. They must also reduce the concentration of power by promoting decentralised decision-making processes and empowering lower-level employees to participate in decision-making. This will encourage a more equitable distribution of authority within organisations. This is important because there is a centrality of power in Nigeria, as observed from the Hofstede dimension, thereby concentrating resources in the hands of a minority. This orientation is also reflected in the business sphere, therefore affecting relationships.

Second, a culture that promotes speaking up in situations of abuse must be engineered and supported from the top. People who speak up and report situations of abuse should be rewarded and encouraged rather than talked down. Companies should develop and enforce policies that protect whistleblowers and encourage employees to report unethical behaviour without fear of retaliation. It is important to institutionalise anonymous reporting mechanisms to ensure confidentiality and safety for those who speak up. Additionally, supervisors found to be perpetrators of abuse should be punished appropriately.

Third, policies guiding the usage of power and what is adjudged as a misuse and abuse of power should be recognised and codified in organisations. This will protect both supervisors and subordinates from undue exploitation. In this way, companies need to implement accountability measures to ensure that leaders are held responsible for their actions and decisions. Leaders also need to be offered training on emotional intelligence and why the dignity of the human person must be respected irrespective of class and status. Having such training as a criterion for leadership positions will likely provide needed orientation on appropriate and acceptable leadership behaviours in the organisational context.

Fourth, organisations must create and promote a culture that discourages abuse and dark behaviours. Implementing measurable checks, such as surveys and employee opinion polls, can help regulate and monitor workplace dynamics. Lastly, establishing organisational values that discourage abuse but promote transparency and respect for every member of the organisation will go a long way in limiting negative manifestations of dark leadership personalities. Managers and organisational leaders must consider the dominant culture in their environment and create a system that manages it effectively.

References

Abdulai, M. (2021). The culture of toxic organisational leadership in sub-Saharan Africa: Why contexts matter. In: Örtenblad, A. (eds) *Debating Bad Leadership. Palgrave Debates in Business and Management*. Palgrave Macmillan. https://doi.org/10.1007/978-3-030-65025-4_18

Adeola, O., Adisa, I., & Obileye, A. A. (2020). Cultural influence on customer service delivery. In R. Hinson, O. Adeola, R. Lituchy, & A. Amartey (Eds.), *Customer Service Management in Africa: A Strategic and Operational Perspective*. New York: Routledge.

Adewale, A. A. (2020). Model of virtuous leadership in Africa: Case study of a Nigerian firm. *Journal of Business Ethics*, *161*, 749–762. https://doi.org/10.1007/s10551-019-04340-3

Bustamante, S., & Ogunyemi, K. (2021). Nigeria. In: Bustamante, S., Pizzutilo, F., Martinovic, M., Herrero Olarte, S. (eds) *Corporate Social Responsibility and Employer Attractiveness. CSR, Sustainability, Ethics & Governance*. Springer. https://doi.org/10.1007/978-3-030-68861-5_30

Carlson, J., Kurato, Y., Ruiz, E., Ng, K. M., & Yang, J. (2004). A multicultural discussion about personality development. *The Family Journal*, *12*(2), 111–121.

Ciulla, J. B. (2020). Ethics and effectiveness: The nature of good leadership. In: *The Search for Ethics in Leadership, Business, and beyond. Issues in Business Ethics* (Vol. 50). Springer. https://doi.org/10.1007/978-3-030-38463-0_1

Côté, J. E., & Levine, C. G. (2014). *Identity, Formation, Agency, and Culture: A Social Psychological Synthesis*. Psychology Press.

Hofstede, G. (1998). Attitudes, values and organizational culture: Disentangling the concepts. *Organization Studies*, *19*(3), 477–493.

Hofstede, G. (2011). Dimensionalizing cultures: The Hofstede model in context. *Online Readings in Psychology and Culture*, *2*(1), 8.

Johnson, K. A., Hill, E. D., & Cohen, A. B. (2011). Integrating the study of culture and religion: Toward a psychology of worldview. *Social and Personality Psychology Compass*, *5*(3), 137–152.

Ma, G. X., Born, M. P., Petrou, P., & Bakker, A. B. (2021). Bright sides of dark personality? A cross-cultural study on the dark triad and work outcomes. *International Journal of Selection and Assessment*, *29*(3–4), 510–518.

National Bureau of Statistics. (2018). National Nutrition and Health Survey (NNHS) 2018. https://www.nigerianstat.gov.ng/pdfuploads/NNHS_2018_Final%20 Report.pdf

Nguyen, H. H. D., Le, H., & Boles, T. (2010). Individualism–collectivism and cooperation: A cross-society and cross-level examination. *Negotiation and Conflict Management Research*, *3*(3), 179–204.

Nuzulia, S., & Why, F. Y. P. (2020). When the dark shines: The role of dark personality traits in leadership role occupancy and hiring decisions in a collectivistic culture. *Social Psychological and Personality Science*, *11*(8), 1089–1100.

Oyewunmi, A. E., Akinnusi, D. M., & Oyewunmi, O. A. (2018). Of predators and preys: Corporate psychopathy and employee burnout as parallels. *Periodica Polytechnica Social and Management Sciences*, *26*(2), 149–156.

Oyewunmi, A. E., Esho, E., & Oyewunmi, O. (2021). Spiritual intelligence and employee outcomes in an African sample. *Journal of Management, Spirituality & Religion*, *18*, 151–71.

Oyewunmi, A. E., & Oyewunmi, O. A. (2022). Speaking silence: Abusive supervision, subordinates' citizenship behavior, and whistleblowing intention. *SAGE Open*, *12*(1), 21582440221079912.

Paulhus, D. L., & Williams, K. M. (2002). The dark triad of personality: Narcissism, Machiavellianism, and psychopathy. *Journal of Research in Personality*, *36*(6), 556–563.

Puni, A., & Anlesinya, A. (2017). Whistleblowing propensity in power distance societies. *Journal of Global Responsibility*, *8*(2), 212–224.

Schyns, B., Gauglitz, I. K., Wisse, B., & Schütz, A. (2022). How to mitigate destructive leadership

Human resources-practices that mitigate Dark Triad leaders' destructive tendencies. In D. Lusk & T. Hayes (Eds.), *Overcoming Bad Leadership in Organizations: A Handbook For Leaders, Talent Management Professionals, and Psychologists* (pp. 251–276). (The SIOP professional practice series). Oxford: Oxford University Press. https://doi.org/10.1093/oso/9780197552759.003.0013

Spence, J. T., & Buckner, C. (1995). Masculinity and femininity: Defining the undefinable. In P. J. Kalbfleisch & M. J. Cody (Eds.), *Gender, Power, and Communication in Human Relationships* (pp. 105–138). Lawrence Erlbaum.

Srivastava, S., Singh, S., & Dhir, S., 2020. Culture and International business research: A review and research agenda. *International Business Review*, *29*(4), 101709.

Tiwari, M., & Jha, R. (2022). Narcissism, toxic work culture and abusive supervision: A double-edged sword escalating organizational deviance. *International Journal of Organisational Analysis*, *30*(1), 99–114.

Volmer, J., Koch, I. K., & Göritz, A. S. (2016). The bright and dark sides of leaders' dark triad traits: Effects on subordinates' career success and well-being. *Personality and Individual Differences*, *101*, 413–418.

Wisse, B., & Sleebos, E. (2016). When the dark ones gain power: Perceived position power strengthens the effect of supervisor Machiavellianism on abusive supervision in work teams. *Personality and Individual Differences*, *99*, 122–126.

Chapter 16

Culture and the Politics of Leadership: Insights from Iraqi-Kurdistan

Balen Mohammed

Introduction

The chapter presents a contextual overview of the Kurdish people, their identity, history, and current challenges, emphasising their distinct cultural and linguistic identity and their desire for increased recognition and autonomy (Gurses & Gunter, 2016). Kurds, an ethnic group primarily inhabiting Kurdistan—a territory spanning parts of Turkey, Iran, Iraq, and Syria—have a long history and a strong culture but face political marginalisation and cultural oppression. Iraq, renowned for its extensive heritage, boasts significant diversity in terms of culture and ethnicity. After World War I, the United Kingdom formed Iraq by combining three former Ottoman states: Baghdad, Basra, and Mosul, and Iraq subsequently transitioned from a monarchy to a republic following independence and several political upheavals (Basu, 2011). The Kurds, making up approximately 20% of Iraq's population and primarily residing in the northern Kurdistan region, are identified by their unique culture and language. Kurdish culture, among the oldest in the world, shares similarities with Mesopotamian culture but has faced historical injustices and oppression. The chapter examines Kurdish society's influence on leadership dynamics in Iraqi Kurdistan, the influence of Kurdish leaders, Iraqi-Kurdish culture and ethnic identification, and concluding insights on leadership in a dynamic world.

DOI: 10.4324/9781003475262-19

Iraqi-Kurdish culture and ethnic identification highlight a shared history, mistreatment, and the collective struggle for recognition (Mtani et al., 2023). Ethnic identity significantly influences individuals' behaviours and socialisation patterns. The intensity of ethnic identification often drives people to socialise with those who share their ethnic background, as in-group members are perceived as superior, coupled with an absence of barriers to interaction and nulling the fear of discrimination. Research supports the idea that situational variables, such as the ethnic diversity of a context, can intensify and strengthen ethnic norms. Individuals with similar traits exert a more significant influence on society compared to those with different characteristics, aligning with the social comparison theory. Thus, spending time with individuals from one's ethnic group results in greater consumption of cultural items associated with that group compared to interacting with individuals from various ethnic groups. This consumption is expected to exceed the influence of ethnic identification alone. The theory suggests that the strength of ethnic identification positively impacts the degree of social interaction with individuals from the same ethnic background (Mtani et al., 2023).

Culture and Leadership in Iraqi Kurdistan

Reflecting on the multifaceted nature of Kurdish culture and its impact on leadership in Iraqi Kurdistan reveals several key elements that shape leadership approaches in the region. Kurdish culture is influenced by a combination of factors and is characterised by a strong sense of solidarity and cultural identity, despite being dispersed across countries. Traditional social structures, such as tribal and familial relationships, provide leaders with authority and credibility. Kurdish leaders are often seen as icons of tenacity and resistance, influencing their leadership ideologies. They also demonstrate flexibility and pragmatism in managing political situations while maintaining cultural identity. Unity and cultural identity are central to Kurdish culture. Despite being spread over several nations, Kurds share a common language, cultural heritage, and history, which fosters a strong sense of unity and solidarity. This shared identity frequently manifests in leadership approaches, with Kurdish leaders uniting their people around the cause of Kurdish nationalism and self-determination by emphasising the importance of maintaining Kurdish culture and heritage (Gurses & Gunter, 2016).

Traditional social structures play a significant role in Kurdish society. Leaders often derive credibility and power from their standing within these systems. Tribal elders hold considerable sway in Kurdish communities and play crucial roles in mediating disputes and resolving conflicts (Hama & Abdullah, 2020). Kurdish communities have faced persecution and oppression, fostering a strong sense of perseverance and resolve. Kurdish leaders exhibit both pragmatism and adaptability in their leadership style, balancing their strong cultural identity with practical political manoeuvring. They often form pragmatic alliances and navigate complex political landscapes to further their community's interests. This adaptability reflects Kurdish culture's emphasis on survival and resilience in the face of adversity (Nazarova, 2022). In summary, Kurdish culture emphasises cultural identity, traditional social structures, collective struggle, and adaptability. These elements collectively shape leadership approaches in Iraqi Kurdistan, enabling Kurdish leaders to rally support, navigate political challenges, and advance their community's goals.

Leadership in the Face of Adversity

In 2014, when ISIS (Islamic State of Iraq and Syria) launched a large-scale offensive in Northern Iraq, the Kurdish region of Iraq faced an existential threat. The Kurdish Peshmerga forces, the military branch of the Kurdistan Regional Government (KRG), were thrust into the spotlight as the frontline defence against the encroaching threat. This period of intense conflict provides a rich case study for understanding the unique leadership dynamics within Kurdish society.

The sudden rise of ISIS caught many by surprise, including the Iraqi central government. With the Iraqi army retreating in the face of the rapid advance, Kurdish leaders had to make swift and strategic decisions to protect their people and territory. The Kurdish leadership displayed resilience, adaptability, and pragmatic decision-making. In confronting a common enemy, Kurdish leaders emphasised the importance of unity and cultural identity to rally support and morale among the Peshmerga and the civilian population. This call to unity was not merely rhetorical; it involved practical steps such as coordinating with various tribal and political factions within the Kurdish region to present a united front. The deep-rooted sense of Kurdish identity and solidarity played a crucial role in mobilising the population and the military forces against ISIS. In Kurdish society, traditional social structures, such as tribal affiliations and familial ties, significantly influence leadership credibility. During the crisis, leaders who had strong ties within these traditional structures were able to leverage their positions to secure resources, recruit fighters, and maintain order. Tribal elders and influential families played pivotal roles in local defence efforts and logistical support, demonstrating the continued relevance of these traditional structures in contemporary conflict situations. The Kurdish leaders exhibited a high degree of adaptability and pragmatism. Recognising the need for external support, they quickly forged alliances with international actors, including the United States and other coalition forces. This strategic pragmatism ensured that the Peshmerga received critical military aid, training, and air support, which were instrumental in turning the tide against ISIS.

The Kurdish response to the ISIS threat highlights several key lessons for leaders operating in challenging environments. First, leveraging a shared cultural and ethnic identity can be a powerful tool in rallying people during crises. Second, understanding and utilising traditional social structures can enhance leadership effectiveness and resource mobilisation. Third, leaders must be adaptable, willing to form strategic alliances, and make pragmatic decisions to navigate complex and dynamic situations. Fourth, navigating religious and cultural landscapes with sensitivity can help maintain internal cohesion and support. This case study underscores the interplay between culture, traditional social structures, and pragmatic leadership in times of crisis.

Lessons for Leaders in Challenging Situations

A stormy past, strong social structures, and a deep sense of national identity shape the Kurdish experience, providing insightful lessons for leaders navigating a variety of challenging situations. Unquestionably, one of the most important things to learn from Iraqi Kurdistan is the power of culture when it comes to leadership. Tribal ties continue to be a powerful indicator of legitimacy; leaders who enjoy strong tribal support are frequently at a disadvantage when it comes to building authority. This emphasises how important it is for leaders to fully understand the social structures and cultural norms that are prevalent in the operational contexts in which they operate. A sophisticated understanding of the conventional sources of authority and their potential interactions with formal power institutions is essential for effective leadership. Furthermore, the legacy of Iraqi Kurdistan's resistance activities, personified by the recognisable Peshmerga forces, emphasises the impact of collective struggle on leadership philosophies. The resistance movements that many Kurdish political personalities came from fostered a powerful blend of charisma, tenacity, and steadfast dedication to a cause (Flanagan & Brannen, 2008). Leaders who work in challenging or conflict-ridden workplaces would be wise to recognise the inspirational value of sharing a struggle to create strong relationships between leaders and followers. Nationalism is a powerful force in the Iraqi-Kurdish relationship that demands attention. Within the political realm of the region, Kurdish nationalism functions as a contested space as well as a unifying ideal (Natali, 2005). Leaders who can effectively harness the deep emotional resonance of nationalist goals can mobilise a sizeable base of support. But divergent interpretations of nationalism also highlight an important lesson for leaders to learn to foster a cohesive vision while acknowledging the possibility of internal conflicts and conflicting ideological narratives, politicians must adeptly negotiate the complexity of collective identity.

The demands of modernisation also apply to Iraqi Kurdistan's leadership. The region, like many others, must adjust to modern difficulties such as economic development, regional instability, and growing calls for accountability and transparency, even as traditional cultural values continue to hold significance (Günter, 2018). This changing environment highlights a critical lesson for leaders in a variety of fields: the significance of striking a balance between adherence to tradition and adaptability and a readiness to innovate. Proficiency in technological skills, diplomacy, and responsiveness to the needs and expectations of a more informed and linked connected populace are increasingly necessary for successful leadership in the 21st century. Finally, the politics of leadership in Iraqi Kurdistan provide an engaging case study of how history, culture, and modern conditions interact to influence the ascent, trajectories, and styles of leaders. We must understand deeply ingrained social structures, acknowledge that shared experiences fuel leadership, acknowledge the complexity of identity politics, and adapt conventional leadership paradigms to meet the demands of modern society. Recognising these insights can help leaders working in diverse and demanding contexts improve their awareness of the subtle factors influencing their performance and create more significant avenues for advancement.

Leadership is the skill of inspiring and directing a collective toward the attainment of common objectives, and it is a concept that is constantly changing and developing. Leaders in the present evolving landscape encounter distinct difficulties and prospects. To achieve success, leaders must possess the qualities of adaptability, empathy, and technological proficiency.

An essential lesson for contemporary leaders is the significance of cultivating a culture that promotes collaboration and adaptation. The inflexible and stratified systems of the past are becoming progressively inadequate in a society characterised by perpetual transformation. Leaders should facilitate and encourage their teams to actively participate in generating ideas, displaying initiative, and collaborating to resolve issues. An organisation with a collaborative culture can respond promptly to unforeseen circumstances. The success of organisations such as Spotify and Google can be attributed to their adoption of flat structures and team-oriented practices, which promote creativity and agility.

Modern leaders must prioritise the acceptance and integration of diverse perspectives and individuals. Forming a heterogeneous team composed of individuals with different perspectives, backgrounds, and skill sets yields a plethora of knowledge and ideas and is essential for effectively addressing challenges in a multifaceted environment. Leaders should advocate for inclusive work environments where all individuals feel esteemed and secure in expressing their viewpoints. Research has continuously indicated that teams with a varied range of members typically get better results compared to teams with members who are similar in terms of background and characteristics. This highlights the strategic advantages of fostering inclusion.

Social media platforms such as Twitter and Facebook have disrupted conventional, hierarchical communication, presenting fresh prospects for mobilisation, particularly during periods of crisis. When faced with disputed political circumstances within their nation, leaders strive to enhance or uphold their political authority and take measures to restore or enhance their power equilibrium. The diversionary theory of war posits that leaders may employ alternative tactics to deflect attention away from domestic concerns, such as using force as a threat or participating in escalating rhetoric, rather than directly engaging in a physical fight. Democratic leaders are more motivated to connect with a wider range of voters since they have a higher likelihood of losing their jobs. Democratic leaders are prone to altering their communication tactics in times of popular unrest, especially before an election, in contrast to non-democratic regimes. Leadership as an art and science, combining intuitive and structured approaches. It emphasises the importance of narrative and storytelling, cultural and historical contexts, and ethical considerations. This interdisciplinary approach empowers leaders to navigate challenges.

Conclusion

This chapter provides an overview of the Kurdish people, their identity, history, and the challenges they face. It discusses the influence of Kurdish society on leadership dynamics in Iraqi Kurdistan, emphasising the significance of cultural identity, traditional social structures, and collective struggle. It demonstrates how Kurdish leaders navigate complex political landscapes, leveraging their cultural identity and traditional social structures to garner support and advance their community's goals. The case study of the Kurdish response to the ISIS threat underscores the importance of unity, strategic pragmatism, and cultural sensitivity in leadership. Understanding the intricate interplay between culture, traditional social structures, and pragmatic leadership in times of crisis provides valuable insights for leaders operating in diverse and dynamic contexts. By recognising these lessons, leaders can improve their performance and create more significant avenues for advancement, ensuring effective governance and resilience in times of adversity.

References

Basu, M. (2011). The cultural diversity of contemporary Iraq in the light of security threats and conflicts between its components. *Journal of Conflict Studies, 31*(1), 87–103.

Flanagan, S. J., & Brannen, S. (2008). *Turkey's Shifting Dynamics: Implications for US-Turkey Relations*. CSIS.

Günter, M. M. (2018). *The Kurds: A Modern History*. Markus Wiener Publishers.

Gurses, M., & Gunter, M. M. (2016). *The Kurds: A Modern History*. Markus Wiener Publishers.

Hama, H. H., & Abdullah, F. H. (2020). Political parties and the political system in Iraqi Kurdistan. *SAGE Open, 10*(3), 1–10.

Mtani, W. Z., Kadhim, Q. K., Salim, M. A., Hatim, A., Attiya, J., Al Mahdi, R. A., & Abdelhassan, M. I. (2023). Kurdish ethnicity, conspicuous consumption, and Kurdish cultural apparel consumption in Iraq. *Kurdish Studies, 11*(1), 17–35.

Natali, D. (2005). *The Kurdish Quasi-State: Development and Dependency in Post-Gulf War Iraq*. Syracuse University Press.

Nazarova, F. (2022). Energy factor in Iraqi Kurdistan: Opportunities and geopolitical problems. *International Journal of Management and Humanities, 5*(7), 112–119.

Chapter 17

Unveiling the Unfelt Snakes: Understanding the Dark Side of Leadership in Asian Culture

Samyia Safdar, Namra Mubarak, and Shazia Faiz

Introduction

Dark leadership has been embedded in Asian culture for a long time. The abuse of power by leaders and the suppression of the voice of others is prevalent (Mubarak et al., 2024). While Western literature identifies the consequences of this leadership style, the perception of Asians of despotic leaders is underpinned by cultural processes that deify leaders and overlook their negative tendencies. With this perspective, an array of dark leadership styles is bound to manifest. The authoritarian leadership style combines the centralisation of power, strict control, and limited input from subordinates and often relies on fear and coercion to maintain authority (Hofstede, 2011). Narcissistic leaders exhibit grandiosity, self-centeredness, and a lack of empathy for others. They prioritise their own needs over the well-being of their followers (Lee & Chan, 2009). Hubris Leadership is characterised by arrogance, pride, and self-confidence, leading to irresponsible decision-making (Owen & Davidson, 2009). Dictatorial leaders exert absolute control and often rule through fear and intimidation. They suppress dissent and limit freedoms to maintain power (Smith, Peterson & Schwartz, 2002).

Paternalistic leaders may present themselves as caring and protective figures but can also be controlling and make decisions on behalf of others without their input (Hanges et al., 2016). Despotic leadership is a leadership

 DOI: 10.4324/9781003475262-20

style where the leader exercises absolute power and control over their subordinates, often without regard for their well-being or input (Khan, Mubarak & Jaafar, 2021b). Abusive leadership is characterised by harmful and destructive behaviours toward subordinates, such as bullying, harassment, verbal abuse, and exploitation (Li & Sun, 2015). The tyrannical leadership style is an autocratic and domineering approach where managers ignore employees' well-being and opinions and practice absolute authority and power (Ashforth, 1997). Psychopathic leaders are driven by greed and self-interest, with predatory, unacceptable, and brutal characteristics (Neumann & Hare, 2008). Machiavellian leaders are known for their manipulative and cunning tactics to achieve their goals. They are willing to deceive and exploit others for personal gain (House et al., 2004). This chapter further discusses dark leadership styles in Asian cultures and simultaneously identifies lessons for leaders.

Despotic Leadership

Despotic leadership is one of the many forms of dark leadership styles that has not received enough attention (Schilling, 2009). A despotic leader considers themselves superior, neglecting the rights and interests of their followers (Aronson, 2001). Many references can be seen from the history of Asian culture where the despotic leadership style is depicted. In China, people view a specific president as a dictator considering the policy of concentrating power and suppression of dissent. Similarly, the history of Pakistan shows how democratic values have been suppressed and peoples' voices have been silenced under the watch of despotic leaders. These examples from Asian countries highlight the prevalence of despotic leadership in that cultural context, therefore, it is essential to explore the fundamentals that engender this mode of leadership. It is plausible that a combination of factors, including political structures, cultural norms, and historical precedents have contributed to the suppression of dissent and high-power concentration culture in the Asian countries considered in this chapter.

Consider the case of a well-known private-sector university operating in Pakistan. The leaders practice a despotic leadership style, disregarding employee inputs, demanding absolute obedience, and exercising tight control, which leads to high employee and faculty turnover rates and low morale. This case study exemplifies the tangible influences of leadership styles on employee well-being and organisational health. It emphasises the requirement for bosses to adopt a leadership style that considers subordinates' perspectives and ensures inclusiveness.

Therefore, based on lessons and insights in the Asian context, leaders could gain a better understanding of how their attitudes and actions can empower or suppress their employees. An effective appreciation of the negative outcomes of despotic leadership would promote a respectful environment and enhanced inclusion. Leaders' receptiveness to feedback and open dialogue are useful tools to mitigate the negative outcomes of a despotic leadership approach.

Abusive Leadership

According to Tepper (2000), abusive leadership is also one of the negative sides of leadership. Abusive leaders' words and actions are harmful to the individuals working under their direction or supervision. These include verbal, physical, manipulation, exploitation, etc. They create a hostile and negative environment that erodes the individuality of subordinates and constrains the expression of divergent opinions or perspectives. Nepotism and favouritism by leaders have been identified as forms of abusive leadership. Leaders may show preferential treatment to family members or close associates, leading to resentment and unfair treatment of other employees, which can undermine morale and productivity (Chen & Aryee, 2007). Consider the case of a leading public sector telecommunication company in Pakistan where cultural norms and hierarchical structures primarily allowed abusive leadership practices. Leaders at the departmental level often use intimidation and verbal harassment to enforce strict observance of their directives, creating a hostile work environment that leads to low morale and a high turnover rate of employees. Therefore, the company adopted specific initiatives and launched training programs and workshops to educate both employees and leaders about the significance of a respectful working environment. They also created an anonymous reporting system where anyone can report the abusive behaviour that they have experienced. Consequently, the employee's performance and productivity improved, the turnover rate declined, and a more positive work environment emerged.

These examples of abusive leadership from an Asian context provide cardinal lessons for leaders. It is noteworthy that leaders could promote equality and mitigate the potential abuse by recognising that organisational hierarchy and cultural norms influence their behaviours. Also, it is important to create an inclusive environment by ensuring employee well-being, ethical practices, fairness, and open communication, and designing policies and processes to address power imbalance.

Tyrannical Leadership

Another detrimental facet of leadership style is tyrannical leadership (Boudrias, Rousseau, & Lajoie, 2021). It is the self-serving and negative leadership type in which leaders possess control and use oppressive measures on their employees. Leaders with this kind of style focus more on punitive actions, excessive demands, and lack of empathy. Intimidation and fear are often used by these kinds of leaders, which results in the creation of a demoralising and stifling work environment.

In Pakistan, tyrannical leadership is being practised under the umbrella of an autocratic management style in numerous organisations. They impose strict compliance with their orders and uphold inflexible control over decision-making processes. Employees' attitudes and feelings are negatively impacted damaging the work environment (Zhao et al., 2024). In China, especially in the manufacturing sector, the leaders show the characteristics of tyrannical leadership. They use punitive procedures, need absolute obedience, and impose harsh rules, which results in work withdrawal behaviour and a reduction in task performance (Ahmad, Nauman, & Malik, 2022). For instance, a well-known manufacturing firm in China witnessed a tyrannical leadership style. The top management of this firm demands the enforcement of harsh rules and absolute obedience. After attending the workshop, the top management realised that they needed to modify their leadership style by emphasising inclusion in decision-making, empathy, and employee engagement. Therefore, the CEO created an environment where feedback was appreciated. The constructive feedback mechanism replaced punitive measures. As a result, the firm observed a significant increase in employee retention, productivity, morale, and performance.

Hofstede (2011) asserts that identifiable cultures have different effects on leadership, particularly regarding the concept of dark leadership. High-power distance societies, i.e., Asian countries, show tolerance towards tyrannical leaders because of the cultural focus on hierarchy and authority. While low-power distance societies, i.e., western cultures, show resistance towards tyrannical leaders because of equality and open communication. Therefore, Asian leaders can leverage specific lessons, especially regarding the damaging effects of tyrannical leadership, and create a positive work environment that promotes empathy and inclusion in the decision-making process.

Psychopathic Leadership

Psychopathic leaders are lacking in empathy, manipulative, and charming (Landay, Harms, & Credé, 2019). They are always emotionally detached but are adroit at emotional manipulation. By using deceptive tactics, lying, and backstabbing they create a facade of charisma (Palmen, Kolthoff, & Derksen, 2021). The followers may be drawn by it initially but increasingly feel betrayed.

Asian culture is also evident in this kind of leadership style, as a few of the examples are discussed here. In Pakistan, psychopathic leaders might use deceit and charm to scramble the corporate ladder for personal gain. Initially, followers might get attracted by the charm of the leader. Eventually, followers can identify the leaders' empathy deficient and self-centred behaviour. This realisation reduces employee satisfaction and increases turnover intention (Khan et al., 2021a). In China, multinational firms' psychopathic leaders implement activities for personal gain by using their charm or practising unethical activities. This kind of behaviour creates a hostile environment where employees feel that trust is eroded (Boddy et al., 2020). A China-based Tech start-up once illustrious for its innovative solution and hasty growth became a case study in the menaces of psychopathic leadership. The CEO of that tech start-up initially drew investors and employees by using his manipulative and charismatic tactics. However, he fostered a toxic environment as the firm grew. Due to a lack of empathy and his self-centred nature, the employees reported feeling deceived and morally detached. This caused low employee morale and high turnover rates resulting in company backlash from the public and employees and causing huge reputational damage. Open communication and ethical leadership could engender a productive work environment whilst discouraging psychopathic leadership practices.

Psychopathic leadership can be attributed to the cultural values of individualism and psychopathic traits. Individualistic societies, which prioritise individual accomplishment and success, may enable the manifestations of such behaviours. However, in collectivist societies, which stress social cohesion and group harmony, leaders who exhibit such traits can easily be predictable and vetoed. In these cultures, corporate psychopathy could be effectively addressed by emphasising democratic and open communication processes.

Management should ensure the training programs for the leaders so that they can be able to identify the traits of psychopathic leadership and understand its harmful effects on employee well-being and organisational culture. At the workplace, the presence of empathy and ethical behaviour can also mitigate the detrimental effects of psychopathic leadership. Leaders can encourage open dialogues and transparency to resolve issues at the workplace, which can create trust and a supportive environment resulting in a reduction in turnover and greater employee satisfaction.

Machiavellian Leadership

Exploitation for personal gain, deception, and manipulation are the characteristics of this leadership style (Jonason & Webster, 2010). To attain their objectives, Machiavellian leaders often use strategic tactics and cunning, even if they have to sacrifice other's welfare. They maintain their power and authority by control and manipulation and take ethical considerations for granted to foster their interests. Associated with an environment of fear and distrust undermining collaboration and teamwork. Employees feel undervalued and exploited and their morale and productivity decrease when they work under this kind of leadership (Mertens et al., 2024).

Asian culture abounds with these kinds of examples, a few of which are discussed in this chapter. Machiavellian leaders can manipulate the idea of "guanxi" (relationship and networking), to consolidate control and power. They can use their relationship and networks to gain favours, influence decisions, and sideline opponents, creating a workplace culture that undermines meritocracy (Xing, 2021). In one Chinese multinational company, the regional manager was using Guanxi to secure business deals and build a powerful network through personal favours while sidelining capable workers lacking strong networks. This causes low morale and distrust issues in hard-working employees leading to a toxic work environment and low productivity.

Moreover, the widespread presence of hierarchical structures in Pakistan indicates that leaders with Machiavellian characteristics can exercise power and control through favouritism and manipulation. Using psychological tactics these leaders exploit followers' dependency and loyalty to secure compliance and maintain dominance (Aggarwal et al., 2020). Machiavellian leadership, with deceit, strategic manipulation, and exploitation for personal gain, unfolds differently in both Eastern and Western cultures. In Eastern culture, with harmony, hierarchical respect, and collectivism, Machiavellian leaders go for indirect ways and use guanxi or personal relations to influence decisions, attain their goals, and exert their power. Therefore, to maintain authority and power, leaders sometimes compromise ethical considerations (Liyanagamage & Fernando, 2023). While, in Western culture, leaders with these characteristics adopt direct tactics and manipulation to achieve their benefits. These kinds of leaders' behaviour is sometimes implicitly endorsed in eminent Western business environments, resulting in profitability and success (Muris et al., 2017). This shows that ethical flexibility, manipulation, and strategic exploration are the consistent characteristics of Machiavellianism leaders across cultures (Hussain et al., 2021).

However, significant lessons are provided based on the above discussion of Machiavellian leadership. Leaders should avoid this style considering its destructive impact of exploitation and manipulation on employee productivity and morale. This kind of leadership style also underscores the significance of ethical behaviours at the leadership level. Therefore, leadership should foster a collaborative workplace environment to build trust. Their use of personal networks and relationships should be ethical, devoid of favouritism, and focus on promoting meritocracy.

Conclusion

In Asian culture, the search for dark leadership divulges a multifaceted and complex landscape, emphasising substantial aberrations. The relative prevalence and elusive integration of dark leadership styles, including Machiavellian, tyrannical, despotic, psychopathic, and abusive, into Asian organisational settings, underscore the central role of cultural settings on leadership subtleties. Though Western literature mostly stresses the negative outcomes of dark leadership, including lack of freedom, corruption, and abuse, the insights from Asian contexts often integrate an additional nuanced view, depicting cultural and historical habituation that outlines the manifestation and reception of these leadership styles.

Control and absolute power are characterised as despotic leadership, with adapted examples from Asian countries, namely, Pakistan and China. These kinds of leadership characteristics are reflected in Asian culture because of the well-established cultural and historical norms, i.e., authority and hierarchy. Abusive leadership occurs when cultural values and hierarchical structures enable exploitative behaviour and power imbalance. Punitive measures and harsh control are characterised as tyrannical leadership.

Importantly, high-power distance societies have authoritarian leadership and tolerance, which enable them to practice tyrannical leadership. The emotionally detached and manipulative are characterised as psychopathic leaders, whereas those with exploitation and deceit are characterised as Machiavellian leaders. These kinds of leaders establish the compliance and perseverance of dark leadership styles in numerous Asian settings. These styles frequently influence cultural essentials such as hierarchical respect in Pakistan and China's "guanxi" to exert control and power.

Ultimately, this chapter elaborates on the dark leadership style by examining its numerous types and implications in the Asian context. It challenges the chiefly Western-based approach of dark leadership, supporting a more ethnically nuanced perspective to leadership research. By emphasising dark leadership in the Asian context, this study provides implications for policymakers, leaders, and scholars about the necessity of culturally sensitive leadership development and ethical frameworks for decision-making.

References

Aggarwal, A., Chand, P. K., Jhamb, D., & Mittal, A. (2020). Leader-member exchange, work engagement, and psychological withdrawal behaviour: The mediating role of psychological empowerment. *Frontiers in Psychology, 11*, 423.

Ahmad, R., Nauman, S., & Malik, S. Z. (2022). Tyrannical leader, Machiavellian follower, work withdrawal, and task performance: Missing links in construction projects. *Journal of Construction Engineering and Management, 148*(7), 04022045.

Aronson, E. (2001). Integrating leadership styles and ethical perspectives. *Canadian Journal of Administrative Sciences/Revue Canadienne des Sciences de l'Administration, 18*(4), 244–256.

Ashforth, B. E. (1997). Petty tyranny in organizations: A preliminary examination of antecedents and consequences. *Canadian Journal of Administrative Sciences/Revue Canadienne des Sciences de l'Administration, 14*(2), 126–140.

Boddy, C. R., Malovany, E., Kunter, A., & Gull, G. (2020). Employee well-being under corporate psychopath leaders. In S. K. Dhiman (Ed.), *The Palgrave Handbook of Workplace Well-being* (pp. 1–28). Palgrave Macmillan. https://doi.org/10.1007/978-3-030-30025-8_74

Boudrias, J. S., Rousseau, V., & Lajoie, D. (2021). How lack of integrity and tyrannical leadership of managers influence employee improvement-oriented behaviours. *Journal of Business Ethics, 172*(3), 487–502.

Chen, Z. X., & Aryee, S. (2007). Delegation and employee work outcomes: An examination of the cultural context of mediating processes in China. *Academy of Management Journal, 50*(1), 226–238.

Hanges, P. J., Aiken, J. R., Park, J., & Su, J. (2016). Cross-cultural leadership: Leading around the world. *Current Opinion in Psychology, 8*, 64–69.

Hofstede, G. (2011). Dimensionalizing cultures: The Hofstede model in context. *Online Readings in Psychology and Culture, 2*(1), 8.

House, R. J., Hanges, P. J., Javidan, M., Dorfman, P. W., & Gupta, V. (Eds.). (2004). *Culture, Leadership, and Organizations: The GLOBE Study of 62 Societies*. Sage Publications.

Hussain, G., Samreen, F., Ismail, W. K. W., Riaz, A., & Azhar, J. (2021). From Machiavellianism to unethical behaviour: A cross-level examination of cultural factors. *The Spanish Journal of Psychology, 24*, e46.

Jonason, P. K., & Webster, G. D. (2010). The dirty dozen: a concise measure of the dark triad. *Psychological Assessment, 22*(2), 420.

Khan, N. A., Khan, A. N., Moin, M. F., & Pitafi, A. H. (2021a). A trail of chaos: How psychopathic leadership influence employee satisfaction and turnover intention via self-efficacy in tourism enterprises. *Journal of Leisure Research, 52*(3), 347–369.

Khan, J., Mubarak, N., & Jaafar, M. (2021b). Despotic leadership, negative emotions and project success: The role of Mindfulness. *Academy of Management Proceedings, 1*, 14775.

Landay, K., Harms, P. D., & Credé, M. (2019). Shall we serve the dark lords? A meta-analytic review of psychopathy and leadership. *Journal of Applied Psychology, 104*(1), 183.

Lee, Y. T., & Chan, A. (2009). Leadership styles and cultural values among managers and subordinates: A comparative study of four countries of the Pacific Basin. *Asia Pacific Business Review, 15*(3), 331–348.

Li, Y., & Sun, J. M. (2015). Traditional Chinese leadership and employee voice behaviour: A cross-level examination. *The Leadership Quarterly, 26*(2), 172–189.

Liyanagamage, N., & Fernando, M. (2023). Machiavellian leadership in organisations: A review of theory and research. *Leadership & Organization Development Journal, 44*(6), 791–811.

Mertens, D., Villegas, S. G., Ware, M. G., Vengrouskie, E. F., & Lloyd, R. (2024). Business process reengineering leadership: Princes of Machiavelli. *Journal of Management History, 30*(1), 41–59.

Mubarak, N., Khan, J., Bashir, S., & Safdar, S. (2024). Dark side of leadership and information technology project success: The role of mindfulness. *Journal of Managerial Psychology, 39*(3), 304–322.

Muris, P., Merckelbach, H., Otgaar, H., & Meijer, E. (2017). The malevolent side of human nature: A meta-analysis and critical review of the literature on the dark triad (narcissism, Machiavellianism, and psychopathy). *Perspectives on Psychological Science, 12*(2), 183–204.

Neumann, C. S., & Hare, R. D. (2008). Psychopathic traits in a large community sample: links to violence, alcohol use, and intelligence. *Journal of Consulting and Clinical Psychology, 76*(5), 893.

Owen, D., & Davidson, J. (2009). Hubris syndrome: An acquired personality disorder? A study of US Presidents and UK Prime Ministers over the last 100 years. *Brain, 132*(5), 1396–1406.

Palmen, D. G., Kolthoff, E. W., & Derksen, J. J. (2021). The need for domination in psychopathic leadership: A clarification for the estimated high prevalence of psychopathic leaders. *Aggression and Violent Behaviour, 61*, 101650.

Schilling, J. (2009). From ineffectiveness to destruction: A qualitative study on the meaning of negative leadership. *Leadership, 5*(1), 102–128.

Smith, P. B., Peterson, M. F., & Schwartz, S. H. (2002). Cultural values, sources of guidance, and their relevance to managerial behaviour: A 47-nation study. *Journal of Cross-Cultural Psychology, 33*(2), 188–208.

Tepper, B. J. (2000). Consequences of abusive supervision. *Academy of Management Journal, 43*(2), 178–190.

Xing, L. (2021). Conceptualizing 'meritocracy's ruling legitimacy in the course of China's history, transformation, and global rise. In C. Shei and W. Wei (Eds.), *The Routledge Handbook of Chinese Studies* (pp. 127–145). Routledge.

Zhao, S., Ben-Abdallah, R., Khattak, S. A., & Wang, N. (2024). Examining the effects of tyrannical leadership on workplace incivility: Interplay of employee low morale and supportive organisational culture. *Current Psychology, 43*, 20456–20467.

Chapter 18

Toxic Leadership across Cultures: A Bitter Pill to Swallow

Oluwatobi Omotoye, Emmanuel Mogaji, and Zaccheaus Olonade

Introduction

There is consensus in the literature that toxic leaders exploit and devalue their employees, creating a negative atmosphere that undermines the entire organisation (e.g., Matos et al., 2018; Küçük, 2019). Traits like narcissism, authoritarianism, and manipulation are common among toxic leaders (Hattab et al., 2022; Schmidt, 2008). These behaviours often lead to micromanagement, favouritism, public humiliation, and coercion, making the work environment unbearable (Mackey et al., 2021). In terms of cross-cultural management, the challenge of addressing toxic leadership becomes even more complex. Organisations that operate in diverse cultural settings face several challenges in identifying and mitigating these harmful behaviours. This chapter discusses the psychological traits of toxic leaders and how these traits are perceived across different cultures. By understanding these dynamics, leaders can better navigate the challenges of cross-cultural management and create healthier, more supportive work environments. Practical strategies and insights are offered to promote the recognition of toxic behaviours and foster open communication and accountability. These actions are essential for mitigating the effects of toxic leadership and enhancing both organisational performance and employee satisfaction.

DOI: 10.4324/9781003475262-21

The Concept of Toxic Leadership

The term toxic leadership was first introduced by Whicker (1996), who described toxic leaders as maladjusted, discontent, and often malevolent individuals who tear others down. Lipman-Blumen (2006) expanded on this, defining toxic leaders as those who inflict severe and lasting harm on their followers through destructive behaviour or dysfunctional personal characteristics. The intent is crucial for behaviour to be deemed toxic; these leaders harm others to enhance themselves at the expense of subordinates and organisations (Lipman-Blumen, 2006). Toxic leaders neglect the well-being of their subordinates, often engaging in harmful and abusive behaviours (Schmidt, 2008). They are known for micromanagement, which causes subordinates to feel oppressed and anxious. Additionally, they often exhibit narcissistic and self-centred behaviours, showing little empathy or sensitivity towards their subordinates (Hattab et al., 2022; Schmidt, 2008). These traits disrupt not only the leader-follower relationship but also the entire organisational mechanism (Başkan, 2020). Narcissism is a prominent trait found in toxic leaders. Such leaders possess an inflated sense of their importance and a deep need for excessive attention and admiration (Cragun et al., 2020). They often harbour grandiose fantasies of unlimited success, power, and brilliance, coupled with a lack of genuine empathy for others. This self-centred perspective drives them to prioritise their self-image and personal gains over the welfare of their subordinates and the organisation (Asad & Sadler-Smith, 2020). Their behaviour can create a toxic work environment where employees feel undervalued and demoralised (Cragun et al., 2020).

Machiavellianism is characterised by manipulative, deceitful, and strategic behaviour aimed at personal gain (Genau et al., 2021). Machiavellian leaders are skilled in organisational politics, using cunning tactics to create alliances and manoeuvre situations to their advantage, often at the expense of others' well-being (Xiu et al., 2023). This fosters an environment of mistrust and hostility, severely undermining teamwork and collaboration (Frazier & Jacezko, 2021). A lack of empathy is a defining trait of many toxic leaders. Empathy involves the ability to understand and share the feelings of others, and leaders who lack this trait fail to connect with their subordinates' emotional states (Nowack & Zak, 2020). This results in a dehumanising approach to leadership, where employees are treated as mere instruments for achieving the leader's objectives, fostering a climate of fear and resentment (Sergey et al., 2020). Toxic leadership can have profound and far-reaching effects on organisational culture and climate. One significant consequence is the creation of a hostile work environment characterised by fear, mistrust, and low morale. Toxic leaders often engage in behaviours such as bullying, micromanagement, and favouritism, leading to increased stress and anxiety among employees (Brouwers & Paltu, 2020). These stifle open communication and collaboration as employees focus on self-preservation rather than contributing to organisational goals.

The adverse effects of toxic leadership extend to employee performance and productivity. Toxic behaviours result in decreased job satisfaction and motivation, which are critical drivers of employee performance (Adeoye et al., 2020). The stress and mental health issues caused by toxic leadership, such as burnout and depression, lead to higher absenteeism and presenteeism, further reducing productivity levels (Demerouti et al., 2001). In effect, toxic leadership increases turnover rates and the associated costs. High turnover leads to the loss of valuable institutional knowledge and experience, disrupts organisational stability, and incurs significant recruitment and training costs (Hattab et al., 2022). Toxic leadership is a primary driver of employee turnover intentions, as individuals seek to escape the negative environment (Akca, 2017). The reputation of the organisation can also suffer, making it challenging to attract top talent and perpetuating a cycle of dysfunction and underperformance.

Cross-Cultural Perspectives on Toxic Leadership

Cultural differences play a significant role in shaping the perception and tolerance of toxic leadership. Leadership behaviours considered toxic in one culture may not be perceived the same way in another due to varying cultural norms, values, and expectations. Hofstede's cultural dimensions theory, which includes dimensions such as power distance, individualism versus collectivism, and uncertainty avoidance, provides a useful framework for understanding these variations (Hofstede, 1980). In cultures with high power distance, such as many Asian and Middle Eastern countries, hierarchical structures and unequal power distribution are more accepted. Authoritarian leadership styles may be more tolerated, and behaviours considered toxic in low power distance cultures might be seen as normal or necessary for maintaining order and respect (Hofstede, 2003). For example, in China, where Confucian values emphasise respect for authority and hierarchy, a leader's strict and controlling behaviour might be perceived as a sign of strength and competence rather than toxicity (Xu et al., 2022).

Conversely, in low power distance cultures, such as those in Scandinavian countries, there is a greater emphasis on equality and participative leadership. In these societies, toxic leadership behaviours such as micromanagement, intimidation, and exploitation are less likely to be tolerated. Employees in these cultures expect leaders to be approachable, supportive, and fair, and deviations from these expectations can lead to significant backlash and decreased organisational commitment (House et al., 2004). In Sweden, for instance, organisational practices emphasise flat structures and collaborative decision-making, making it easier to identify and address toxic leadership to maintain a healthy work environment (Brouwers & Paltu, 2020). In individualistic cultures, like the United States, toxic leadership is often recognised through behaviours such as self-promotion, lack of empathy, and manipulation. The highly publicised case of Uber's former CEO, Travis Kalanick, highlights how toxic leadership can manifest in a competitive and individualistic culture. Kalanick's aggressive and often demeaning leadership style led to a toxic work environment characterised by fear and high turnover. Despite his initial success in driving the company's growth, his behaviour ultimately resulted in significant reputational damage and his eventual resignation (Doorley & Garcia, 2015). In collectivist cultures, such as South Korea, toxic leadership might be less overtly challenged due to the cultural emphasis on group harmony and respect for authority. The case of Korean Air's former Vice President Heather Cho illustrates this. Her infamous "nut rage" incident, where she berated and physically confronted a flight attendant over the service of macadamia nuts, exposed the dark side of hierarchical authority in Korean corporate culture (Kim et al., 2019). Although her actions were widely condemned and led to legal consequences, the initial tolerance of such behaviour underscores the complexities of addressing toxic leadership in cultures with deeply entrenched power dynamics.

In cultures with moderate power distance and a mix of collectivism and individualism, such as India, the perception of toxic leadership can vary widely depending on the organisational and regional context. Traditional family-owned businesses may accept authoritative and paternalistic leadership styles, whereas multinational corporations operating in India often expect Western-style participative leadership. This duality is evident in cases where Indian subsidiaries of multinational companies have to adapt their leadership approaches to align with local cultural expectations while adhering to global standards (Budhwar & Bhatnagar, 2008). In many African and Asian countries, high power distance and collectivism often mean a greater acceptance of hierarchical and authoritative leadership styles. However, the influence of multinational corporations and exposure to global organisational practices are gradually shifting expectations towards more ethical and participative leadership (Ogbonna & Harris, 2000). The contrast between traditional and contemporary leadership expectations in Nigeria highlights the ongoing cultural evolution and its impact on organisational dynamics.

In cultures like Japan, known for high uncertainty avoidance and collectivism, toxic leadership can manifest subtly through excessive control and unrealistic expectations. The concept of "karoshi" or death from overwork reflects the extreme consequences of toxic leadership in Japanese organisations. Leaders who impose relentless pressure on employees to meet high-performance standards without considering their well-being contribute to a toxic work environment that can lead to severe mental and physical health issues (Wolor, 2022). The cultural emphasis on loyalty and harmony often discourages open confrontation, making it challenging to address toxic leadership directly. These examples underscore the importance of understanding cultural context when analysing and addressing toxic leadership. While the core behaviours of toxic leaders may be similar, their impact and the organisational response can vary significantly based on cultural values and norms. Organisations operating in multicultural environments must be particularly mindful of these differences and strive to develop culturally sensitive leadership practices that promote a healthy and inclusive work environment (Gelfand et al., 2007).

Understanding cross-cultural perspectives on toxic leadership is crucial for organisations in a globalised world. Cultural differences significantly influence how toxic leadership is perceived and tolerated, affecting organisational culture, employee well-being, and overall performance. By examining examples from various cultural contexts, it becomes clear that while toxic leadership behaviours may be universally detrimental, the specific manifestations and responses to these behaviours can vary widely. Organisations must recognise these cultural nuances and develop strategies to mitigate the impact of toxic leadership, fostering a positive and supportive work environment across diverse cultural settings.

Mitigating Toxic Leadership

Mitigating toxic leadership requires robust organisational policies and practices. One essential policy is the implementation of comprehensive performance evaluation systems, incorporating 360-degree feedback from subordinates, peers, and superiors to provide a holistic view of a leader's behaviour and impact (Murphy, 2020). Such feedback can help identify toxic behaviours not evident in traditional performance reviews. Transparent codes of conduct defining acceptable and unacceptable behaviours within the organisation are crucial. These codes should be well-communicated and integrated into the company culture, with consistent and fair disciplinary actions for violations to reinforce a healthy work environment. Regular training on these codes ensures that all employees, including leaders, understand and adhere to organisational expectations. Organisations should implement whistleblower policies that protect employees who report toxic behaviour. Ensuring anonymity and protection from retaliation encourages employees to speak out against toxic leadership without fear of reprisal (Baraibar-Diez & Odriozola, 2023). Independent ombudsperson offices or ethics committees can handle such complaints, enhancing the credibility and effectiveness of these policies.

Psychological assessments during hiring and promotion processes can also help identify potential toxic leaders. Tools such as personality tests and situational judgement tests can help pinpoint individuals with traits associated with toxic leadership, such as narcissism and Machiavellianism, before they assume critical leadership roles. Training and development programmes are crucial in preventing and mitigating toxic leadership. These programmes should focus on fostering ethical leadership and developing emotional intelligence among leaders. Ethical leadership training emphasises integrity, transparency, and accountability in decision-making processes. By highlighting real-world scenarios, these programmes illustrate the positive impact of ethical leadership on organisational culture and performance. Developing competencies such as spiritual and emotional intelligence, including self-awareness, self-regulation, empathy, and social skills, will help leaders manage their own emotions and positively influence others (Coronado-Maldonado & Benitez-Marquez, 2023). Role-playing, simulations, and feedback can enhance leaders' emotional intelligence, reducing the likelihood of toxic behaviours.

Mentorship and coaching programmes facilitate the development of ethical and emotionally intelligent leaders. Pairing emerging leaders with experienced mentors who exemplify positive leadership traits provides guidance, advice, and modelling of appropriate behaviours (Asmamaw & Semela, 2023). Continuous coaching sessions help leaders reflect on their actions, receive constructive feedback, and develop improvement strategies. Leadership development programmes should include modules on cultural competence, especially in multinational corporations. Understanding and respecting cultural differences can prevent misunderstandings and reduce the likelihood of behaviours being perceived as toxic in diverse work environments (Minkov et al., 2023). Training in cultural competence also enhances leaders' ability to manage diverse teams effectively and inclusively. Human Resources (HR) and senior management play pivotal roles in addressing and mitigating toxic leadership. HR departments are often the first line of defence against toxic behaviours, responsible for implementing and enforcing policies related to leadership conduct and employee well-being. HR should actively monitor workplace dynamics through regular surveys, focus groups, and exit interviews to identify signs of toxic leadership (Kaiser et al., 2008). The data collected can inform targeted interventions and policy adjustments. HR should also facilitate ongoing training and development programmes, ensuring they are accessible to all organisational leaders. Additionally, HR can play a crucial role in succession planning by identifying and nurturing high-potential employees who exhibit positive leadership traits, creating a pipeline of ethical leaders for the future (Salas et al., 2012).

Senior management, including the CEO and executive team, must demonstrate a commitment to ethical leadership and set the tone for the entire organisation. Leaders at the top must model the behaviours and values they wish to see throughout the organisation. This commitment can be demonstrated through transparent communication, ethical decision-making, and accountability (Grojean et al., 2004). Senior management should also ensure clear channels for reporting and addressing toxic leadership behaviours, fostering a culture where feedback is valued and acted upon. Regular town hall meetings, open-door policies, and anonymous feedback mechanisms can encourage employees to voice their concerns without fear (Oyewunmi & Oyewunmi, 2022). Senior management should periodically review and assess the effectiveness of leadership development programmes and make necessary adjustments based on feedback and evolving organisational needs. This continuous improvement approach ensures that the strategies in place remain relevant and effective in fostering a positive leadership culture.

Lessons for Leaders

Understanding and addressing toxic leadership is essential for fostering a healthy organisational environment. Leaders play a pivotal role in shaping workplace culture. Hence, timely recognition of toxic leadership indicators and implementation strategies to mitigate their effects will contribute to significant improvements in employee well-being and organisational performance. The first step in mitigating toxic leadership is recognising its signs. Leaders must be aware of behaviours such as excessive control, manipulation, and a lack of empathy. Toxic leaders often prioritise their interests over those of the team and the organisation, leading to a hostile work environment. Regular feedback from employees, anonymous surveys, and open communication channels can help identify these harmful behaviours early. Also, empathy and respect are foundational to a healthy workplace culture. Leaders should actively cultivate an environment where employees feel valued and respected. This involves listening to employee concerns, acknowledging their contributions, and providing support when needed. Empathetic leadership fosters trust and loyalty, reducing the likelihood of toxic behaviours taking root.

Training and development programmes are essential in promoting ethical leadership and preventing toxic behaviours. These programmes should focus on building emotional intelligence, effective communication, conflict resolution, and ethical decision-making skills. By equipping leaders with these tools, organisations can foster a more positive and supportive work environment (Oyewunmi et al., 2021). Apt and well-communicated policies are crucial in managing and preventing toxic leadership. These policies should outline acceptable behaviours, consequences for violations, and procedures for reporting and addressing toxic behaviour. Ensuring that these policies are consistently enforced helps maintain a fair and respectful workplace.

Open communication is vital in addressing and preventing toxic leadership. Leaders should encourage a culture where employees feel comfortable voicing their concerns without fear of retaliation. Regular town hall meetings, suggestion boxes, and anonymous reporting systems can facilitate this open communication. Accountability and transparency are key in mitigating the effects of toxic leadership. Leaders should be transparent about their decision-making processes and hold themselves and others accountable for their actions. This builds trust and reinforces a culture of integrity within the organisation, and in the long term, will engender a more robust outlook on organisational performance, employee well-being, and satisfaction. In effect, a firm and functional understanding and implementation of the requisite strategies is non-negotiable in the overall narrative of managing the varied dimensions of toxic leadership.

Conclusion

This chapter illuminates the pervasive issue of toxic leadership within cross-cultural management, highlighting its detrimental impact on organisational health and employee well-being. By examining the psychological traits of toxic leaders and exploring how these traits are perceived across different cultural contexts, we gain a comprehensive understanding of the complexities involved in managing toxic leadership globally. The chapter has provided practical lessons for leaders, emphasising the importance of recognising toxic behaviours, promoting empathy and respect, and implementing comprehensive training programmes. Additionally, fostering open communication and accountability is crucial in mitigating the effects of toxic leadership and cultivating a positive and supportive work environment.

References

Adeoye, S. O., Ayeni, D., & Egbuta, O. U. (2020). Toxic leadership and organisational silence: An appraisal of selected faith-based organisations in Ogun State, Nigeria. *Human Resource Management, 10*, 67–05.

Akca, M. (2017). The impact of toxic leadership on intention to leave of employees. *International Journal of Economics, Business and Management Research, 1*(4), 285–298.

Asad, S., & Sadler-Smith, E. (2020). Differentiating leader hubris and narcissism on the basis of power. *Leadership, 16*(1), 39–61.

Asmamaw, A. T., & Semela, T. (2023). Exploring the influence of leader emotional intelligence on faculty engagement in Ethiopian higher education. *Cogent Education, 10*(2), 2277547.

Baraibar-Diez, E., & Odriozola, M. D. (2023). Implementation of whistleblowing policies: The case of listed companies in Spain. *International Journal of Business Governance and Ethics, 17*(1), 79–98.

Başkan, B. (2020). Toxic leadership in education: A systematic review. *International Journal of Educational Administration, Management, and Leadership, 1*(2), 97–104. https://doi.org/10.51629/ijeamal.v1i2.11

Brouwers, M., & Paltu, A. (2020). Toxic leadership: Effects on job satisfaction, commitment, turnover intention and organisational culture within the South African manufacturing industry. *SA Journal of Human Resource Management, 18*(1), 1–11.

Budhwar, P. S., & Bhatnagar, J. (Eds.). (2008). *The changing face of people management in India*. Routledge.

Coronado-Maldonado, I., & Benítez-Márquez, M. D. (2023). Emotional intelligence, leadership, and work teams: A hybrid literature review. *Heliyon, 9*, e20356.

Cragun, O. R., Olsen, K. J., & Wright, P. M. (2020). Making CEO narcissism research great: A review and meta-analysis of CEO narcissism. *Journal of Management*, *46*(6), 908–936.

Demerouti, E., Bakker, A. B., Nachreiner, F., & Schaufeli, W. B. (2001). The job demands-resources model of burnout. *The Journal of Applied Psychology*, *86*(3), 499–512.

Doorley, J., & Garcia, H. F. (2015). *Reputation management: The key to successful public relations and corporate communication*. Routledge.

Frazier, M. L., & Jacezko, M. C. (2021). Leader Machiavellianism as an antecedent to ethical leadership: The impact on follower psychological empowerment and work outcomes. *Journal of Leadership & Organizational Studies*, *28*(2), 154–168.

Gelfand, M. J., Erez, M., & Aycan, Z. (2007). Cross-cultural organisational behaviour. *Annual Review of Psychology*, *58*, 479–514.

Genau, H. A., Blickle, G., Schütte, N., & Meurs, J. A. (2021). Machiavellian leader effectiveness. *Journal of Personnel Psychology*, *21*, 1–10.

Grojean, M. W., Resick, C. J., Dickson, M. W., & Smith, D. B. (2004). Leaders, values, and organisational climate: Examining leadership strategies for establishing an organisational climate regarding ethics. *Journal of Business Ethics*, *55*, 223–241.

Hattab, S., Wirawan, H., Salam, R., Daswati, D., & Niswaty, R. (2022). The effect of toxic leadership on turnover intention and counterproductive work behaviour in Indonesian public organisations. *International Journal of Public Sector Management*, *35*(3), 317–333.

Hofstede, G. (1980). Culture and organisations. *International Studies of Management & Organisation*, *10*(4), 15–41.

Hofstede, G. (2003). What is culture? A reply to Baskerville. *Accounting, Organisations and Society*, *28*(7–8), 811–813.

House, R. J., Hanges, P. J., Javidan, M., Dorfman, P. W., & Gupta, V. (Eds.). (2004). *Culture, leadership, and organisations: The GLOBE study of 62 societies*. Sage Publications.

Kaiser, R. B., Hogan, R., & Craig, S. B. (2008). Leadership and the fate of organisations. *American Psychologist*, *63*(2), 96.

Kim, H. K., Baik, K., & Kim, N. (2019). How Korean leadership style cultivates employees' creativity and voice in hierarchical organisations. *Sage Open*, *9*(3), 2158244019876281.

Küçük, B. A. (2019). *The impacts of toxic organisational climate, narcissistic leader and workplace envy on individual outcomes of counterproductive work behaviour, work exhaustion and contextual performance: The roles of perceived self-esteem and self-control*. Marmara Universitesi (Turkey).

Lipman-Blumen, J. (2006). *The allure of toxic leaders: Why we follow destructive bosses and corrupt politicians--and how we can survive them*. Oxford University Press.

Mackey, J. D., Ellen III, B. P., McAllister, C. P., & Alexander, K. C. (2021). The dark side of leadership: A systematic literature review and meta-analysis of destructive leadership research. *Journal of Business Research*, *132*, 705–718.

Matos, K., O'Neill, O., & Lei, X. (2018). Toxic leadership and the masculinity contest culture: How "win or die" cultures breed abusive leadership. *Journal of Social Issues*, *74*(3), 500–528.

Minkov, M., Sokolov, B., Tasse, M. A., Jamballuu, E., Schachner, M., & Kaasa, A. (2023). Transposition of the Minkov-Hofstede Model of culture to the individual level of analysis: Evidence from Mongolia. *Cross-Cultural Research*, *57*(2–3), 264–293.

Murphy, K. R. (2020). Performance evaluation will not die, but it should. *Human Resource Management Journal*, *30*(1), 13–31.

Nowack, K., & Zak, P. (2020). Empathy enhancing antidotes for interpersonally toxic leaders. *Consulting Psychology Journal: Practice and Research*, *72*(2), 119.

Ogbonna, E., & Harris, L. C. (2000). Leadership style, organizational culture and performance: Empirical evidence from UK companies. *The International Journal of Human Resource Management*, *11*(4), 766–788. https://doi.org/10.1080/09585190050075114

Oyewunmi, A. E., Esho, E., & Oyewunmi, O. A. (2021). Spiritual intelligence and employee outcomes in an African sample. *Journal of Management, Spirituality and Religion*, *18*, 151–171.

Oyewunmi, A. E., & Oyewunmi, O. A. (2022). Speaking silence: Abusive supervision, subordinates' citizenship behaviour, and whistleblowing intention. *Sage Open*, *12*(1), 215824402210799. https://doi.org/10.1177/21582440221079912

Salas, E., Tannenbaum, S. I., Kraiger, K., & Smith-Jentsch, K. A. (2012). The science of training and development in organisations: What matters in practice. *Psychological Science in the Public Interest*, *13*(2), 74–101.

Schmidt, A. A. (2008). *Development and validation of the toxic leadership scale*. University of Maryland.

Sergey, B., Boris, K., & Nadiia, R. (2020). Modelling of empathy, emotional intelligence and transformational leadership to the project success. In *Mathematical modeling and simulation of systems: Selected papers of 14th international scientific-practical conference, MODS*, June 24–26, 2019, Chernihiv, Ukraine (pp. 209–222). Springer International Publishing.

Whicker, M. (1996). *Toxic leaders: When organisations go bad*. Ouorum Books.

Wolor, C. W., Ardiansyah, A., Rofaida, R., Nurkhin, A., & Rababah, M. A. (2022). Impact of toxic leadership on employee performance. *Health Psychology Research*, *10*(4), 57551.

Xiu, L., Lv, F., & van Dierendonck, D. (2023). The interplay of servant leadership behaviours and Machiavellianism on perceived leader effectiveness: The role of team conflict management. *European Journal of Management and Business Economics*, *33*, 289–305.

Xu, X., Xu, Z., Lin, C., & Hu, Y. (2022). Confucian culture, gender stereotype and female entrepreneur: Evidence from China. *Applied Economics Letters*, *30*(18), 2565–2575. https://doi.org/10.1080/13504851.2022.2099796

CONTEMPORARY AND EMERGING ISSUES

IV

Chapter 19

The Invisible Manager: The Dark Side of Digital Leadership in the Nordic Context

Kateryna Maltseva Reiby and Ingvild Sagberg

Introduction

Lene Hansen, 34, an Associate Professor at a university in Oslo, opens her email inbox at 7:07 a.m. while taking the train to her office. The virtual assistant connected to her Outlook account informs her that she has not replied to two emails she received four days ago. Shortly after she replies to these, she logs into *Eduvision*, the educational platform used by her university, to check whether any of her students have contacted her. She answers three student inquiries and uploads an educational video for her students. For the next 3 minutes of her journey, Lene catches up with the most recent posts on *Workplace*, the communication and sharing platform her university uses, having been guilted into doing so by an automatic notification about them. As she scrolls through her feed, she presses the "like" and "share" buttons to show engagement with various colleagues' posts. Next, she receives an automatic reminder from her university's research-management platform, *Collaboratum*, that she needs to send the final version of one of her manuscripts for proofreading by 10:00 a.m. to a coauthor from a different

DOI: 10.4324/9781003475262-23

department. As the train pulls into Oslo Central Station at 07:42 a.m., her fitness app, *TopWalk*, sends her a notification informing her that today is the last day of the interdepartmental steps competition. Feeling a little shamed because she knows her colleagues will probably have seen how little she has been moving in the last eight weeks, Lene opts to walk to her office rather than take the bus.

In the space of just over half an hour, Lene had interacted with five different digital information systems. She was reminded about replying to emails and meeting deadlines; she felt obliged to be socially active and collegial on an internal social platform (*Workplace*); and she was nudged to walk more. Lene's story is, of course, fictional, but it might well seem real to many. Today's workplaces are highly digitalised, with organisations employing a variety of digital tools to plan, organise, conduct, delegate, and manage work. These tools take various forms, among them chatbots, facial recognition software, performance management information systems, and virtual assistants. Some are standalone applications, while others are features integrated into software suites. Many (if not all) digital tools implemented at workplaces have monitoring and surveillance capabilities that allow management to observe how work is being done and what progress is being made (Negrón, 2021). Such digitalisation of the workplace allows leadership behaviours such as planning, role clarification, employee onboarding, and even emotional support to be outsourced to digital tools (Quaquebeke & Gerpott, 2023).

Our objective in this chapter is to provide a critical reflection on how delegating or outsourcing leadership roles to digital tools might lead to darker leadership behaviours, namely passivity or avoidance of responsibility and neither informing employees about the tools' true purposes nor including employees in decision-making processes about tool implementation. We argue that digital leadership might make a manager omnipresent yet less visible – a notion we refer to as "the invisible manager". We discuss this darker side of digital leadership in the context of the Nordic model of work organisation and leadership (Gustavsen, 2007), outlining how it may infringe some of the Nordic model's important principles – for instance, participative decision making, trust, and decision-making autonomy.

The chapter is organised as follows. First, we outline the principles of the Nordic model of work organisation and leadership, as well as elaborate on which leadership behaviours are consistent with the Nordic model. We then discuss the concept of digital leadership and outline with specific examples how digital tools are heavily aiding managers to engage in certain leadership behaviours. We then reflect on how digital tools undermine the principles of the Nordic model. Finally, we offer lessons for leaders and concluding remarks, in which we encourage managers to engage with digital tools in a mindful manner consistent with the Nordic model.

Leadership Models and the Nordic Context

Managers are generally responsible for a wide range of tasks, goals, and functions in their workplaces – for example, planning, decision-making, problem-solving, internal and external communication, productivity, development, deployment of financial and material resources, and, of course, taking care of the organisation's employees (Mintzberg, 2013; Yukl, 2012). In this chapter, we primarily focus on leadership, which we define as using "noncoercive influence to direct and coordinate the activities of an organised group toward the accomplishment of group objectives" (Jago, 1982, p. 315). Leadership entails the capacity to influence people and their performance by equipping them with the resources and capabilities required to achieve organisational goals (Vroom & Jago, 2007). It can be constructive and effective – but also destructive and dark. Destructive leadership comes in many forms; a manager's leadership behaviour can take several of them simultaneously. But before elaborating on the differences between constructive leadership and destructive leadership, we will describe the key principles of the Nordic model of work organisation and leadership.

The Nordic Model of Work Organisation and Leadership

By the "Nordic model" of work organisation and leadership, we refer to a set of principles according to which leaders (or managers) in the Nordic countries – that is, Denmark, Finland, Iceland, Norway, and Sweden – behave towards their employees. The Nordic model's principles, which include participative decision-making, trust, decision-making autonomy, collaborative work, innovation, and meaningfulness are intended to promote employees' personal and professional development (Andreasson & Lundqvist, 2018; Gustavsen, 2007; Lindell & Arvonen, 1996; Torp & Reiersen, 2020).

- *Participative decision-making*: Decision-making processes are decentralised, creating a high level of employee involvement (Gustavsen, 2007; Torp & Reiersen, 2020). Leaders are attuned to the input provided by employees and motivated to listen carefully to it (Andreasson & Lundqvist, 2018).
- *Trust*: The relationship between management and employees is characterised by high levels of trust (Torp & Reiersen, 2020), and this trust often encourages friendship between these two groups (Lindell & Arvonen, 1996). Trust is enabled by the values of openness and professional integrity, which guide Nordic leadership (Andreasson & Lundqvist, 2018). Relationships between managers and employees are trusting because the former function primarily as "motivating and inspiring coaches" rather than as a single source of authority (Andreasson & Lundqvist, 2018).
- *Decision-making autonomy*: Employees have significant power, influence, and responsibility when it comes to the work they do (Andreasson & Lundqvist, 2018). In one survey conducted in Norway, for instance, employees reported that they can decide for themselves "the order of work tasks, working methods, and pace of work" (Torp & Reiersen, 2020, p. 8), indicating they have high levels of decision-making authority and autonomy.
- *Collaborative work*: Consensus seeking and cooperation (rather than competition) among employees and between employees and leaders are important notions within the Nordic model (Andreasson & Lundqvist, 2018). Torp and Reiersen (2020) report that employees in Norway, for example, experience high levels of support from colleagues and managers.
- *Innovation*: Nordic leadership is highly oriented towards innovation (Lindell & Arvonen, 1996). Leaders facilitate working environments that are not hierarchical, encouraging employees not to fear using their problem-solving abilities, experimenting, and innovating (Torp & Reiersen, 2020).
- *Meaningfulness*: The Nordic model implies that the workplace must be physically safe and psychologically meaningful. For instance, one of the goals of the Norwegian Working Environment Act (2006, Section 1-1) is "to secure a working environment that provides a basis for a healthy and meaningful working situation." Managers act on behalf of the employer during everyday work and are responsible for the quality of their subordinates' working environment.

Leadership Types: Constructive and Inspirational vs. Dark and Dysfunctional

Of the leadership types theorised in the literature, the one whose intended outcomes correspond closest to the principles outlined above is transformational leadership. First described by Burns (1978), transformational leadership consists of a relational process that motivates and inspires people to work towards a common purpose. In the Nordic context, it has been demonstrated to be effective in supporting employees' basic psychological needs for autonomy, relatedness, and competence, as well as in providing a good learning climate (Hetland, Skogstad, Hetland, & Mikkelsen, 2011; Hetland, Hetland, Schou Andreassen, Pallesen, & Notelaers, 2011) and a work environment that benefits innovation and change (Lofquist & Matthiesen, 2018). Further, the Nordic leader is characterised by being oriented towards collaboration, democracy, consensus-oriented decision-making processes, informality, and equality, resulting in a high level of trust and a good social climate for negotiations and collaborations between employers and employees (Berg, Børve, & Røkenes, 2023).

The influential "full-range leadership model" (Bass, 2000) further elucidates transformational management and provides a suitable starting point for pinpointing behaviours that fall within the dark/destructive side of leadership. It breaks leadership down into various behavioural components and characterises these as transformational, transactional, or passive, with transformational leadership positioned as the superior leadership style. The model's transformational components are mostly interpersonal and aimed at inspiring employees, providing them with intellectual stimulation so they can learn and develop at work, as well as with individualised consideration through coaching and mentoring to motivate them and make work meaningful to them. Its transactional components are more task-related and fall into two subcategories: contingent rewarding (i.e., successful completion of tasks is rewarded) and active or passive management by exception (based on monitoring and corrections). At the end of the behaviour range lies passive leadership, whose components are mainly focused on avoiding the duty of leading and refraining from intervening and solving problems (Bass, 2000).

Whereas both transformational leadership and leadership based on contingent rewards may be constructive, management by exception is not recommended for a learning organisation (Bass, 2000). It has been demonstrated that passive leadership (also referred to as "passive-avoidant" or "laissez-faire" leadership) is not merely "non-leadership" or "zero-sum" leadership (Czakert & Berger, 2022) but is actually a type of destructive (dark) leadership that contributes to a stressful, conflictual, and detrimental work environment (Aasland, Skogstad, Notelaers, Nielsen, & Einarsen, 2010; Skogstad, Einarsen, Torsheim, Aasland, & Hetland, 2007). Destructive leadership behaviour is defined as "systematic and repeated behaviour by a leader, supervisor or manager that violates the legitimate interest of the organisation by undermining and/or sabotaging the organisation's goals, tasks, resources, and effectiveness and/or the motivation, well-being or job satisfaction of his/her subordinates" (Einarsen, Aasland, & Skogstad, 2007, p. 208). Managers act destructively when they avoid taking due responsibility for a safe and meaningful working environment for their subordinates – for example, when employees experience significant role stress or work overload, or when interpersonal conflicts develop among colleagues.

Digital technologies, particularly decision-making systems based on artificial intelligence, have changed the roles of employees and managers in organisations (Harms & Han, 2019; Quaquebeke & Gerpott, 2023). In the next part of this chapter, we discuss how digital technologies might change leadership and unleash certain dark aspects that undermine the Nordic principles of work organisation and leadership.

Digital Leadership: Is There Anybody in There?

In recent years, terms such as "algorithmic leadership", "e-leadership" "automated leadership", "computers as leaders", "AI leaders", and "digital leadership" have been introduced to mark a fundamental change in organisational science: the delegation of leadership tasks to artificially intelligent systems (Quaquebeke & Gerpott, 2023). We use the term "digital leadership" in this chapter to refer to the use of digital tools to perform leadership functions automatically and without immediate human oversight (Harms & Han, 2018).

A wide range of leadership tasks and behaviours can now be delegated to digital tools, from completing routine administration to motivating and inspiring employees (Quaquebeke & Gerpott, 2023; Wesche & Sonderegger, 2019). Below, we draw on the three meta-categories from the taxonomy of leadership behaviours formulated by Yukl (2012) – that is, task-oriented behaviours, relations-oriented behaviours, and change-oriented behaviours – to describe examples of digital tools that are now extensively being used to aid and support human managers' engagement in different leadership behaviours.

Task-oriented behaviours are geared toward ensuring "that people, equipment, and other resources are used in an efficient way to accomplish the mission of a group or organisation" (Yukl, 2012, p. 460). This category of behaviours includes clarifying, planning, monitoring operations, and problem-solving. Performance management information (PMI) systems such as monday.com, Wrike, and Trello are an example of a tool that handles task-oriented behaviours (Maltseva Reiby & Sagberg, in press). PMI systems enable project planning and team participation without direct managerial oversight, and they can amend project goals, delegate tasks, keep track of deadlines, and send reminders and feedback to teams based on instantly available data about their performance. Such systems extensively scrutinise employees' performance by enabling monitoring and surveillance of their work, as well as actively suggesting how the work should be conducted by means, for instance, of integrated templates for different projects (Maltseva Reiby & Sagberg, in press). Digital tools that enable leaders to instantly monitor employee performance to organise work processes have been branded as "bossware" in the media (Corbyn, 2022) because they are used to spy on employees to measure their productivity. Bossware can take the form of software, apps, platforms, or hardware (Negrón, 2021). One bossware software suite, called "ActivTrak", has been designed to enable managers to monitor remote workers (Coworker, 2021). Not only can it track employees' mouse use without obtaining their consent to do so, but it can also categorise mouse activities according to the amount of productive or unproductive use of time, or to what types of activities the employee engaged in (e.g., emails, meetings, or social media use), or to whether the employee's work was multitasking or focused (ActivTrak, n.d.).

Relations-oriented behaviours encompass support, development, recognition, and empowerment of employees. Leadership behaviours in this category are considered to comprise "true" leadership as they are concerned with motivating, engaging, supporting, and inspiring people and fostering good relationships among employees and between employees and management (Quaquebeke & Gerpott, 2023; Yukl, 2012). Social platforms such as *Workplace* are a good example of how managers can delegate some relations-oriented behaviours to a digital tool. Although *Workplace* is marketed primarily as a communication and collaboration tool, it lets leaders track and manage employees' online presence and interactions (Workplace, n.d.a). Managers can obtain analytics on the posts, activities, and engagement levels of their employees in the form of sentiment analysis, network analysis, and indices such as employee experience score or employee net promoter score. Behavioural insights that managers obtain from such platforms and tools are often accompanied by recommendations on how to further engage, motivate, and inspire employees. One of the platform's add-ons, *Grytics* for *Workplace*, allows managers to "implement engagement strategies and measure employee sentiment, identify inactive members, and connect influencers with community members" (Workplace, n.d.b). Another example of outsourcing important relations-oriented leadership behaviours to digital tools is the emotion-recognition tool *Affectiva*, which can be used to track employee engagement and measure job applicants' emotional intelligence (Coworker, 2021).

Change-related behaviours are oriented toward facilitating innovation and group learning, and they encompass "advocating change, articulating an inspiring vision, encouraging innovation and collective learning" (Yukl, 2012, p. 462). Until recently, creativity, problem-solving, and innovation had been considered skills that AI could not effectively assist human leaders with (Quaquebeke & Gerpott, 2023), but generative AI has radically called this belief into question. The use of ChatGPT has quickly evolved from being private and experimental into being an integral part of professional knowledge work (Retkowsky, Hafermalz, & Huysman, 2024). While the long-term effects of using tools like ChatGPT are yet to be investigated, business media outlets such as *Forbes* recommend managers use ChatGPT to "spark innovation at work" by deploying different prompting techniques that engage employees during brainstorming and problem-solving sessions, product-development activities, and so on (Wells, 2023).

Leadership by Proxy: The Darker Side of Digital Tools

Digital leadership changes the role of the leader as well as employee–leader relationship dynamics. Though there are positive ways in which digital leadership can contribute to a meaningful work environment (see Tigre, Curado, & Henriques, 2023), we would like to critically reflect on the darker aspects of digital leadership.

We believe that the root of digital leadership's so-called "darkness" in the context of the Nordic model is that by giving managers both invisibility and omnipresence, it encourages leadership behaviours that run counter to the model's principles. Dark or destructive leadership can manifest itself in passive or active ways. While passive leadership, as we discussed earlier, is characterised by avoiding responsibility and refraining from intervening (Bass, 2000), active destructive leadership includes behaviours like manipulation, deception, bullying, hostility, aggression, and harassment (Einarsen et al., 2007; Skogstad et al., 2007; Tafvelin, Lundmark, von Thiele Schwarz, & Stenling, 2022). We argue that both active and passive destructive leadership behaviours might arise through digital leadership. In our example with Lene, we show how digital tools keep track of a range of details about her professional life – and even some personal details (e.g., her location and physical activity). Digital leadership supposes surveillance and monitoring. Often, the digital tools characterised as "bossware" are imposed on employees without their explicit consent and without information being given to them about how the tool works and what it is used for (Negrón, 2021). This is contrary to the principles of participative decision-making because employees do not have a voice in discussions about using the tool, and they are often not aware of its purposes. This exclusion and opacity, we believe, change the dynamics between employees and managers. While managers gain more power in the sense of having more data and information about their employees, the employees are kept in the dark about how their digital behaviour is recorded, interpreted, and acted upon. Withholding information and preventing employees from participating in organisational development are further examples of active, destructive leadership behaviours (Lundmark, Nielsen, Hasson, von Thiele Schwarz, & Tafvelin, 2020).

When digital tools of the kind we have described in this chapter are deployed in workplaces, surveillance, and monitoring are accompanied by a certain steering of employees to work in a certain way. In our fictional example, Lene receives multiple reminders from various tools and platforms, and these steer her to perform tasks. Similarly, PMI systems steer employees to organise work using certain templates (Maltseva Reiby & Sagberg, in press). Moreover, digital leadership explicitly or implicitly encourages employees to commit to certain behaviours. For example, the tools and platforms remind them to be social and collegial, as well as when and how to do their work. Steering day-to-day professional activities in this way limits employees' decision-making autonomy, an important principle of the Nordic model. Employees are encouraged to fit their working day into the fabric of digital tools that are often foisted on them and might limit their professional freedom.

Trust is another area that these digital tools can impact. Trust is a product of credibility and benevolence (Ganesan, 1994). New and insightful data about employee behaviours, mental states, and performance might increase managers' credibility in the sense that they will arguably be more capable of making informed decisions. However, the lack of a physically present manager who listens and empathises with his or her employees might undermine benevolence. Digital encouragement and support through "likes" and "shares" might have limited authenticity compared to human interaction (Colbert, Yee, & George, 2016). Managers who (voluntarily or not) "resign" and leave leadership tasks to digital technology could be accused of being passive, particularly if the lack of active, interpersonal leadership results in meaninglessness, disregard of workplace democracy, or an otherwise bad work environment.

Lessons for Leaders

Digital leadership challenges organisational roles and relationship dynamics, and it can elicit dark leadership behaviours. However, digital tools that enable digital leadership are now an inevitable part of the workplace, and artificial intelligence will clearly keep playing an increasingly significant role in organisations (Quaquebeke & Gerpott, 2023). It is not our intention to warn organisations or managers against using these tools. Instead, to encourage effective, mindful, and sustainable leadership behaviours, we would like to propose strategies for alleviating the potentially dark effects of the invisible, omnipresent manager. We developed these recommendations in line with the general requirements for a responsible and health-affirming workplace as well as with the Nordic model's general principles.

Learn the law and adhere to it: The Nordic model places responsibility for enacting workplace laws and regulations on management. In Norway, for example, organisations must comply with extensive rules on employees' rights to privacy. At the same time, PMI systems such as monday.com are finding their way into Norwegian workplaces (Monday.com, n.d.). Understanding the nuances of how particular uses of certain digital tools can diminish decision-making autonomy or undermine participatory decision-making in an organisation can be challenging. Investing in familiarising oneself with state-of-the-art data practices by consulting independent agencies is a good way to audit the existing processes. In Norway, *Datatilsynet*, the Norwegian data protection authority, is an independent public organisation responsible for protecting individuals' right to privacy (Datatilsynet, n.d.). *Datatilsynet* provides various consultancy services on legal, technical, and security issues, as well as on different tools that can be used to facilitate the responsible use of digital technologies in private and public organisations. Similar institutions exist in other Nordic countries.

Increase digital literacy among managers and employees: A deeper understanding of how digital tools are implemented and what opportunities and risks they pose to employees is a prerequisite for transparent communication and trusting relationships between managers and employees (Tigre et al., 2023). Digital literacy is a concept that denotes the "abilities of employees in utilising digital technologies in work-related practices" (Cetindamar Kozanoglu & Abedin, 2020, p. 1660). In the Nordic countries, various initiatives exist to increase digital literacy among the population. Norway, for example, has a national strategy to improve its population's digital participation and competence (Ministry of Local Government and Modernisation, 2022). Its purpose is to prevent digital exclusion. Employees in various public and private organisations can access digital-literacy training programs that, among other things, educate participants about digital technologies, clarify employees' and technologies' respective roles, and assist with the implementation and use of technology.

Be an active manager: To motivate people to engage in achieving organisational goals, active leadership is needed, not passive or avoidant leadership. Active leadership involves building meaningfulness, trust, and participation during times of change (e.g., when implementing new tools) and involving employees in important decisions that will affect their work situation. Automated leaders can make decisions, but they cannot understand the complex social interactions that make groups and organisations work: "To entirely remove the human leader from the scene would take out the heart (i.e., the human element) in what is ultimately a quintessentially human activity" (Parry, Cohen, & Bhattacharya, 2016, p. 587). A lack of active leadership may give rise to an unhealthy work environment characterised by conflicts, stress, and bullying (Skogstad et al., 2007).

Conclusion

Digital tools are unquestionably valuable in many aspects of managing work processes. Across the world, including in the Nordic countries, they will continue to shape work processes and organisations. In this chapter, we highlight that a major challenge lies in not letting digital leadership turn into passive or active dark leadership. A manager who just lets technology happen is either engaging to some degree in laissez-faire leadership or outsourcing important aspects of leadership to an invisible and inhuman artificial manager lacking strategic, ethical, and human awareness. Digital tools create scope for employees to be treated irresponsibly – for instance, by monitoring them extensively without their knowledge, or by depriving them of the kind of feedback, coaching, and interaction they need. Leaders are not "ordinary" organisation members: the decisions they make in areas such as hiring and remuneration have a great impact on the organisation and the lives of their subordinates (Wesche & Sonderegger, 2019). Whether it is based on human thought or machines' calculations, leadership has enormous consequences. Our point is not that digital leadership necessarily will be dark or destructive in itself. We do not yet fully know how it will affect work and organisations. However, its dark side is unleashed *when new practices are introduced passively* – that is, without employee involvement or conscious consideration of meaningfulness, practical value, and ethical consequences. Invisible managers may deprive the organisation of its very real and visible employees by undermining a psychologically safe and meaningful working climate. Within the Nordic model of work, dialogue, and employee involvement are at the centre of transparent organisational processes. A competent leader should not be controlling, but present, accessible, and visible – not necessarily physically but certainly psychologically – so he or she can provide the *whys* rather than merely the *hows*. In other words, competent leaders should be anything but invisible.

References

Aasland, M. S., Skogstad, A., Notelaers, G., Nielsen, M. B., & Einarsen, S. (2010). The prevalence of destructive leadership behaviour. *British Journal of Management*, *21*(2), 438–452. https://doi.org/10.1111/j.1467-8551.2009.00672.x

ActivTrak. (n.d.). *Productivity reports: Gain insight into work habits to increase employee productivity across your organisation*. Retrieved 14 April 2024 from https://www.activtrak.com/product/productivity-reports/

Andreasson, U., & Lundqvist, M. (2018). *Nordic leadership*. Nordic Council of Ministers.

Bass, B. M. (2000). The future of leadership in learning organisations. *Journal of Leadership Studies*, *7*(3), 18–40. https://doi.org/10.1177/107179190000700303

Berg, T. E., Børve, H. E., & Røkenes, F. M. (2023). The Nordic model and management in international corporations: A scoping review. *Nordic Journal of Working Life Studies*, *14*(1). https://doi.org/10.18291/njwls.141901

Burns, J. M. (1978). *Leadership*. Harper & Row.

Cetindamar Kozanoglu, D., & Abedin, B. (2021). Understanding the role of employees in digital transformation: conceptualisation of digital literacy of employees as a multi-dimensional organisational affordance. *Journal of Enterprise Information Management*, *34*(6), 1649–1672. https://doi.org/10.1108/JEIM-01-2020-0010

Colbert, A., Yee, N., & George, G. (2016). The digital workforce and the workplace of the future. *Academy of Management Journal*, *59*(3), 731–739. https://doi.org/10.5465/amj.2016.4003

Corbyn, Z. (2022). *'Bossware is coming for almost every worker': The software you might not realize is watching you*. Guardian. https://www.theguardian.com/technology/2022/apr/27/remote-work-software-home-surveillance-computer-monitoring-pandemic

Coworker. (2021). *Bossware and employment tech database*. Coworker. https://home.coworker.org/worktech/

Czakert, J. P., & Berger, R. (2022). The indirect role of passive-avoidant and transformational leadership through job and team level stressors on workplace cyberbullying. *International Journal of Environmental Research and Public Health*, *19*(23), 15984. https://doi.org/10.3390/ijerph192315984

Datatilsynet. (n.d.). *About us*. Retrieved 30 April 2024 from https://www.datatilsynet.no/en/about-us/

Einarsen, S., Aasland, M. S., & Skogstad, A. (2007). Destructive leadership behaviour: A definition and conceptual model. *The Leadership Quarterly*, 18, 207–216.

Ganesan, S. (1994). Determinants of long-term orientation in buyer-seller relationships. *Journal of Marketing*, *58*(2), 1–19. https://doi.org/10.1177/002224299405800

Gustavsen, B. (2007). Work organisation and the Scandinavian model. *Economic and Industrial Democracy*, *28*(4), 650–671. https://doi.org/10.1177/0143831X070822

Harms, P. D., & Han, G. (2018). Algorithmic leadership: The future is now. *Journal of Leadership Studies*, *12*(4), 74–75. https://doi.org/10.1002/jls.21615

Hetland, H., Hetland, J., Schou Andreassen, C., Pallesen, S., & Notelaers, G. (2011b). Leadership and fulfilment of the three basic psychological needs at work. *Career Development International*, *16*(5), 507–523. https://doi.org/10.1108/13620431111168903

Hetland, H., Skogstad, A., Hetland, J., & Mikkelsen, A. (2011a). Leadership and learning climate in a work setting. *European Psychologist*, *16*(3), 163–173. https://doi.org/10.1027/1016-9040/a000037

Jago, A. G. (1982). Leadership: Perspectives in theory and research. *Management Science*, *28*(3), 315–336. https://doi.org/10.1287/mnsc.28.3.315

Lindell, M., & Arvonen, J. (1996). The Nordic management style in a European context. *International Studies of Management & Organisation*, *26*(3), 73–91. https://doi.org/10.1080/00208825.1996.11656689

Lofquist, E. A., & Mathiesen, S. B. (2018). Viking leadership: How Norwegian transformational leadership style effects creativity and change through organisational citizenship behaviour (OCB). *International Journal of Cross-Cultural Management, 18*(3) 309–325.

Lundmark, R., Nielsen, K., Hasson, H., von Thiele Schwarz, U., & Tafvelin, S. (2020). No leader is an island: Contextual antecedents to line managers' constructive and destructive leadership during an organisational intervention. *International Journal of Workplace Health Management, 13*(2), 173–188. https://doi.org/10.1108/IJWHM-05-2019-0065

Maltseva Reiby, K., & Sagberg, I. (in press). The digital design of work: The implications of project management information systems for the meaningfulness of work. In M. Orel, M. Černe, & S. I. Wong (Eds.), *Humanizing the digital workplace: Creativity, innovation, and leadership in the age of technology*. Springer Nature.

Ministry of Local Government and Modernisation. (2022). *Digital throughout life: National strategy to improve digital participation and competence in the population*. https://www.regjeringen.no/contentassets/8f8751780e9749bfa8946526b51f10f4/digital_throughout_life.pdf

Mintzberg, H. (2013). *Simply managing: What managers do – and can do better*. Berrett-Koehler Publishers.

Monday.com. (n.d.). *Find a partner*. Retrieved 29 April 2024 from https://monday.com/p/find-a-partner/?country=norway

Negrón, W. (2021). *Little tech is coming for workers: A framework for reclaiming and building worker power*. Coworker. https://home.coworker.org/wp-content/uploads/2021/11/Little-Tech-Is-Coming-for-Workers.pdf

Parry, K., Cohen, M., & Bhattacharya, S. (2016). Rise of the machines: A critical consideration of automated leadership decision making in organisations. *Group & Organisation Management, 41*(5), 571–594. https://doi.org/10.1177/1059601116643442

Quaquebeke, N. V., & Gerpott, F. H. (2023). The now, new, and next of digital leadership: How artificial intelligence (AI) will take over and change leadership as we know it. *Journal of Leadership & Organisational Studies, 30*(3), 265–275. https://doi.org/10.1177/15480518231181731

Retkowsky, J., Hafermalz, E., & Huysman, M. (2024). Managing a ChatGPT-empowered workforce: Understanding its affordances and side effects. *Business Horizons, 67*, 511–523. https://doi.org/10.1016/j.bushor.2024.04.009

Skogstad, A., Einarsen, S., Torsheim, T., Aasland, M. S., & Hetland, H. (2007). The destructiveness of laissez-faire leadership behaviour. *Journal of Occupational Health Psychology, 12*(1), 80–92. https://doi.org/10.1037/1076-8998.12.1.80

Tafvelin, S., Lundmark, R., von Thiele Schwarz, U., & Stenling, A. (2023). Why do leaders engage in destructive behaviours? The role of leaders' working environment and stress. *Journal of Occupational and Organisational Psychology, 96*, 165–181. https://doi.org/10.1111/joop.12413

Tigre, F. B., Curado, C., & Henriques, P. L. (2023). Digital leadership: A bibliometric analysis. *Journal of Leadership & Organisational Studies, 30*(1), 40–70.

Torp, S., & Reiersen, J. (2020). Globalization, work, and health: A Nordic perspective. *International Journal of Environmental Research and Public Health, 17*(20), 1–20. https://doi.org/10.3390/ijerph17207661

Vroom, V. H., & Jago, A. G. (2007). The role of the situation in leadership. *American Psychologist, 62*(1), 17. https://doi.org/10.1037/0003-066X.62.1.17

Wells, R. (2023). *18 ChatGPT prompts to spark innovation at work*. Forbes. https://www.forbes.com/sites/rachelwells/2023/11/19/18-chat-gpt-prompts-to-spark-innovation-at-work/?sh=2468d6c16d12

Wesche, J. S., & Sonderegger, A. (2019). When computers take the lead: The automation of leadership. *Computers in Human Behaviour, 101*, 197–209. https://doi.org/10.1016/j.chb.2019.07.027

Working Environment Act. (2006). *Act relating to the working environment, working hours and employment protection, etc. (Working Environment Act)* (LOV-2005–06–17–62). Lovdata. https://lovdata.no/dokument/NLE/lov/2005-06-17-62

Workplace. (n.d.a). *Launching workplace insights. A new way to understand your company*. Retrieved 14 April 2024 from: https://www.workplace.com/blog/employee-engagement-and-workplace-insights

Workplace. (n.d.b). *Grytics for workplace*. Retrieved 14 April 2024 from: https://en-gb.workplace.com/integration/grytics-for-workplace?app_id=704461486418496

Yukl, G. (2012). Effective leadership behaviour: What we know and what questions need more attention. *Academy of Management Perspectives, 26*(4), 66–85. https://doi.org/10.5465/amp.2012.0088

Chapter 20

My Boss Is Horrible: A Cursory Social Media Content Analysis of Perceptions and Perspectives of the Dark Side of Leadership in the Workplace

Ebes Aziegbe-Esho

Introduction

For a long time, leadership has been idealised, and leaders idolised. Research and discourse on leadership were \focused extensively on the various forms of "positive" leadership styles and their different characteristics. Concepts such as transformational, charismatic, and ethical leadership styles dominate the discourse. The erstwhile implicit assumption was that leadership connotes the "good", "moral", and all sorts of positives in behaviours and attitudes. However, the reality is that not all leadership styles are positive, and leaders can indeed have negative traits and behaviours that adversely affect others. In other words, leaders are not always "good" and may sometimes portray some dark and socially undesirable behaviours. These types of leaders are known as leaders who exhibit the dark side of leadership or simply as dark side leaders.

 DOI: 10.4324/9781003475262-24

Table 20.1 Different Forms of Dark Leadership

Exploitative Leadership	*Despotic Leadership*	*Abusive Supervision*
Authoritarian leadership	Psychopathic leadership	Narcissistic leadership
Leader Machiavellianism	Autocratic leadership	Coercive leadership
Aversive leadership	Destructive leadership	Toxic leadership
Unethical leadership	Abusive leadership	Close monitoring
Aversive leadership	Corrupt leadership	Derailed leadership
Evil leadership	Insincere leadership	Insular leadership
Negative leadership	Personalised charismatic leadership	Pseudo-transformational leadership
Petty tyranny	Tyrannical leadership	Bad leadership
Controlling leadership	Directive leadership	Dysfunctional leadership
Hubristic leadership	Laissez-Faire leadership	Managerial tyranny
Malevolent leadership	Passive leadership	Self-serving leadership
Managerial derailment	Strategic bullying	Dark leadership

Source: Author's compilation from the literature.

Generally, a leader who exhibits the dark side of leadership has one of three negative personality traits - narcissism, psychopathy, and Machiavellianism (Fouts, 2020). These three personality traits are generally referred to as the "dark triad of personality" and form the core personality traits of dark leadership (Elbers et al., 2023; Fouts, 2020; Furtner et al., 2017). This dark triad was first introduced by Paulhus and Williams in 2002 to reflect personality traits of malevolent character with tendencies for self-promotion, emotional coldness, duplicity, and aggressiveness (Elbers et al., 2023; Paulhus & Williams, 2002). However, narcissism, psychopathy, and Machiavellianism manifest in diverse ways, and some research suggests that they may even have some positive effects. Nevertheless, the overwhelming evidence from extant literature is that dark leadership has serious effects on followers, employees, or subordinates in the workplace, and on the organisation. Dark leadership has both negative psychological and physiological effects on employees in the workplace (Dagistan, 2023).

However, what specific behaviours of leaders do employees regard as dark in the workplace? Are perceptions of dark leadership behaviours the same regardless of context? To provide answers to these related questions, this chapter presents the perceptions and perspectives on dark leadership behaviours in Nigerian workplaces using publicly available data from the social media platform, Twitter, henceforth "X". Nigeria has been classified as having a culture with a relatively high-power distance (Clearly Cultural, n.d.; Hofstede Insights, 2024). Academic literature suggests that certain negative behaviours associated with dark leadership may be more acceptable or even expected in contexts with high-power distance cultures (Den Hartog & Dickson, 2018; Mehraein et al., 2023). The perspectives of a social media sample of employees in Nigeria sheds light on the acceptance or non-acceptance of the dark side of leadership in contexts with high power-distance cultures.

Dark leadership is an eclectic term that is used to describe different types of leadership styles which are associated with some negative behaviours and attitudes of leaders (see Table 20.1). There is no consensus on what dark leadership is or on how it should be defined (Mackey et al., 2021; Mehraein et al., 2023). The several forms of dark leadership have been defined in different ways even when the same form is being referred to by different studies. Einarsen and colleagues (2007, p. 208) initially defined destructive leadership as "the systematic and repeated behaviour by a leader, supervisor or manager that violates the legitimate interest of the organisation by undermining and/or sabotaging the organisation's goals, tasks, resources, and effectiveness and/or the motivation, well-being or job satisfaction of subordinates". This conceptualisation of dark or destructive leadership was only from the perspective of harm to the organisation. More recently, Krasikova et al. (2013, p. 1310) defined destructive leadership as "volitional behaviour by a leader that can harm or intends to harm a leader's organisation and/or followers by (a) encouraging followers to pursue goals that contravene the legitimate interests of the organisation and/or (b) employing a leadership style that involves the use of harmful methods of influence with followers, regardless of justifications for such behaviour". This formal definition has gained some traction in the literature (Mackey et al., 2021). It acknowledges that dark leadership can also cause harm to employees, not just to the corporate entity.

The concept of dark leadership may seem to be mutually exclusive with other positive leadership styles. However, Bass (1990) and Conger (1990), two seminal research works on the concept, portray dark leadership as the negative side of transformational leadership and charismatic leadership respectively. This suggests that leadership styles are not mutually exclusive. It has also long been argued that transformational leadership and transactional leadership styles are not mutually exclusive but interrelated and interdependent (Asrar-ul-Haq & Anwar, 2018; Bass, 1985; Northouse, 2004). Some argue that dark leadership has two sides: a dark or negative side with negative behaviours, and a good or bright side consisting of positive behaviours (Furtner et al., 2017; Judge et al., 2009; Maccoby, 2000; Rosenthal & Pittinsky, 2006). Consequently, leaders with dark leadership styles can display both negative and positive attitudes and behaviours, and even display some aspects of other positive leadership styles, such as transformational and charismatic leadership (Zhang et al., 2020). So, the concept of dark leadership does not necessarily equate to a leader being "all-out evil". Mehraein et al. (2023), in their review of studies on the effect of the dark side of leadership on creativity and innovation, found that 19 out of 106 studies found positive effects. In addition, seemingly successful people in leadership positions that display dark leadership may have other traits that may have contributed to their attaining positional leadership, and the present success of the organisation. As noted by Dagistan (2023), unfortunately, a dark leader's negative attributes or qualities may have inadvertently contributed to their present success. Nevertheless, research shows that such success is hardly sustainable.

Much of the research on dark leadership has focused on the triad personality traits of narcissism, psychopathy, and Machiavellianism. Each of these three personality traits has been associated with varying degrees of callousness, impulsivity, manipulation, criminality, and grandiosity (Furtner et al., 2017; Paulhus, 2014). Dark leaders usually have a high drive for power, dominance, and humiliation, which may be due to fear and anxiety (Furtner et al., 2017; Mehraein et al., 2023). They can be controlling and undermine the autonomy and competence of employees (Mehraein et al., 2023). The triad personality traits of dark leaders often overlap (Paulhus & Williams, 2002). Consequently, they are not mutually exclusive traits. Leaders can display the three personality traits to different degrees. The overarching feature of all forms of dark leadership is that they are associated with negative behaviours toward their followers. Dark leadership can cause psychological and physical harm to employees in the workplace, and, indeed, to other members of the organisation. It stems from personality traits and the influence of environmental factors and other dynamics (Dagistan, 2023; Kellerman, 2004). The drive for success can also push a leader to exhibit dark behaviours (Dagistan, 2023; Conger, 1990).

Academic literature distinguishes the different forms of dark leadership, but employees who work with dark leaders may find these distinctions irrelevant. What is most concerning for employees and followers is the negative effects of the behavioural characteristics associated with dark leadership. Although the dark triad seems to dominate extant literature, dark leadership is a broad term that encompasses several negative behavioural characteristics. While scholars continue the conversations on dark leadership, its various forms, and whether it has positive dimensions, it is pertinent to consider the negative behaviours associated with such style. Employees may not see the so-called positive effects that have been identified by some research. Consequently, it is important to understand employees' perceptions and perspectives of the kind of behaviours that constitute dark leadership, especially in a high-power distance culture like Nigeria, where it has been suggested that dark leadership behaviours may be more acceptable by the culture (e.g., Oyewunmi & Oyewunmi, 2022).

Social Media Perspectives of Dark Leadership in the Workplace

The data for this chapter was sourced from Twitter posts with the hashtags "horrible bosses" (#horriblebosses), horrible boss (#horribleboss), and horrible employees (#horribleemployees), which first trended in Nigeria between March and April 2022, and again in May 2024. The data was collected in May 2024, and a total of 397 tweets were analysed.

The nuances and complexity of social media platforms present peculiar challenges to using social media data for research. One, social media posts can be altered or deleted. Two, social media inherently biases the sample to only those who use social media platforms, thus potentially biasing the findings. Three, the issues of ethics, privacy, and copyrights on the use of social media data for research are yet to be fully delineated (Chen et al., 2023; Taylor & Pagliari, 2018); many institutions are yet to set specific guidelines on using social media data for research. While there are some general guidelines, there are generally no accepted standards for the use of social media data for research. Finally, social media users can be sensitive to the use of their data for research without their consent (Hemphill et al., 2022). Consequently, this study adheres primarily to some of the practical recommendations of Dym and Fiesler (2020) and other social media research guidelines (e.g., Chen et al., 2023; Taylor & Pagliari, 2018). Only a summary of the general themes of the tweets from the social media platform, 'X', is presented as it was not feasible to obtain informed consent from specific human participants' tweets included in the study. Therefore, to minimise the risks associated with using social media data, the findings do *not* include the direct quotes from "X". They also do *not* include paraphrases of the tweets even though recommendations on the use of social media data allow and encourage the use of paraphrasing to navigate the issues of not obtaining consent and other complexities. Moreover, since the chapter presents the perceptions and perspectives of social media users, only the themes of the publicly available tweets are summarily presented.

The analysed tweets can be classified into five major themes. Apart from the descriptions of negative dark leadership behaviours, four other themes emerged from the analysis. Employees were focused on the causative factors, racial and ethnic profiling of leaders, the sectors and occupations most affected, and possible solutions to dark leadership.

Theme 1: Perceived Dark Leadership Behaviours

Employees' perception of dark leadership behaviours ranged from staff layoffs and abrupt termination of appointment without the necessary due notice, use of explicit abusive and condescending language, running of errands unrelated to official job functions, working continuously without any breaks for long hours, and coming to the office for official work during national and state public holidays. Others include the setting of unrealistic targets, long extended working hours and late office closure times, sleeping overnight in the office, and sexual harassment. Poor remuneration and outright refusal to pay salaries were also perceived as indications of dark leadership. Of the dark triad, only narcissism was specifically mentioned. However, words such as "wicked" and "wickedness" were rampantly used to describe the negative behaviours of leaders in the workplace.

Theme 2: Perceived Causative Factors

Several factors were perceived as being responsible for dark leadership behaviours. The lack of laws, legal framework, and regulatory institutions, widespread poverty, lack of effective internal governance processes, and the high unemployment rate were regarded as the major causative factors of the perceived dark leadership behaviours. In their tweets, several users emphasised the ineffectiveness of HR units in performing their functions.

Consequently, leaders and managers were perceived as taking undue advantage of employees. Others suggested that most HR units were completely subject to the control of senior management and Chief Executive Officers (CEOs) and could offer little or no help in reducing dark leadership behaviours. A few users argued that some employees displayed a high sense of entitlement, thus insinuating that certain situations require dark leadership behaviours. While many perceived that the country had weak labour laws, others believed that the existing laws only needed enforcement. Socio-cultural values such as deference to elders and those in authority and a culture of silence were cited as enablers of dark leadership behaviours. Finally, from their tweets, many users held the perception that persons who had been victims of dark leadership behaviours might be more prone to exhibiting such traits when they assume leadership roles.

Theme 3: Industries, Professions, and Occupations

Dark leadership was perceived to be prevalent in a wide range of industries, professions, and occupations. However, the phenomenon was observed to be more rampant in start-ups, ICT, law healthcare, education, hospitality, manufacturing, and fashion industries. Therefore, the perception is that dark leadership is not limited to "blue" collar jobs, as doctors, lawyers, and teachers, were reported to have been subject to dark leadership behaviours. Employees of owner-managed organisations seemed to be the most affected by dark leadership behaviours. Interns and those serving under the country's National Youth Service Corps (NYSC)[1] were particularly vulnerable to dark leadership behaviours in the workplace. While the focus was on leaders and workers in formal settings, dark leadership was perceived to also extend to informal workplaces such as family households. Domestic workers, known colloquially as "house helps" were also mentioned as being particularly subjected to dark leadership behaviours.

Theme 4: Racial and Ethnic Profiling of Dark Leadership

The perception was that dark leadership behaviours are common in organisations with leaders and senior management from certain ethnic groups and nationalities. However, contrary to the trending hashtags, some tweets mentioned specific examples of local and foreign organisational leaders perceived to demonstrate positive leadership behaviours.

Theme 5: Perspectives of Possible Solutions

A final theme was the provision of possible solutions. Amid a rather pessimistic attitude towards the political, economic, and socio-cultural context, the perceived solutions can be summarily grouped into three. One, there is a need for employees to educate themselves on the existing labour laws, regulatory frameworks, and international best practices. The perception was that dark leadership was rampant because many employees were not equipped with adequate knowledge of labour laws and regulations. Two, a call to human resource and industrial relations professional bodies to play a more active role in educating, guiding, and defending employees. Finally, a need for counselling and other employee assistance initiatives to ameliorate the effects of dark leadership behaviours.

Reflections from Social Media Perspectives

Employees' perceptions of dark leadership in a high-power distance culture are not very different from what exists in extant literature. The perspectives on dark leadership are very similar to those found in the review of the literature by Mackey et al. (2021) and Mehraein et al., (2023). Destructive leadership styles include abusive supervision, the sustained display of hostile verbal and non-verbal behaviours; aversive leadership, the use of intimidation, threats, and punishment; despotic leadership, the use of personal dominance; exploitative leadership, when leaders pursue their self-interests; and narcissistic leadership style when leaders are primarily motivated by their egomaniacal needs and relentless pursuit of their vision (Conger, 1990; Mackey et al., 2021).

Dark leadership is dark leadership and is not acceptable even in high-power distance cultures. Although the allusion to the effect of high-power distance was one of the perceived causes of dark leadership behaviours, the negative behaviours were not perceived as accepted forms of behaviour. In fact, from the perspectives on social media, some of the perceptions of dark leadership, such as poor remuneration and late closures from the office may not be construed as dark leadership in other contexts. Perhaps this might be because of more effective laws and regulatory frameworks in place and other institutional and contextual factors.

Moving Forward: Interpreting and Clarifying Perspectives

The grammar and language used on social media, such as "X" vary. Users do not always use polished or grammatically correct language. Therefore, in analysing the data collected, many times, the language used was sometimes the local lingua franca and other forms of the vernacular. Thankfully, the researcher is quite familiar with "pidgin" English and their meanings. Nevertheless, there is still a need to note that the meanings of some tweets were, therefore, subjectively interpreted. Consequently, the actual meaning of some tweets may have been inadvertently misinterpreted. Other researchers interested in this study and the broad subject of dark leadership are welcome to explore and replicate this research in the same, similar, or different social media and other contexts to corroborate, compare, or dispute the findings. Use of the "X" API is particularly welcome if and when it becomes available to researchers.

It is also important to note that social media platforms such as "X" may not be the true representation of any group or population. Therefore, the study sample may not be a true representation of the employee population in Nigeria. Moreover, it is difficult to confirm that the authors of the tweets are employees in Nigeria. In addition, compared to the 25,000 tweets reported by the media (Ladipo, 2022), the sample analysed is rather small. Consequently, the perspectives presented above need to be taken with the necessary caution. Nevertheless, the perspectives provide fruitful insights into the perceptions of dark leadership. They also provide some fertile avenues for more research on the issue, as some of the themes that emerged from the research are yet to be fully explored or even considered in extant research.

Lessons for Business and Organisational Leaders

Paradoxically, visionary leaders may be more prone to having a dark side than non-visionary leaders. In a rephrase of the apt words of Conger (1990), the very qualities that distinguish the visionary leader may contain the potential for disaster. Therefore, dark leadership is not necessarily synonymous with failed leadership, at least in the short term. A person could lead an organisation towards some form of success and applause in the industry and marketplace but still portray dark traits which very often can only be seen by those within close working range. Leaders may become so driven and passionate about their visions that they become emotionally detached and begin to display negative attitudes and behaviours. Unfortunately, it is the workers who bear the brunt of such unsavoury attitudes and stress-causing behaviours. Despite what may seem like success in the short term, the organisation may also ultimately suffer some severe consequences as a result.

Leaders, especially those in the workplace, will therefore do well to take note of five main lessons. First, communicate the organisation's vision so that everyone understands, buys in, and runs with the vision with minimal complaints. Second, it is important to set achievable targets, and these should be complemented with appropriate rewards for diverse performance levels. Third, the success that stems from dark leadership is not sustainable in the long haul and is not amenable to the sustainability of the business and organisation. Fourth, create room and opportunities for employee feedback, and take necessary action to address concerns. Leaders should provide necessary explanations to employees when corrective action(s) on negative feedback can inevitably not be taken. Finally, leaders should periodically embark on training by taking leadership and other management courses to enhance leadership and managerial knowledge and skills.

Conclusion

At best, it may be more worthwhile to assume that leadership is neither inherently 'good' nor 'bad'. Leadership is, perhaps, value-free as asserted by Kellerman (2004). Regardless, employees' perception of leaders in the workplace is crucial not only for the long-term sustainability of the business but also for sustainable competitive advantage. The short-term success of leadership and the business may tempt business and organisational leaders to ignore employees' perceptions. However, the human capital of employees (their knowledge, skills, abilities, and other characteristics of employees) are key input to organisational success, and competitive advantage that is sustainable is based on people and their human capital (Esho & Verhoef, 2020). Consequently, leaders must create workplaces that are conducive for employees to perform optimally. To conclude, regardless of the results of a few research on some positive correlational effects of dark leadership personality traits, in the words of Cunha and colleagues (2024), "drawing on the dark triad to teach effective leadership is dangerous, irresponsible, and bad theory". A perception of dark leadership is dangerous and bad for the long-term success and sustainability of businesses and is outrightly irresponsible if it is truly dark leadership.

Note

1 NYSC is a scheme for youths that aims to inculcate the spirit of unity and selfless service to the community. It is usually undertaken for one year upon graduation from some tertiary educational institutions by Nigerian youths below a certain age.

References

Asrar-ul-Haq, M., & Anwar, S. (2018). The many faces of leadership: Proposing research agenda through a review of the literature. *Future Business Journal*, *4*(2), 179–188.

Bass, B. M. (1985). *Leadership and Performance beyond Expectations*. New York: Free Press.

Bass, B. M. (1990). From transactional to transformational leadership: Learning to share the vision. *Organisational Dynamics*, *18*, 19–36.

Chen, Y., Sherren, K., Smit, M., & Lee, K. Y. (2023). Using social media images as data in social science research. *New Media & Society*, *25*(4), 849–871. https://uk.sagepub.com/en-gb/journals-permissions

Clearly Cultural. (n.d.). Making sense of cross-cultural communication. Available at https://clearlycultural.com/geert-hofstede-cultural-dimensions/power-distance-index/

Conger, J. A. (1990). The dark side of leadership. *Organisational Dynamics*, *19*(2), 44–55. https://psycnet.apa.org/doi/10.1016/0090-2616(90)90070-6

Cunha, M. P. E., Clegg, S., Rego, A., & Simpson, A. V. (2024). Drawing on the dark triad to teach effective leadership is dangerous, irresponsible, and bad theory. *Academy of Management Learning and Education*, *23*, 626–651. https://doi.org/10.5465/amle.2022.0326

Dagistan, U. (2023). The phenomenon of dark leadership: A conceptual evaluation. *Anadolu University Journal of Social Sciences*, *23*(4), 1071–1090.

Den Hartog, N. D., & Dickson, M. W. (2018) Leadership, culture, and globalization. In *The Nature of Leadership*, Antonakis, J., Cianciolo, A. T., & Sternberg, R. J. (Eds.), Thousand Oaks, CA: Sage, pp. 327–353.

Dym, B., & Fiesler, C. (2020). Ethical and privacy considerations for research using online fandom data. In *Fan Studies Methodologies*, Largent, J. E., Popova, M., & Vist, E. (Eds.), *Transformative Works and Cultures*, No. 33. https://doi.org/10.3983/twc.2020.1733

Elbers, A., Kolominski, S., & Aledo. P. S. B. (2023). Coping with dark leadership: Examination of the impact of psychological capital on the relationship between dark leaders and employees' basic need satisfaction in the workplace. *Administrative Sciences*, *13*(4), 96. https://doi.org/10.3390/admsci13040096

Einarsen, S., Aasland, M. S., & Anders Skogstad, A. (2007). Destructive leadership behaviour: A definition and conceptual model. *The Leadership Quarterly*, *18*(3), 207–216. https://doi.org/10.1016/j.leaqua.2007.03.002

Esho, E., & Verhoef, G. (2020). A holistic model of human capital for value creation and superior firm performance: The strategic factor market model. *Cogent Business & Management*, *7*(1), 1737347.

Fouts, M. (2020). The dark side of leadership: How to identify and steer clear of it when job hunting. *Forbes*. Available at https://www.forbes.com/sites/forbescoachescouncil/2020/10/07/the-dark-side-of-leadership-how-to-identify-and-steer-clear-of-it-when-job-hunting/?sh=187c93701bd7

Furtner, M. R., Maran, T., & Rauthmann, J. F. (2017). Dark leadership: The role of leaders' dark triad personality traits. In M. G. Clark & C. W. Gruber (Eds.), *Leader Development Deconstructed* (pp. 75–99). Springer International Publishing/Springer Nature. https://doi.org/10.1007/978-3-319-64740-1_4

Hemphill, L., Scholpke-Gonzalez, A., & Panda, A. (2022). Comparative sensitivity of social media data and their acceptable use in research. *Scientific Data*, *9*, 643. https://doi.org/10.1038/s41597-022-01773-w

Hofstede Insights. (2024). The culture factor group. Country comparison tool. Available at https://www.hofstede-insights.com/country-comparison-tool?countries=nigeria

Judge, T. A., Piccolo, R. F., & Kosalka, T. (2009). The bright and dark sides of leader traits: A review and theoretical extension of the leader trait paradigm. *The Leadership Quarterly*, *20*, 855–875.

Kellerman, B. (2004). *Bad Leadership: What It Is, How It Happens, Why It Matters.* Boston, MA: Harvard Business School Press.

Krasikova, D. V., Green, S. G., & LeBreton, J. M. (2013). Destructive leadership: A theoretical review, integration, and future research agenda. *Journal of Management*, *39*(5), 1308–1338.

Ladipo, E. (2022). Workers call out #horriblebosses in Nigerian tech ecosystem. *Business Day*. https://businessday.ng/technology/article/workers-call-out-horrible-bosses-in-nigerian-tech-ecosystem/

Maccoby, M. (2000). Narcissistic leaders: The incredible pros, the inevitable cons. *Harvard Business Review*, *78*, 68–77.

Mackey, J. D., Parker Ellen, B. III, McAllister, C. P., & Alexander, K. C. (2021). The dark side of leadership: A systematic literature review and meta-analysis of destructive leadership research. *Journal of Business Research*, *132*, 705–718. https://doi.org/10.1016/j.jbusres.2020.10.037

Mehraein, V., Visintin, F., & Pittino, D. (2023). The dark side of leadership: A systematic review of creativity and innovation. *International Journal of Management Reviews*, *25*, 740–767.

Northouse, P. G. (2004). *Leadership: Theory and Practice*. Thousand Oaks, CA: Sage.

Oyewunmi, A. E., & Oyewunmi, O. A. (2022). Speaking silence: Abusive supervision, subordinates' citizenship behavior, and whistleblowing intention. *Sage Open*, *12*(1), 215824402210799. https://doi.org/10.1177/21582440221079912

Paulhus, D. L. (2014). Toward a taxonomy of dark personalities. *Current Directions in Psychological Science*, *23*, 421–426.

Paulhus, D. L., & Williams, K. M. (2002). The dark triad of personality: Narcissism, Machiavellianism, and psychopathy. *Journal of Research in Personality*, *36*, 556–563.

Rosenthal, S. A., & Pittinsky, T. L. (2006). Narcissistic leadership. *The Leadership Quarterly, 17(6), 617–633. https://doi.org/10.1016/j.leaqua.2006.10.005*

Taylor, J., & Pagliari, C. (2018). Mining social media data: How are research sponsors and researchers addressing ethical challenges? *Research Ethics*, *14*(2), 1–39.

Zhang, X., Liang, L., Tian, G., & Tian, Y. (2020). Heroes or villains? The dark side of charismatic leadership and unethical pro-organisational leadership behaviour. *International Journal of Environmental Research and Public Health*, *17*, 5546. https://doi.org/10.3390/ijerph17155546

Chapter 21

Combating Digital Manipulation: A Cross-Cultural Analysis of Enterprise Leadership in China and the United Kingdom

Yuan Zhai

Introduction

Business and political leaders have been able to use digital technologies speedily and cheaply to reach out to constituents and stakeholders in ways impossible a generation ago because socioeconomic communication and data processing had been slow and labour-intensive (Andreas & Haenlein, 2010). On popular platforms such as Facebook, Twitter- (now known as X), Instagram stream, or even WhatsApp – business and political leaders can swiftly communicate with their employees, customers, shareholders, and the wider public (Iddris, 2018). By reaching more people in faster timeframes with far greater consistency and reliability, wielders of dark influence have more reach than ever before (Bradshaw & Howard, 2018). If these 'enemies' have the desire or an inclination towards deception; if they have a secret political, commercial, or other objective such as sabotaging a business deal or a country's economy, disrupting a political campaign, or undermining a

DOI: 10.4324/9781003475262-25

leader's reputation – then today's mighty arsenal of tools and tactics is virtually limitless (Elbers et al., 2023).

'Dark' goals refer to latent motivations that lead to deceptive or manipulative communication tactics (King et al., 2017). For instance, leaders may promote political ideologies, undermine rivals, attack business competitors, or distract the public from a crisis. Other dark goals include expanding governmental control of various aspects of society (Molter & Diresta, 2020; King et al., 2017). In China, many executives of state-owned enterprises (SOEs) need to balance the interests of all three components of the 'iron triangle' – Communist Party, state, and business – resulting in dark goals (Brødsgaard et al., 2017). While less likely in the UK, British leaders are also vulnerable to the temptation of 'dark' goals – i.e., for leaders and their companies or political causes to profit from misinformation intended to harm rivals, deflect blame from their own failures, or secure support for policies they favour (Bastos & Mercea, 2018). Without proper oversight, UK leaders could use such platforms and algorithms to strategically shape public opinion while shrouding their intentions in secrecy. Strong traditions of freedom of the press, which have remained relatively robust in the UK, and strong norms of accountability may dissuade it, but there are new ways in which leaders might attempt to escape responsibility for their actions in the age of social media (Hern, 2019). Indeed, there are scandals surrounding the role of social media companies in aiding the spread of misinformation whether by malicious intent or by algorithm. Tech giants such as Facebook have come under scrutiny for their role in allowing deliberate misinformation targeted 'for profit or to influence' as well as for 'unintended harm', including unintended algorithmic amplification (Ofcom, 2021).

The cultural dimensions theory advanced by the Dutch organisational psychologist Geert Hofstede (Hofstede, 2001) could give some indication of why the public might be more or less susceptible to digital manipulation by leaders. For example, the relatively high-power distance index (PDI) in China might make people more deferential to hierarchical leadership attempts at digital persuasion. At the same time, deference can turn into severe backlash once the veil of deception is lifted and the trust in the leaders is shattered (Zhang, 2019). In the UK, individuals tend to hold a critical attitude towards leadership claims due to a high level of individualism, except if they fall under the influence of charismatic leaders within their respective groups (Collinson & Collinson, 2009). This chapter further examines the risks and potential benefits of digital technologies for leader engagement and communication with stakeholders by examining case studies of digital communication in China and the UK through a comparative cross-cultural lens. It draws on nuanced differences in patterns of public receptiveness to digital communication, as well as organisational accountability, to shed light on the complex interplay between leadership, technology, and culture in shaping digital communication practices. It concludes by offering targeted interventions for each cultural context to enhance responsible leadership communication and counter the negative effects of misinformation and polarisation.

Chinese State-Owned Enterprise Executives' Digital Engagement: Navigating the Iron Triangle and Talent Management Challenges

The political and economic environment in which China's SOEs operate makes it hard for executives to balance their various constituencies. In these SOEs, the Communist Party is the central pillar of political governance. As Brødsgaard et al. (2017) and Brødsgaard (2012) point out, the Party's cadre management system gives it control over SOE executives' appointments, evaluations, and promotions. Other scholars have also identified four pillars supporting the political governance structure in Chinese SOEs: state ownership, the Party cadre management system, the Party's participation in corporate decision-making, and intra-party supervision (Jin et al., 2022). Taken together, these mechanisms turn Chinese SOE leaders into 'quasi-officials' who are always keen to manoeuvre business objectives, and social and political goals (Wang, 2014). However, this unique governance structure also raises concerns about the incompatibility between the Party's political objectives and the economic efficiency and competitiveness of SOEs.

In an analysis of China's recent SOE reforms, Yu (2019) concludes that, while the 2013 reformist rhetoric indicates a government commitment to market-oriented reforms to enhance SOE efficiency/competitiveness, the practice of the reforms has largely involved mergers and acquisitions designed to consolidate party-state control over SOEs and institutionalise the leadership role of the Communist Party in SOE governance. In the process, the reforms have generated still larger 'national champions' and further fragmented the market for corporate control while also subjecting SOEs to tighter Party control, with the Party writing its leadership into corporate charters and making top executives more accountable to Party committees (Rosen et al., 2018). Some critics have urged that these reforms marked a renunciation of the once-elaborated market economy system of SOE reforms in favour of prioritising political imperatives over economic efficiency, such that carrying them to realisation will further undermine the long-term competitiveness of Chinese SOEs in global markets. For instance, Zhang (2019) argued that the latest SOE reforms would undo a lot of progress made in the earlier reform periods.

The distinctive political governance structure of Chinese SOEs – reinforced by recent reforms – shapes executives' digital engagement strategies with the public. On the one hand, as Brødsgaard et al. (2017) detailed, although social media leadership offers new opportunities for SOEs to earn public trust by connecting corporate messaging to national priorities, SOE leaders are incentivised to prioritise political and administrative experience over financial performance to advance their careers. This pressure creates complexity for executive public engagement strategies: the political governance model of SOEs means that their executives may be at higher risk of damaging public trust by providing inaccurate or non-transparent information on digital platforms, both in terms of their personal reputations and those of their SOEs (Rosen et al., 2018). Additionally, the extra layer of political vetting focusing on political loyalty and ideological conformity may discourage SOE executives from engaging in highly open, authentic communicative exchanges with the public, limiting the effectiveness of their digital engagement strategies (Leutert, 2020).

Furthermore, the literature also reveals extensive talent management challenges that Chinese SOEs are facing. Brown (2014) has suggested a model of talent management for leader-managers of SOEs to achieve stronger human capital and human resources (or HR) strategies. However, effective talent management implementation generally faces challenges stemming from the specific organisational culture of Chinese SOEs and the Communist Party's role in hindering the desired merit-based talent management reform (Zhang, 2019). This means that efforts to change the decision-making process in SOEs can be constrained by the party-state and its relentless emphasis on political loyalty and connections, rather than professional competence, which often yields a talent pool of SOE executives who can be much less suited to dealing with today's agile market in comparison to their Western counterparts (Lin et al., 2020).

These perspectives speak to the message that organisational structure and ownership are central to shaping firm performance. This provides further impetus for tailored talent management that is informed by the unique challenges and opportunities of the SOE setting. This structure and ownership may affect China's approach to managing its SOEs' talent, which, in turn, may shape the orientation of executives about digital engagement strategies. Unless they have a steady pipeline of competent leader-managers, SOEs will not succeed at building public trust in their organisations or successfully engaging with the public through digital means. This, in turn, calls for a critical rewrite of talent management practices in Chinese SOEs, or to be precise, hiring and developing leaders who are fit for the new challenges of building and managing modern SOEs while navigating the 'iron triangle' (Brødsgaard et al., 2017).

Chinese SOE executives' digital engagement strategies are framed by the intricate political governance structure of their organisations and the talent challenges they face. As Yu (2019) states, the current SOE reform agenda is again prioritising the political imperatives over economic efficiency and competitiveness, adding another layer of complexity to the environments in which SOE executives are operating. Questions arising from this context are how sustainable and robust the SOEs are going to be in an ever-globalising market and continuing competition with their private peers. As the technological landscape is evolving, China's public is increasingly demanding more attention to issues of transparency and accountability (Hao et al., 2020). SOEs will have to find a solution to address these issues, develop and apply flexible strategies to navigate the 'iron triangle', and gain more trust and support from the public in the coming decade.

Accountability for UK Enterprise Leaders in the Digital Age

The UK's highly individualistic culture and the long-standing tradition of a free press provide important protection against manipulation by enterprise leaders. Yet, untruths and falsehoods continue to disseminate widely, and the efficacy of this protection is open to debate. The culture has long encouraged its citizens to pursue their own interests and question authority when necessary. Such a context might facilitate a greater readiness to challenge the claims made by enterprise leaders. If exposed as misleading, these leaders could suffer reputational damage (Hambleton et al., 2022). But how much of this, in practice, is translated into effective accountability of enterprise leaders? The UK's leadership culture is perhaps best conceptualised as a 'blend of individualism and collectivism' with a complexity that does not align with the linear model of the hierarchy (Collinson & Collinson, 2009).

The media environment is far from impeccable, British media has tended to maintain greater standards of journalistic integrity and fact-checking than is the general practice in many other countries (Hambleton et al., 2022). As Sweeting and Hambleton (2020) note, the polarising nature of social media exchanges and the emergence of echo chambers can lead to opinion diversity in some segments of the population, making them more vulnerable to manipulation. Moreover, the UK's media environment appears to be increasingly fractured, creating a growing divide between traditional news sources and alternative media that tend to prioritise partisan agendas over factual reporting (Sweeting et al., 2020).

Leadership practice in the UK is dynamic (Collinson & Collinson, 2009). The ideal is a 'blended leadership' in which aspects of the individualistic and the collectivist models are combined in the hope of producing a more adaptive and responsive leadership style that is better suited to modern organisations. However, this is not always common practice. Many enterprise leaders do not display the ethical calibre necessary to build trust and resilience in the face of digital manipulation (Linkov et al., 2018). The UK government has recently brought forward the development of the Online Safety Bill, which gives social media platforms legal responsibility for harmful content on their sites (Sweeting et al., 2020). However, others have pointed out that this strategy is insufficient to address the underlying problems – particularly the business models that encourage engagement over the veracity of social media companies (Hambleton et al., 2022). Moreover, initiatives designed to improve the public's digital literacy or use of critical-thinking skills to resist emotional manipulation online (Sweeting et al., 2020) are not well-evaluated. Journalists' lobbying for evidence-based policy may seem self-interested, and the gendered rhetoric used in political UK discourse (Harmer et al., 2017) might further hinder accountability by prioritising 'masculine' leadership forms over more transparent approaches.

Power Distance and Deference to Hierarchy in China

China's high PDI (Hofstede, 2001) fosters greater tolerance of inequality in organisations (e.g., social stratification). Thus, the public is socialised to defer to top-down leaders with less questioning because leaders are perceived as 'only expected to serve the collective interest' (Brødsgaard et al., 2017). Compounding this cultural feature is the 'iron triangle' of complex relationships between the Communist Party, the state, and

China's multipronged business interests (Brødsgaard et al., 2017). First, the arm's-length managerial control between different government ministries is weak, allowing SOE executives to take advantage of regulatory benefits. Second, SOE managers' loyalties to the party sometimes contradict their duties to the state. Third, SOEs are often acting in a manner aligned with the interests of the Communist Party (Brødsgaard et al., 2017). The Party's cadre management system still controls SOE executives' actions (Jin et al., 2022), and the state's recent reforms of SOEs may further consolidate party-state control (Yu, 2019), solidifying top-down hierarchical structures and public deference to these structures. This cultural and political context makes it easier for members of the public to defer to authority or nationalist objectives. In effect, this makes it easier for SOE executives to harness platforms of social media and digital communication to spread their propaganda and political agendas as an effective way to reach many people simultaneously (Blanchette & Polk, 2020).

While higher PDI in China might help to explain the initial public acceptance of manipulative narratives, the lower uncertainty avoidance in China might make the public more willing to confront the unexpected (or ambiguous) once misleading information is exposed (Zhang & Zhou, 2014). The discussion points to the risk for SOEs' executives engaging with the public through digital channels, as failure to provide accurate and transparent information could damage public trust, and thus result in serious public backlash (Brødsgaard et al., 2017). Such implications are important to consider given the mounting challenges in talent management for Chinese SOEs that still emphasise political loyalty over professional competence (Zhang, 2019). This prioritisation of political loyalty over professional competence in talent management might make it difficult for executives of Chinese SOEs to navigate the nuanced demands of digital engagement. If public demands for transparency and accountability intensify, SOEs must develop adaptive strategies to build public trust and support, as well as manage the possibility of public backlash in the face of deception being exposed (Yu, 2019).

Collectivist Values Promote Conformity and Shared Interests

China's collectivist culture emphasises family, national, and group interests. The salience of collectivist values means that the Chinese public is not only more amenable to confirmation bias but also more inclined to accept that their leaders' interests are aligned with 'the greater good'. This conformity to collective interests is facilitated by the political governance structure of Chinese SOEs, which requires executives to balance business, social, and political goals (Brødsgaard, 2012), thereby allowing executives to invoke the preservation of 'collective interests' as a rationale for their digital engagement strategy. The scarcity of viewpoints debating the 'objective truth' on Chinese digital spaces (Blanchette & Polk, 2020) also sustains confirmation bias, promotes 'groupthink', and consequently creates fertile grounds for digital misinformation and propaganda.

UK Culture Values Skepticism and Individual Needs

By contrast, the highly individualistic culture in the UK suggests that citizens are more likely to give primacy to personal interests and express skepticism about appeals to the 'greater good'. The views of UK enterprise leaders are relatively more likely to be subject to intense inspection, and the public is also more likely to push back against policy narratives that do not advance their interests. This makes it more likely that leaders' attempts at digital manipulation are more likely to be exposed, picked apart, and criticised. These checks are not perfect, considering the increasing fragmentation and polarisation of the UK's media landscape (Sweeting & Hambleton, 2020). China's more collective cultural orientation and the public's greater propensity to defer to authority render the citizens more susceptible to digital manipulation for purposes of enhancing collective interests compared with UK culture.

Overall, the cross-cultural qualitative and comparative study of digital manipulation by enterprise leaders in China and the UK demonstrates how cultural dimensions help shape public susceptibility and explain organisational responsibility. With its high-power distance, greater reliance on collectivist values, and lower uncertainty avoidance, China is more susceptible to top-down political manipulation. Indeed, digital manipulation appears local within China because SOE executives can leverage social media for political purposes, carrying out their mandates and propagating government policies, and leaders assume that the public agrees with their views and actions. In contrast, the UK's highly individualistic culture and robust free press traditions provide some protections against digital manipulation but the fragmentation of the media landscape and more random practice of power, leadership, and management in independent, privately owned firms also mean that challenges with digital manipulation will continue. As the information ecosystem continues to evolve, both nations will presumably need tailored interventions to safeguard against threats of digital manipulation and other risks, while promoting responsible and constructive online engagement.

Lessons for Leaders

Chinese and British societies face unprecedented difficulties due to the increasing prevalence of digital manipulation. Our response to digital challenges requires fundamental changes to digital space management and leadership approaches. We must stop thinking of digital literacy as a simple task that can be checked off a list. Sustained engagement combined with real-world practice is necessary for communities to successfully navigate the modern complex information landscape. The solution requires collaboration between community leaders and education specialists along with technology experts to establish interactive environments which enable people to learn about manipulation strategies in a secure way.

Existing platform regulation methods fail to deliver effective results. We need to shift our emphasis from reactive content moderation toward proactive strategies that offer platforms and incentives to encourage constructive communication. Current trends demonstrate the worry that digital spaces manipulate public conversations. Protecting traditional media is important but we must also transform our methods of information sharing and validation for today's digital landscape. Online platforms and local journalism initiatives can work together to develop and assess new methods for community-led story verification and fact-checking.

Leaders must take ownership to establish the right tone. Instead of focusing on compulsory training programs, we should establish a leadership culture that prioritises genuine digital engagement. Leaders could establish peer networks to share their online trust-building experiences while creating mentorship programs that allow new digital leaders to learn from experienced communicators.

These issues cross borders and cultures. The exchange of experiences between China and the UK allows us to create sophisticated and effective methods for building trust in our globally connected society. The future demands innovative thinking and dedication from every segment of society. Building trust requires creating spaces where transparency and trust grow organically instead of following a predetermined set of solutions.

Conclusion

The cross-cultural analysis in this chapter shows that the risks posed by technological platforms are similar in Chinese and UK contexts. As the world of digital communication progresses into even more immersive and augmented interactions, societies will need enlightened and empowered stakeholders who are equipped with the critical thinking skills to evaluate and interpret information online and hold leaders accountable for how they communicate. By calibrating the right mix of non-technical digital literacy campaigns, platform accountability rules, and ethics training, policymakers, industry leaders, and civil society can build a more robust and responsible digital commons. Indeed, the war against digital manipulation will always be a work in progress, with all actors scrutinising and adapting so that advancements in technology do not correspond with opportunities for deception and exploitation.

References

Andreas, M. K., & Haenlein, M. (2010). Users of the world, unite! The challenges and opportunities of social media. *Business Horizons*, *53*(1), 59–68.

Bastos, M., & Mercea, D. (2018). The Brexit botnet and user-generated hyperpartisan news. *Social Science Computer Review*, *37*(1), 38–54.

Blanchette, J., & Polk, A. (2020). Dual circulation and China's new hedged integration strategy. Center for Strategic and International Studies (CSIS). https://www.csis.org/analysis/dual-circulation-and-chinas-new-hedged-integration-strategy (Accessed 20 May 2024).

Bradshaw, S., & Howard, P. N. (2018). Challenging truth and trust: A global inventory of organized social media manipulation. The Computational Propaganda Project. University of Oxford. https://demtech.oii.ox.ac.uk/wp-content/uploads/sites/12/2018/07/ct2018.pdf (Accessed 20 May 2024).

Brødsgaard, K. E. (2012). Politics and business group formation in China: The party in control? *The China Quarterly*, *211*, 624–648.

Brødsgaard, K. E., Hubbard, P., Cai, G., & Zhang, L. (2017). China's SOE executives: Drivers of or obstacles to reform? *The Copenhagen Journal of Asian Studies*, *35*(1), 52–75.

Brown, L. M. (2014). A proposed talent management model for leader-managers in state-owned enterprises in China. *International Journal of Human Resource Studies*, *4*(3), 198–213.

Collinson, D., & Collinson, M. (2009). 'Blended leadership': Employee perspectives on effective leadership in the UK further education sector. *Leadership*, *5*(3), 365–380.

Elbers, A., Kolominski, S., & Blesa Aledo, P.S. (2023). Coping with dark leadership: Examination of the impact of psychological capital on the relationship between dark leaders and employees' basic need satisfaction in the workplace. *Administrative Sciences*, *13*(4), 96.

Hambleton, R., Sweeting, D., & Oliver, T. (2022). Place, power and leadership: Insights from mayoral governance and leadership innovation in Bristol, UK. *Leadership*, *18*(1), 81–101.

Hao, Z., Liu, Y., Zhang, J., & Zhao, X. (2020). Political connection, corporate philanthropy and efficiency: Evidence from China's anti-corruption campaign. *Journal of Comparative Economics*, *48*(3), 688–708.

Harmer, E., Savigny, H., & Ward, O. (2017). 'Are you tough enough?' Performing gender in the UK leadership debates 2015. *Media, Culture & Society*, *39*(7), 960–975.

Hern, A. (2019). Revealed: How TikTok censors videos that do not please Beijing. *The Guardian*. https://www.theguardian.com/technology/2019/sep/25/revealed-how-tiktok-censors-videos-that-do-not-please-beijing (Accessed 22 May 2024).

Hofstede, G. (2001). *Culture's Consequences: Comparing Values, Behaviors, Institutions, and Organizations across Nations* (2nd ed.) Sage Publications.

Iddris, F. (2018). Digital supply chain: Survey of the literature. *International Journal of Business Research and Management*, *9*(1), 47–61.

Jin, X., Xu, L., Xin, Y., & Adhikari, A. (2022). Political governance in China's state-owned enterprises. *China Journal of Accounting Research*, *15*(2), 100236.

King, G., Pan, J., & Roberts, M. E. (2017). How the Chinese government fabricates social media posts for strategic distraction, not engaged argument. *American Political Science Review*, *111*(3), 484–501.

Leutert, W. (2020). State-owned enterprises in contemporary China. In T. Wright (Ed.), *Handbook of China's Political Economy* (pp. 207–223). Edward Elgar Publishing.

Lin, K. J., Lu, X., Zhang, J., & Zheng, Y. (2020). State-owned enterprises in China: A review of 40 years of research and practice. *China Journal of Accounting Research*, *13*(1), 31–55.

Linkov, I., Trump, B. D., Poinsatte-Jones, K., & Florin, M. V. (2018). Governance strategies for a sustainable digital world. *Sustainability*, *10*(2), 440.

Molter, V., & Diresta, R. (2020). Pandemics & propaganda: How Chinese state media creates and propagates CCP coronavirus narratives. *Harvard Kennedy School Misinformation Review*, *1*(3).

Ofcom. (2021). Understanding online false information in the UK. Economist Discussion Paper Series, 2. https://www.ofcom.org.uk/__data/assets/pdf_file/0027/211986/understanding-online-false-information-uk.pdf (Accessed 15 May 2024).

Rosen, D. H., Leutert, W., & Guo, S. (2018). Missing Link: Corporate Governance in China's State Sector. Asia Society Special Report. Rhodium Group. https://asiasociety.org/sites/default/files/inline-files/ASNC_Rhodium_SOEReport_0.pdf (Accessed 18 May 2024).

Sweeting, D., & Hambleton, R. (2020). The dynamics of depoliticisation in urban governance: Introducing a directly elected mayor. *Urban Studies*, *57*(5), 1068–1086.

Sweeting, D., Hambleton, R., & Oliver, T. (2020). *Mayoral Governance in Bristol: Has It Made a Difference?* University of Bristol.

Wang, J. (2014). The political logic of corporate governance in China's state-owned enterprises. *Cornell International Law Journal*, *47*(3), 5.

Yu, H. (2019). Reform of state-owned enterprises in China: The Chinese Communist Party strikes back. *Asian Studies Review*, *43*(2), 332–351.

Zhang, X. (2019). Integration of CCP leadership with corporate governance leading role or dismemberment? Touching the proverbial elephant: The multiple shapes of Chinese law. *China Perspectives*, *2019-1*, 55–63.

Zhang, X., & Zhou, J. (2014). Empowering leadership, uncertainty avoidance, trust, and employee creativity: Interaction effects and a mediating mechanism. *Organisational Behaviour and Human Decision Processes*, *124*(2), 150–164.

INTERVENTIONIST PARADIGMS

V

Chapter 22

Navigating the Dark Side of Leadership: Insights from Nigeria's Public Sector

Sheriff F. Folarin, Ugochukwu D. Abasilim, and Mostafa M. Jalal

Introduction

Leadership is one of the prime determinants of organisational culture, productivity, and success. It is classically represented by inspirational vision, strategic insight, and motivational prowess, with claims that it can transform and lead any organisation toward its goals (Amah & Ogah, 2023). However, beneath this very conventional view lies a darker reality threatening organisational harmony and efficiency. Dark leadership is an under-recognised but not rare occurrence in organisational lives and comprises traits such as narcissism, psychopathy, and Machiavellianism (Cesinger et al., 2023). Specifically, it refers to traits typically signified by self-serving motives, manipulative behaviours, and declining levels of trust, morale, and operational effectiveness observed in organisations (Wilhau & Karau, 2021).

The dimensions of dark leadership in the Nigerian public sector take unique directions, as shaped by cultural norms, historical legacies, and institutional frameworks (Aniche, 2021). Nigeria's public sector landscape provides fertile ground for dark leadership behaviours, especially against the backdrop of bureaucratic complexities and governance challenges (Inuwa & Ononiwu, 2020). Consequently, it impairs decision-making processes and

DOI: 10.4324/9781003475262-27

perpetuates a culture of impunity and inefficiency (Pensky, 2008). Empirical evidence from recent studies refers to the pervasiveness and dark, destructive consequences of leadership in the public agencies of Nigeria (Akanle & Shittu, 2022; Àkànle & Nkpe, 2021). It shows that leaders in such contexts gain increasing influence to the detriment of organisational integrity and employee well-being. Similarly, such behaviours erode trust, suppress innovation, and retard organisational adaptation to dynamic sociopolitical environments.

Therefore, the chapter interrogates the concept of dark leadership within Nigeria's public sector, specifically discussing its prevalence, manifestations, and consequences on organisational dynamics. Drawing from case studies and empirical data, the chapter elaborates on how dark leadership practices materialise in decision-making processes, organisational cultures, and employee engagement levels. The intricate relationship between dark leadership, cultural norms, and institutional contexts is also discussed, given its implications for organisational resilience and sustainable development. This chapter furthers ongoing conversations on the subject and details practical ways to mitigate the negative consequences of dark leadership. Ethical leadership practices, transparency, and accountability will help generate organisational environments characterised by trust, integrity, and operational excellence. These insights are instrumental to policymakers, practitioners, and scholars who attempt to understand the cultural contexts underpinning leadership in Africa and strive for effective governance and sustainable organisational outcomes.

Understanding Dark Leadership

Leadership plays a pivotal role in organisational success by fostering employee coordination, goal alignment, and enhanced performance. With effective leadership, organisations can avoid chaos and inefficiency. The concept of "dark leadership" has sparked debates in literature, with researchers highlighting its toxic, destructive, and abusive manifestations (Padilla et al., 2007). Behaviours associated with dark leadership include victimising employees, lying to them, blaming the wrong person for mistakes, and discrimination. Research indicates that dark leadership correlates with decreased employee performance, increased psychological distress, and low levels of job satisfaction and commitment.

Additionally, higher levels of abusive leadership are linked with increased work-family conflict. Despite these negative attributions, dark leaders often avoid dealing with the repercussions of their behaviours. This relatively dismissive attitude towards dark leaders can be attributed to prevailing perceptions of leadership. Traditionally, leaders have been idealised as possessing positive traits that contribute to organisational success. However, recent research challenges this notion, suggesting leaders may exhibit unethical behaviours and possess dark characteristics (Herbst, 2014). Various terminologies describe leadership's negative aspects, including toxic, destructive, tyrannical, and dysfunctional (Padilla et al., 2007; Ashforth, 1994).

Leadership decisions significantly impact organisational structures, and leaders may only sometimes act in the organisation's best interests. Negative leader attitudes can lead to adverse consequences for followers, including disappointment, stress, unhappiness, decreased self-confidence, and disengagement from work (Ashforth, 1994). While much research has focused on positive leadership styles and their benefits, there has been a notable neglect of the darker aspects of leadership. Recent developments in leadership research emphasise the need to acknowledge and understand the negative impacts of leadership on employees and organisations.

This shift in perspective has led to increased attention to the dark side of leadership, prompting a surge of studies examining its various dimensions. However, the ambiguity surrounding the concept of dark leadership presents challenges in delineating its scope and constituent leadership styles. The lack of theoretical integration further complicates understanding, highlighting the need for clarity in comprehending dark leadership and its implications. Addressing this issue is crucial for advancing knowledge and effectively addressing the challenges of dark leadership in organisations.

Dark leadership encompasses behaviours and traits that harm both followers and organisations, reflecting the dysfunctional aspects of a leader's personality. Various terms have been introduced in the literature to describe this phenomenon, including petty tyranny (Ashforth, 1994), abusive supervision (Tepper, 2000), dark side leadership (Conger, 1990), evil leadership (Delbecq, 2001), toxic leadership (Lipman-Blumen, 2005), and bad leadership (Kellerman, 2004). For instance, petty tyranny refers to leaders' oppressive, capricious, and vindictive use of power and authority (Ashforth, 1994). This behaviour is characterised by arbitrariness, belittling of subordinates, lack of consideration, protracted or constrained conflict resolution, discouragement of initiative, and non-contingent punishment. Similarly, abusive supervision involves sustained displays of hostile behaviours towards subordinates, such as hostile verbal and nonverbal actions (Tepper, 2000). Dark leadership, on the other hand, encompasses negative leadership behaviours characterised by traits such as narcissism, Machiavellianism, and psychopathy. Narcissism, for example, is at the core of dark leadership, with narcissistic leaders exhibiting self-absorption, entitlement, hostility, arrogance, and a superficial view of themselves (Judge et al., 2009).

While some argue for positive aspects of narcissism, such as productivity and inspiration (Maccoby, 2004), others emphasise its negative impacts on followers and organisations (Judge et al., 2009). Similarly, Machiavellianism involves using lies, manipulation, coercion, and force by leaders to motivate followers (Judge et al., 2009). This behaviour may lead to negative organisational outcomes, such as poor follower perceptions and workplace deviance (Tepper et al., 2006). Psychopathy, on the other hand, refers to operating with psychopathic traits below the level required for diagnosis as psychopaths (Boddy, 2011).

Psychopathic leaders may engage in workplace bullying and demonstrate a lack of emotional intelligence (Lishner et al., 2011). The consequences of dark leadership are significant and far-reaching. Research has shown that employees under abusive supervisors experience lower levels of organisational commitment, life and job satisfaction, and perceptions of organisational justice. They also engage in fewer organisational citizenship behaviours and are more likely to experience turnover, conflict between work and family, emotional exhaustion, and psychological distress (Ashforth & Lee, 1997; Tepper, 2000; Duffy et al., 2002; Tepper et al., 2006).

Of particular concern is the impact of dark leaders on employees' organisational commitment and turnover intentions. As conceptualised by Meyer and Allen (1997), organisational commitment consists of three dimensions: affective, continuance, and normative commitment. Affective commitment is highly predictive of employee retention and job performance (Meyer et al., 2002). Dark leaders who diminish their employees' affective commitment risk losing valuable personnel and may experience declines in job performance.

The job embeddedness model (Mitchell & Lee, 2001) and the unfolding model (Lee & Mitchell, 1994) offer theoretical frameworks to understand employee turnover. According to the job embeddedness model, employees are likelier to remain with an organisation if they have strong connections to the organisation and the community. Dark leaders undermining employees' affective commitment may weaken their sense of connection to the organisation, increasing the likelihood of turnover. Similarly, the unfolding model suggests that employees often leave a job due to a "shock" event. Over time, dark leaders may subject their subordinates to numerous shocks, ultimately motivating them to leave the organisation.

Thus, dark leaders can impact employee turnover through job embeddedness and unfolding models. To comprehend dark leadership, one must explore theoretical frameworks that dive into the intricacies of bad leadership practices and their effects on individuals and institutions. Various theoretical views offer valuable insights into the concept of dark leadership. The Social Learning Theory (Bandura, 1977) is a well-known theoretical framework that suggests individuals acquire knowledge and skills by observing, imitating, and modelling conduct. Within the framework of dark leadership, this idea posits that leaders may acquire abusive or manipulative tendencies by observing other leaders or being exposed to and encouraged in such activities within their organisational environment.

Subordinates, in response, may internalise these habits and continue them inside the organisation. The Trait Theory of leadership is another significant paradigm that proposes that specific personality qualities make persons more likely to become leaders (Peters, 2023). Within the realm of dark leadership, bad leadership practices have been linked to qualities such as narcissism, Machiavellianism, and psychopathy (Judge et al., 2009). Leaders with these characteristics may demonstrate a greater propensity to partake in abusive or exploitative actions towards their subordinates.

The Dark Triad paradigm, consisting of narcissism, Machiavellianism, and psychopathy (Paulhus & Williams, 2002), provides a focused perspective for comprehending dark leadership. Studies have demonstrated that persons with elevated levels of these characteristics are more prone to displaying manipulative, exploitative, and abusive behaviours while in positions of leadership (Jonason & Webster, 2010). Knowing how these characteristics interact with leadership behaviours will help you better understand the mechanics underlying dark leadership. Moreover, the perspective of Role Theory highlights the impact of societal norms and expectations on personal conduct (Biddle, 1979).

Leaders have a specific social position within organisations with associated expectations and obligations. Dark leaders, however, have the potential to act contrary to these standards by taking actions that harm both the organisation and their followers. The elements contributing to the genesis and persistence of bad leadership behaviours can be clarified by investigating the role dynamics under dark leadership circumstances.

Impact of Dark Leadership on Employees' Well-being and Organisational Culture

There has been a noticeable increase in the study of dark leadership and its impact on organisational effectiveness in recent years. This illustrates a growing realisation of the damage and often catastrophic effects of toxic leader behaviours on organisational outcomes. Narcissism, Machiavellianism, and psychopathy characterise dark leadership; it adversely impacts the welfare of employees and the culture of organisations. It detrimentally impacts trust, morale, and productivity in the work atmosphere, reducing creativity and efficiency. Emotional and psychological impact on followers, corrosion of trust, and encouragement of unethical behaviour have identified challenges against organisational health and effectiveness (Nicolaides & Duho, 2019).

Research studies on the damage that can be caused to an organisation's outcomes because of a toxic executive have grown in recent years. A perusal of these dark-side factors provides an understanding of their pernicious effects and the importance of interventions for organisational culture and performance. The following section elaborates on this perspective by depicting how traits of dark leadership, such as narcissism, psychopathy, abusive supervision, and Machiavellianism, all negatively affect organisational effectiveness.

Abusive Supervision and Employee Well-being

Abusive supervision is among the most studied aspects of dark leadership. Tepper (2000) pioneered the systematic study of the effects of abusive supervision. According to his findings, employees who are victims of abusive monitoring exhibit more stress and poorer job satisfaction. Lower job satisfaction implies decreased commitment to the organisation and productivity. Further research has reiterated and corroborated these findings by proving that staff under abusive supervision have adverse effects such as emotional exhaustion, disengagement, and a reduction in performance (Wu & Hu, 2009; Oyewunmi & Oyewunmi, 2022). This damaging effect is further amplified, and the effectiveness of the business further decreases by the toxic work environment, which is usually characterised by mistrust and terror.

Narcissism and Decision-Making

It has been shown that leaders who are highly egotistic and predisposed to idolisation negatively influence organisational decisions and their strategic orientation. Narcissistic leaders put themselves ahead of the organisation's image to promote their interests and take risks (Rosenthal & Pittinsky, 2006). This self-serving behaviour may endanger the organisation's long-term sustainability and survival. Additionally, it has been indicated that narcissistic employers can create an atmosphere in the workplace where workers become scared to give their ideas or criticise. This results in a faulty decision-making process, often leading to poor strategic decisions (Judge et al., 2009).

Machiavellianism and Manipulative Behaviour

Machiavellian leaders are manipulative, deceitful, and exploitative; they often use unethical tactics to accomplish predetermined goals. Dahling et al. (2009) explored how Machiavellian leadership obstructs cohesiveness and effective organisational decision-making by fostering an illusory and untrustworthy climate. They will be more likely to engage in unethical behaviour and propagate a manipulative environment throughout the organisation (Ashforth & Anand, 2003). Machiavellianism is associated with an increased level of poor organisational performance, as attested to by low morale, negative employee sentiments, and feelings of exploitation and abandonment.

Psychopathy and Organisational Stability

The impulsiveness, lack of regret or guilt, and superficial appeal of psychopaths can seriously jeopardise the stability of organisations and their capacity to generate revenue. Babiak and Hare (2006) investigated how psychopathic leaders behaved in corporate settings. They concluded that the organisation faces financial hazards due to its careless decisions about the economy and its disregard for morality. Psychotic leaders continue in their use of bullying and other abusive actions in work and organisational environments, creating a hostile work environment that disrupts organisational procedures and only serves to raise employee attrition (Oyewunmi et al., 2018). The leader's incapacity to build sincere connections and trust inside the business contributes to the ensuing organisational instability, creating a turbulent and inefficient operational climate.

Erosion of Ethical Standards

The ethical climate of an organisation is also heavily influenced by leadership. The presence of a dark figure as a leader in an organisation makes corrupt practices more common in an organisation, and as a result, the ethical norms of working are weakened. The authors of a study by Padilla et al. (2007) discussed the "toxic triangle" model in which "settings conducive to the unleashing of dark side behaviour" are combined with destructive leaders and susceptible followers. The normalisation of corruption by dark leaders affects organisational culture. It has long-term negative consequences on the efficiency of the organisation's performance, as elaborated in a report by Ashforth and Anand (2003). When ethical standards are not maintained, employees, stakeholders, and consumers lose trust in a corporation.

Impact on Employee Turnover and Organisational Costs

There is a high correlation between abusive supervision and voluntary employee turnover, according to Tepper et al. (2006). Employees who are victims of dark leadership are more likely to leave the organisation due to the negative implications they experience. High turnover rates disrupt organisational processes, as most turnovers are likely to be accompanied by high costs in training, hiring, and knowledge loss. Turnover has a significant impact not only on the current production of the organisation but also on the long-term strategic capacity of the organisation.

The body of research on the subject clearly illustrates that dark leadership makes organisational effectiveness challenging and increasingly unrealised. This aligns with the view articulated in this chapter that a toxic work environment impairs employee well-being, decision-making, ethical standards, and financial performance due to abusive supervision, narcissism, psychopathy, and Machiavellianism. However, these dimensions should be considered to fully appreciate what these practices look like and how they impact the organisation's results.

Dark Leadership in Government Agencies: A Reflection

Dark leadership, manifested by traits such as narcissism, Machiavellianism, and psychopathy, can result in profound implications for the well-being of individuals at work and for the culture in general within an organisation. The effect of dark leadership is often felt more in the public sector; usually, it causes reduced efficiency, low morale, and a decline in the ethical standards in an organisation. Such case studies involve the failures and other pathologies brought about by dark leadership, which are destructive to several government agencies across contexts. This reflection discusses unethical incidences in selected government agencies in Nigeria. These are isolated cases, and in no way erode the credible contributions of the agencies to the well-being of the public. However, important lessons can be learned for improved institutional outcomes and necessary public policy reforms.

The Federal Inland Revenue Service (FIRS) is responsible for collecting taxes and revenue to fund government operations and public services. Despite its critical role in economic development, the FIRS has been plagued by allegations of corruption and unethical behaviour among senior officials. A landmark case typifying the influence of dark leadership is one whereby a senior staff of the agency was implicated in bribery and tax evasion activities by the Independent Corrupt Practices and Other Related Offences Commission (ICPC). The defendants were found guilty of bribery and tax evasion. It was alleged that the company bribed the senior staff to fraudulently reduce its tax liability. The senior staff was said to have solicited and accepted a cash gratification thereby constituting abuse of office (Okereke & Okoli, 2022).

There are some implications from this case as it pertains to organisational culture and effectiveness. The case brought to light the erosion of trust, ethical standards, and operation disruption. This suggests that the cases of bribery and tax evasion erode citizens' confidence in the agency and its ability to administer the tax regime fairly. Also, it provides critical insights into the need for reform to enhance integrity and transparency.

The Federal Road Safety Corps (FRSC) is responsible for ensuring safety on Nigeria's roads through the enforcement of traffic regulations, education, and rescue operations. However, the agency has faced specific challenges casting some degree of aspersion on the character of leadership. The Independent Corrupt Practices and Other Related Offences Commission charged two officials of the agency to court over allegations of extortion of motorists. The Commission accused the defendants of forcefully collecting unauthorised "fees" without a traffic offence being charged. The defendants were said to have used their positions for personal gain by accepting gratification from motorists. The counts bordered on offences contrary to specific sections of the Corrupt Practices and Other Related Offences Act of 2000. The duo pleaded not guilty and were later granted bail (Okereke & Okoli, 2022) . These allegations mirror many other issues connected to public trust and institutional integrity within the agency and further dimensions.

The involvement of the officials in corrupt practices diverts attention and resources from performing the key role of the enforcement of traffic laws. The diversionary effects of mitigating corruption incidents erode effectiveness and compromises and relatively limited operational capabilities. The charges against the officials have some legal implications. Conviction may attract very stiff penalties, including imprisonment without the option of a fine, and adverse publicity for the case seriously dents the reputation of the FRSC. This will affect the Commission's ability to recruit and retain competent personnel and negatively impact public support for its programs. The case calls for wholesale reforms within the FRSC to address corruption and enhance transparency and accountability. Among the reforms should be strengthening internal controls, anti-corruption training, and promoting a culture of integrity to restore public trust and ensure that FRSC conducts all its activities based on high ethical standards.

Unethical practices have a negative multiplier impact on the society. Bribes constitute an additional financial cost, and they distort economic activities due to uncertainty and lack of trust. Consequently, this also impedes the general investment climate and prospects of sustainable economic development. Therefore, the effect of reported corruption and extortion by agency officials extends beyond some particular cases; it represents a vote of no confidence on the institution's integrity and the credibility required to deliver on stipulated statutory obligations. Such issues must be dealt with, taking into cognisance aspects of strict enforcement of anti-corruption laws, constant monitoring, and ethical conduct.

Lessons for Leaders

The cases of dark leadership in government agencies examined bring out valuable lessons for leaders at all levels. Leaders must be ethical and lead with integrity. The cases presented how unethical behaviour undermined the trust level within an organisation and hampered its effectiveness. The maintenance of ethical standards for an excellent working culture is a means to enhance the public trust and credibility of organisations. Leaders should set up strong transparency measures, including regular audits, clear whistleblowing mechanisms, and public disclosure around activities within the institution. Strengthen accountability frameworks that put leaders and employees under scrutiny for their actions. Leaders must be role models, set the tone, and articulate expectations for ethics-based behaviour throughout the workforce. Employees at all levels in the organisation should be frequently exposed to and provided with ethics and compliance training to help bring organisational values to life and support ethical decision-making. Internal controls are a fundamental safeguard against corruption and misbehaviour. Leaders need to invest in an efficient internal control system that monitors financial transactions, procurement processes, relations with stakeholders, etc. All these controls help identify and avert unethical behaviour at its early development stages before it becomes severe. Leaders should establish confidential reporting channels and, vice versa, protect whistleblowers from any retaliatory measures. Allowing employees to report unethical behaviour empowers them to lead a culture of accountability and is a strong signal of commitment to ethical governance. As the governance and leadership landscape changes, leaders must be informed about the emerging risks and best practices in ethical leadership. Continuous learning and adaptation enable leaders to respond to new challenges and support high governance standards.

These lessons can help leaders control the risks associated with dark leadership and build a culture of integrity, enabling institutions to follow their mandates more effectively and resiliently in serving the interests of all stakeholders.

Conclusion

This chapter on dark leadership in the public sector underlines how bad leadership harms organisational culture, operational effectiveness, and citizens' trust. Leaders should set an example by being advocates of ethical standards, creating transparent climates, and taking every measure possible to ensure the establishment of adequate control mechanisms. The standards call for leaders to demonstrate ethical behaviour, offer ongoing ethics and compliance education, and establish sound internal controls to monitor and prevent destructive behaviours. Whistleblower protection is critical to identifying improper actions and acting upon them (Manesh et al., 2024). This encourages accountability, transparency, and openness within the organisation. Once leaders keep a continuous learning and adaptive posture, they will remain current with emerging risks and ethical practices.

Strengthening governance structures, ethical leadership development, and anti-corruption laws are essential to reducing the risks of dark leadership. Of importance in rebuilding trust would be open communication with stakeholders on efforts to rectify past misconduct and set in motion necessary reforms. Continuous monitoring and assessment are fundamental to ensure that the governance frameworks and ethical standards remain effective and responsive. These lessons and practices can reduce the risks of dark leadership, improve ethical behaviour, and build a culture of integrity and trust in organisations. The onus lies on leaders to implement processes that will ensure enhanced organisational performance, positive societal impact, and sustainable development.

References

Àkànle, Ọ., & Nkpe, D. O. (Eds.). (2021). *Corruption and development in Nigeria* (1st ed.). Routledge. https://doi.org/10.4324/9781003178637

Akanle, O., & Shittu, O. S. (2022). The unending development question of Nigeria. *The European Journal of Development Research*, *34*(1), 321–342.

Amah, O. E., & Ogah, M. (2023). *Leadership and organisational effectiveness post-COVID-19*. Springer Books.

Aniche, E. T. (2021). Institutions, inequality and crisis of developmental regionalism in Africa. In E. T. Aniche & T. Falola (Eds.), *Rethinking Institutions, Processes, and Development in Africa*. Rowman and Littlefield International.

Ashforth, B. E. (1994). Petty tyranny in organizations. *Human Relations*, 47(7), 755–778.

Ashforth, B. E., & Anand, V. (2003). The normalization of corruption in organizations. *Research in Organizational Behavior*, 25, 1–52.

Ashforth, B. E., & Lee, R. T. (1997). Burnout as a process: Commentary on Cordes, Dougherty and Blum. *Journal of Organizational Behavior*, 18(6), 703–708.

Babiak, P., & Hare, R. D. (2006). *Snakes in suits: When psychopaths go to work*. HarperCollins.

Bandura, A. (1977). *Social learning theory*. Prentice Hall.

Biddle, B. J. (1979). *Role theory: Expectations, identities, and behaviors*. Academic Press.

Boddy, C. R. (2011). The corporate psychopaths theory of the global financial crisis. *Journal of Business Ethics*, 102, 255–259.

Cesinger, B., Gundolf, K., Hughes, M., Khedhaouria, A., & Montani, F. (2023)The bright and dark sides of the Dark Triad traits among senior managers: Effects on organizational commitment. *Review of Managerial Science*, 17, 1731–1763. https://doi.org/10.1007/s11846-022-00571-3

Conger, J. A. (1990). The dark side of leadership. *Organizational Dynamics*, 19(2), 44–55.

Dahling, J. J., Whitaker, B. G., & Levy, P. E. (2009). The development and validation of a new Machiavellianism scale. *Journal of Management*, 35(2), 219–257.

Delbecq, A. L. (2001). Evil and the nature of executive leadership. *The Executive*, 15(2), 58–59.

Duffy, M. K., Ganster, D. C., & Pagon, M. (2002). Social undermining in the workplace. *Academy of Management Journal*, 45(2), 331–351.

Herbst, T. H. (2014). Examining the dark side of leadership: Insights from psychology. *Frontiers in Psychology*, 5, 1123.

Inuwa, I., & Ononiwu, C. G. (2020). Traditional and information technology anti-corruption strategies for curbing public sector corruption in developing economies of Sub-Saharan Africa: A systematic literature review. *The African Journal of Information Systems*, 12(2), 218–246.

Jonason, P. K., & Webster, G. D. (2010). The dirty dozen: A concise measure of the dark triad. *Psychological Assessment*, 22(2), 420–432.

Judge, T. A., LePine, J. A., & Rich, B. L. (2009). Loving yourself abundantly: Relationship of the narcissistic personality to self and other perceptions of workplace deviance, leadership, and task and contextual performance. *Journal of Applied Psychology*, 94(4), 935–944.

Kellerman, B. (2004). *Bad leadership: What it is, how it happens, why it matters.* Harvard Business Review Press.

Lee, T. W., & Mitchell, T. R. (1994). An alternative approach: The unfolding model of voluntary employee turnover. *Academy of Management Review*, 19(1), 51–89.

Lipman-Blumen, J. (2005). *The allure of toxic leaders: Why we follow destructive bosses and corrupt politicians–and how we can survive them.* Oxford University Press.

Lishner, D. A., Hong, P. Y., Jiang, J. Y., & Gagnon, S. (2011). Psychopathy, narcissism, and borderline personality: A critical review of self-report instruments. *Personality and Individual Differences*, 51(3), 390–395.

Maccoby, M. (2004). Narcissistic leaders: The incredible pros, the inevitable cons. *Harvard Business Review*, 82(1), 92–101.

Manesh, M., Tavakoli, A., Oyewunmi, A. E., & Pillay, S. (2024). Ethical decision-making in East Africa: predictors of whistleblowing intention. *Society and Business Review*, 19(3), 424–454. https://doi.org/10.1108/SBR-03-2022-0067

Meyer, J. P., & Allen, N. J. (1997). *Commitment in the workplace: Theory, research, and application.* Sage Publications.

Meyer, J. P., Stanley, D. J., Herscovitch, L., & Topolnytsky, L. (2002). Affective, continuance, and normative commitment to the organization: A meta-analysis of antecedents, correlates, and consequences. *Journal of Vocational Behavior*, 61(1), 20–52. http://dx.doi.org/10.1006/jvbe.2001.1842

Mitchell, T. R., & Lee, T. W. (2001). The unfolding model of voluntary turnover and job embeddedness: Foundations for a comprehensive theory of attachment. *Research in Organizational Behavior*, 23, 189–246.

Nicolaides, A., & Duho, K. C. T. (2019) Effective leadership in organizations: African ethics and corruption. *Modern Economy, 10*, 1713–1743. https://doi.org/10.4236/me.2019.107111

Okereke, E. U., & Okoli, U. R. (2022). Anti-corruption fight by independent corrupt practices and other related offences commission (ICPC) and sustainable development in Nigeria. *African Journal of Politics and Administrative Studies, 15*(2), 135–155.

Oyewunmi, A. E., Akinnusi, D. M., Oyewunmi, O. A. (2018). Of predators and preys: Corporate psychopathy and employee burnout as parallels. *Periodica Polytechnica Social and Management Sciences*, 26(2), 149–156. https://doi.org/10.3311/PPso.11810

Oyewunmi, A. E., & Oyewunmi, O. A. (2022). Speaking silence: Abusive supervision, subordinates' citizenship behaviour, and whistleblowing intention. *Sage Open*, 12(1), 215824402210799. https://doi.org/10.1177/21582440221079912

Padilla, A., Hogan, R., & Kaiser, R. B. (2007). The toxic triangle: Destructive leaders, susceptible followers, and conducive environments. *Leadership Quarterly*, 18(3), 176–194.

Paulhus, D. L., & Williams, K. M. (2002). The dark triad of personality: Narcissism, Machiavellianism, and psychopathy. *Journal of Research in Personality*, 36(6), 556–563.

Pensky, M. (2008). Amnesty on trial: impunity, accountability, and the norms of international law. *Ethics and Global Politics*, 1(1–2), 1–40.

Peters, M. A. (2023). Who leads, who follows? Critical review of the field of leadership studies: From the 'Great Man'& trait theory to equity & diversity leadership in the biodigital era. *Beijing International Review of Education*, 5(1–2), 25–50.

Rosenthal, S. A., & Pittinsky, T. L. (2006). Narcissistic leadership. *Leadership Quarterly*, 17(6), 617–633.

Tepper, B. J. (2000). Consequences of abusive supervision. *Academy of Management Journal*, 43(2), 178–190.

Tepper, B. J., Duffy, M. K., Henle, C. A., & Lambert, L. S. (2006). Procedural injustice, victim precipitation, and abusive supervision. *Personnel Psychology*, 59(1), 101–123.

Wilhau, A. J., & Karau, S. J. (2021). Gender differences in entrepreneur values and venture mission. *Journal of Business Diversity, 21*(1). https://doi.org/10.33423/jbd.v21i1.4075

Wu, T. Y., & Hu, C. (2009). Abusive supervision and employee emotional exhaustion dispositional antecedents and boundaries. *Group & Organization Management, 34*, 143–169. http://dx.doi.org/10.1177/1059601108331217

Chapter 23

Leadership and the Bankruptcy of Integrity

Matthew N. O. Sadiku and Janet O. Sadiku

Introduction

Every one of us is a leader in some sense. Parents have an obligation to lead their children in the right way. A priest is a spiritual leader in his congregation. A college president is an academic leader. A manager leads within the context of a firm, company, or industry. The ability to lead effectively has a cumulative effect on others because, at its core, leadership is influence. Our influence is like a pebble thrown into a pool, causing concentric circles to expand in ever-widening circles. How we perform in our respective leadership capacities has a ripple effect on how we perform as a nation. Leaders are important people and provide clear direction for the entire group or organisation. Everything either rises or falls on leaders. A lot is expected of a leader but certainly, no leader is perfect. However, to whom much is given, much is expected, and actions speak louder than words.

Good leadership is imperative considering the scope of leadership crises in the family, academia, political arena, para-church ministries, and the corporate world. Nevertheless, good leaders are hard to find despite the several colleges that train people for leadership positions. The increasing lack of credible leadership is not an indication that there are no people who want to lead. However, there is a growing decline in accessing dependable and responsible leaders. Are leaders made? In our opinion, the answer is 60% yes and 40% no. The ability to lead is a talent, such as the natural aptitude to be

DOI: 10.4324/9781003475262-28

good in math. It is worth noting that the measure of aptitude varies from person to person. We believe that the general range of our leadership potential is impacted by genetic factors, but within that range, practice and continual training can make a big difference between someone who has leadership potential and someone who is a great leader. Thus, we all have leadership potential, but great and effective leaders exhibit higher levels of potential than the rest of us (Sadiku, 2009). Integrity is an essential quality for leaders because it sets the tone for the entire team. A leader with integrity is someone who can be trusted to do what is right, even when no one is watching. Leaders with integrity are trustworthy, honest, and ethical. They are committed to doing the right thing, even when it is not easy, popular, or convenient. Laws, codes of conduct, and ethical standards are three major ways in which followers assess the integrity of their leader. Followers may find it easier to follow a leader with integrity on account of the increased confidence in the moral basis of the leader's actions (Moorman & Grover, 2009).

This chapter essentially examines the problem of leadership without integrity. It begins with a brief review of the concepts of leadership and integrity and highlights the factors that contribute to a lack of integrity. Case studies are discussed and lessons for leaders are prescribed.

Leadership: A Brief Overview

Leadership is one of the most extensively studied topics in the social sciences. It is at the heart of every group or organisation. The importance of leaders is brought to the in many social contexts, including the workplace, religious and secular communities, schools, colleges, classrooms, business, healthcare, government, politics, law enforcement, military, organisations, and families. It influences the way we work and live and defines our behaviour in definite respects. Leaders are aware that they are not perfect, are aware of their strengths and weaknesses, and strive for continuous improvement (Sadiku et al., 2020). For decades, there have been questions about leaders being born or made. In the past, individual differences such as cognitive intelligence, traits of personality, and demographic characteristics dictate who leads. This approach suggests that "leaders are born." Today, leadership is regarded as a process of social influence in which one person can work cooperatively with others in the accomplishment of a common task. This lends credence to the view that leadership is an art and is learned over time.

Leadership is regarded as the heart of every organisation and demands various levels of accountability. It is a process of leading followers and influencing the activities of an organised group toward goal achievement. Great leaders move us in the right direction, ignite our passion, and inspire the best in us. Integrity is one of the top attributes of a good leader; it implies being honest, having moral principles, and consistent ethical standards (Karthikeyan, 2017). People look for business savvy, analytical skills, experience, charisma, communication skills, and vision as important traits in a leader or an aspiring leader. While these are important, they are only the baseline and complement the characteristics of a leader. There is a tendency to overlook the soft skills found in the most successful leaders, particularly the role of emotional intelligence. The emotional intelligence approach is a radical departure from the traditional leadership style. Emotional intelligence refers to a set of verbal and nonverbal abilities that allows all individuals (especially leaders) to use their emotions to guide thinking and action (Sadiku & Olaleye, 2020).

Leadership is regarded as the single, most crucial factor that determines the success or failure of an organisation. Leadership effectiveness can be divided into two broad categories: getting along behaviours (teamwork and empowerment of others) and getting ahead behaviours (visioning, energising, designing, and rewarding). The different types of leadership include transformational, transactional, servant, charismatic, pastoral, primal, innovation, authentic, inspirational, etc. These different styles can be regarded as a continuum, with each type of leadership style adaptable to a specific situational demand. Whether leading a meeting, project, team, or an entire organisation, one might consider adopting a leadership style. The role of emotional intelligence is relevant to the effective appreciation of leadership. Also, it has emerged as one of the crucial components of leadership effectiveness in different contexts.

In this chapter, we are interested in the less palatable side of leadership. It is time to acknowledge the darker side of leadership. A leader whose personality is composed of a trio of negative personality traits — narcissism, psychopathy, and Machiavellianism — is considered a dark leader. The challenge is a dark leader can be very charming and adept at masking their underlying dark side, making it difficult to identify a dark leader. A dark leader is overbearing, dominating, and aggressive, and you cannot reason with them. For such leaders, control is often the overriding factor (Fouts, 2020). The dark side of leadership manifests itself in destructive leadership, toxic leadership, exclusive leadership, leadership without integrity, dark triad personalities (narcissists, Machiavellians, and psychopaths), micro-managers, etc. Besides creating an unhealthy work environment, dark side leaders can cause good employees to leave, eroding overall performance and impacting employee morale.

The Concept of Integrity

We all know people who cannot keep their word, people who cheat, people who lie, deceive, or exaggerate, and people who take advantage of our trust until they have no credibility left. It takes most of us a long time to realise that one of the most important things we have is our word. If people cannot trust our words, what can they trust? To walk in integrity means we act by what we know and believe to be right. It means refusing to yield under pressure toward mediocrity. In his commentary, Dr. Lloyd Ogilvie wrote "integrity is the moral dimension that separates wisdom from intelligence and cleverness" (Ogilvie, 1990). Integrity is what motivates us to practice what we preach and be held accountable accordingly. Having integrity is like having air, water, or currency and propels strength of character in difficult circumstances. Our integrity is tested by how we react to adversity or prosperity. In times of adversity, integrity shows how strong or weak we truly are.

Before World War II, Nora Waln wrote a book titled *Reaching for the Stars*, exposing Hitler's Nazi plot. She mailed the manuscript to an American publisher, but it was intercepted on its way. She had to flee to London and rewrite the book from memory. When she sent copies of the book to Heinrich Himmler, the Nazi hangman, seven of Nora's friends were imprisoned. She came back to Germany and offered her life so that her friends could be freed. She was asked to rewrite the book to make Hitler appear good. In refusing, Nora said, "I am willing to forfeit my life, but not my beliefs" (Tan, 1979). That is integrity, not yielding under pressure. Integrity provides several benefits to both leaders and organisations. Leaders with integrity do what is morally and ethically right and avoid questionable practices. They make a promise and keep it. This includes meeting deadlines and fulfilling commitments to coworkers. When you sacrifice your integrity, you sacrifice your most precious leadership tool.

There are four types of integrity: personal, moral, ethical, and intellectual. Personal integrity is the adherence to personal values in day-to-day behaviour. People are drawn to leaders with personal integrity because they know that they are genuine and authentic. Moral integrity is about doing what is right. Ethical integrity is about being honest and transparent in all dealings. Leaders with intellectual integrity are logical and reasonable. If leaders follow the principle of integrity in every situation, they will be saved from a lot of trouble and shame.

Leading without Integrity

Many leaders aspire to have integrity, but it can be difficult to achieve due to outside influences such as peer pressure. Leaders lacking integrity often crumble under pressure or in the face of adversity. Leadership without integrity can be attributed to the following factors:

Lack of character: A leader without integrity lacks character. A leader with sound character shows professional competence, courage, and integrity, and sets high personal standards for himself before he can rightfully demand it from others. Before you can expect your followers to perform, they must know what is expected of them. Integrity is seen as the quality of acting in accordance or harmony with relevant moral values, norms, and rules. A wise person perceives that the fundamental basis of life is relational. The only adequate relationship between persons is based on sound character. Nothing is more valuable to an individual than the character associated with a person's name. Building sound character is a continuous and lifelong process that will cause us to live above reproach.

Lack of trust: Integrity is the most important trait of leadership in our society because people will not follow someone unless they have attributed a certain level of trust to them. A trustworthy leader does what they say they are going to do. Trust is a fundamental element of inclusive leadership. Trust is generated by leaders who are authentic and open about their weaknesses as well as their strengths. Integrity in leadership based on mutual trust positively impacts personal credibility. Leadership without integrity destroys trust and legitimacy at exponential costs to all. Where integrity and trust are relegated or lacking in leadership, leaders' performance is constrained and falls below expected standards. A sub-optimal performance of leadership can be illustrated by health services weakening, life expectancy slumping, people going hungry, schooling standards falling, civil society becoming more beleaguered, the quest for personal and national prosperity slowing, crime rates accelerating, and overall security becoming more tenuous.

Lack of accountability: Leaders are constantly defining the path for the organisation. By holding themselves accountable, they inspire everyone down the line to take responsibility for their actions. Leaders who hold themselves accountable for their actions can earn their colleagues' respect. Without accountability, however, organisations tend to suffer from misalignment, lack of ownership, and failure to execute strategic initiatives. Accountability suggests that leaders answer to someone or something and practice what they preach. By aligning company values with specific behavioural and performance expectations, HR leaders can help leaders understand what accountability looks like and how to live it within the organisation. Accountable leaders drive vertical alignment of individuals' goals to overall business objectives. They set goals that align with the business' priorities. Leaders undermine their integrity when they fail to take personal accountability for mistakes.

Corruption: This is one of the major practices of leaders without integrity. Corruption is the abuse of entrusted power for private use or gain. To some, corruption is limited to government officials/civil servants or politicians in positions of authority who naturally believe that they are in a position to embezzle the funds entrusted to their office. To others, corruption is using public/corporate funds or resources for private/personal use. Corrupt political leaders typically treat public funds and property with relatively low regard and fail to give due account as required. It is acting in parochial interest because of advantages promised or given, engaging in forms of favoritism and conflict of interest (Huberts, 2018). Corruption erodes trust, weakens democracy, hampers economic development, and further exacerbates inequality. Integrity is dignity, while corruption brings a sense of conflicting values, cognition, emotions, and beliefs.

Toxic leadership: A toxic leader is often pretentious. They believe their opinion is the only thing that matters, leading them to make poor decisions. A toxic leader can also be manipulative. They may try to control other people by toying with their emotions, making it difficult for others to trust them. They lack empathy and struggle with the process of aligning with the feelings of others. A toxic leader may also have an inability to take criticism well. Another prominent quality of a toxic leader is intolerance, which can manifest itself in a leader's need for control. Toxic leaders can harm employee morale, especially regarding criticism, micromanagement, and a general lack of respect. A toxic leader can harm an organisation exponentially, impair morale and cause high turnover.

Leadership without Integrity: A Reflection

All societies have codes of ethics. A code of ethics is a set of standards that guide the conduct of members. It is a set of principles designed to regulate decision-making and distinguish right from wrong. Thus, we have codes of ethics for educators, lawyers, scientists, engineers, doctors, nurses, dentists, accountants, psychologists, social workers, religious ministers, researchers, politicians, etc. A leader must act in accordance with societal laws and professional codes. These codes of conduct and ethical standards drive business actions and decisions within a given industry. These codes are often created and reinforced by professional associations and societies. A leader without integrity fails to act according to these stipulated benchmarks, and such behaviour contravenes the spirit and intents of the provisions.

A follower deciding on which candidate to vote for would benefit from the ability to know exactly whether the candidate would raise taxes, balance the budget, enact health care reforms, or strengthen national defence. Issues of the candidate's personality or character would become less important the more the voter knew about guaranteed outcomes. Since the results of a political leadership effort only occur in the future, the following is based on predictions of what may come true. Followers are thus always in the position of having to decide to engage with less-than-perfect information about what may happen. Apart from the confidence they gain from attributions of leader integrity, followers seek information about whether the leader is credible. In this case, following is a risky business that requires some degree of faith in the leader and the leader's words. For a leader without integrity, his actions, now and in the future, will be inconsistent with the expectations of their followers (Moorman & Grover, 2009). Some national leaders deliver far less in performance and may be regarded as leaders without integrity. Under their stewardship, nothing seems to work. Indeed, the prevailing cultural, economic, and legal factors contribute in significant respects to a nation's profile and thus undermine its corporate viability and actual existence (Prentis & Igoni, 2016). This depiction places a corresponding burden on the citizenry to demand an alternative acceptable leadership behaviour.

Lessons for Leaders

Leadership skills are needed in the workplace, schools, politics, organisations, and families. Leadership is regarded as the single, most crucial factor that determines the success or failure of an organisation. It is all about setting a vision for a group and engaging them in carrying out the vision. Leaders are generally responsible for planning, organising, delegating, problem-solving, team building, consulting, goal setting, and rewarding subordinates. A leader's actions are central to integrity, but followers and stakeholders are responsible for appraising the level of integrity. Integrity is the most important trait of leadership because people will only follow those they trust. As a leader, the values you promote define your character, and ultimately define the core of who you are. In sharing your values with your followers, you become publicly accountable to them. Integrity is the perceived pattern of alignment between a leader's words and deeds. Leaders with integrity set a good example and inspire their followers to follow their example. Deception or lying to followers results in a loss of leadership credibility. When leaders fail to maintain the confidence of followers, effective communication and the flow of useful information become hampered. Leading without integrity can severely damage trust. Although nobody is perfect, and certainly no leader is perfect, when a breach of personal integrity becomes obvious, effective leadership ceases. Leaders who lose their integrity always find it challenging to gain the trust and respect of others.

References

Fouts, M. (2020). The dark side of leadership: How to identify and steer clear of it when job hunting. https://www.forbes.com/councils/forbescoachescouncil/2020/10/07/the-dark-side-of-leadership-how-to-identify-and-steer-clear-of-it-when-job-hunting/

Huberts, L. W. J. C. (2018). Integrity: What it is and why it is important. *Public Integrity*, *20*(sup1), S18–S32. https://doi.org/10.1080/10999922.2018.1477404

Karthikeyan, C. (2017). A meta-analytical study on leadership integrity: A leadership ethics perspective. *International Journal of Management, IT & Engineering*, *7*(4), 240–263.
Moorman, R. H., & Grover, S. (2009). Why does leader integrity matter to followers? An uncertainty management-based explanation. *International Journal of Leadership Studies, 5*(2), 102–114.
Ogilvie, J. (1990). *The Communicator's Commentary: Hosea-Jonah*. Word Books, Dallas, TX, pp. 62–63.
Prentis, E. L., & Igoni, S. E. (2016). Leadership: A case study on the importance of ethics and trust. *Journal of Business, 1*(2), 17–30.
Sadiku, M. N. O. (2009). *Wisdom: Your Key to Success*. Covenant Publishers, Houston, TX, pp. 205–206.
Sadiku, M. N. O., & Olaleye, O. D. (2020). *Emotional Intelligence and Its Applications*. Author House, Bloomington, IN, pp. 41–54.
Sadiku, M. N. O., Olaleye, O. D., & Musa, S. M. (2020). Emotional intelligence in leadership. *International Journal of Trend in Research and Development, 7*(1), 177–180.
Tan, P. L. (1979). *Encyclopaedia of 7700 Illustrations*. Assurance Publishers, Rockville, MD, pp. 616–617.

Chapter 24

Self-Awareness: A Path to the Bright Side of Leadership

Mahadih Kyambade, Bridget Namubiru,
Afulah Namatovu, Monica Tushabe, and Rehema Kagere

Introduction

Self-awareness is a crucial aspect of psychological development and emotional intelligence. It is defined as the conscious knowledge of one's own character, feelings, motives, and desires. It involves an individual's ability to introspect and recognise themselves as separate entities from their environment and other individuals. Self-awareness is fundamental to personal growth, effective communication, and emotional regulation. The concept of self-awareness is built on several key assumptions. Self-reflection assumes that individuals can reflect on their own thoughts, emotions, and behaviours. This reflective capacity enables people to understand how their inner experiences influence their actions and interactions with others (Silvia & Duval, 2001). Self-distinction implies that individuals can distinguish between themselves and others, recognising their own thoughts and feelings as separate from those of other people. This differentiation is essential for empathy and social interactions (Morin, 2006). Metacognition assumes that individuals possess metacognitive abilities, meaning they can think about their own thinking processes. This higher-order thinking skill is crucial for problem-solving and decision-making (Flavell, 1979). Self-regulation is the ability to control one's emotions, thoughts, and behaviours in the face of temptations and impulses. It is essential for goal-directed behaviour and

 DOI: 10.4324/9781003475262-29

personal discipline (Carver & Scheier, 1981). Personal identity contributes to the formation and maintenance of a coherent sense of personal identity. Understanding oneself is key to developing a stable and consistent self-concept over time (Baumeister, 1999).

Self-awareness is a foundational element of emotional intelligence (EI), which has been extensively linked to effective leadership (Goleman, 1995). Leaders with high levels of self-awareness can better understand their strengths and weaknesses, leading to improved decision-making and problem-solving capabilities. Boyatzis and McKee (2005) suggest that leaders who possess self-awareness are more adept at creating resonant leadership environments characterised by empathy, transparency, and trust. Effective decision-making requires a deep understanding of one's cognitive processes and biases. Self-aware leaders are more likely to engage in reflective practice, which involves continuous self-examination and learning from experiences (Schön, 1983). This reflective approach helps leaders to recognise and mitigate their biases; leading to more objective and well-considered decisions (Ehrlinger et al., 2016). Decisions often have far-reaching implications in organisations and the ability to reflect and learn from past experiences is particularly valuable. The ability to manage and resolve conflicts is essential for leaders given the diverse and often competing interests within work environments. Self-awareness enhances leaders' ability to empathise with others and understands different perspectives, which is crucial for effective conflict resolution (Rogers, 1961). Studies have shown that self-aware leaders are better at navigating interpersonal dynamics and fostering a collaborative and inclusive organisational culture (Gardner et al., 2005).

Authenticity in leadership is strongly associated with self-awareness. Authentic leaders are those who remain true to their values and principles, fostering an environment of trust and integrity (Avolio & Gardner, 2005). Authentic leadership has been linked to positive outcomes in organisational settings, including higher levels of employee engagement, satisfaction, and performance (Walumbwa et al., 2008). In the context of institutional leadership, authenticity can help build a strong identity and culture, which are crucial for long-term success. Despite its importance, developing self-awareness in leadership poses several challenges. Cognitive biases, such as the Dunning-Kruger effect, can hinder accurate self-assessment (Dunning, 2011). Emotional avoidance, where leaders shy away from confronting negative aspects of their behaviour, also impedes the development of true self-awareness (Leary, 2007). Moreover, organisational cultures that do not prioritise transparency and feedback can further inhibit self-awareness among leaders (Schein, 2010).

Assumptions of Self-Awareness as a Remedy to Dark Leadership

Counteracting Narcissism

Dark leadership often involves narcissistic traits, such as excessive self-admiration and a lack of empathy (Rosenthal & Pittinsky, 2006). Self-awareness helps leaders recognise these tendencies and focus on the needs and contributions of others. Through self-reflection, leaders can develop humility and a balanced sense of self-worth, mitigating narcissistic behaviours.

Mitigating Machiavellianism

Machiavellian leaders are manipulative and exploit others for personal gain (Christie & Geis, 1970). Self-awareness encourages ethical behaviour and integrity by helping leaders understand the long-term consequences of their actions. Metacognitive strategies allow leaders to assess the morality of their decisions and align their actions with ethical standards.

Reducing Psychopathy

Psychopathic traits in leaders include impulsivity, callousness, and a lack of remorse (Boddy, 2011). Self-awareness enhances emotional regulation and empathy, which are crucial for controlling impulsive behaviours and developing compassionate leadership. By fostering an understanding of their emotional triggers, leaders can avoid actions that harm others and the organisation.

Improving Ethical Decision-Making

Dark leadership is often marked by unethical decision-making driven by personal gain or power (Kellerman, 2004). Self-aware leaders are more likely to engage in ethical decision-making as they are conscious of their values and the broader impact of their actions. Reflective practices help leaders to evaluate the ethical implications of their decisions and to act in ways that benefit the organisation.

Enhancing Interpersonal Relationships

Dark leaders often create toxic environments that damage relationships and trust (Einarsen et al., 2007). Self-awareness fosters empathy and effective communication, which are essential for building and maintaining positive relationships. Leaders who understand their own emotional states and those of others can navigate conflicts more effectively and create a supportive organisational culture.

Promoting Authentic Leadership

Authentic leadership, characterised by self-awareness, transparency, and ethical behaviour, is the antithesis of dark leadership (Avolio & Gardner, 2005). By developing self-awareness, leaders can cultivate authenticity, leading to increased trust and credibility among stakeholders. Authentic leaders are more likely to inspire and motivate others, contributing to a positive and productive environment. The presence of dark leadership characterised by narcissism, Machiavellianism, and psychopathy poses significant challenges in work settings. These leadership traits can undermine trust, morale, and productivity. However, fostering self-awareness among leaders offers a potential remedy to mitigate these destructive behaviours.

Self-awareness is built on the assumption that leaders engage in self-reflection, a process that enables them to examine their own thoughts, emotions, and behaviours critically. Self-reflection helps leaders recognise their ethical and moral responsibilities. According to Schön (1983), reflective practice is essential for professionals to learn from their experiences and improve their practices continuously. Self-reflection can help leaders identify and correct narcissistic behaviours by fostering humility and ethical decision-making. For example, research by Gino and Ariely (2012) demonstrates that reflective practices can reduce unethical behaviour by increasing moral awareness. The ability to distinguish oneself from others is another key assumption of self-awareness. This self-distinction helps leaders to understand their unique perspectives and biases while recognising the viewpoints of others. Empathy, a crucial component of effective leadership, is enhanced by this self-other distinction. Leaders who are aware of their own emotions and can empathise with others are less likely to engage in Machiavellian behaviours, which are manipulative and self-serving (Christie & Geis, 1970). Research by Kellett et al. (2006) highlights that empathic leaders are better at building trust and positive relationships, countering the divisive tactics of Machiavellian leaders.

Metacognitive abilities are fundamental to self-awareness. These abilities enable leaders to evaluate their cognitive processes and adjust their strategies for better outcomes. Dark leadership often involves impulsive and irrational decision-making, particularly in psychopathic leaders (Boddy, 2011). By fostering metacognitive skills, leaders can improve their decision-making processes, ensuring they are rational and aligned with ethical standards. Research by Dunning (2011) supports the notion that metacognitive strategies help individuals recognise and correct their cognitive biases, leading to more balanced and informed decisions.

Self-awareness assumes that individuals can regulate their emotions effectively. Emotional regulation is crucial for maintaining composure, particularly in high-stress environments. Dark leaders often exhibit poor emotional control, leading to volatile and harmful behaviours (Kellerman, 2004). Self-aware leaders, on the other hand, can manage their emotions, reducing the likelihood of impulsive and destructive actions. Goleman (1995) emphasises that emotional regulation is a key component of emotional intelligence, which is associated with effective leadership. Leaders who can regulate their emotions are better equipped to handle conflicts and crises constructively. A coherent sense of personal identity and integrity is another assumption of self-awareness. Leaders who possess a strong sense of self are more likely to act consistently with their values and principles, promoting authenticity in their leadership. Authentic leadership, characterised by transparency and ethical behaviour, is the antithesis of dark leadership (Avolio & Gardner, 2005). Authentic leaders inspire trust and commitment among their followers, creating a positive organisational culture. Walumbwa et al. (2008) found that authentic leadership is linked to higher levels of employee engagement and ethical behaviour, which are critical for counteracting the negative effects of dark leadership.

Dark leadership often results in toxic work environments and damaged interpersonal relationships (Einarsen et al., 2007). Self-aware leaders, by understanding their own emotional states and those of others, can foster empathy and effective communication. This ability to navigate interpersonal dynamics is crucial for building a supportive and collaborative organisational culture. Research by Gardner et al. (2005) suggests that self-aware leaders are more successful in creating resonant leadership environments, which enhance team cohesion and organisational performance.

The assumptions underlying self-awareness, that's self-reflection, self-distinction, metacognition, emotional regulation, and a coherent personal identity, offer significant remedies to dark leadership in work contexts.

By fostering these aspects of self-awareness, leaders can counteract the destructive behaviours associated with narcissism, Machiavellianism, and psychopathy. Previous studies support the effectiveness of self-awareness in promoting ethical decision-making, empathy, rationality, emotional stability, and authenticity in leadership. As organisations continue to navigate complex challenges, developing self-awareness among leaders will be essential for fostering positive, ethical, and effective leadership.

Lessons for Leaders

Leaders should cultivate the habit of self-reflection to understand their own thoughts, emotions, and behaviours. This practice helps in recognising and correcting narcissistic tendencies and promotes ethical decision-making. Reflective practices, such as journaling and mindfulness meditation, can be effective tools for this purpose. Understanding one's unique perspective and biases while recognising the viewpoints of others is crucial. Leaders should strive to enhance their empathy by actively listening to others and considering different perspectives. This approach mitigates manipulative behaviours and fosters a more inclusive and supportive environment. Leaders need to cultivate metacognitive abilities to evaluate and adjust their cognitive processes. This includes being aware of one's thought patterns and biases and making rational, ethical decisions. Training programs focused on critical thinking and decision-making can help leaders develop these skills. Effective leaders must regulate their emotions to maintain composure in high-stress situations. Techniques such as emotional intelligence training, stress management programs, and mindfulness can help leaders manage their emotions, preventing impulsive and destructive actions. Leaders should aim to develop a coherent sense of personal identity and integrity. Acting consistently with one's values and principles promotes authenticity in leadership. Authentic leaders inspire trust and commitment, creating a positive organisational culture. Engaging in values-based leadership training and receiving regular feedback from peers can support this development. Strong interpersonal relationships are essential for a healthy organisational culture. Leaders should work on their communication and conflict-resolution skills to build trust and collaboration within their teams. Regular team-building activities and open communication channels can enhance these relationships.

Self-awareness is a journey rather than a destination. Leaders should commit to ongoing personal and professional development. Participating in leadership development programs, seeking mentorship, and engaging in continuous education can help leaders stay aware of their behaviours and impact on others. Creating an environment where feedback is valued and encouraged can help leaders gain insights into their leadership style and areas for improvement. Implementing 360-degree feedback systems can provide comprehensive insights from various stakeholders, helping leaders adjust their behaviours accordingly. Leaders should prioritise ethical behaviour and decision-making. This involves being transparent, honest, and fair in all interactions. Leaders can benefit from ethics training and establishing clear codes of conduct within their institutions to guide behaviour. Leaders should model the behaviours they wish to see in others. By demonstrating self-awareness, empathy, emotional regulation, and authenticity, leaders can set a positive example for their teams. This approach helps to create a culture of trust, respect, and ethical behaviour throughout the organisation.

Although previous studies have explored the effects and manifestations of the dark side of leadership, this chapter offers a nuanced understanding by outlining workable solutions and the reasoning behind them. A more comprehensive approach to addressing leadership challenges is offered by the emphasis on self-reflection, self-distinction, metacognition, self-regulation, and personal identity. This viewpoint expands the scholarly conversation on leadership and offers useful advice to promote a more inclusive, cooperative, and healthy atmosphere.

References

Avolio, B. J., & Gardner, W. L. (2005). Authentic leadership development: Getting to the root of positive forms of leadership. *The Leadership Quarterly*, *16*(3), 315–338.

Baumeister, R. F. (1999). *The Self in Social Psychology*. Psychology Press.

Boddy, C. R. (2011). The corporate psychopath's theory of the global financial crisis. *Journal of Business Ethics*, *102*(2), 255–259.

Boyatzis, R. E., & McKee, A. (2005). *Resonant Leadership: Renewing Yourself and Connecting with Others through Mindfulness, Hope, and Compassion*. Harvard Business School Press.

Carver, C. S., & Scheier, M. F. (1981). *Attention and Self-Regulation: A Control-Theory Approach to Human Behaviour*. Springer.

Christie, R., & Geis, F. (1970). *Studies in Machiavellianism*. Academic Press.

Dunning, D. (2011). The Dunning–Kruger effect: On being ignorant of one's own ignorance. *Advances in Experimental Social Psychology*, *44*, 247–296.

Ehrlinger, J., Johnson, K., Banner, M., Dunning, D., & Kruger, J. (2016). Why the unskilled are unaware: Further explorations of (absent) self-insight among the incompetent. *Organisational Behavior and Human Decision Processes, 105*(1), 98–121.

Einarsen, S., Aasland, M. S., & Skogstad, A. (2007). Destructive leadership behaviour: A definition and conceptual model. *The Leadership Quarterly, 18*(3), 207–216.

Flavell, J. H. (1979). Metacognition and cognitive monitoring: A new area of cognitive-developmental inquiry. *American Psychologist, 34*(10), 906.

Gardner, W. L., Avolio, B. J., Luthans, F., May, D. R., & Walumbwa, F. (2005). "Can you see the real me?" A self-based model of authentic leader and follower development. *The Leadership Quarterly, 16*(3), 343–372.

Gino, F., & Ariely, D. (2012). The dark side of creativity: Original thinkers can be more dishonest. *Journal of Personality and Social Psychology, 102*(3), 445.

Goleman, D. (1995). *Emotional Intelligence: Why It Can Matter More Than IQ.* Bantam Books.

Kellerman, B. (2004). *Bad Leadership: What It Is, How It Happens, Why It Matters.* Harvard Business Review Press.

Kellett, J. B., Humphrey, R. H., & Sleeth, R. G. (2006). Empathy and complex task performance: Two routes to leadership. *The Leadership Quarterly, 17*(5), 516–529.

Leary, M. R. (2007). How the self became involved in affective experience: Three sources of self-reflective emotions. In J. L. Tracy, R. W. Robins, & J. P. Tangney (Eds.), *The Self-Conscious Emotions: Theory And Research* (pp. 38–52). The Guilford Press.

Morin, A. (2006). Levels of consciousness and self-awareness: A comparison and integration of various neurocognitive views. *Consciousness and Cognition, 15*(2), 358–371.

Rogers, C. R. (1961). *On Becoming a Person: A Therapist's View of Psychotherapy.* Houghton Mifflin Harcourt.

Rosenthal, S. A. & Pittinsky, T. L. (2006). Narcissistic leadership. *The Leadership Quarterly, 17*, 617–633.

Schein, E. H. (2010). *Organizational Culture and Leadership.* John Wiley & Sons.

Schön, D. A. (1983). *The Reflective Practitioner: How Professionals Think in Action.* Basic Books.

Silvia, P. J., & Duval, T. S. (2001). Objective self-awareness theory: Recent progress and enduring problems. *Personality and Social Psychology Review, 5*(3), 230–241.

Walumbwa, F. O., Avolio, B. J., Gardner, W. L., Wernsing, T. S., & Peterson, S. J. (2008). Authentic leadership: Development and validation of a theory-based measure. *Journal of Management, 34*(1), 89–126.

Chapter 25

Strategic Interventions for Addressing Dark Side Leadership

Deasi-Ann Williamson

Introduction

An interventionist approach to leadership emphasises proactive and deliberate actions to foster ethical and inclusive leadership. Effective leadership is recognised as a multifaceted phenomenon, requiring leaders to adapt to evolving environments and cultivate supportive and inclusive workplace cultures. Examining intersectionality enhances the understanding of complex leadership dynamics, empowering leadership practitioners. Coined by Crenshaw (1989), intersectionality examines how different social identities, such as race, gender, class, and sexuality, intersect to create unique modes of discrimination and privilege. Intersectionality theory provides a critical framework for understanding how various power systems interact and shape individual and collective experiences.

The interconnected dynamics inherent in these power struggles are often obscured by dominant narratives, which perpetuate a culture of silence and complicity. Thus, the intersectional nature of dark leadership becomes a critical aspect of the inquiry, highlighting how leaders use their position to further entrench systemic inequalities and oppression (Crenshaw, 1989). There is a paucity of research in these areas, indicating the need for theoretical and methodological advancements (Skouteris et al., 2023).

DOI: 10.4324/9781003475262-30

The synchronisation of strategic interventions and intersectionality serves as a salient nomological dynamic, offering insight into the enduring presence of disparities within leadership behaviours, policy, legislation, systemic reform, and resource accessibility.

Championing Intersectionality

Intersectionality posits that considering a single axis of inequality is insufficient. Instead, it advocates for the simultaneous consideration of multiple axes of (dis)advantage (Tinner et al., 2023). This multifaceted concept is essential for addressing dark-side leadership behaviours. Applying intersectionality within leadership studies exposes how dark-side leadership behaviours are influenced by individual traits and broader systemic and structural inequalities. This approach reveals how overlapping identities compound the effects of systemic oppression, marginalising certain groups while privileging others. The view captured by Mathews (2019) highlights how race and gender can intersect and influence employment decisions, making it difficult for black women to access equal opportunities.

This nuanced understanding is crucial for developing effective intervention strategies, reflecting the dynamic nature of individual circumstances, and creating simulations to understand the implications of strategic decision-making (Yildiz, 2018). Therefore, strategic interventions should aim to transform organisational cultures and perpetuate diversity, equity and inclusion. By incorporating intersectionality, strategic interventions can identify the root causes of inequality and address the specific needs of diverse groups within organisations (Ghasemi et al., 2021). Intersectionality has been adopted as a theoretical innovation for the explanation of power structures and procedures. The intersectional nature of dark leadership behaviours becomes a critical area of inquiry, as it focuses on leadership motivations and standards in assessing how leaders approach to power and use their positions to entrench systemic inequalities and oppression (Burns, 1978). The World Health Organisation (2024) recognises that organisations prioritising intersectionality in their policies and practices are better equipped to foster diverse, ethical, and inclusive leadership. By doing so, organisations enhance their nomological approach, fostering transformation and challenging perfunctory compliance. Also, Skouteris et al. (2023), underscore the significance of researching intersectionality dimensions, coupled with the complexities and cultural nuances. This highlights the need for theoretical and methodological advancements to enhance engagement with intersectionality in developing leadership practice.

As a precursor to the subsequent discussions, it is important to emphasise the critical roles of epistemology and ontological innovation within leadership dimensions. Epistemology concerns the continuous scope of theory and concept development. Wong et al. (2011) state that epistemology investigates the nature of knowledge and its conceptualisation as truth within specific contexts. Conversely, ontology concerns itself with the practical application of theoretical knowledge, testing its efficacy in real-world scenarios and refining strategies based on outcomes. El Bassiti (2017) explains key concepts within this sub-ontology. "Trigger Concept," describes events that lead to core-idea generation. The "Process Concept" defines task and activity networks organised in phases, stages, and iterations to transform an idea into a successful innovation. Finally, the "Deliverables Concept," denotes the outcomes at each stage of the innovation life cycle. Interdependence among organisations necessitates collective capabilities to collaborate effectively, resulting in innovative, widely recognised, and critically acclaimed advancements. Epistemology and ontology are undergoing a renaissance, driven by the demand for effective leadership practices.

A Reflection: Leadership Challenges in the National Health Service (NHS) England

Citing the NHS Enquiry, Robert (2013) states that managers introduced "controlling and reporting" systems that directed front-line staff to prioritise target data, particularly related to persistent and complex issues termed as wicked problems. The challenges encompassed attracting and retaining skilled professionals, addressing staff satisfaction, and rectifying poor leadership practices. According to Ahmed et al. (2022), the NHS advertised over 84,000 vacancies in March 2020, costing the organisation £4.8 million to supply temporary staffing. This highlights the need for effective leadership practices that address the root causes of these challenges. Northouse (2021) cites the importance of viewing leadership as a dynamic, collective, situated, and dialectical phenomenon, providing valuable insights into the complexity of leadership in multifaceted contexts. Similarly, Kuppler (2014) emphasises that leaders focusing solely on cultural change may overlook underlying issues critical to organisational success.

Consider the scenario of being promoted as an Operational Executive in the NHS, a role largely responsible for managing operational service contracts and supporting healthcare experts struggling to achieve their departmental key performance indicators (KPIs). Despite lacking commercial training, the position was secured based on extensive service within the NHS. Transitioning from a senior front-line practitioner to focusing on audit outcomes and commercial data management was a significant departure from previous experience. By adopting a democratic leadership style, operational processes and productivity were enhanced as well as consensus-building and engagement. In essence, addressing commercial performance can be regarded as merely treating surface-level symptoms of systemic challenges. Consequently, engagement with management and stakeholders became necessary to formulate a collaborative support plan. This interaction elicited contradictions of opinions regarding role capability and leadership competencies. A lack of consensus on fundamental institutional practices and internal governance processes indicated the intersecting barriers of age, gender, and organisational dynamics that can impede career advancement. Taylor (2019) asserts that intersectionality recognises that individuals experience discrimination and oppression uniquely, considering various factors that can marginalise them. Yet, the integration of intersectional frameworks within public health studies remains limited (Bowleg, 2012). Addressing dark leadership behaviours requires a comprehensive approach beyond surface-level solutions, emphasising the importance of effective and inclusive leadership practices in resolving complex problems (Burns, 1978).

It is noteworthy that following sub-optimal leadership and poor service standards, The Care Quality Commission (CQC), was established in April 2009 to replace three former regulatory bodies. Under the Health and Social Care Act 2008, the CQC is responsible for registering, inspecting, and monitoring health and adult social care providers, including independent providers, to ensure they meet fundamental standards (House of Commons, 2024).

Strategic Interventions and Lessons for Leaders

A comprehensive assessment of current leadership capabilities fosters development at all levels of the organisation. These assessments lead to more diverse, equitable, and effective outcomes. This process can be implemented via surveys, focus groups, interviews, 360-degree feedback loops, self-assessment tools, and performance evaluations. Mielianti et al. (2021)

highlight that such assessments provide reliable data to identify opportunities and challenges within the organisation's leadership. Furthermore, this process recognises support needs and facilitates the development of effective strategies for success, demonstrating alignment with Maslow's Hierarchy of Needs. To enhance leadership capabilities, leaders must cultivate environments conducive to skill testing and review through structured programs and continuous learning practices. Methods such as individual performance reviews, simulation exercises, benchmarking against industry standards, and feedback loops can be employed.

Incorporating indigenous practices such as "Talk Circles" and "Think Tanks" can provide valuable insights. These techniques engage collaboration and diverse perspectives, fostering a deeper sense of community and belonging among team members. Sheard et al. (2013) emphasise the importance of organisations investing in equipping people with resources to improve their leadership capabilities. Promoting a culture of open communication and constructive feedback can be implemented via anonymous peer evaluations, 360-degree feedback tools, surveys, and suggestion boxes. This also provides a comprehensive understanding of current leadership effectiveness and skills. While peer evaluations can be a valuable tool, it is not without limitations. According to Barroga (2020), peer review can be imperfect, and careful management is necessary to mitigate potential biases and issues. Notably, the absence of a cohesive integration of leadership development, suggests that further work is needed to bridge these gaps (Meuser et al., 2016). Feedback mechanisms require emotional intelligence. Tuckman's Group Development model provides a framework for understanding team progress and enhancing collaboration, which can guide this process. Using feedback mechanisms to address dark side behaviours can serve as a learning tool, promoting transparency and fostering a constructive organisational culture.

Establishing a consistent leadership pipeline involves identifying high-potential employees and providing targeted training and development. Raelin (2003) underscores the importance of cultivating authentic leadership capabilities across all members of an organisation, rather than confining leadership to a select few. This necessitates customised ongoing training, secondments, shadowing opportunities, mentoring, and coaching to enhance skills. Training should also focus on transferable capabilities such as strategic thinking, adaptability, and emotional intelligence. This aligns with Kolb's Experimental Learning model.

As an organisation establishes its leadership pipeline, it promotes cultural shifts through reforming systems and structures. Leadership development then becomes a strategic imperative that promotes organisational succession planning. Individuals should be encouraged to share the experience associated with being a leader, working towards shared visions and common objectives. Leadership should be distributed across the group and individuals should assume leadership roles according to capabilities to meet specific needs. Weber and Karman (1991) assert that this integrated approach improves maturity, competence, and motivation while also boosting team morale, driving innovation, enhancing productivity, fostering strong relationships, and promoting appreciation of shared ideas and abilities. Leaders can foster practical intelligence through leadership development programs and problem-solving workshops, empowering leaders to be equipped to handle future complex, real-world scenarios and challenges. This competency involves understanding one's learning process, assessing situations accurately, and modifying actions to achieve desired outcomes. Brockbank and McGill (2007) posit that reflection enables individuals to create meaning around their experiences. This approach prepares leaders to navigate transformational learning concepts to implement Indigenous practices and policy reforms effectively. By reflecting on problem-solving strategies and outcomes, leaders can effectively apply the knowledge.

Creative intelligence involves the ability to generate novel and effective solutions to problems through reflective practice. Leaders can participate in improvisational exercises, journaling, and storytelling to develop this form of intelligence. These activities align with Cynefin's storytelling framework, which supports leaders in reflecting on their experiences to identify successes and shortcomings, thereby enhancing creative thinking skills applicable to leadership challenges (Snowden et al., 2007). A continuous learning culture can be implemented as a comprehensive development program that promotes ongoing learning and self-improvement to significantly enhance analytical leadership capacity. This might include training sessions, reflection workshops, benchmarking hubs, and mentoring programs. Developing a data-driven, decision-making process that integrates reflective practices, such as scenario planning and risk analysis, helps leaders make informed decisions. This approach involves collectively and concurrently sharing learning, considering multiple perspectives, and assessing potential impacts.

Emotional intelligence is pivotal for leaders in recognising their emotional strengths and shortcomings, thereby facilitating balanced decision-making.

Daniel Goleman's Theory, highlights there are correlations between emotional intelligence and quantifiable business outcomes (Goleman, 1995). Organisations characterised by individualistic cultures may be focused on personal achievements rather than relational dynamics, potentially diminishing emphasis on emotional intelligence (Dulewicz & Higgs, 2003). However, as leaders advance, emotional intelligence should become a strategic necessity. Leaders should adopt practices like mindfulness, reflective journaling, coaching, and peer feedback to manage emotions and behaviours effectively. Effective leaders are aware of their strengths and weaknesses as well as those of their team members and use this self-awareness to plan for future growth and advancement (Bass & Avolio, 1995). This can unearth dark traits of leadership practises, prompting leaders to take actionable measures to mitigate them. Effective leaders possess distinct interests, abilities, and personality traits, with emotional intelligence being a governing factor for success. Leaders can promote brainstorming hubs, problem-solving, and conflict-resolution workshops to enhance self-awareness and navigate challenges. Leaders who engage emotional intelligence foster genuine connections and authenticity, address biases, and enhance trust within teams, thus driving organisational cohesion and innovation. These initiatives align with contemporary leadership principles and can foster a culture of self-regulation and self-awareness that ultimately benefits organisations (Maccoby, 2004).

Pairing leaders with mentors versed in emotional intelligence enhances their ability to manage complex situations effectively. Mentorship fosters resonant leadership whereby emotional intelligence fuels standardised organisational dynamics. Goleman (1995) validates that effective leaders can positively influence emotions and bring out the best in their followers through proper resonance utilisation. Mentorship programs can address comprehensive leadership development by emphasising emotional literacy, active listening, empathy, and reflective exercises to enhance self-regulation. Leaders can also incorporate work-life balance, mental health and mindfulness support in their mentorship plans. According to Goleman (1995), we can create a positive impact by training individuals to be emotionally intelligent and empathetic, encouraging them to widen their sphere of concern. This can lead to a transformation of organisations from within.

Indigenous wisdom emphasises ethical behaviour, community support, and deep-rooted cultural traditions, all essential for establishing a resilient and adaptable organisational framework. These practices necessitate sustainable solutions that ally cultural values and promote communal well-being. According to Downs and Swailes (2013), indigenous principles enhance operational effectiveness, particularly in talent management. Similarly, Miller (2022) argues that such principles cultivate empathetic and culturally sensitive leadership practices, which are pivotal for driving organisational change. Immersing leaders in indigenous organisational cultures can assist them in internalising principles of communal well-being and ethical behaviour, fostering a profound connection to these values. Leaders can develop a value-based culture that champions diversity, equity, and inclusion, thus aligning with value creation. Participation in work retreats, attending workshops led by Indigenous community leaders, and engaging in collaborative projects with Indigenous groups benefit leadership development. Furthermore, incorporating community-based learning and ethical decision-making frameworks provides a counterbalance of promoting ethical community values and mutual respect.

In the context of the emergence of digital transformation, indigenous practices facilitate global connections, remote benchmarking opportunities, cultural exchange via collaborative projects, and a sense of global interconnectedness driven by shared goals. Boulton (2021) argues that embracing digital transformation requires organisations to re-evaluate how they utilise technology, people, and processes to innovate and drive revenue growth. To leverage these insights, leaders should organise regular training sessions on emerging technologies and practices, encouraging cross-functional collaboration that integrates these elements.

The NHS case study underscores significant challenges in intersectionality, dark-trait leadership, and strategic solutions. Applying indigenous principles to problem-solving demonstrates how theoretical frameworks can yield practical solutions, highlighting the efficacy of contextualising theory in real-world scenarios (Kahn et al., 2006). Like many large organisations, the NHS faces difficulties in identifying and addressing intersectional dynamics among its workforce and patient population. The NHS has enhanced its approach by engaging stakeholders across various sectors such as finance, business, construction, health and safety, policing, religious community-based groups, and charitable institutions.

Positive organisational culture and effective management are pivotal in executing core capabilities. Barriers, once perceived as obstacles can serve as catalysts for innovation and change (Isaksen, 2023). Furthermore, workshops and brainstorming sessions can nurture high-quality relationships and create effective strategic environments (Murrell et al., 2021). Through initiatives focusing on communal well-being and ethical behaviour, leaders can develop empathetic and culturally sensitive practices crucial for fostering an inclusive organisational culture that respects intersectional identities. Additional investment in executive programs reflects growing recognition of the effectiveness of education and leadership development in implementing critical strategic initiatives (Fulmer & Vicere, 1996). Organisations could benefit from investing in cultural consultants, policy leads, and other experts to establish mandatory online and in-person training, workshops, campaigns, and rallies.

According to Grint (2010), change management acknowledges the obsolescence of traditional business methods and emphasises the importance of adaptability and innovation in leadership, thus creating a foundation for sustainable change. Various stakeholders may have different priorities and concerns. Managing and aligning these diverse objectives and perspectives within the organisational vision is critical for the successful implementation of change. Dweck (2006) expounds that cultivating a growth mindset can enhance problem-solving and decision-making capabilities by fostering a belief in the capacity for improvement. By incorporating indigenous practices, organisations can develop a more holistic approach to change management. Kurt Lewin's Change Theory suggests that leaders can develop specific skill sets and lean toward traits that suit stakeholders' needs, thereby mitigating risks. Murrell et al. (2021) posit such an environment is necessary for critical "identity work," allowing individuals to scrutinise, challenge and redefine traditional leadership definitions, thereby advancing inclusive decisions and notions that incorporate diverse social identities. Furthermore, respecting diversity, equity, and inclusion endorses systems thinking, innovation, and new perspectives among teams. This aligns with design thinking which Verganti et al. (2021) described as a process that transforms individual understanding into actionable outcomes through iterative, human-centric approaches. The iterative process is beneficial in tackling ill-defined problems by reframing issues in human-centric ways and generating numerous ideas through brainstorming (Buchanan, 1992).

Leaders can develop "think labs" where experienced leaders are paired with new or developing leaders to nurture leadership maturity. These labs can include drop-in and feedback sessions to monitor progress, solicit ideas and provide guidance. This concept aligns with the idea of "holding environments" which underpin high-quality relationships and effective mentoring (Murrell et al., 2021). Organisations can also create task forces to review and revise company policies, ensuring that processes are formalised and structures are established. Proficient decision-making is a vital managerial capability, equipping individuals to interpret and scrutinise the information they convey, thereby providing valuable learning outcomes (Gavin, 2020).

Balancing traditional leadership styles with contemporary execution requires emotional intelligence, agility, flexibility, and adaptability. These traits are essential for supporting stakeholders, mitigating risks, and resolving complex problems.

Conclusion

This chapter has examined the synergy between strategic solutions and intersectionality, demonstrating their efficacy in fostering critical thinking as a foundation for organisational and systemic change. By merging epistemological and ontological innovations, the importance of active learning and innovative action has been underscored. By reflecting on work experiences critical learning points such as discrimination and intersecting identities were highlighted. This depiction provided a backdrop for a comprehensive exploration of leadership capabilities, reflective practice, emotional intelligence, and change management. These elements highlight the importance of sustainable leadership practices. In a world where change is the only constant, organisations must continually evolve to stay relevant and competitive. By integrating these key principles, leaders can foster inclusive, adaptive, and innovative cultures that drive long-term success.

References

Ahmed, S., Hossain, M. H., Shamszaman, Z. U. (2022). A statistical analysis of the staff data to evaluate the influence of the retention factors in NHS England. In *14th International Conference on Software, Knowledge, Information Management and Applications (SKIMA)*, Phnom Penh, Cambodia, pp. 251–260. https://doi.org/10.1109/SKIMA57145.2022.10029576..

Barroga, E. (2020). Innovative strategies for peer review. *Journal of Korean Medical Science*, *35*(20), e138. https://doi.org/10.3346/jkms.2020.35.e138

Bass, B. M., & Avolio, B. J. (1995). Multifactor Leadership Questionnaire (MLQ) [Database record]. APA PsycTests. https://doi.org/10.1037/t03624-000

Boulton, C. (2021). What is digital transformation? A necessary disruption. CIO. Retrieved from: https://www.cio.com/article/230425/what-is-digital-transformation-a-necessary-disruption.html

Bowleg, L. (2012). The problem with the phrase women and minorities: Intersectionality-an important theoretical framework for public health. *American Journal of Public Health*, *102*(7), 1267–1273. https://doi.org/10.2105/AJPH.2012.300750

Brockbank, A., & McGill, I. (2007). *Facilitating reflective learning in higher education* (2nd ed.). Maidenhead: Open University Press McGraw-Hill.
Buchanan, R. (1992). Wicked problems in design thinking. *The MIT Press*, *8*(2), 5–8. Retrieved from: https://www.jstor.org/stable/1511637
Burns, J. M. (1978). Leadership. New York: Harper & Row.Care Quality Commission. (2011). Internal management review of the regulation of Winterbourne View. CQC, pp. 4–28. Retrieved from: https://www.cqc.org.uk/sites/default/files/documents/20120730_wv_imr_final_report.pdf. (Accessed: 1 June 2022).
Crenshaw, K. (1989). Demarginalising the intersection of race and sex: A Black feminist critique of antidiscrimination doctrine, feminist theory and antiracist policies. *University of Chicago Legal Forum*, *1*, 139–167.
Downs, Y., & Swailes, S. (2013). A capability approach to organisational talent management. *Human Resource Development International, 16*(3), 267–281.
Dulewicz, V., & Higgs, M. (2003). Leadership at the top: the need for emotional intelligence in organisations. *The International Journal of Organisational Analysis*, *11*(3), 193–210.
Dweck, C. S. (2006). *Mindset: The new psychology of success*. New York: Random House Publishing Group.
El Bassiti, L. (2017). Generic modular ontology for innovation domain. a key pillar towards 'innovation interoperability'. *Journal of Entrepreneurship, Management and Innovation*, *13*(2), 105–126, 2017, Available at SSRN: https://papers.ssrn.com/sol3/papers.cfm?abstract_id=3105535
Fulmer, R. M., & Vicere, A. A. (1996). An analysis of competitive forces. *Planning Review*, *24*(1), 31–36. Retrieved from: https://doi.org/10.1108/eb054541
Gavin, M. (2020). 5 ways managers can use finance to make better decisions. Harvard Business School. (Online). Retrieved from: https://online.hbs.edu/blog/post/financial-decision-making
Ghasemi, E., Majdzadeh, R., Rajabi, F., Vedadhir, A., Negarandeh, R., Jamshidi, E., Takian, A., & Faraji, Z. (2021). Applying Intersectionality in designing and implementing health interventions: A scoping review. *BMC Public Health*, *21*(1), 1407. https://doi.org/10.1186/s12889-021-11449-6
Goleman, D. (1995). *Emotional intelligence: Why it can matter more than IQ*. Bantam Books. Retrieved from: https://www.danielgoleman.info
Grint, K. (2005). Problems, problems, problems: The social construction of human relations. *Human Relations*, *58*(5), 1467–1494.
House of Commons. (2024). The statutory role and powers of the Care Quality Commission (CQC). Commons Library. Retrieved from: https://commonslibrary.parliament.uk/research-briefings/cbp8754/#:~:text=The%20CQC%20was%20established%20in,and%20Social%20Care%20Act%202008 (Accessed: 16 June 2022).
Isaksen, S. G. (2023). Developing creative potential: The power of process, people, and place. *Journal of Advanced Academics*, *34*(2), 111–144. https://doi.org/10.1177/1932202X231156389

Kahn, P. E., Young, R., Grace, S., Pilkington, R., Rush, L., Tomkinson, C. B., & Willis, I. (2006) The role and effectiveness of reflective practices in programmes for new academic staff: A grounded practitioner review of the research literature. Higher Education Academy, York, [Online, 1st October 2006]. www.heacademy.ac.ukhttp://www.heacademy.ac.uk/4885.htm

Kuppler, K. (2014). Leadership and culture: A review of the literature. *Journal of Management Development, 33*(1), 34–51.

Maccoby, M. (2004). Narcissistic leaders: The incredible pros, the inevitable cons. Harvard Business Review. Retrieved from: https://hbr.org/2004/01/narcissistic-leaders-the-incredible-pros-the-inevitable-cons

Mathews, L. A. (2019). Why intersectionality matters in corporate settings. *Harvard Business Review*, *97*(4), 104–113.

Meuser, J. D., Gardner, W. L., Dinh, J. E., Hu, J., Liden, R. C., & Lord, R. G. (2016). A network analysis of leadership theory: The infancy of integration. *Journal of Management*, *42*(5), 1374–1403. https://doi.org/10.1177/0149206316647099

Mielianti, S., Ernawati D., Naya R., & Bates I. (2021). A country-level national needs assessment of the Indonesian pharmacy workforce. Research in Social and Administrative Pharmacy (RSAP), pp. 2–3. Retrieved from: https://discovery.ucl.ac.uk/id/eprint/10124651/3/Bates_RSAP%20paper_v7_CLEANED.pdf

Miller, H. (2022). Learn the seven distinct leadership styles. Retrieved from: https://leaders.com/articles/leadership/leadership-styles/

Murrell, A. J., Beard, B. S., & Porter, D.M. Jr. (2021). The importance of peer mentoring, identity work and holding environments: A study of African American leadership development. MDPI. Retrieved from: https://www.mdpi.com/1660-4601/18/9/4920.

Northouse, P. G. (2021). *Leadership: Theory and practice* (9th ed.) Los Angeles, CA: Sage Publications.

Raelin, J. A. (2003). *Creating leaderful organisations: How to bring out leadership in everyone.* San Francisco: Berret Khoeler Publishers Inc.

Robert, F. (2013). Report of the Mid Staffordshire NHS Foundation Trust public inquiry. Asset Publishing Service, pp. 1–11. Retrieved from: https://assets.publishing.service.gov.uk/government/uploads/system/uploads/attachment_data/file/279124/0947.pdf (Accessed 20 March 2023).

Sheard, A. G., Kakabadse, N., & Kakabadse, A. (2013). Destructive behaviours and leadership: The source of the shift from a functional to dysfunctional workplace? *International Journal of Social Science Studies*, *1*(1), 73–89.

Skouteris, H., Ananda-Rajah, M., Blewitt, C., & Ayton, D. (2023). No one can see us in positions of power: The intersectionality between gender and culture for women in leadership. BMJ Leader. Retrieved from: https://bmjleader.bmj.com/content/8/1/63#

Snowden, D., & Boone, M. (2007). A leader's framework for decision making. Harvard Business Review. Retrieved from: https://hbr.org/2007/11/a-leaders-framework-for-decision-making

Taylor, B. (2019). Intersectionality 101: What is it and why is it important? Woman Kind Worldwide. Retrieved from: https://www.womankind.org.uk/intersectionality-101-what-is-it-and-why-is-it-important/

Tinner, L., Holman, D., Ejegi-Memeh, S., & Laverty, A. A. (2023). Use of Intersectionality theory in interventional health research in high-income countries: A scoping review. *International Journal of Environmental Research and Public Health*, *20*(14), 6370. https://doi.org/10.3390/ijerph20146370

Verganti, R., Dell'Era, C., & Swan, K. C. (2021). Design thinking: critical analysis and future evolution. *Journal of Product Innovation Management*, *38*, 603–622. https://doi.org/10.1111/jpim.12610

Weber, M. D., & Karman, T. A. (1991). Student group approach to teaching using the Tuckman model of group development. *Advances in Physiology Education*, *261*(6), S12. https://journals.physiology.org/doi/abs/10.1152/advances.1991.261.6.S12

Wong, K.M., Musa, G., & Wong, E.S.K. (2011) A review of philosophical assumptions in management research. *African Journal of Business Management*, *5*(29), 11546–11550.

World Health Organisation. (2024). WHO results report - Programme budget 2018–2019- Leadership and enabling functions. World Health Organisation. Retrieved from: https://www.who.int/about/accountability/results/2018-2019/leadership

Yıldız, A. C. (2018). Development of a dynamic strategy map incorporating scenario analysis and system dynamics: A simulation test on an international construction company, Master's thesis. The Graduate School of Natural and Applied Sciences of Middle East Technical University. Retrieved from: https://etd.lib.metu.edu.tr/upload/12622571/index.pdf

Chapter 26

Afterword

This compendium has brought together a diverse array of perspectives, case studies, and theoretical insights, all shedding light on the shadowy aspects of leadership. The various contributions have highlighted the complexity of dark leadership, illustrating how personality traits, cultural contexts, and organisational environments can converge to create toxic leadership dynamics. From the exploration of destructive and narcissistic leaders to the examination of abusive supervision and corporate psychopathy, our contributors have provided a comprehensive overview of the different forms of dark leadership.

One of the key themes that emerged from this compendium is the importance of context. The interplay between national culture, organisational culture, and individual leader characteristics is crucial in understanding how dark leadership manifests and how it can be mitigated. This cross-cultural perspective has enriched our understanding and echoed the importance of bespoke interventions, taking into consideration cultural and contextual factors. All the sections offer practical strategies for preventing and addressing dark leadership. These insights are invaluable for practitioners, researchers, and consultants who are on the front lines of fostering healthier and more ethical organisational environments. As we look to the future, the study of dark leadership will continue to evolve. Emerging issues such as digital manipulation and the spread of misinformation by leaders in the digital age present new challenges that require ongoing research and innovative solutions. The dynamic nature of leadership and the ever-changing corporate landscape mean that our understanding of dark leadership must also adapt and evolve.

DOI: 10.4324/9781003475262-31

In closing, we hope that this compendium serves as a valuable resource for those seeking to address the dark side of leadership. By bringing together a wealth of knowledge and multidisciplinary experience, we aim to inspire further research, conversations, and action in this critical area. Let us continue to strive for leadership that not only avoids the pitfalls of the dark side but also champions the bright side, fostering enabling environments for ethical, compassionate, and effective leadership.

Index

Note: *Italic* page numbers refer to figures and page numbers followed by 'n' refer to notes.

abuse of power 27, 47, 111, 162, 180, 182, 192
abusive leadership 193–195, 198, 259
abusive supervision 21, 177, 237, 259, 262, 264
active leadership 225
Africa 178–181
antisocial behaviour 84, 122
Asian culture 192, 196–198
  abusive leadership 194–195
  dark side of leadership 192–199
  despotic leadership 193–194
  Machiavellian leadership 197–198
  psychopathic leadership 196–197
  tyrannical leadership 195–196
assertive followership 12
authenticity 281
authentic leaders 281
authentic leadership 281, 283, 284
authoritarian leadership 199
authority 27

bad apples 8
bad barrel makers 8
bad barrels 8
blended leadership 248
bright side leaders 79
bright side of leadership 280–286
business ethics 97, 99, 126
business leaders 96, 121, 124, 140, 141

calculative thinking 95, 98–99
capitalism 3
capitalist system 133–142
career-damaging criticism 109
categorical error 25–32
  lessons for leaders 31–32
change management 296, 297
charismatic leadership 232–233
Charity Commission 153–154
China
  collectivist values promote conformity and shared interests 249–250
  culture values skepticism and individual needs 250–251
  enterprise leadership, cross-cultural analysis 243–252
  iron triangle and talent management challenges 245–247
  lessons for leaders 251
  power distance and deference, hierarchy 248–251
  state-owned enterprise executives' digital engagement 245–247
codes of ethics 277
collaborative work 218
collectivism 9, 176, 180, 181, 197, 204, 205, 247
collectivist cultures 51, 176, 181, 205
Colombia 70–79
communication skills 4, 6, 126, 273
community camouflage 144–157
Community of Practice (CoP) 59, 64–65
competent leaders 226, 247
conducive environments 7, 86–87, 89, 110, 147
Confucianism 11

contextual variables 101
convergent calculative thinking 94–102
corporate culture 7, 40, 122
corporate ecosystem 9
corporate governance 126
corporate prey playbook 11
corporate psychopaths 8, 34, 39–41, 146
  largest fraud, USA history 36–38, 40
corporate psychopathy 39–40, 196
corruption 276
counterproductive work behaviour 52, 85
creative intelligence 293
criminal psychopaths 3
cultural/cultures 7, 8, 12, 13, 20, 22, 29, 40, 51, 52, 87–90, 106–110, 122, 140, 141, 145–146, 148–150, 152, 170, 173–182, 185, 188, 191, 195, 197, 202–210, 234, 236, 245, 246, 292, 293
  competence 207
  and dark leadership 177–178
  differences 51, 52, 176, 177, 204, 206, 208
  dimensions theory 174, 176–177, 179, 244
  factors 9, 53, 178
  of fear 89–90, 125, 155, 168
  of followership 9–12
  heritage 168, 186
  and Hofstede theory 175–177
  identity 186, 187, 191
  of integrity 209, 266, 267
  management 202, 210
  norms 163, 166, 188, 193, 204, 257
  politics of leadership 185–191
  toxic leadership 202–210
  values 9, 11–12, 87, 109, 177, 196, 198, 206, 236, 294

dark behaviours 47–53, 182, 233
dark entrepreneurs 137–140
dark entrepreneurship 133–142
  capitalist imperative and unequal playing field 138–139
  definition and characteristics 134–136
  glimpse into 139–140
  lessons for leaders 140–141
'dark' goals 244
dark leaders 31, 70, 72, 85–90, 111, 152, 164, 166, 233, 235, 259, 260, 264, 273
dark leadership 18–23, 31, 32, 53, 70, 72, 82, 85–87, 110, 111, 145–150, 152, 162, 164, 168, 169, 173–182, 195, 198–199, 230–239, 257–267, 282, 283, 288, 291
  behaviours 88, 175, 178, 224, 232, 234–236, 257, 289
  Colombian militia, case 73–76
dark leadership (*Cont.*)
  conducive environment 87
  and culture 177–178
  culture influence 173–182
  destructive leaders 86
  factors associated with 85–87
  forms of **231**
  lessons for leaders 23
  process of 59–66
  in Star Wars 18–23
  styles 192, 199, 232
  susceptible followers 86–87
  through discursive practices 73–76
  toxic triangle model of 109
  toxic triangle of 89–90
  triad 174–175
dark personalities 91, 110
dark personality traits 83–85
  everyday sadism 85
  Machiavellianism 84
  narcissism 83–84
  psychopathy 84–85
dark-side behaviours 8
dark side leaders 8, 47–53, 70–79, 162, 230, 274
  authority 78
  cross-cultural perspective of 51–52
  discursive practices of 70–79
  encouragement 77
  guidance 77–78
  hope/hopelessness 76
  intergenerational 76–77
  kindness 78
  lessons for leaders 52–53, 76–79
  obedience 78
  past and future 79
  personality of 48–49
  in practice 71–72
  reflection from Pakistan 71–72

shadows, organisation 50–51
trust 78–79
dark side of leadership 4, 8, 13, 22, 25, 31, 32, 35, 38, 42, 48–49, 51, 71, 73, 78–79, 107, 109–110, 162, 163, 166–170, 192–194, 231, 257–268; *see also individual entries*
categorical error and 25–32
dark traits 8, 47, 85, 89, 175
dark triad 19, 48, 51, 53, 83–85, 110, 117–128, 138, 231, 234, 235, 239
concepts and components 118–120
family business leadership, causes and consequences 123–126
and leadership 117–128
traits 118, 122, 124, 125
decision-making autonomy 217
despotic leaders 72, 76, 192, 237
despotic leadership 193–194, 198
destructive actions 150, 284, 285
destructive leaders 71, 86, 110, 146, 155, 264
destructive leadership 50, 82, 86, 90, 110, 145, 146, 155, 217, 222, 273; *see also* dark leadership
behaviour 220, 223
styles 72, 151, 237
toxic triangle of 110
digital engagement strategies 246, 247, 250
digital leadership 216, 217, 220–222
digital literacy 225, 248
campaigns 252
digital manipulation 243–252
digital technologies 220, 224, 225, 243, 244
digital tools 216, 217, 220–224
digital transformation 295
discursive practices 70, 72, 76, 79

Edison machine 10
effective leadership 22, 62, 118, 188, 239, 258, 278, 281, 283, 285, 288
emotional intelligence 126, 182, 207, 209, 222, 260, 273, 280, 284, 292–294, 297
emotional regulation 280, 282, 284
empathy skills 62
employee involvement 218, 226
employee well-being 35
Enron 36–38
success 38–42
entrepreneurs 133–137, 139, 141
entrepreneurship 134–138, 141
innovation, dark side 137
innovation and exploitation, duality 136–137
pull factors and opportunity 136
push factors and necessity 136–137
ethical behaviour 89, 94–102, 135, 178, 197, 198, 267, 282–283, 286, 294
calculative *vs.* meditative ethical thinking 98–99
convergent *vs.* divergent ethical thinking 97–98
lessons for leaders 101
ethical/ethics 23, 39, 53, 62, 84, 94, 97, 99, 126, 133, 234, 267, 277
climate 179, 264
codes 13, 94, 96, 101
conduct 134, 135, 141, 266
leaders 62, 207
relativism 95
responsibilities 23
standards 145, 156, 264, 266, 267, 272, 282, 284
training 286
ethical leadership 95–96, 101, 155, 170, 174, 196, 207, 267
at agency level 95–96
ethnic identification 186
ethnic identity 186, 188
everyday sadism 85
exploitative leadership 151, 237

family business environments 117–128
leadership and dark triad in 121–123
lessons for leaders 126–127
family businesses 72, 117, 119, 121–125, 127
family business leaders 118, 123, 124, 127
family business leadership 118, 123–127
dark triad in 126–127
family dynamics 121, 127
family leaders 122, 124
Federal Inland Revenue Service (FIRS) 265
Federal Road Safety Corps (FRSC) 265
fiscal responsibility 37
followership 9, 12, 14, 27, 31
culture of 9–12

gatekeeping 167
global financial crisis 8
Godfatherism 166
guanxi 197, 199

high power distance 174, 176, 179, 204, 205
Hitler, Adolf 35
Hofstede, Geert 173–182
Holmes, Elizabeth 10
Horatio Alger Award 38
Hubris Leadership 192

Indigenous wisdom 294
individual differences 87, 272
individualism *vs.* collectivism 176, 204
individualistic cultures 51, 205, 247, 250, 294
innovation 20, 21, 51, 118, 127, 133–136, 141, 176, 217–218, 222, 258, 293–296
institutional leadership 281
interests 28–31
internal whistle-blowers 40
interpersonal relationships 120, 125, 179
intersectionality 288, 291, 295, 297
invisible manager 215–226
Iraqi-Kurdistan 185–191
  culture and leadership in 186–187
  lessons for leaders, challenging situations 188–190
iron triangle 244–247
ISIS (Islamic State of Iraq and Syria) 187

Kurdish communities 187
Kurdish culture 185–187
Kurdish leadership 187
Kurdish people 185, 191
Kurdish relationship 189
Kurdish society 187

lack of accountability 276
lack of character 275
lack of trust 275–276
leader-follower exchange 9
leader-follower process 9
leader-follower trust 13
leaders 12–13
leadership 31–32, 121–123
  adversity and 187–188
  bankruptcy, integrity 271–278
  behaviours 20, 150, 181, 204, 216, 217, 220, 222, 260, 277, 289
  brief overview 272–274
  and dark triad 117–128
  development 13, 125, 292, 295
  disruption and influence 106–112
  effectiveness 188, 273, 292
  ethics 22
  integrity, concept of 274–275
  leading without integrity 275–277
  lessons for leaders 278
  morality of 108–109
  personalities 110, 173, 174, 178
  philosophical analysis of 161–171
  positions 29, 31, 32, 47, 74, 108, 146, 181, 233, 271
  practices 90, 248, 290
  process 88, 163, 174
  psychopathy 20
  strategies 106, 108
  styles 19–22, 29, 31, 71, 109, 112, 147, 187, 192–198, 205, 230, 232, 273, 286
  theories 61, 147
  toxic triangle of 82–91
  traits 118, 174, 283
  values 79
  without integrity 276
leader traits 87, 88
Lucas, George 18

Machiavellianism 19, 48–49, 52, 53, 72, 82–85, 88, 90, 110, 117–118, 125, 127, 138, 173–175, 178–181, 198, 203, 207, 231, 233, 257, 260–264, 273, 282, 283, 285
Machiavellian leadership 197–198
Mandela, Nelson 28
meaningful leadership 100–101
meaningfulness 218
meditative thinking 95, 98–100
metaphoric language 3
Military Communities of Practice (MCoPs) 59–66
  critical and theoretical reflections 61–63
  lessons for leaders 65–66
  reflection 60–61

samhandling in 64–65
short story 60
toxic leadership behaviour 63–64
military leadership 61, 62
military organisations 71, 72
modern leadership 100–101
modern management policies 28
moral behaviour 95, 96
moral relativism 101
motives 28–31
multinational corporations 205, 207

narcissism 19, 20, 48, 51, 53, 82–86, 88, 90, 109–111, 117–119, 123, 125, 127, 138, 173–175, 177, 178, 202, 203, 207, 231, 233, 235, 257, 260–264, 282, 283, 285
narcissistic personality 48, 119
narcissistic traits 119, 123, 282
national cultures 89, 90, 176
National Youth Service Corps (NYSC) 236, 240n1
negative behaviours 162, 232–235, 237
negative personality traits 48, 82, 273
NGO Halo Effect 152
Nigeria 139, 164, 166, 173, 178–181, 232, 234, 238, 257, 265
arts and entertainment
dark side of leadership 166–169
lessons for leaders 169–170
overview 164–166
case of 178–181
cultural dimensions and implications **180**
entertainment industry 164–169
Hofstede exploration of 173–182
lessons for leaders 181–182
Nigeria's public sector
abusive supervision and employee well-being 262
dark side of leadership 257–268
employee turnover and organisational costs 264
ethical standards, erosion 264
government agencies, dark leadership 264–266
lessons for leaders 266–267
Machiavellianism and manipulative behaviour 263
narcissism and decision-making 263
organisational culture 262–264
psychopathy and organisational stability 263
Nollywood 167
Nordic context
constructive and inspirational *vs.* dark and dysfunctional 219–220
darker side of digital tools 222–224
dark side of digital leadership 215–226
digital leadership 220–222
leadership by proxy 222–224
leadership models and 217–224
leadership types 219–220
lessons for leaders 224–225
work organisation and leadership 217–218
Nordic leadership 218, 222, 226
Nordic model 216–218, 222, 223
Norges Bank Investment Management (NBIM) 61
Norway 59–66

open communication 195, 196, 202, 204, 209, 267, 292
organisational change 6, 295
organisational coherence 22
organisational culture 7, 90, 118, 122, 125, 127, 175, 197, 203, 206–207, 257, 262–265, 282, 295
organisational dynamics 206, 291
organisational politics 203
organisational structure 22, 91, 125, 246

Pakistan 70–79
participative decision-making 217
participative leadership 205, 206
paternalism 11
perceptions 6, 230–240
performance management information (PMI) systems 221
personal identity 281, 284, 285
personal integrity 275, 278
personality traits 30, 48, 82, 84, 88, 117, 118, 123, 126, 174, 231, 233, 294

political campaigns 27
political personalities 189
political psychopaths 35
  loss of life, human history 35
popular culture 18, 20, 22
power 18–23, 27, 32, 47, 49, 84, 86, 89, 90, 96, 98, 109–111, 120, 122–123, 125, 145, 152, 154, 162–167, 169, 176, 180, 187, 188, 192, 197, 198
power distance 9, 174, 176, 179, 181, 204, 232, 237, 248, 250
power distance index (PDI) 244
pragmatic leadership 188, 191
predation 3, 5
predator playbook 5–8
predator-prey interaction 5, 8
predatory leaders 11
psychological factors 96, 98
psychopathic behaviours 8, 52
psychopathic leaders 3–14, 33, 34, 43, 49, 193, 196, 199, 260, 263, 284
psychopathic leadership 3–14, 33–43, 196
  lessons for leaders 43
  longitudinal nature of failure 33–43
psychopathic organisational leadership 35
psychopathic tendencies 4, 10, 12
psychopathic traits 4, 8, 34, 42, 43, 51, 123, 124, 196, 260
psychopaths 3, 33, 34, 38, 49, 51, 84, 146, 260, 263
  functional traits of 4
psychopathy 6, 19, 48–49, 52, 82–84, 88, 90, 110, 117–118, 125, 127, 173, 174, 231, 233, 257, 260–264
psycho-social dispositions 26
public consciousness 23
public trust 147, 246–247, 249, 265, 266
Pup Enterprises 89
Pygmalion syndrome 77

regulations 50, 63, 88, 95, 134, 138, 154–157, 207, 224, 280, 294
resonant leadership 62, 294
revised leadership process model 87–89, *88*
rude awakening 28

samhandling 59, 64–66
self-aware leaders 281
self-awareness 280–286
  authentic leadership 283–285
  ethical decision-making 282
  interpersonal relationships 283
  lessons for leaders 285–286
  Machiavellianism 282
  narcissism 282
  psychopathy 282
self-preservation 4
self-regulation 280
senior management 208, 236
Skilling, Jeffrey 38
small and medium-sized family businesses (SMEs) 125
social distancing 108, 110
social interactions 51, 64, 186
social learning theory 8
social media 120, 237, 244, 248, 250
  content analysis 230–240
social media perspectives
  interpreting and clarifying perspectives 238
  reflections from 237–238
  workplace, dark leadership 234–237
social media platforms 190, 232, 234, 238, 248–250
social pressure 96, 138
social structures 96, 188
Splitstrike Conversion 42
Star Wars 18–23
  dark leadership in 18–23
state-owned enterprises (SOEs) 244–250
strategic interventions 288–297
  intersectionality, championing 289–290
  and lessons for leaders 291–297
  National Health Service (NHS) England, leadership challenges 290–291
structural ethics 94
susceptible followers 86–87
sustainable development 268

talent management 246, 249, 295
toxic behaviours 162, 202, 207, 209
toxic leaders 40, 42, 65, 66, 73, 162, 202–210, 276–277
toxic leadership 38, 50, 61, 63–64, 146, 170, 178, 202–210, 259, 274, 276–277
  concept of 203–204

cross-cultural perspectives 204–206
lessons for leaders 208–209
mitigating 206–208
toxic organisational leadership 178
toxic triangle 85, *86*, 89, 90, 109, 147, 155
of dark leadership 88
model 109, 264
toxic triangle, leadership 82–91, *86*
lessons for leaders 90–91
toxic work culture 177
transformational leadership 73, 106, 109, 111, 219, 232
dark side 109–110
employee welfare risks, dark side 111
lessons for leaders 111–112
pandemic partying and misleading the house, case study 107–108
transformative mindsets 108
trust 28–29, 31, 32, 62, 64, 66, 78–79, 120–122, 134, 196, 198, 209, 216–219, 223, 225, 244, 246–248, 257, 262–267, 274–276, 278
tyrannical leadership 195–196, 198

UK VCSE 145, 147–150, 157; *see also* voluntary, community and social enterprise (VCSE) sector
dark times in 147–150
unethical practices 8, 40, 48, 134, 137, 140, 178, 266
unethical pro-organisational behaviour (UPOB) 109, 150, 157
United Kingdom
enterprise leadership, cross-cultural analysis 243–252
enterprise leaders in digital age, accountability 247–248
lessons for leaders 251

Vader, Darth 18
leadership style of 19–22
voluntary, community and social enterprise (VCSE) sector 144–157
context-dependent dark leadership 146–147
darkness deeper, shadows 150–152
events, behaviour and change 147–150
lessons for leaders 156–157
regulation 153–156
voluntary veils 144–157

white-collar crimes 8
workplace
dark side of leadership in 230–240
industries, professions, and occupations 236
lessons for business and organisational leaders 238–239
perceived causative factors 235–236
perceived dark leadership behaviours 235
possible solutions, perspectives 237
racial and ethnic profiling, dark leadership 236
social media perspectives, dark leadership 234–237
work-related stress 29
world population 26

FSC
www.fsc.org
MIX
Papier | Fördert gute Waldnutzung
FSC® C083411

Kolibri 360 GmbH
Ferdinand-Jühlke-Straße 7
99095 Erfurt, Deutschland
produktsicherheit@kolibri360.de